Simon Cameron
Lincoln's Secretary
of War

Simon Cameron Lincoln's Secretary of War

A Political Biography

ERWIN STANLEY BRADLEY

Philadelphia
University of Pennsylvania Press

Published in Great Britain, India, and Pakistan
by the Oxford University Press
London, Bombay, and Karachi

Library of Congress Catalogue Card Number: 65-20756 3/28/68

7507

Printed in the United States of America

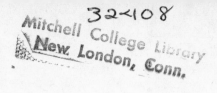
To the Memory of my Mother

Ida Bradley Diehl

Her children arise up and call her blessed

—Proverbs, XXXI: 28.

Preface

The Bard once wrote that the evil that men do lives after them, while the good is oft interred with their bones. Sometimes this evil not only maintains its existence, but, nurtured and magnified over the span of succeeding generations by those wishing to believe the worst in men, continues to grow. Such was the fate of a modern Caesar of politics, Simon Cameron.

Writers have usually focused their attention on certain phases of Cameron's career, those largely negative in character, and have thereby presented a distorted overall picture. The purpose of the writer of this political biography is not to play the role of a revisionist but rather to present the story as he believes he has found it.

Simon Cameron, secretary of war in Lincoln's cabinet, minister to Russia, four times United States Senator, and czar of a state political hierarchy, enjoyed an active political life extending from 1820 to 1877.

This man of humble origin, well on his way in the 1830's to becoming one of America's wealthiest entrepreneurs, concentrated his energy and talents on politics during the turbulent Jacksonian era. At first a follower of James Buchanan, he became disgruntled at the tardy recognition accorded his services, played the role of an opportunist (a stamp which the public eye continued to impose upon him during the remainder of his public career), and catapulted himself into the Senate.

Dissatisfied with the tariff policies of the Democratic

Party, ostracized by party leaders, and determined to secure political dominance in his own state, the politico, already possessed of a numerous, loyal clientele, took advantage of the depressing effect imposed upon political parties by the sectional controversy in the 1850's and via the Know-Nothing route emerged a state leader of the new Republican party. His election in 1857, in the face of a Democratic majority in the General Assembly, to the United States Senate, accorded him recognition on the national level and allowed him to contend for the Presidential nomination in 1860. After his retirement from Lincoln's cabinet and upon the termination of his brief Russian mission, Cameron sought political rehabilitation by becoming Lincoln's man in Pennsylvania. He executed this plan of action successfully.

A large part of Cameron's political career from 1855 to 1872 was occupied by a personal and political feud with Governor Andrew G. Curtin for control of the Commonwealth's Republican organization. The struggle ended with the exit of the defeated Curtin from the party and with Cameron, the exponent of militant conservative Republicanism, in control of the greatest political machine the state had yet witnessed. In 1877, when Cameron chose to retire from the Senate, he experienced no difficulty in transferring his scepter of power to his political heirs, J. Donald Cameron and Matthew Quay.

A. Howard Meneeley's characterization of Simon Cameron is definitive: "No politician of his generation understood the science of politics better than Simon Cameron; none enjoyed greater power; none had more success."

ERWIN STANLEY BRADLEY

Union College
Barbourville, Kentucky
May, 1965

Acknowledgements

Completion of this work was made possible through the assistance provided by the American Philosophical Society and by Union College, Barbourville, Kentucky.

The writer acknowledges the assistance and many courtesies extended to him by the staffs of the Manuscript Division of the Library of Congress; the Pennsylvania Historical and Museum Commision; the Pennsylvania State University Library; the Historical Society of Pennsylvania; Lancaster Newspapers, Incorporated; Pennsylvania State Library; Blair County Historical Society; Western Pennsylvania Historical Society; and the Free Library of Philadelphia.

Special thanks is due to Mr. and Mrs. Henry L. Haines, IV, for use of the Cameron letters of Captain Henry Haines, and to Cathell C. Crippen for the Cameron notes of the late Dr. Lee F. Crippen.

The illustrations were provided through the courtesy of the Library of Congress, Donald H. Kent of the Pennsylvania Historical and Museum Commission, the Reformed Church of Maytown, Mr. J. G. Bradley, and the Wisconsin State Historical Society.

The revised manuscript was completed through the typing, labor, and patience of the author's wife, Vivian Wright Bradley.

Contents

Illustrations

The illustrations appear as a group following page 224.

Abbreviations

The following abbreviations have been used to designate manuscript repositories frequently mentioned in the notes:

DCC   Dauphin County Historical Society, Collection, Harrisburg, Pennsylvania.

DCL   Dickinson College Library, Carlisle, Pennsylvania.

HSP   Historical Society of Pennsylvania, Philadelphia, Pennsylvania.

HSWP   Historical Society of Western Pennsylvania, Pittsburgh, Pennsylvania.

LC   Manuscripts Division, Library of Congress, Washington, D.C.

PHMC   Pennsylvania Historical and Museum Commission, Harrisburg, Pennsylvania.

WHGS—Wyoming Historical and Geological Society, Wilkes-Barre, Pennsylvania.

Simon Cameron Lincoln's Secretary of War

1
The Earlier Years

IN THE QUAINT OLD CEMETERY AT DONEGAL SPRING, WITHIN sight of the Cameron country home only a few miles from Harrisburg, Pennsylvania, lies the grave of the Reverend Colin McFarquhar, new pastor of the local church in 1776, who died in 1822 at the advanced age of ninety three.

When this Presbyterian minister migrated from Gairlock, Scotland, in the fall of 1775, there came with him several families of Highlanders, including that of Donald Cameron of Perth, a partisan of the Young Pretender to the English throne. Donald's sons, John and Simon worked as tenants (gillies) on the extensive Donegal farms under the direction of the Reverend McFarquhar. John left for Lebanon Valley while Simon remained on the *glebe* with his wife, the former Ann McKenzie, a relative of his pastor's wife.

A legal record of the theft in 1777 by Ann Monroe, spinster, of a 40-shilling coat from Simon Cameron and of hard money and linen from Donald Cameron, indicates that Simon was taking care of his aged father. About the year 1790 Simon Cameron suddenly fell ill in the fields during the hot July harvest season, succumbed, and was buried close to the little church he had helped to build.[1]

Not long after his father's death, Charles, Simon's eldest son, left the Donegal farms to learn a trade and establish himself as a tailor and tavern keeper on the public square of nearby Maytown. There, in a log house, on March 8, 1799, the subject of this biography, Simon Cameron, was born to Charles' wife, Martha Pfoutz Cameron, a descendant of Palatinate Germans.[2]

The poor tailor Charles Cameron fought a losing lifetime fight against poverty. An erratic seasonal trade, a limited rural clientele, and finally the sale of his household goods in 1808 to satisfy the claims of creditors induced Simon's father to try his fortune northward in Sunbury, the thriving little county seat of Northumberland; but the passing of two years found Charles Cameron and wife, now bereft of their six children, still living in

[1] Herbert H. Beck, "The Camerons of Donegal," Lancaster County Historical Society Paper, LVI, No. 4 (1952), 85-109; interview of Simon Cameron by Frank Burr, Philadelphia Weekly Press, April 13, 1882; "Report" on the early history of the Camerons by investigators for family, 1897; Samuel Evans to Simon Cameron, January 5, 1877, Simon Cameron Papers, Library of Congress. Hereafter cited as Cameron MSS. Simon Cameron, owner of a 200-acre farm in Lancaster County in 1782, could not have been the grandfather of the great political leader, because the latter remained on the Donegal farms until his death. There was a Simon Cameron of Donegal who in 1776 appealed his non-attendance to militia duty on the grounds that his wife had lately died, leaving him four small children. See Records of Militia Appeal Docket for Lancaster County, Archives Division, Pennsylvania State Library.

[2] Maytown's list of taxables for 1790 does not include Charles Cameron. Unlike the two oldest children, Simon was not born at the tavern. A small vacant lot (1964) next to the Lutheran parsonage in Maytown marks the site of Cameron's birthplace. Simon's grandmother Pfoutz died in 1828 at the age of 91, leaving him "her blessing and $50."

squalid surroundings across the Susquehanna river in Lewisburg. Because Charles Cameron did not long survive this last move it was fortunate that the children had been left with the more prosperous families in Sunbury.[3]

Charles Cameron's third son, Simon, age eleven, had been received into the home of Dr. Peter Grahl, a Jewish physician practicing in the Sunbury area. The childless doctor showed genuine affection for his ward, often taking him along on his rounds and, on certain occasions, finding himself not sufficiently far removed from his cups, entrusted his protégé with the delivery of medicine to patients. On his part, young Simon was not long in seizing the opportunity to continue the limited education which his devoted mother had begun with borrowed books at Maytown. The youth's avid reading of the physician's and his neighbors' libraries made him acquainted with Plutarch's *Lives* and *Don Quixote*, leading favorites of the age.

A record of Simon Cameron's formative years would not be complete without mention of Lorenzo Da Ponte, a baptized Jewish-Italian émigré lately of Vienna, London, and New York. "Poet to the Italian theater" at the brilliant Austrian Court of Joseph II, Ponte wrote librettos for Mozart's *Le Nozze di Figaro* and other famous works. After twelve years of writing for Drury Lane Theater he moved to New York to do tutoring in Italian.[4] Da Ponte moved to Sunbury because his wife

---

[3] Beck, "The Camerons," 86. Charles Cameron, remembered for his "democratic style of speech," with two of his sons, William and James, is buried at Lewisburg. His inscription reads: Charles Cameron—died Jan. 16, 1811—Aged 46 years.

[4] *Webster's Biographical Dictionary* (Springfield, Massachusetts, 1953), 388.

wished to be near her sister, Mrs. Grahl. This remarkable gentleman of culture rapidly broadened the vistas of the receptive Simon. A never-to-be-forgotten experience of this youth of fourteen was his trip to Philadelphia with Ponte during the Christmas season. Cameron's kindness to one of Ponte's sons almost two decades later illustrates one key to the famous politico's success—never to forget a favor or fail to repay a debt. Ponte's late pamphleteering in London could easily have provided one factor in determining Simon's decision to become a printer; the other was the decline of Dr. Grahl's fortune and health. In fact, Simon's apprenticeship to Andrew Kennedy, publisher of the Northumberland *Gazette*, was accomplished less than a month before the death of his great benefactor. From this date in May, 1816, Simon Cameron was on his own. Surely this stripling of seventeen could not have realized the potentialities of journalism as a stepping-stone into the political world, but very likely Dr. Grahl and Lorenzo Da Ponte did and so urged this course for him.[5]

Cameron completed his apprenticeship at Harrisburg under James Peacock, editor of the Harrisburg *Republican*, rising to assistant editor. While boarding in the home of his employer, Simon had the good fortune to meet Samuel D. Ingham, Secretary of the Commonwealth. Evidence of Ingham's faith in Cameron's abilities is shown by his invitation to take charge of the Doylestown *Bucks County Messenger* for the purpose of conciliating local factions within Jefferson's old Demo-

[5] Lorenzo Da Ponte, *My 2 Friends*, printed pamphlet in receipt book of Cameron and Krause, Cameron MSS, LC. Cameron came into possession of the indenture in 1878. See "interview" in *New York Times*, June 3, 1878.

cratic-Republican Party. The next year, 1822, found
Cameron earning $10 a week for Congressional printers
Gales and Seaton. He went back to Pennsylvania when
he heard Peacock's paper was for sale. The opportunity
for part ownership in the *Republican* led to Cameron's
first important business transaction. A thrifty uncle furnished $400 from a tattered coat and the new business
man, Simon Cameron, shortly afterward merged his enterprise with Charles Mowry's *Pennsylvania Intelligencer.*
Cameron ended his career as an active journalist in 1827,
becoming a silent partner as part owner of the *Pennsylvania Reporter,* successor to the *Intelligencer.*[6] Cameron's
career as a journalist, although short, had been very
profitable. It had given him opportunity to become
acquainted with the leading current political figures at
Harrisburg and Washington; as well, he had amassed a
fortune of $20,000.

Having secured a stake in a profitable business enterprise, the junior editor saw the way open to marriage.
On October 16, 1822, the Reverend Dr. Lochman joined
Simon Cameron in matrimony to Miss Margaretta Brua,
daughter of Peter Brua, a director of the Harrisburg
bank. Ten children were born of this marriage, six of
which grew into maturity.[7]

Cameron could hardly have entered the political arena
under tutelage superior to that supplied by Samuel D.
Ingham. Recognized in state political circles as spokesman for a political clique, the Family, Ingham was one

[6] Philadelphia *Weekly Press,* April 13, 1882. Unless otherwise
noted, the material for this introductory chapter is taken from
Lee F. Crippen, *Simon Cameron: Ante-Bellum Years* (Oxford,
Ohio, 1942).

[7] Harrisburg *Pennsylvania Intelligencer,* Oct. 17, 1822.

well versed in all the arts of poltical chicanery; a chieftain who not only prided himself on this particular type of learning but also as one well disposed to teach these arts to eager novices and confederates alike.[8]

The young ambitious Cameron also benefited through the election of John Andrew Shulze, his early friend, to the gubernatorial chair in 1823. The Family had aided in securing Shulze's nomination, but the stolid German failed to follow the Family line, with its pronounced Calhoun leanings, after taking office and partly through the influence of Cameron became an Adams man before the end of his first term. The failure of Calhoun's followers to have their leader endorsed for the Presidency at the State Convention of 1823, together with Governor Shulze's coolness, required a new type of political strategy. It was decided to hitch Calhoun to Jackson, who was experiencing a meteoric rise in the state. State political leaders were not slow in claiming credit for the Jackson boom in spite of its known grass-roots origin beginning as early as 1822 with local editors and political leaders. Old Federalist veterans such as Andrew Gregg and James Buchanan joined with Independent-Republicans and numerous personal admirers of Old Hickory to mount the Jackson bandwagon with the immediate aim of capturing the State Republican Convention of 1824 for their hero.[9]

The Harrisburg State Convention of 1824 made a memorable impression upon Cameron, a young Demo-

[8] Philip Shriver Klein, *Pennsylvania Politics, 1817–1832: A Game Without Rules* (Philadelphia, 1940), 127. It was John Cameron, not Simon, who was Governor Shulze's brother-in-law. See W. H. Egle, *History of Dauphin and Lebanon Counties*, 474.

[9] Klein, *Pennsylvania Politics*, 120-22.

cratic delegate from Dauphin County with a delegation he had sought to bring unpledged. Uncommitted delegations were the best advantage that the Calhoun men could have hoped for, what with a convention filled with ardent Jackson admirers. It was here that Cameron witnessed the magnificent stand of the venerable Jonathan Roberts standing alone "like a gnarled old oak before the Jackson hurricane." [10] The Calhoun men derived some comfort from their man's nomination for second place on the Jackson ticket.

With rapidly growing business interests before he attained the age of thirty, Cameron was becoming more and more concerned over the necessity of a protective tariff for American industry. If one is looking for a theme of consistency in the long political career of Simon Cameron (which at first glance appears to be only that of a political opportunist), he can discern it in Cameron's staunch advocacy of candidates pledged to protection. This attitude could explain Cameron's coolness to Calhoun as a result of the Vice-President's deciding vote against the Woolens Bill early in 1827. Although actually the bill would have been of doubtful value to most of the Keystone State, a vote against the Woolens Bill was interpreted by tariff men as a vote against the best interests of the state. Strangely, the Calhoun men were proscribed, although the Congressmen from Pennsylvania who voted against the bill were Jacksonians. Cameron's lukewarm support of Jackson in 1828 was evidence of his distrust of the tariff orthodoxy proclaimed by the general's supporters. However, before the end of another four years Cameron was foremost in the Jackson ranks.

Cameron, because of his youthfulness, political im-

[10] *Ibid.*, 165.

maturity, and close gubernatorial ties, was concerned in the late 1820's chiefly with political developments within Pennsylvania. Here, where Governor Shulze's easy re-election had indicated a political truce, there followed a fierce battle between the factions for control of the old battered Jeffersonian tree now literally bursting with fresh buds. The benign attitude of the governor lent encouragement to the Adams men while a last ditch battle was being fought between the Family-Calhoun faction and the Amalgamators for control of the Jackson camp. Cameron, ostensibly silent, was busily keeping himself informed of the latest developments and passing on his information to Congressman James Buchanan, the perennial representative of the Lancaster County locale. This up-and-coming Jackson man had already suffered a public drubbing for his vote against the Woolen Bills and hovered dangerously close to political eclipse for his part in practically forcing Jackson to eat his own words after the President had cited Buchanan as the "member of Congress of high respectability" who had transmitted information to him of an evil offer from Henry Clay shortly before the House Presidential election of 1825.[11] Nevertheless, Cameron hitched himself to the Jackson star via the Buchanan route.

The entrance of Samuel D. Ingham, high priest of Calhounism, into the cabinet of the triumphant Jackson encouraged the South Carolinian's followers in their hopes of capturing the gubernatorial chair the following year through the post-election magic of Jackson's coattails. Although Cameron professed to believe that Shulze stood a good chance for a third try at the governorship, his

[11] John T. Morse, *John Quincy Adams* (Boston and New York, 1899), 185.

candidacy could hardly be taken seriously in light of the late offer of the Adams men in 1828 to support him for second place on the Adam's Presidential ticket.

A Family man, George Wolf, won the Democratic nomination,[12] and went on to defeat Joseph Ritner, protectionist, inveterate enmey of Masons, and champion of the underprivileged. This presaged a final national Calhoun victory a few years hence when it was expected that tired Old Hickory would carry out his Presidential one-term philosophy and retire designating Calhoun his successor. But by 1831, Calhoun, broken by a rejuvenated Jackson, was no longer a candidate; and in the meantime Samuel D. Ingham had fallen a victim to the Peggy Eaton imbroglio. The crestfallen secretary departed ingloriously from Washington under cover of darkness after writing Jackson's bosom friend, Major John Eaton, "that you must be a little deranged, to imagine that any blustering or yours could induce me to disavow the past immoral conduct of Margaret Eaton what all the inhabitants of this city know. . . ."[13]

Post election lulls found Cameron busy with lucrative Pennsylvania canal-building contracts and a mid-summer (1829) appointment as adjutant-general of the Commonwealth.[14] This honorable appointment was probably an eleventh-hour expression of friendship from the retiring governor, John Andrew Shulze. Cameron could expect few favors from the incoming governor, George Wolf, because he had done nothing to earn them. According to

[12] Some attributed Wolf's nomination to Masonic intrigue. See Marguerite P. Bartlett, *The Chief Phases of Pennsylvania Politics in the Jacksonian Period* (Allentown, 1919), 22.

[13] *Autobiography of Peggy Eaton* (New York, 1923), 154. Sometimes quoted as "*not* a little deranged."

[14] *Pennsylvania Archives*, 9th Series, IX, 7010.

Cameron's own words, all the new governor's important appointments were made, or so it seemed, with the purpose of furthering Calhoun's future candidacy within the state, and were dictated through Ingham.[15] At any rate his rank of adjutant-general of militia explains Cameron's lifelong title of "general." Cameron's departure from the Commonwealth for an extended stay the following summer made his resignation imperative.

Cancellation of a state canal contract led to his superintendency of the Mississippi-Lake Ponchartrain project. This Louisiana development scheme removed Cameron from the political scene of his native state until the spring of 1832, but constant communication with political leaders kept him well informed. Such was his enthusiasm for political intrigue that from this remote station he endeavored to promote a third term boom for his friend, Shulze.

Acceptance of the Jackson fiat—Martin Van Buren as his running mate in 1832—was an especially bitter pill for the general's followers in Pennsylvania to swallow. After the hero's retirement the Keystone State would occupy no place of prominence and be forced to play second fiddle to the new foreordained concert meister, the Little Magician from New York. The support given Jackson in the last two Presidential elections by their state, argued the Pennsylvanians, entitled them to no less recognition than a Jacksonian Vice-President. Passing through the imaginative minds of the various factional leaders were rapturous pictures of a Dallas, a Buchanan, or perhaps a Wilkins seated in the highest seat which his Jacksonian majesty's favor could bestow. William

[15] Cameron to J. A. Alix, July 17, 1833, quoted in Klein, *Pennsylvania Politics*, 296.

Wilkins, a western Pennsylvanian, was designated the choice of the state Democracy after a lengthy fight at the state nominating convention at Harrisburg. The Pennsylvania delegation left for the National Democratic Convention pledged to vote first for Wilkins, next for Dallas, but never for Van Buren as the Vice-Presidential candidate of the party.

Never was Jackson's mailed fist more clearly revealed than at the this Democratic National Convention, called for one purpose only—to force Van Buren's acceptance on the ticket. Under the circumstance the state managers selected to carry out Jackson's unpopular mandate at the national convention had to be men of unquestionable loyalty, able to cope with the rebellion anticipated from the anti-Van Buren delegates.

By the spring of 1832 no prominent Pennsylvania Democrat had succeeded in retaining the necessary confidence of the narrowed Jackson oligarchy. "Well might John Binns have published a new set of coffin handbills with the black boxes labeled: Ingham, Bernard, Baldwin, Buchanan, Wilkins, and Dallas." [16] This best explains why a new man from Pennsylvania was chosen for strategic convention leadership. Apparently Simon Cameron was selected for the key post because both Ingham and Buchanan, men formerly in Jackson's confidence, had testified to his worth.[17] In his interview with Frank Burr in 1882, Cameron did not make clear whether he knew in advance of his acceptance that he would be required, contrary to State Convention instructions, to whip the

[16] *Ibid.*, 350.
[17] In addition Cameron was credited with initiating in his own state, on the suggestion of J. B. Lewis, a draft-Jackson movement for a second term not long after the beginning of his first term.

Pennsylvania delegation into line for Van Buren.[18] Very likely he was uninformed because Major John Eaton, from whom Cameron had received his instructions when in New Orleans, was not himself aware of it until after his arrival at Baltimore for the Convention.[19] A unanimous vote from Pennsylvania's delegation for Van Buren at the National Democratic Convention testified to a perfectly lubricated Jacksonian machine with Cameron functioning as the Commonwealth's critical cog.

As was to be expected from his conduct at the convention, Simon Cameron became a favorite subject of Democratic editorials dwelling at length upon his treason at the Baltimore convention and including revelations of his late ephemeral loyalty to the national factional leaders, Calhoun and Adams, followed by his sudden switch to Jackson. This much may be said in Cameron's favor: at least all three of these men pretended to represent the same party and at one time or another expressed sentiments much in agreement with Cameron's ideas. In addition one could hardly expect political maturity from a novice just out of his twenties. However, his gamble for recognition at the Presidential level in defiance of Democratic State Convention instructions provides an excellent picture of Cameron's political philosophy. He had appeared in the guise of an opportunist—a role he was to play again and again with astonishing success in his long political career. Such action was always heralded by his

---

[18] Philadelphia *Weekly Press*, April 13, 1882.

[19] Edward Stanwood, *A History of the Presidency from 1788-1897* (Boston and New York, 1898), 160. Cameron was offered the permanent chairmanship of the convention. See Harrisburg *Telegraph*, June 27, 1889; Philadelphia *Weekly Press*, April 13, 1882.

enemies as the prelude to certain downfall. But the
prophetic utterings of his political opponents proved, with
few exceptions, false, and Cameron would emerge
stronger than ever until finally the myth of Cameron's
invincibility became established. This myth took root
among the rank and file voters long before it was realized
by his leading political opponents.

Cameron actually enjoyed his feat of administering
nauseating doses of Van Burenism to recalcitrant Pennsylvanians. To it must be added the pleasure of contemplating the future rewards likely to be bestowed upon him by
the gratified heir presumptive to Jackson's throne. Van
Buren's ability to deliver these rewards depended in
large measure, as everyone realized, upon the continued
existence of an ailing, failing President who could guarantee the Little Magician's succession. Here again
Cameron was gambling on odds which at that time were
considered poor.

With Van Buren safely established in the Vice-Presidential seat, Cameron proceeded to take out more political
insurance. Continued amiable relations with the influential Buchanan could hardly fail to pay off and, secondly,
some way must be found to conciliate the powerful Wilkins faction that was branding him a traitor for his
action at the Baltimore Convention. The first opportunity
appeared in December, 1833, when Cameron worked to
throw the United States Senatorial election to Buchanan,
lately returned from Russia, reluctantly blessed by Jackson, and unprepared for the fray; but Samuel McKean,
Governor Wolf's friend won the Senatorial prize, partly,
so claimed Cameron, because the Clay men supported
him. However, McKean's biographer attributed his

victory to the winner's opposition to national conventions.[20]

Cameron continued his strategy the following year. William Wilkins, the senior United States Senator from Pennsylvania had been elected in 1830 by a coalition determined to stop the rise of Anti-Masonry. In the Senate Wilkins proved a devoted supporter of Jackson during the nullification controversy and struggle over removal of the United States deposits, but his stand on the bank question had angered many of his constituents. Wilkins, realizing the necessity of a cooling off period, accepted Cameron's aid in securing the Russian mission. This move rehabilitated Cameron with the Wilkin's faction besides providing for a Senatorial vacancy for Buchanan. Cameron was not long in informing Van Buren of his own part in Buchanan's victory, in keeping with his policy of maintaining a heavy correspondence with important political leaders—lest they forget! It is doubtful whether Cameron knew of Jackson's personal aversion to Buchanan or he may not have so ardently pushed the latter's cause in the Jacksonian camp.

In view of Cameron's policy of advancing others, it must have been somewhat of a blow when he failed at his first attempt to secure a share of the federal patronage in the summer of 1834. Death had made vacant the office of governor of Michigan Territory. James Buchanan, on whom Cameron placed much reliance, wrote to the President on the candidate's behalf. Besides noting Cameron's general qualifications for the office, the cunning

---

[20] *Dictionary of American Biography*, XII, 78. Cameron's partisan reasons are likely correct, as McKean did not openly state his position until a week after his election. See Henry R. Mueller, *The Whig Party in Pennsylvania* (New York, 1922), 20.

ex-Congressman was careful to drop a hint Jackson could hardly fail to note—Cameron was already exerting a powerful influence within the state party ranks. To make doubly sure of the prize, Cameron had written the preceding month to a prominent Philadelphia political leader citing his opposition to the United States Bank (?) and arranged to have the chief executive deluged with a flood of letters on his behalf,[21] but, unfortunately, one powerful figure, Governor Wolf, gave him no support.[22]

The next several years were rather inactive ones politically for Cameron. What with lucrative canal contracts, growing railroad interests, new iron partnerships, and his position as cashier of his bank at Middletown, one wonders how he found any time for active participation. Political conditions in Pennsylvania were in a chaotic, practically fluid state: federalism had lately been laid to rest, Anti-Masonry recently had raised its self-righteous head, and the divergent horns of Jeffersonianism, now matured, were recognizable under the appellations of Whigs and Democrats. Confusion was worse confounded when the state Democrats in 1835 ran concurrently two candidates for governor, to the great delight and profit of the Anti-Masonic candidate, Joseph Ritner. However, at the next gubernatorial election the reunited Democrats defeated the Whig-Anti-Masonic coalition, gaining, in addition, the lower house of the legislature. But refusal of the frustrated coalition, under the leader-

[21] In his notes (no. 32, p. 252), Professor Crippen cited this letter as an example of how Cameron showed "himself perfectly capable of catering to the views of the opposition in order to further his own purposes."

[22] The later appointment of Wolf by Jackson to the office of Comptroller of the Treasury is indicative of the President's high regard for him.

ship of the pugnacious Thaddeus Stevens, Thomas Burrowes, Governor Ritner, and others, to concede victory to the Democrats led to that disgraceful episode in Pennsylvania's political history known as the Buckshot War. This event, besides marking the swan song of Anti-Masonry in the Keystone state, brought Stevens, along with his Adams County "Tapeworm," the serpentine Gettysburg Railroad, national attention.[23]

Simon Cameron had been absent in the west during the exciting campaign of 1838, returning just about the time the Buckshot War terminated, so he appears to be innocent of any participation in the episode. But Cameron did fulfill one civic duty during this period in his capacity as delegate to the Friends of the Integrity of the Union meeting in Harrisburg on the eve of the Constitutional Convention of 1837. The purpose of this newly organized society was to plan organized opposition to abolitionist influence in the coming Constitutional Convention, and more specifically to block any antislavery clause Thaddeus Stevens might undertake to insert into the Constitution. This indomitable chieftain was seeking to reactivate his wobbly Anti-Masonic party with a shot of abolitionism.[24]

A pseudo delegate from Adams county, Stevens made an auspicious entrance into the convention, gained the floor, and loaded enemy resolutions with ridiculous amendments which metamorphosed the orderly gathering into bedlam. At the finale of this opera bouffe the voice of delegate Simon Cameron could be heard faintly above the din seeking recognition from the chair. Stevens responded with a mocking burlesque of respect for the

[23] Wayland F. Dunaway, *History of Pennsylvania* (New York, 1948), 386.

[24] Ralph Korngold, *Thaddeus Stevens* (New York, 1955), 48.

delegate's wishes, expressing hope for courteous treatment for Cameron from the convention.[25] By his presence Cameron indicated his willingness to consort openly with the avowed enemies of abolitionism and to prevent any such taint from creeping into Pennsylvania's new constitution. As a good organization man, Cameron saw the wisdom of excluding disruptive influences likely to rent the party with factional strife.

Viewed through Cameron's rose-colored glasses, the Presidential election of 1836 was no ordinary one. Victory for Jackson's designated successor, Van Buren, spelled the spoilsman's reward for one who had worked successfully to sustain the New Yorker when his popularity was at a low ebb within the Keystone state. Cameron's services at the 1836 Democratic National Convention were not needed, nor was he a delegate. True, the Pennsylvania Democratic State Convention, rent by the feud between the Wolf and Muhlenberg factions, failed to come to an agreement on selection of delegates and sent two Van Buren delegations to Baltimore.[26] This appears not to have created much of a tactical problem for the Little Magician. Both sets were seated with each being alloted half the state's vote. An amused spectator in Baltimore on May 20, 1835, the opening day of the national convention, Cameron noted sarcastically how only three years ago barely one-third of a Van Buren delegation from Pennsylvania could be sent but now the entire state "was fighting the honor of singing his praise." [27]

Although a narrow state margin of 4,000 votes for Van

[25] Elsie Singmaster, *I Speak for Thaddeus Stevens* (Cambridge, Mass., 1947), 214.

[26] Bartlett, *The Chief Phases of Pennsylvania Politics*, 93.

[27] Cameron to Buchanan, quoted in Charles M. Snyder, "Pennsylvania Politics, 1833-1847" (Ph.D. Thesis, University of Pennsylvania, Philadelphia. 1949), 111.

Buren over Harrison gave the Commonwealth's Democratic leaders little to brag about in the exciting Presidential election of 1836, they were unanimous in their
expectation that Pennsylvania was to be rewarded with
a place in the Presidential cabinet. Cameron, agreeing
that his state had been badly paid in the past, joined in
the chorus. Van Buren successfully resisted immediate
pressure from all sides, filling only one main vacancy.
Later the state spoilsmen could find little solace in foreign
missions for George M. Dallas and Henry Augustus P.
Muhlenberg.[28] At any rate, Cameron experienced some
comfort in seeing David R. Porter elected to the gubernatorial chair the following year.

The Van Buren administration was still young when the
opportunity presented itself for the president to offer
"tangible evidence," as Cameron aptly stated it, of his
wish to remember the early and efficient services rendered
him by Cameron.[29] Agents would be required to adjust
the debts due the Winnebago Indians and the claims of
their half-breed relatives living in Wisconsin Territory.
Cameron sought federal appointment as Commissioner
through his usual intermediary, James Buchanan.
Allegedly, the petitioner was looking forward to the
pleasures of office rather than any material remuneration
it might offer. Although Cameron's Congressman, Dr.
Luther Reily, registered a strong protest against the appointment, the suppliant secured it from Van Buren
without difficulty. Before setting out on his duties the

---

[28] The latter had rejected an opportunity to go into the Cabinet
as Secretary of the Navy. When he again showed gubernatorial
aspirations which might cause party disharmony he was "hustled"
off to Europe by Van Buren. See *ibid.*, 221-22.

[29] Crippen, *Simon Cameron*, 32.

revengeful Cameron vindicated himself before his constituents by first grabbing the Democratic caucus nomination from Reily, who was seeking re-election, and then
resigning early in the campaign. Cameron at this stage
had "great confidence" in his "own exertions when
centered on a single object." [30]

High waters prevented Cameron and his co-commis-
sioner, General James Murray, from reaching their
destination, Prairie du Chien, on schedule. Contrary to
instructions specifying that each individual claimant
should receive a certificate making drafts payable to him
only, many certificates were issued to third parties acting
for the petitioners. The third parties, unfortunately, were
not required to give bond for their trust. On the basis
of disregard of instructions by the commissioners, the
military disbursing agent of the territory suspended payment of drafts and notified the War Department of his
action, the consequence of which was to bring a new
commissioner on the scene to supplant Cameron.

Cameron certainly would not have received such
notoriety from this affair if it had terminated under the
above circumstances. But enemy journalists hailing him
as Old Winnebago, or the Great Winnebago Chieftain,
and muckraking reformers vying with each other in a
contest for scandalous revelations of the past, with not
even cursory examination of the facts, quoted this
episode as a prime example of corruption in government.
This charge against Cameron resulted largely from the
letters of General Joseph M. Street, Indian Agent in the
territory. Cameron, he alleged, was using $60,000 worth
of Middletown bank notes to buy at a heavy discount
the drafts issued to the half-breeds. In addition, Cameron

[30] Cameron to Buchanan, July 5, 1838, quoted in *ibid.*, 34.

was accused of collaborating with a notorious speculator, Daniel M. Brodhead, who experienced no difficulty in squaring his conscience with the ethics of his methods. These accusations of Street's were based not on sworn witnesses, but solely upon opinions, impressions, and gossip.

A careful study of the Winnebago episode was made by Professor Lee Crippen in his ante-bellum biography of Cameron. His conclusions contribute much toward rehabilitating Cameron's reputation in the affair—a phase that badly needed it. In defense of Cameron's disregard of instructions it was pointed out that the Indian payments did not arrive on schedule, the Indians were anxious to get back on their reservations, the claimants had signified their desire to have a third party act for them, and finally these procedures were approved by Henry Dodge, Superintendent of Indian Affairs for the territory. Cameron's innocence in the incident as expressed by his successor, Judge John Fleming, is evidence not to be overlooked in the case.

A study of the life of Joseph Montfort Street reveals in a striking way the general's passion for making reckless charges. In Kentucky, Aaron Burr, John Brown, Harry Innes, and Christopher Greenup had suffered from the journalistic venom of his *Western World*. In the case of Greenup, Street retracted his accusations, but he did not emerge so easily in his libel suit with Innes, which he lost. Soon after moving to Wisconsin Territory he had tried without success to have Dodge removed for alleged malfeasance in office. Later, in another case, he was fined for exceeding his authority.[31] Briefly, Cameron's part in the Winnebago affair may be stated as follows: he did

[31] Katherine E. Crane, "Joseph Montfort Street," in *Dictionary of American Biography*, XVIII, 136-137.

exceed his instructions and showed poor business acumen in failing to require bond of the third parties intrusted with the certificates; but the charges of Joseph Street remain unproved. Cameron did admit some land investments in the vicinity and reported to Buchanan of the opportunity here offered to reap a fortune.[32] Moreover, a letter to an iron partner in Pennsylvania has an incriminatory tone: "I wish Headley was here, the country would suit him all to pieces and he would soon have a good share of it. He would too have had an opportunity of give me some aid." [33] Recent scholars of the Civil War era still look upon this episode as a smear on Cameron's record.[34]

The year 1839 opened with Cameron in a state of political eclipse. Both James Buchanan and his mouthpiece, editor John W. Forney of the Lancaster *Intelligencer* ostracized him, ostensibly because of his Winnebago notoriety. Cameron, who placed personal loyalty first, must have suffered deeply this rebuff, but he concealed his pride, carried on a heavy correspondence with the Senator, exerted his influence over Governor Porter in Buchanan's behalf, and was happy to see both reelected in 1841 and 1843, respectively. In fact, Porter had been hailed by the opposition Whig organs as the Cameron candidate for governor.[35] This is an admission from the Whig camp of the power which the Camerons (Simon and James) had already built up within the state.

Cameron was now associated with a wing of the victo-

[32] Crippen, *op. cit.*, 254, note 80.

[33] Simon Cameron to Thomas McNair, Oct. 8, 1838, quoted in James B. McNair, *Simon Cameron's Adventures in Iron* (Los Angeles, 1949), 86.

[34] Burton J. Hendrick, *Lincoln's War Cabinet*, 54.

[35] Bellefonte *Democratic-Whig*, July 10, 1841, quoting Harrisburg *Chronicle*.

rious state Democratic power known as the Improvement men. As the name implied, the group favored continued public improvements, a protective tariff, a state bank, and the Relief Bill which forced banks to aid the state treasury and authorized notes pledged by the state. The nadir of Pennsylvania's financial history was at hand and only drastic measures could maintain the Commonwealth's credit.[36] Other Improvement men were Hendrick B. Wright, Muhlenberg, Forney (a silent partner), and, finally, Governor Porter.[37] Sometimes they were known as the Harrisburg *Keystone* clique.

Cameron's failure to support the Van Buren candidate for Speaker of the State House indicated that he considered the time propitious to detach himself from the slipping ex-President. Governor Porter himself was beginning his descent with his second term. Trouble which started in his administrative family led to the resignations of Henry Petriken and Francis R. Shunk, his successor in the gubernatorial chair.[38]

The coming Senatorial, gubernatorial, and Presidential elections brought renewed political interest and participation for Cameron. Some of the Improvement men had started a boom as early as March, 1842, for former Vice-President Richard Johnson of Kentucky through their mouthpiece, the Harrisburg *Keystone*. In January of 1844, a Johnson rally was held at Harrisburg where "General Simon Cameron of Middletown known as one of the most consistent and influential Democrats in the State presided." His speech allegedly produced "unbounded enthusiasm"

[36] Dunaway, *History of Pennsylvania,* 391.
[37] Snyder, "Pennsylvania Politics," 287, 296.
[38] Cameron to Hendrick B. Wright, Nov. 1, 1841, quoted in *ibid.,* 288.

for the taker of Tecumseh's scalp.[39] A polite reply from the Kentucky Colonel to General Cameron indicated a neutral stand in his proposed candidacy until time of the national convention.[40] Cameron's friend, Governor Porter, had allowed himself to be tied with the unpopular President Tyler through his brother's nomination for a cabinet post. Now, in the light of editor Forney's new Presidential boom for Buchanan, Cameron was placed in the ridiculous position of a Porter man working for Buchanan.[41] The situation was relieved by Buchanan's withdrawal as a candidate; later, in January, 1843, Porter's men absented themselves from the caucus which renominated Buchanan for another term as Senator.

At the State Convention, March, 1844, Cameron was disappointed in seeing Van Buren chosen over Johnson as the Democratic state choice for the Presidential nomination. Although Buchanan had already withdrawn his name the preceding December in the interest of party harmony, his friends were determined to keep open every possible avenue for his re-entry into the Presidential race. Van Buren's lack of enthusiasm for southwestern expansion lessened his chances of election, said many political leaders, and in addition he was distasteful to the Pennsylvania protectionists. Cameron was among the group which again began agitating in May for Buchanan's candidacy. The most they could wring from the conscience-stricken Pennsylvania Senator at the last minute was his consent to enter the lists only after Van Buren had a trial heat at the National Convention. About the same time Buchanan made his announcement, Cameron,

[39] Harrisburg *Democratic-Union,* Jan. 27, 1844.
[40] *Ibid.,* March 2, 1844.
[41] Snyder, "Pennsylvania Politics," 310, 313.

in conjunction with John M. Read, called a hurried meeting of the Democratic State Central Committee for the purpose of releasing the Van Buren pledge delegates. Lack of a quorum prevented success and Cameron set out at once for Baltimore to play the part of observer-strategist.

With Improvement man Hendrick B. Wright of Pennsylvania in the chair, this strange, exciting Van Buren convention adopted the two-thirds rule with the aid of "Van Buren" votes from Pennsylvania, thus practically insuring the New Yorker's defeat.[42] What followed was a deadlock between Van Buren and Lewis Cass with the remainder of the vote split between Buchanan and Johnson; and then the prearranged "surprise" candidate, James K. Polk, stampeded the convention. A long shot of the Cameron men that Buchanan or Johnson would emerge as the compromise candidate paid off badly. The second-hand choice of George M. Dallas, Philadelphia blueblood, as Polk's running mate raised orthodox eyebrows among the Democrats who had lately heard a Democratic National Convention pass resolutions against a new National Bank.[43]

A protectionist Democrat, it would seem easier for an ironmaster of Cameron's caliber to support Clay, the Whig Presidential candidate rather than the Democratic one. Polk's letter of June 19, to John K. Kane, a citizen of Philadelphia, was obviously intended to allay the

[42] Thomas H. Benton, *Thirty Years in the United States Senate* (2 vols., New York, 1856), II, 593. The Pennsylvania delegation voted 13-12 to sustain the two-thirds rule. According to Benton, the Pennsylvania delegates "may be said to have decided the nomination."

[43] J. W. Forney confided to Buchanan his fear of Dallas as a drag on the national ticket. See Mueller, *Whig Party in Pennsylvania*, 104.

fears of Pennsylvania protectionists and at the same time garner votes from the free traders. This letter, a masterpiece of equivocation, contained a phrase sanctioning "moderate discriminating duties" which would produce needed revenue and "afford reasonable incidental protection."[44] At any rate, Cameron, as a party regular, worked in a lukewarm fashion for Democratic success in November, and even opened a correspondence with the party nominee. Polk, whether because of his superlative political calisthenics, or perhaps because of Old Hickory's embodied ghost, carried the state with a safe majority.

The choice of Henry Augustus Muhlenberg for the Democratic gubernatorial nomination was much more to Cameron's liking. After a desperate struggle over the seating of delegates at the state convention, Francis Shunk withdrew from the field.[45] Instead of healing wounds this only added more to the ones first contributed by Muhlenberg when he ran as a bolting candidate in 1835.[46] The Improvement men, however, received a bad jolt when Muhlenberg died in mid-August, leaving his convention opponent, Shunk, the logical last minute choice of the party. Fears that a vindictive Shunk might emerge with the governorship led the Muhlenberg men to seek guarantees of a conciliatory administrative policy together with a fair share of the patronage. Buchanan, playing the role of chief pacificator obtained a "reluctant promise from Cameron to get into line," and a pledge from Shunk if elected to office to practice no discrimination against the Muhlenberg faction.[47]

[44] *Ibid.*, 103, quoting *Niles Register*, LXVI, 295.
[45] Snyder, *op. cit.*, 330.
[46] Alexander K. McClure, *Old Times Notes of Pennsylvania*, (2 vols., Philadelphia, 1905), I, 88.
[47] Snyder, *op. cit.*, 335.

The state Whigs, on their part suffering from evident lack of leadership, had separated hero Joseph Markle from his plow in Westmoreland County in order for him to pave the way in October, 1844, for a far more glorious Clay victory in November. This western Pennsylvania Cincinnatus established new campaign strategy by stumping for the gubernatorial prize mounted on his steed. However, these unorthodox campaign tactics of the general failed to pay off and Markle's defeat by Shunk presaged a victory for "Polk, Dallas, and the Tariff of 1842," or so the top Democratic echelon pretended to believe. Polk and Dallas did win, but not the Tariff of 1842, as was perceived soon after the Presidential election.

Announcement of Shunk's cabinet confirmed the fears of the Muhlenberg faction. The governor-elect chose a small coterie of private friends to fill the offices of Secretary of Commonwealth, attorney-general, and auditor-general. One of these appointees, John K. Kane, recipient of Polk's famous tariff letter, was especially offensive to the Muhlenberg men. In light of Buchanan's glowing description of Cameron as the "life and soul of the Muhlenberg party," [48] it is little wonder that he should consider himself the first on Shunk's proscription list; or that he should lend a willing ear to Whig cries for a "champion supported by a sufficient number of virtuoutous [sic] Democrats," to uphold their interests. [49]

Simon Cameron, who championed the Pennsylvania

[48] Buchanan to Shunk, Aug. 15, 1844, quoted in Crippen, *op. cit.*, 56. McClure sarcastically identified this faction as the one "that usually managed to control the canal board and political plunder of the state," *Old Time Notes*, 1, 92.

[49] Philadelphia *United States Gazette*, Dec. 7, 1844, quoted in Snyder, *op. cit.*, 343.

Whig interests of tariff protection and internal improvements, now endorsed the Northern Conscience Whig's
antipathy to the spread of slavery,[50] and realized at once
the potentialities of the call for new alignments under
new leadership.

A hint of Cameron's aspirations to achieve a United
States Senatorial seat through regular party channels is
seen in his letter of December 7, 1844, to Buchanan, reporting in somewhat schoolboy fashion the favorable
notice he was receiving from "several gentlemen" who
were hoping to see him replace Daniel Sturgeon in the
Senatorial election of January, 1845.[51] Not unlikely this
letter was sent with the hope of getting Buchanan's blessing for such a move. Rather amusingly, Cameron's correspondence with Buchanan and his friends, during the national post-election interim betrays an unusual solicitude
for Buchanan's political welfare; no doubt with the hope
of stimulating its beneficiary to reciprocate in like manner.

The Shunk-Muhlenberg factional strife was again evident when the legislative Democrats went into caucus to
select their Senatorial nominee. Neither of the factions
could decide the contest in favor of their candidates and
the incumbent, Daniel Sturgeon, emerged the winner.
The Shunk faction, however, got its man for state treasurer
while the Muhlenberg men gained nothing. Sturgeon's
scant majority in the caucus was indicative of the dissatisfaction within party ranks. Through Buchanan,
Cameron transmitted what could be considered a virtual

[50] McClure had no doubt of Cameron's antislavery proclivities
at this stage of his career. See *Notes* I, 92.

[51] Snyder, *op. cit.*, 346. Crippen made no mention of the Sturgeon
vacancy and accepted this letter as indicative of Cameron's hope
to succeed Buchanan when the latter stepped into Polk's cabinet.
This was ten days before Polk made the appointment.

ultimatum as to the future course of the Muhlenberg
men—because no favors could be expected by acting with
the Shunk group his men were preparing "to resist further
attempts of the Administration to reward favorites with
office." [52] A Democratic legislative majority of thirteen
over the combined Whigs and Native Americans brought
about the re-election of Sturgeon, the "silent senator." [53]

Within two months, the entrance of Buchanan into
Polk's cabinet again gave the Democrats an opportunity
to fill another vacant Senatorial seat. The Muhlenberg
malcontents, under the leadership of Cameron, now had
the opportunity of pulling the proverbial rabbit out of
their hats—that is, of course, if they possessed the magic.
Hindsight makes it evident that Cameron proceded as
carefully and secretly as possible. A coup could be
executed successfully only with the help of the frustrated
minority Whigs. Cameron's letter to Buchanan, more than
a month before the election, in which he expressed his
ability to name Buchanan's successor was more than a bid
for help—it was the boast of a proud political warrior
already confident of success. A week later John Y. James,
Pennsylvania legislator, disclosed Cameron's plan to
Buchanan. His strategy called for the Democratic insurgents to boycott their caucus and ally themselves with
the Whigs.[54] Two weeks before the election, Cameron was
marshalling every possible resource in his own behalf. To
his former iron partner he wrote: "If you can aid me with
Mr. Morley and Mr. Campbell I will remember it with

[52] Cameron to Buchanan, Jan. 20, 1845, quoted in Snyder, *op.
cit.*, 344.

[53] Sturgeon is said to have made only one speech in his Senatorial
career. Appleton's *Cyclopedia of American Biography*, V, 734.

[54] Snyder, *op cit.*, 345.

gratitude. Their aid might secure the election and it would place me in a situation where I should have many opportunities of serving my friends." [55]

The composition of the nominating Democratic caucus which chose G. W. Woodward, the Shunk candidate of the January caucus, its Senatorial nominee, consisted of only 48 of the full roster of 73 legislative Democrats.[56] Even with the Cameron coterie absent, the Woodward men had much difficulty in nominating their candidate. Hendrick B. Wright and William Ross secured lobbyists to reveal Woodward's alleged Nativist and free-trading inclinations.[57] Woodward's winning caucus vote of 25 represented approximately one-third of the Democratic strength in the legislature.

It could hardly be considered a coincidence that on the same day Woodward was nominated, a group of Whigs addressed a letter to Cameron regarding his views on the tariff, alien qualifications for citizenship, and the distribution of the proceeds from public land sales. In accordance with prearranged plans, Cameron's replies were consistent with Whig views, but the wary Whigs had no intention of supporting a bolting Democrat without two important guarantees: the first consisting of a public written statement of Cameron's future policies as a Senator and, secondly, proof of the bolter's Democratic strength without Whig help. Failure to select a caucus candidate gave the Whigs freedom to maneuver as they saw fit.

[55] Cameron to Thomas McNair, February 26, 1845, quoted in McNair *op. cit.*, 97. Both these gentlemen were representatives from Luzerne County, where factionalism was rife. See Snyder, *op. cit.*, 345.

[56] Harrisburg *Democratic-Union*, April 2, 1845.

[57] Snyder, *op. cit.*, 345.

On March 13, 1845, the legislative houses chose Buchanan's successor. The Woodward party regulars mustered their full strength from the beginning and their candidate's vote varied only by two through five ballots. Cameron, starting with 11 Democratic votes on the first ballot, increased it to 25 on the second. The Whigs now had proof of the bolter's Democratic strength and began throwing their votes to Cameron, who captured the election on the fifth ballot, 67 votes to Woodward's 55. The Harrisburg *Democratic-Union* announced with "regret that a combination of fortuitous circumstances thwarted the wholesome usages of the party," but derived comfort from the fact that the interests of the party "are committed to a Democrat every way worthy of the honor." [58]

Few Senatorial elections in Pennsylvania's political history have created more interest or excitment than the election of Simon Cameron to the Senate of the United States in 1845. Buchanan's bombastic mouthpiece, John Wien Forney, greeeted news of the political bombshell with a "God save the Commonwealth." [59] Addresses to the Democracy of Pennsylvania excoriated the unorthodox and disorganized conduct of Cameron "whose pledge to Whigs and natives should . . . sever him from association and confidence of the Democratic party." [60] Buchanan, who had privately expressed his disgust of Cameron's boast of being able to name the next Pennsylvania Senator,[61] remained aloof from the clamor. Vice-

[58] March 15, 1845.
[59] John W. Forney to Morton McMichael, March 14, 1845, John W. Forney Papers, LC.
[60] Crippen, *op. cit.*, 61, 62.
[61] Eugene E. Savidge, *Life of Benjamin Harris Brewster* (Philadelphia, 1891), 71.

President Dallas, because of his position as president of
the Senate, also refrained from direct abuse of Cameron,
but could hardly find words strong enough to denounce
those who would enter into an alliance with the professed
enemies of the Democracy.[62]

Cameron on his part professed to disbelieve that one
(Buchanan) he had served for 12 years as a "son serves
a father" could be guilty of connivance with the vilifiers.
Cameron's further observation that he had never asked
any aid from Buchanan must have created some kind of
stir within the Democratic sage. The letter to Buchanan
ended with a veiled threat: Cameron preferred peace to
war but such a war could not remain one-sided.[63] The
leaders of the Democratic Party evidently considered the
revolt dangerous and salved the matter over by pleading
for party harmony.

The first phase of Cameron's political career came to
a close with his entrance upon the national scene. Here
was first demonstrated within the Commonwealth the
ability of an individual who never submitted his name
to the voters in a public election to build up a personal
following at the risk of jeopardizing the political careers
of its members and of achieving victory in a manner
heretical to the dogmas of his own party.

[62] Harrisburg *Democratic-Union*, June 25, 1845.
[63] Cameron to Buchanan, March 27, 1845, quoted in Crippen,
op. cit., 62. In June, 1878, Cameron told a correspondent of the
New York Times that he ran in 1845 because of the disparaging
remarks that had been made about him and the pleas he received
from a group of manufacturers.

2
Man of Affairs

SIMON CAMERON, HIGHLY SUCCESSFUL BUSINESS MAN OF 1845, was a product of the very erratic formative years of American industry. The embryo tycoons of Protestant America, so it seemed, in agreement with the Calvinistic bourgeois philosophy of the day could see no sin in the practice of crushing competitors in their world of business six days of the week and sharing the spoils on the seventh with a benevolent deity. Thus, through the keen business acumen usually attributed to those of thrifty Scot Covenanter ancestry, he had succeeded in gaining a place of recognition in several phases of economic endeavor. Living comfortably in middle class style at Middletown, not far from the state capital, Harrisburg, this highly successful entrepreneur, happily married, was busy with the task of rearing his five children, engaging in many business activities over a wide area, and participating in civic affairs, with time to spare for intense, sporadic political activity.

In the early 1830's the Cameron family moved from Harrisburg into living quarters at the Middletown Bank building. Their second son, William Brua, born in 1826, graduated from Princeton two years after his father's election to the Senate, assisted in the family enterprise at Middletown, and became paymaster in the Union Army with the coming of the war.[1] John Colin, Ann Eliza, Mary, and James Buchanan died in childhood, while the youngest son, Simon, lived at a school for mentally retarded children. The sixth child, James Donald ("Don"), born in 1833 also graduated from Princeton, was soon intrusted with much of his father's business and finally in 1877 inherited the greatest political machine the Commonwealth had yet seen. Rachel, the eldest daughter, married a leading lawyer of Bellefonte, James Burnside, president judge of twenty-fifth judicial district of Pennsylvania. The citizens of Centre County came to know Simon Cameron intimately because he periodically visited his daughter and delivered political talks in Bellefonte. Rachel was widowed in 1859 when Judge Burnside was killed by a fall from his carriage.[2] Two other daughters, Virginia Rolette,[3] and Margaretta were married to prominent Pennsylvanians, Wayne MacVeagh (1866) and Richard S. Haldeman (1870), respectively.

Although observers at a distance usually regarded Cameron somewhat antisocial, aloof, and lacking the human interest touch usually attributed to successful political leaders, he actually was quite pleasant and congenial within small groups. Three years prior to the time when editor John Wien Forney had besought the deity's aid upon hearing of Cameron's first election to

[1] Egle, *History of Dauphin and Lebanon*, 473.

[2] Bellefonte *Central Press*, July 7, 1859.

[3] Virginia's middle name, "Rolette," is of special interest because Jean Joseph Rolette, pioneer fur trader was chief justice for Crawford County, Wisconsin Territory at Prairie du Chien in 1838, where Cameron lived during the Winnebago affair.

the Senate, that worthy had accompanied Simon Cameron
on a delightful spring trip through Pennsylvania's lush
southeastern counties. Concerning Cameron's affability in
1842, Forney related:

We . . . enjoyed the scenery, the weather, and the conversation of the people, with whom General Cameron was, even
at that early day, on the most familiar terms. It was very
pleasant to notice how intimately he understood the habits
and history of the people of the whole country-side through
which we passed—how at intervals, he would stop the carriage, hail the passer-by, ask about his health, joke with him
on politics, inquire about his wife, sons, daughters by name,
and enter into a familiar speculation as to the coming crops.[4]

Although Simon Cameron at that time possessed no
statewide political organization he had already laid some
foundations upon which to build his future pyramidal
political hierarchy.

Along with his amiable qualities, Cameron retained a
curtain of commanding reserve the components of which
few could fathom. It was this "peculiar manner"[5] which
enabled him to metamorphose an apparently pleasant
request into a peremptory enjoiner. Recalcitrant political
leaders, usually of the stolid local type, learned to know
and dread his reputed occult powers and there were few
indeed who failed to emerge from one of those Cameronian "conferences" duly chastened.

The new Senator of 1845, tall, erect in bearing, his
high broad forehead crowned with luxuriant greying hair
matching keen grey eyes,[6] presented a dignified appearance even in presence of such an august body as the

[4] John W. Forney, *Anecdotes of Public Men* (New York, 1873),
66.

[5] *Ibid.*, 67.

[6] A Howard Meneely, *The War Department*, 1861 (New York,
1928), 84.

Senate. Fifteen years later William H. Russell, war correspondent of the London *Times*, upon meeting the new Secretary of War at a White House reception was impressed with the "idea of a person of ability and adroitness." [7]

By 1845 Simon Cameron had investments in a variety of interests, *viz.*, newspapers, printing, public works, banks, railroads, and iron. Journalism and printing marked his entrance into the business world. Although he ended his career as an editor in 1827, Cameron continued as a silent partner of S. C. Stambaugh in the Harrisburg *Pennsylvania Reporter*. With various partners Cameron received, through Governor Shulze's influence, lucrative state printing contracts, beginning in 1824 and ending in 1829, totaling approximately $7,000.[8] When Simon became adjutant-general in 1829 the state printing contracts were made out in the name of his brother James.[9] With the coming of the Wolf regime, Cameron lost the state printing patronage. Shortly after his election to the Senate, Cameron owned one-fourth interest in the Washington *Union*.

Upon completion of Governor Clinton's "ditch," the Erie Canal, in New York State, the canal craze hit Pennsylvania head on. The "Pennsylvania Public Works" system in 1840, which at first consisted of horse railways and a portage in addition to the 600 miles of canals, had cost the Commonwealth $32,000,000, over six times the original estimate.[10] This tremendous state burden led to

[7] William Howard Russell, *My Diary North and South* (New York, 1954, edition by Fletcher Pratt), 27.

[8] McNair, *op. cit.*, 10, 11, 12.   [9] *Ibid.*, 12.

[10] Arthur Cecil Bining, *Rise of American Economic Life* (New York, 1949), 214.

rumors of repudiation of debt. In conjunction with various partners Simon Cameron was awarded contracts for several canal sections both in the eastern and western divisions. He began work in 1826 on the section between Harrisburg and Northumberland. All of Cameron's canal contracts were awarded during the terms of his friend, Governor Shulze, his last one being awarded the same year Schulze left office.[11] It is also of interest to note that Charles Mowry, his first printing partner, was a canal commissioner in charge of two eastern divisions.[12] In addition, the firm of McCord and Cameron was awarded a contract to construct the New Orleans Lake Ponchartrain Canal, a tremendous project for its day. The firm was relieved of its obligations because of McCord's financial failure, but Cameron was retained as superintendent. Regarding his financial remuneration for this work, Cameron wrote: "If Hulings had never come here I should have made such a fortune as would have satisfied a much more avaricious man than myself—as it is I shall not grumble." [13] Cameron was also one of the managers of the Susquehanna and Tidewater Canal extending on the left bank of the Susquehanna river from Columbia, a canal-railroad junction, to the tidewater.

Hard on the heels of the canal mania came the railroad era, the chief factor leading to the early decline of canals. Work began on railroads within Pennsylvania at a time when horses still provided the locomotive power. In 1832 a charter was granted for a railroad extending from Lancaster to Harrisburg via Portsmouth. The latter town was located on the Susquehanna and because of its location the proposed eastern branch could be considered a

[11] McNair, *op. cit.*, 14.   [12] *Ibid.*, 14.
[13] Cameron to Ayres, Jan. 9, 1831, quoted in *ibid.*, 17.

competitor to the railway section of the state works. As this rail line was projected to go through Cameron's town of Middletown, it is no surprise to find his name among those pushing subscriptions and on the 1840 list of directors. The Cameron brothers, William and James, were given contracts for parts of the construction. In 1836 the portion between Middletown and Harrisburg was completed and first runs were initiated with an English locomotive appropriately dubbed "John Bull."

With the Lancaster-Harrisburg railroad incompleted and subscriptions exhausted the company sought a $200,-000 loan from the successor of the United States Bank at Philadelphia. The line was completed probably the next year (1837) and Cameron was elected its president. Cameron was also interested in two other lines; the Susquehanna running northward from Harrisburg, and the Cumberland Valley, extending south. He was largely instrumental in organizing the first and "gave encouragement" [14] to the latter. These two roads later became part of the Northern Central, known commonly as the Cameron road. With the new presidency of Cameron in 1853, the Lebanon Valley Railroad prospered. James Cameron, superintendent of motive power on the state Columbia Railroad, was in a position to assist connecting lines such as the Harrisburg-Lancaster. During the heat of a political campaign, James Cameron was charged with profiting to the extent of $100,000 from the Columbia road.[15] The bid of four partners, two of whom were Simon

[14] Egle, *op. cit.*, 563.

[15] In 1840 Cameron was removed from the Board of the Harrisburg-Lancaster line because he publicly proclaimed the railroad "dangerous to life and property." The resolution was soon repealed and he was reelected. See copy of April 8, 1889, Cameron MSS, LC.

and William Cameron, to buy (1842) the State railroad from Columbia to Philadelphia for the then enormous sum of $3,000,000 testified to the huge collateral then available to the Camerons.[16] Simon Cameron took advantage of his nearness to the legislative halls at Harrisburg, to lobby actively for railroad legislation [17] both for himself and his friends.

Although Cameron was often termed an ironmaster by the press, his early investments in this field do not appear considerable. Heavy commitments concurrently in railroads, together with the economic conditions of the late 1830's, can explain his difficulty in raising funds for even small enterprises in the iron business. In view of the heavy demands for this type of ware required by newly chartered railroads it is easy to visualize the added profits to be gained by selling iron from privately owned forges to the construction contractors.

In 1837, Cameron, S. F. Headley, and Thomas McNair bought the Foundryville forge near Berwick in Columbia County for $15,000. One hundred more dollars brought the addition of 400 acres to be used as a source of wood fuel. The Bank of Northumberland accepted the note which the partners gave to its former owner in partial payment for the property. The furnace was in operation by the following summer turning out castings, hollow ware and stove iron. Cameron took out time from his other duties to visit various furnaces, noting the more efficient production of the hot blast furnace. In November, 1839, Cameron sold his interest to McNair. In partnership with his brother, James, Cameron bought

[16] Most of the information on railroads is taken from McNair, *Cameron's Adventures in Iron.*

[17] Snyder, *op. cit.,* 158.

Nescopeck Forge just across the line from Berwick in
Luzerne County. This forge was sold at a loss of $1,000
in the early 1840's when economic conditions within the
Commonwealth were at their lowest ebb. A few years
later when prosperity returned to the iron industry
Cameron commented to his former partner: ". . . we were
unfortunate to be in business at the worst time." [18]

Banking, one of Cameron's earliest business ventures,
continued to interest him many years but with declining
active participation after his son, James Donald, became
his partner. The Bank of Middletown was organized during Cameron's first year of residence in the town. No
doubt his heavy subscription of 78 shares in the enterprise had a bearing on his selection as cashier after his
future iron partner refused the position. The Middletown
bank, evidently well managed, soon began paying divi-
dends and was accepted as a depository for state funds.
The policy of allowing private banks to use state funds
for private investment remained one of the perennial
scandals of Pennsylvania state government for many
years. Following the collapse of the Second United States
Bank, the bank at Middletown was also favored with
federal deposits, labeling it one of the "pet" banks of the
Democratic administration. Along with the Whigs,
Cameron was glad to see passage of a resolution in the
state legislature requesting a postponement in Congress
of the Independent Treasury Bill. Such passage was described to banker Gratz as a "great and glorious victory."[19]

Two factors made it especially difficult for the Bank
of Middletown to survive. The first was the terrible panic

[18] McNair, *op. cit.*, 97.
[19] Cameron to Simon Gratz, Feb. 12, 1838, quoted in Snyder,
op. cit., 184.

of 1837 which continued with variations through 1841. The other was Cameron's proclivity for making loans to friends without sufficient collateral to guarantee repayments. The later policy, unorthodox as it may have been from the viewpoint of sound banking, constituted a contributing factor in Cameron's rise to political success. However, Cameron was not lax in keeping an eye on proposed banking legislation. When an anti-bank bill was pending which would require bank stock to be sold at auction, excessive bank profits to be surrendered to the state, and stockholders to be personally liable for bank obligations, Cameron camped in Harrisburg for the entire session of the legislature. When reminded by Cameron that this was also their fight, Philadelphia bankers contributed to his "expenses." At Harrisburg one could not live on the winds.[20]

Although the Middletown Bank successfully weathered the panic years, its position was still insecure when James Donald Cameron returned from Princeton in 1852. He gradually assumed a place of leadership in the bank and ended the policy of leniency practiced by his father. Half a century after its founding the Cameron Bank in Middletown was doing business as usual, with Don its president.

When the new Senator, representing the business interests of the Commonwealth, appeared in Washington in the middle of March, 1845, the Senate was concluding its special session; consequently there was little for Simon Cameron to do as a national legislator beyond taking his oath of office and returning to Middletown to await the assembling of the Twenty-ninth Congress in December. Senator Benton in his comments on the freshmen Senators of the new Congress did not see fit to include Cameron

[20] Cameron to Gratz, *ibid.*, 186-87.

on the list of those later to achieve eminence.[21] Ernest
Bates noted the new Pennsylvania Senator as "the first
of the long line of political bosses to hold despotic rule
over the vote of that unhappy state."[22] Although he had
not been elected as the Democratic party candidate
Cameron was anxious to secure recognition again as a
party regular; and so attempted to inform President Polk
through his fast cooling political liasion agent, James
Buchanan.[23] At a White House evening visit after the
December presidential message, Cameron again reassured
the President: "We Pennsylvanians may scratch a little
about the tariff but we will not quarrel about it."[24]

However when an administration measure to alter the
protective tariff of 1842 was proposed in the Senate,
Cameron did much more than "scratch"; in fact he became the acknowledged leader of the Senate protectionist
bloc which sought, futilely, to kill it.[25] The so-called
Compromise Tariff of 1833 had actually maintained protective features until the beginning of 1842 when it
suffered a drastic reduction. The protectionists Whigs
allowed the tariff to remain only very briefly at its rock
bottom rate of 20 per cent. The Tyler-Whig political feud
is credited with producing the ill-considered, hasty tariff
legislation of 1842.[26]

Because this controversial tariff of 1842 was definitely

[21] Benton, *op. cit.*, II, 655.

[22] Ernest S. Bates, *Story of Congress: 1789-1935* (New York,
1936), 173.

[23] Crippen, *op. cit.*, 69.

[24] Allen Nevins, ed., *Polk, The Diary of a President* (New York,
1952), 30-31.

[25] George P. Garrison, *Western Extension, 1841-1850* (New
York, 1906), 186.

[26] F. W. Taussig, *Tariff History of United States* (New York,
Fifth Edition, 1909), 113.

protective in nature, the industrialists were prepared to fight to maintain the *status quo* under an administration pledging itself to revision. The proposed tariff legisla- iton of 1846 was framed by Secretary of the Treasury Robert J. Walker, a gentleman well known for his free trade inclinations; but actually the bill under Schedule C provided for a 30 per cent duty on such controversial articles as iron, manufactured metals, woolens, leather, glass, wood, etc.[27]

Cameron, a professed Democrat, might be censured for fighting against a Democratic administration measure but two factors were in his favor: he owed no debts to the new Polk regime and he was representing the sentiments of his own state. In January, before the Walker Bill was introduced in the House, the Pennsylvania legislature passed a resolution requesting all its members in Congress to oppose any modification of the Tariff of 1842. As in- structed, Pennsylvania's Congressmen, both Whig and Democratic, voted against Walker's bill with the excep- tion of David Wilmot, who remembered that his Congres- sional constituents placed agricultural interests first. With passage of the bill in the House, no time was lost in bringing it to the floor of the Senate for action.

In the course of lengthy consideration of the bill in the upper house, Cameron delivered what is generally considered his greatest oratorical effort in his long career as Senator. His speech of July 22, read from a manuscript, occupied approximately eight pages of the *Congressional Globe.* Starting in the somewhat stereotyped style of the time, with an elaborate glorification of American political institutions, and interjected with quotations from Wash- ington, Adams, Jefferson, Monroe, and lastly Jackson,

[27] *Ibid.,* 114.

whom he characterized as the most remarkable man of his age, Cameron developed the thesis of a democratic protective tariff. Agricultural interests were inseparable, said Cameron, from those of industry, and the interest of the laborer was bound to that of the industrialist. The recent industrial prosperity within his state was due largely to the protective tariff of 1842. The Keystone State, now producing over half the nation's iron, would soon be in position to compete with Britain. Cameron labeled anti-protectionist principles those of the "Southern Democracy [which] would rob the poor man of his labor, and make him dependent on the capitalists of England for his scanty subsistence." [28] In answer to the observations of Senator Ambrose H. Sevier of Arkansas, who made caustic remarks on the character of Pennsylvania's labor, Cameron replied that "he desired to learn no new democracy from gentlemen who compared his laboring fellow citizens with the Negro laborers of the South."

Inasmuch as Cameron was treading on dangerous ground in attempting to sectionalize the vote on the tariff, he was also accepting a gambler's chance that tariff legislation detrimental to *free labor*, which in the popular mind of many Northerners existed only in the North, could be defeated with Northern votes. That Cameron was taking into consideration all contingencies of the situation is shown by his pointed remarks directed to his fellow Pennsylvanian, Dallas, seated in the Senate presidential chair, who, in event of a deadlock would be required to cast the deciding vote. After quoting from an eight-year-old speech of Dallas lauding the protective system, Cameron must have caused the Vice-President to

[28] *Cong. Globe*, 29 Cong., 1 Sess., Appendix, 1133.

squirm by adding that "No native Pennsylvanian would dishonor his state by supporting the bill." [29]

As Cameron correctly divined, the Vice-President was required to vote; not on its final passage but on a third reading which made possible final action. The bill then passed the Senate with amendments and was accepted by the House. Dallas defended his affirmative vote on the tariff on the basis of national interests in preference to those of one state, Pennsylvania.[30] With characteristic persistence, Cameron on his part refused to accept the act as final. He characterized the new tariff worthy of British statesmanship with repeal coming from the enraged laborers and mechanics.[31]

The question seizing the imagination of the American public in 1846 was not the commonplace tariff, the intricacies of which few could fathom; instead it was the growing pains of a boisterous youthful nation, confident in its ultimate destiny of spreading the new-found glories of democracy over the North American continent, and now, so it seemed, about to resume its inexorable march. A party pledged to annexing Texas to the Union in addition to extending the nation's territory contiguous to Russia's Alaska, had come into power under the leadership of a President who know what he wanted and eventually got just that. The southward thrust could easily lead to war with Mexico, while even the most genial of John Bulls could hardly be expected to acquiesce in such an unreasonable face-losing demand as the cession of all of Oregon to the greedy Yankee.

With Texas already annexed, and the Congressional decision to agree to terminate the joint occupation of

[29] *Ibid.*, 1136.   [30] Snyder, *op. cit.*, 358.
[31] *Cong. Globe,* 29 Cong., 1 Sess., 1157.

Oregon, north-western states expansionsts, including Lewis Cass, Stephen A. Douglas, and abolitionist Joshua Giddings, pressed for all of Oregon.[32] There was general feeling among the Northerners that the Southerners, especially the slavocracy, having accomplished their goal of slavery expansion in Texas, were now willing to accept a mere mess of pottage for the nation's birthright in the far northwest. Cameron, in agreement with the Northern expansionists, believed "our title only terminates where the Russian line begins, at 54 degrees 40." [33] His vote later against the pending Oregon settlement with Britain indicated his belief in again postponing a final settlement of the Oregon question.

At the time Cameron made his statement on April 23, 1845, the wisdom of not closing the door to further negotiations with Britain over the Oregon question was evident. Relations with Mexico were at the breaking point, and only a fortnight later Polk discovered that Mexico, violating the sovereign boundary rights of a free nation had caused American soil to run red with American blood. Here at last was sufficient cause for a righteous war of conquest resulting in not only an inflated Texas, blown up to bursting proportions, but also a huge expanse, much of its wasteland, commonly known as the Mexican Cession, inhabited by Mexicans, Indians, and Gila monsters in addition to a few stray Yanquis.

The decision to bring Texas into the Union had aroused the ire of antislavery elements everywhere. The new Senator, Simon Cameron, seriously considered himself a tribune of his constitutents, and in this capacity he found himself presenting petitions from citizens of Philadelphia and Lancaster praying the rejection of Texas or in fact

[32] Turner, *op. cit.*, 551-52.   [33] *Ibid.*, 551-52.

any slave state.[34] Significantly, he did not publicly project his own ideas on the subject and registered no protest or comment when such petitions were immediately tabled in the Senate. Cameron was one of the forty Senators voting promptly for war with Mexico upon the request of President Polk, and later he "agreed in every particular" with the manner in which the administration had prosecuted the war.[35] In the midst of the Mexican War, during the course of extended remarks in the Senate, March 1, 1847, he expressed his determination to cheerfully obey the mandate of the Pennsylvanians and their legislature, who were united in their opposition to the acquiring of more slave territory. In accordance with instructions, Cameron voted the following day for the Wilmot Proviso.[36]

At this point Cameron was doing an excellent job of ambidextrous political gymnastics. To ignore the vote of 133 Pennsylvania state legislators, many of whom were likely to pass on his re-election to the Senate, was unthinkable—hence the statement: ". . . the agent was bound to carry out in good faith the wishes of his principal." [37] On the other hand Cameron had no wish to be classed as a free-soiler and evidently considered himself at heart a Democratic regular; consequently his assertion that he would never hesitate in giving up his *own opinion* and adopting those of his state. He followed this with the temporizing statement that the people of Pennsylvania did not wish to interfere with the Southern institutions and many believed the South would abolish slavery in

---

[34] *Ibid.*, 24.   [35] *Cong. Globe*, 30 Cong., 1 Sess., 95.
[36] *Ibid.*, 29 Cong. 2 Sess., 551, 555-56.   [37] *Ibid.*, 551.

due time. His fight the following year against the free-
soilers of his own state[38] is proof of his wish to keep
Democratic state factions free of such taint.

A steady stream of petitions from groups representing
a great variety of interests poured in upon the freshman
Senator. He never seemed to tire in the presentation of
them although many were repetitious or dilatory in nature.
His efforts on behalf of Mexican War veterans evoked
commendatory remarks from various Pennsylvania groups,
and even the New York *Tribune* paid tribute to him as
a devoted public servant.[39] His numerous, almost daily
memorials before the Senate praying for the relief of
indigent Pennsylvanians became somewhat of a scandal
even in that repeatedly beseeched body. According to
Senator Sevier of Arkansas, the usual procedure in the
Senate consisted of prayers, reading the "Journal" followed
by an hour and half "consumed in the recital of a sort of
funeral dirge from the pensioners of Pennsylvania." [40]
This charge provoked an angry retort from the Pennsylvania senator.

Cameron's hottest encounter in the Senate occured on
the last day of the thirtieth Congress. It was after the
stroke of midnight, with Senatorial nerves strained to the
breaking point, that Cameron, the lame duck, sought to
bring the wrangling to an end. The captious three-time
duelist, Henry S. Foote of Mississippi, fortified with
alcoholic stimulants, challenged Cameron's right to speak,
and thrusting his fist into the speaker's face shouted,

[38] Allen Nevins, *Ordeal of the Union* (2 vols. New York, 1947),
I, 190.
[39] December 11, 1847, quoted in Crippen, *op. cit.*, 88.
[40] *Cong. Globe*, 29 Cong., 1 Sess., 1132.

"That's false." Cameron's lightning-like blow knocked Foote "on his back like a deadman." While the fallen senator's friends were engaged in carrying the body into the Senate lobby, Cameron calmly concluded his remarks. A Harrisburg paper reported an encounter in Cameron's favor.[41] The *Congressional Globe* glossed over the incident as "something approaching a personal collision." [42]

Undoubtedly the national Democratic administration of 1845-49 best remembered Senator Cameron not for his unsolicited support as an expansionist, nor even for his war on the Walker Tariff, but rather for his encounter with President Polk involving such questions as the patronage, the custom of Senatorial courtesy, and especially Cameron's status as a Democratic party regular, in the course of which the junior Senator from Pennsylvania administered a humiliating defeat to a chagrined President and in the process possibly widened the breach with his old political confidant, James Buchanan. This conflict centered around Polk's nomination of George W. Woodward to the Supreme Court and that of Henry Horn to the very lucrative post of Collector of the Port of Philadelphia.

George W. Woodward, it will be recalled, the regular caucus nominee of the state Democratic party in 1845 had been defeated for the Senatorship by a coalition of Whigs and tariff Democrats supporting bolter Simon Cameron. President Polk's failure to secure Cameron's approval in advance for the Woodward appointment was more than the practice of ignoring irregularly elected

[41] W. Dudley to Cameron, Sept. 4, 1884, Cameron MMS, LC. Cameron expected an "affair of honor"; instead, Foote apologized.
[42] *Cong. Globe*, 30 Cong., 2 Sess., 686-87.

officers such as Cameron; it was a direct slap at Cameron, or, as Alexander McClure aptly characterized it, an attempt to vindicate Woodward.[43]

Fascinating questions bearing on this case arise from a study of Polk's *Diary*. Did Secretary of State Buchanan connive with Cameron in bringing about Woodward's rejection by the Senate; and if he did so was it because his ego could not permit an important Pennsylvania appointment without his own knowledge or approval? Did he sympathize with Cameron? Was he disappointed because one John M. Read had not been nominated, or did he desire the appointment for himself? Buchanan on his part labeled his reputed alliance with Cameron "such stuff as dreams are made of." [44]

Cameron brought about Woodward's rejection through the aid of the Whig vote in addition to six Democratic Senators totaling four more votes than he actually needed. Six days later, on January 28, 1846, the President's *Diary* recorded a visit from the victorious Cameron, who "put on a smiling and hypocritical air and acted as though he had been one of my friends." A fortnight later Cameron, in the course of a long private conversation with Polk, attempted to justify his opposition to Woodward's appointment, but to no avail, and on his part received a lecture on the indignities suffered by the President who allegedly had been given a "d——d drubbing" by the Senators in order to teach Polk, like an unruly Negro, how to behave himself.[45] In early August, the irresolute

[43] *Old Time Notes*, I, 99.

[44] Buchanan to C. E. Lester, Jan. 30, 1846, quoted in Snyder. *op. cit.*, 352n.

[45] According to David Wilmot, Cameron was the one who had made the remark about drubbing Polk in the manner of an unruly Negro. See Polk's *Diary*, 46n. Cameron denied saying it, *Diary*, 49.

Buchanan having decided that he did not care for his immediate appointment to the Supreme Court bench— the President nominated another Pennsylvanian, Robert C. Grier, who was acceptable to Cameron.[46]

The case of Henry Horn especially illustrates the importance Cameron attributed to a measure of control over the national patronage. Here was a freshman Senator who had hopes of laying the foundation of a personal political machine. Nothing could sooner bring about his collapse then the realization that its patron was not in position to reward friends with remunerative positions and to oust or at least prevent enemies from procuring such positions. In the case of a potential client from Bradford County, Cameron remarked: "I say make him a watchman [at the Capitol]. This will feed him and a man with a full belly is not half as troublesome as hungry ones."[47] Cameron, who was to fill many bellies in the course of his long career, was determined that the first rich political plum of his career on the national level should be his, to be bestowed as he saw fit.

Henry Horn for years had headed the Jackson Hickory Club in Philadelphia and like Cameron had been a Muhlenburg man. Later, as a Van Buren lieutenant in that city, he remained faithful to the New Yorker in 1844, at a time when Cameron had thrown him into the rubbish heap. He had visited Polk in late December, 1845, for the purpose of soliciting the collectorship of the port of Philadelphia. Cameron, evidently not certain of his strength as in the Woodward case, waited until several

---

[46] James G. Blaine believed that Cameron forced this nomination upon the President. James G. Blaine, *Twenty Years of Congress* (2 vols., Norwich), I, 196.

[47] Quoted in Snyder, *op. cit.*, 372.

Democratic Senators were absent before calling up Horn's nomination before the Senate. With the aid of two additional Democratic votes, Cameron defeated Polk's nomination of Horn for the post. At this point Polk now considered Cameron little better than a Whig—a "managing tricky man in whom no reliance can be placed." [48] This comment is somewhat surprising in view of Cameron's candid opposition to Horn. Later, when Polk renominated Horn, after receiving another warning from Cameron, Polk suffered his second defeat in the Senate.

Cameron's enemies could hardly deny his tactics worthy of a master strategist in the field of political maneuvering. His resolution calling upon Polk for the recommendations upon which Horn was appointed was a most unusual procedure. Moreover, his presentation of a protest against Horn's appointment signed by Pennsylvania's Congressmen amounted to an extra trump card. Through all this maneuvering, Polk refused Cameron recognition as a Democratic member of the Senate, but nevertheless the Pennsylvania Senator fought the top Democratic echelon to a standstill and proved his power, if not his right, to dispense party patronage.

About the time Cameron concluded his short term in the Senate, first rumblings were heard of a very questionable business transaction in connection with the establishment of Polk's new journalistic mouthpiece, the Washington *Union*, which had supplanted the old Jackson administrative organ, the *Globe*. Of Cameron's participation in the various phases of its labyrinthine course there can be no doubt.

In 1844, when James Buchanan recommended that

[48] *Diary*, I.

government monies be deposited in Cameron's Middletown bank, he secreted away a $50,000 skeleton in his family closet. In November of the same year, on order of George M. Bibb, Tyler's secretary of the treasury, $50,000 was transferred from a Philadelphia bank, so the choleric Thomas A. Benton observed, "to a village [Middletown] bank in the interior of Pennsylvania, where there was not public use for it, and where safety was questionable." [49] In 1856, Buchanan's $50,000 skeleton emerged to haunt him during his quest for the Presidency. Although nonchalant in tone, his letter to Horatio King revealed his uneasiness over the matter.[50] Whether or not Buchanan in 1844 possessed foreknowledge of the intended use of these funds is a moot question.

At any rate, James Buchanan, then a member of the inner coterie of the Democratic Presidential candidate's associates during the campaign of 1844, must have been acquainted with the proposal to establish a new Democratic organ in place of the old Washington *Globe*, at that time under the editorship of Francis P. Blair and John C. Rives. Blair, Polk revealed in his *Diary*, was especially obnoxious to the President, who resolved that Blair must be ousted. The details of how this change in personnel was accomplished is not pertinent to the Cameron story, but the same cannot be said for the alleged financial trickery it involved. In March, 1846, both Cameron and Polk wrote to Andrew Jackson Donelson asking him to accept the editorship of the proposed administration organ. Donelson, refusing the offer because of his sympathies for Blair, turned the Cameron letter over to the

[49] Thomas H. Benton, *Thirty Years in the Senate*, II, 651.
[50] William E. Smith, *The Francis Preston Blair Family in Politics* (2 vols., New York, 1933), I, 334.

dying Jackson, who in spite of his bodily torments wrote long letters concerning the matter to his friend, Blair. Upon the ousting of Blair and Rives, Thomas Ritchie of Richmond, Virginia, was installed editor of the new paper, the *Union*, with Major John P. Heiss of Tennessee as business manager.

The question most pertinent to the establishment of the Washington *Union* is the source from which payment for it was made. The plant of the *Globe*, including all equipment, was assessed at $35,000. However, it is likely that Blair and Rives expected to received $5,000 more than the assessed value because Cameron, on the very day of the sale, had written to an intermediary, L. S. Coryell: "if only one-third [the down payment] of $40,000 is needed, it will be easily arranged." Polk in his letter of March 28 to Donelson had explained that a "business partner" would advance all the money, while in Cameron's letter to Donelson, according to the prejudiced Benton, the writer had $50,000 in his hands for the purpose of establishing the new paper. On one point all agreed: neither Ritchie nor Heiss had the necessary funds to consumate the transaction. On April 9, Jackson had asked of Blair if "that renegade politician, Cameron, who boasts of his $50,000" was one of the purchasers. Technically, the sale was made to Major John P. Heiss, agent, for $35,000 on April 12, 1845. The other partners besides Heiss were Ritchie, Cameron, and J. Knox Walker, a relative of President Polk.

Undoubtedly Cameron provided funds for the purchase because on May 28, 1847, he thanked Heiss for paying the note, which was likely a last installment. Cameron then proceded to sell his share to Heiss (although the share was later listed in Coryell's name) for $14,000.

Certainly Cameron, a private banker, had the right to advance funds for such an enterprise if he wished, but Cameron's accusers charged him with manipulating federal funds intrusted to his care for the purpose of establishing, at public expense, a profit-making political mouthpiece for the Democratic administration.

The secrecy and denials involved in what appears to be a bewildering maze, whereas only simplicity was required, makes the case appear all the more suspicious. For example, Heiss denied (and lied) that Cameron had ever made him a loan. The new editor, Ritchie, was in absolute ignorance, so he testified, of the source of the funds used to buy the paper of which he was editor and of which he held one-fourth ownership. And only before a Congressional committee, in closed session, according to Rives and Senator Benton, did Cameron admit his advance of funds to Heiss. If, as charged by Cameron's enemies, his share had originally cost him nothing, he had netted the tidy sum of $14,000 on the deal. The reader must bear in mind the lack of proof of these accusations.

On the floor of the Senate, Cameron had shown unusual solicitude for the welfare of Ritchie and Heiss. On one occasion he moved to amend an amendment by directing the secretary of the treasury to pay the amount deducted from their accounts by the Committee of the two houses for public printing prior to the passage of the law fixing the rate of compensation.[51] On another occasion, when a resolution was before the Senate to allow the editor of the *Union* the freedom of the floor, Cameron amended it to include the publishers, namely Heiss.[52] At that time Cameron happened to be serving

[51] *Cong. Globe*, 29 Cong., 2 Sess., 506.
[52] *Ibid.*, 20 Cong., 1 Sess., 147.

on two convenient committees, the one on printing and the other for the District of Columbia. Apparently no one has yet answered this very important question: at what time did the United State Treasury reclaim the $50,000 loaned to the Middletown Bank? Keeping in mind the absence of proof of misuse of public funds in this case, and the possibility of private sources, the end result was to add to the mystery already surrounding the Winnebago affair, to the charges of bribery in connection with Cameron's first election to the Senate, and to the building up in the public eye the idea that corruption was a corollary of any questionable Cameron transaction.[53]

In early March, 1849, Simon Cameron returned to private life, inaugurating an eight-year period of partial political eclipse from the national scene. During this period he remained a very important figure in the local and state political life of the Commonwealth. Having arrived at the mid-century mark of an unusually long life span, this seemingly repudiated Democratic leader had hardly begun the fight which was to bring him recognition as the greatest political figure of the Commonwealth. In James G. Blaine's opinion, Cameron's recent successful tactics against the strong administration forces of President Polk in the Senate revealed the "secret of his future remarkable career as a party manager in the field." [54] To Alexander K. McClure's way of thinking the retiring Senator had proved he could be a dangerous foe as well as a valuable friend. His fight for a protective tariff had

[53] The *Globe-Union* transaction is discussed in Benton, *op. cit.*, II, 650-55; William E. Smith, *op. cit.*, I, 177-81; Crippen, *op. cit.*, 63-68. The last reference presents much pertinent evidence from the "Papers of John P. Heiss," appearing in *Tennessee Historical Magazine*, June, September, 1916.

[54] Blaine, *op. cit.*, I, 196.

gained for him not only much good will among industrialists and laboring men of his own state but attention from like groups in neighboring states.

Cameron certainly aspired to succeed himself in the role of a regular Democratic candidate for the full term of six years. Strenuous efforts on his behalf in the Philadelphia area testified to Cameron's ability to build a strong following in regions likely to prove most effective. Evidently at this time no reputable state Democratic leader felt he could afford to support a bolter who after his appearance in the Senate had maintained only a pseudo Democratic record of regularity. Apparently his name was not even presented before the Democratic Senatorial caucus in 1849 because no votes were recorded for him. Gratifying as such a nomination could have been interpreted—recognition of his efforts in Congress on behalf of the Commonwealth's welfare, and his acceptance as a party regular—it could not have brought about his election.

The Pennsylvania Whig Party, now in possession of comfortable majority on joint ballot of the two houses of the General Assembly, was in position to elect a bona fide Whig leader without resorting to any coalitions. It is difficult to picture Cameron, in 1849 the regular Democratic candidate, bargaining for a half-dozen votes from a Whig majority. The Whigs elected their choice, James Cooper, a part-time neighbor of the "Wooly Head" candidate, Thaddeus Stevens, who earned only three votes. Throughout the balloting the Democrats maintained an unbroken front for their losing man, Richard Brodhead.

Not many miles from Middletown, former secretary of state James Buchanan was enjoying his newly acquired estate, "Wheatland." The events of the past four years had wrought a change in the relationship between him and Cameron. A few more years was to reveal Cameron a dangerous opponent of his old chieftain, seeking to dislodge Buchanan from his place of leadership in the State Democracy. For Buchanan this was a respite of four years from public life during the victorious Whig interlude.

3
The Making
of a Political Boss

A STUDY OF PENNSYLVANIA POLITICS THROUGH THE PERIOD 1845 to 1857 presents many baffling problems and not a few anomalies. Tariff orthodoxy was particularly difficult to maintain among the state's Democracy, with the state titular leader James Buchanan in the unenviable position of endeavoring to make the national administration dish palatable to his brother Pennsylvanians, while at the same time trying to ease Washington's hand. Containment of the spread of slavery was an idea gradually fastening itself upon many Keystone Democrats; and while they were willing to accept the truce of 1850, events of 1854 brought open rebellion within their ranks. An old skeleton, Nativist religious-race prejudices, formerly centered in Philadelphia locale, emerged in new cloth to haunt a state Democracy dedicated to capturing the Catholic foreign vote.

This indecisiveness among the voters of the Commonwealth is well illustrated by following briefly the shifting political strength from year to year. In the state legislative elections of 1845, the Democrats carried the state with a very comfortable majority of 40 in the state legislature, but the next year the Whigs beat the Democrats better than two to one in the Congressional elections. In 1847 the Democrats elected their gubernatorial candidate, Francis R. Shunk, by 18,000 votes, and secured a substantial majority in the lower house of the legislature. But the following year the Whigs came back with a triple victory; the governorship, the legislature, and a majority for Zachary Taylor. The Democrats had another short period of control from 1850 to 1854 and then the impossible happened—a Whig governor and a Democratic canal commissioner were each elected by over a majority of 100,000 votes. In the legislature, a majority of members seated themselves in the caucus of the minority party, the American-Know-Nothing.

It was in such a witches' brew of chaotic state politics that highly controversial state and national problems of the time had to be discussed. An adroit manipulator could hardly have asked for a more favorable political medium in which to operate. Here was furnished the opportunity for a skilled political craftsman to shape a hierarchy founded not on the shifting, ephemeral issues of the day, but rather on a personal loyalty not likely to suffer from such vicissitudes.

Simon Cameron was slow in arriving at the momentous decision to build a political machine ostensibly Democratic in substance but whose members swore liege loyalty to him. To act in such a capacity Cameron must no longer deal with Buchanan in the manner a lieutenant deals with his chieftain, but rather like one equal antagonist pitted against the other, struggling for recognition as the state Democracy's generalissimo. Eventually such a contest without compromise or quarter must lead to the downfall of one of the antagonists; but in this particular struggle such was not to be the case, because in the midst of the strife Simon Cameron departed from the party scene, carrying with him, like Lucifer, his quota of fallen angels.

For a period after his election to the Senate in 1845, little was heard of Cameron's activities within state political circles, where he was generally considered a traitor by Democratic leaders, while the Whigs viewed him with contempt, disgust, and lack of confidence. However, Cameron's courageous stand in the Senate for what appeared the best interests of both the industrialists and many thousands of working men brought about a reaction in his favor. He resumed his efforts to ingratiate himself with Buchanan, giving what was likely unsolicited advice, suggesting Buchanan for governor in 1848, and at the same time opposing his former mentor on various issues.

In the fall of 1846 Pennsylvania's Congressional voters, it was believed, would have an opportunity to show how they felt on the question of the Walker Tariff of 1846, an item still very much in the news of the Commonwealth. The election of 16 Whigs to 7 Democrats to Congress that same year was looked upon as evidence of the electorate's disfavor of Congress for not retaining the Tariff of 1842.[1] This was a peculiar interpretation in light of Pennsylvania's solid vote in Congress for the older tariff; that is, with the exception of notorious David Wilmot, whose constituents, according to the humorous alleged observation of former Governor David R. Porter,

---

[1] Mueller, *Whig Party in Pennsylvania*, 133n.

were in need of only one kind of protection, a species of immunity from officers of justice seeking the stolen lumber used to manufacture the area's sole product—shingles. Both Cameron and Buchanan hoped to see the Freesoiler defeated for re-election. A plan to defeat Wilmot by running a bolting protectionist Democrat with Whig backing failed, and the chagrined Cameron reported to Buchanan a Wilmot victory as part of the general Democratic success. To Cameron, a Democratic gain in his Whig-held home county of Dauphin appeared significant. Actually, the most meaningful aspect of the election was the disinterestness of the average voter. Somehow the Whigs had been able to arouse the most interest.

Had it not been for his Senatorial duties during the winter of 1845-46, Cameron might again have camped at the state's legislative doorstep, where a tremendous battle loomed over the question of granting charters and operating privileges to railroads. The western and southwestern interests of the Commonwealth preferred to grant rights for an extension of the Baltimore and Ohio Railroad to Pittsburgh, while the eastern interests, fearful of losing markets, fought for a central line extending from Philadelphia to Pittsburgh. There was plenty of business, argued Cameron, to sustain both lines. His Northern Central Railroad, the chief connecting link between the two lines, could enjoy maximum profits only if both lines were provided with satisfactory termini. The affair apparently ended with grudging concessions allotted to both competing lines, but the following year the Baltimore and Ohio had its franchise annulled.[2]

Cameron indicated some intent to dispute Buchanan's

[2] McClure, *Old Time Notes*, I, 129.

leadership of the state Democracy when he resorted to
underhand efforts in 1847 to defeat Governor Shunk's
renomination, in opposition to Buchanan's hearty endorsement of another term for the honest governor. Anti-Shunk
resolutions of local Democratic conventions in favor of
one term for governor were attributed to the machinations of Cameron. Shunk's renomination, wrote Cameron,
could be defeated if only the Philadelphia delegation
could be brought into line.[3] Cameron's war on Shunk was
a carry-over from the days of the Muhlenberg-Shunk feud
when he had served as a Muhlenberg lieutenant and was
consistent with the declaration he had made after Shunk
failed to apportion his faction its share of the spoils.
After Shunk's renomination Cameron did nothing in behalf of the governor's re-election beyond announcing his
intention of doing his duty at the polls for his party.

The Whig gubernatorial candidate, General James
Irvin, a Centre County ironmaster, was, it must be admitted, a man more likely to attract protectionists of
Cameron's stamp. Cameron's enemies, sensing this common interest which he shared with the Whig candidate,
accused him of countenancing Irvin's election. Shortly
after Shunk's re-election, the New York *Tribune* published a fantastic account of how the Whigs of Pennsylvania had suffered themselves to be duped by the old
Muhlenberg faction. This plan, according to the *Tribune*,
called for a quiet campaign on the part of the Whigs,
creating no stir among the electorate while the anti-
Shunk Democrats brought about his defeat; but miscar-
riage of the dastardly plot had resulted in Shunk's re-
election. Granted the truth of the *Tribune's* version,

[3] Snyder, *op. cit.*, 366.

Cameron, the cunning arch-manipulator, had significantly, if innocently, contributed to his enemy's victory. These blasé accusations must have given Cameron considerable discomfort because he humiliated himself sufficiently to appeal through Buchanan for a public denial of the truth of the charges in John W. Forney's organ, the *Pennsylvanian*.[4]

The Democratic gubernatorial victory of 1847 proved to be short lived. Shunk's ill health led to his resignation the following summer. In the following special election William Freame Johnston, the Whig governor *pro tempore*, emerged the victor by a scant 300 votes over Morris Longstreth.[5] Johnston, a former protectionist Democrat, was able to garner votes in the industrial coal and iron regions. Johnston's triumph was just a part of the triple victory scored by the Whigs in Pennsylvania that year. It included also a comfortable margin for the Presidential candidate, Zachary Taylor. Long before the treaty of peace was signed ending the war with Mexico, mushrooming local political clubs of both major parties were urging the hero's nomination in spite of their ignorance of his Presidential qualifications or political affiliations, both of which were moot indeed.

Cameron joined with the former Democratic Improvement leaders in establishing a Presidential boom for Taylor. On June 1, 1847, the Philadelphia *Pennsylvanian* printed a letter of Cameron to Samuel D. Patterson, the purpose of which was to establish Taylor's Democratic leanings.[6] At a local Democratic meeting held at New

[4] Crippen, *Simon Cameron*, 98.
[5] Charles M. Snyder, *The Jacksonian Heritage* (Harrisburg, 1958), 226.
[6] *Ibid.*, 209.

Berlin, Pennsylvania, in September, 1847, Cameron men attempted an endorsement of Taylor but were easily beaten by Shunk's faction, whereupon the Cameron malcontents walked out of the meeting.[7] A successful "Old Rough and Ready" meeting planned by Cameron, Richard Vaux, John M. Read, and Henry A. Muhlenberg, Jr., was held three days later in Harrisburg. Naturally, this group experienced no internal opposition to its enthusiastic endorsement of Taylor. By early January, 1848, however, Cameron had conceded Taylor's capture by the Whigs. The Democracy must look elsewhere for choice Presidential timber.

Two prominent Pennsylvania Democrats, James Buchanan and George M. Dallas, contested for Presidential backing from the state's Democratic leaders. Between the two Cameron had little choice. Dallas when Vice-President had delivered a vicious public attack upon Cameron because of his unorthodox methods of getting himself elected United State Senator in 1845, and had opposed the Improvement men.[8] Cameron mounted the bandwagon of his old friend Buchanan, who had long coveted the Presidential prize. The State Democratic caucus endorsed Buchanan and instructed the delegation (of which Cameron was a member) to support him at the national convention. Now as in the days of yore, Cameron became an active, enthusiastic Buchanan lieutenant. At the national convention it would be his duty to spar with the opposition, watching and interpreting every move with the eye of a veteran political strategist until the propitious time arrived when a favorable bargain

---

[7] Crippen, *Simon Cameron*, 101.
[8] Snyder, *Jacksonian Heritage*, 191, 206.

could be struck for his candidate, in addition to reporting every convention detail to his chieftain.

Adoption of the usual two-thirds rule by the national Democratic Convention at Baltimore did little to prolong its proceedings; Lewis Cass, the leading contender, captured the prize on the fourth ballot. Buchanan's failure to achieve the nomination could hardly be attributed to lack of effort on the part of Cameron in view of Pennsylvania's unit vote on each ballot for Buchanan,[9] although its twenty-six members included some Cass men. At home the ostracized David Wilmot was having his revenge by drumming up trade for the Free Soil team of Van Buren and Adams.

Following the November defeat of Cass by Taylor within Pennsylvania, Cameron was ready with his usual stock explanation for any Democratic reverse, the Walker Tariff of 1846. Cameron was thus discounting the important element of Taylor's personal popularity, a factor which had led Cameron himself to be drawn toward the hero. After thirty years of hindsight, James Blaine, if he was not blowing Cameron's horn in retrospect, concurred in placing the blame on the tariff for the defeat of Cass. Hendrick B. Wright, a contemporary, named both "gunpowder and the tariff." [10]

Cameron's course of action in 1848 when he supported Buchanan contrasted with that of 1852 when he pursued an opposite course amounting to an about face, provides ones of those numerous puzzles surrounding the famous

[9] Blaine, *Twenty Years*, I, 194. Buchanan's position was weakened when Pennsylvania's delegation named Cass its second choice. See Andrew McLaughlin, *Lewis Cass* (Boston and New York, 1899), 236.

[10] Snyder, *Jacksonian Heritage*, 218.

politico's long career. In 1852, the discredited Cass was the weaker candidate to whom Cameron transferred his allegiance. The key to this riddle lay in the Commonwealth's Senatorial election of 1849. No one was in better position in 1849 to influence the outcome of a Democratic state caucus nomination than was James Buchanan, recognized leader of the state's Democracy. To Simon Cameron, who possessed a strong sense of personal loyalty, Buchanan could not deny him support for the Senatorial caucus nomination in view of his own strong efforts for Buchanan in 1848. From Buchanan's view, Cameron was a troublesome party bolter who had refused to accept the party's verdict in 1845 and who had lately come to Buchanan's aid only because he was seeking to rehabilitate himself as a party regular. Moreover the "Old Buck" could hardly have forgotten Cameron's late underhand efforts to defeat Governor Shunk's renomination. At this juncture when Cameron realized there could be little, if any, assistance forthcoming from his old chieftain, Cameron decided to take the most unusual step of challenging Buchanan's leadership.

As already noted, Cameron had shown signs of restlessness because of the Muhlenberg-Shunk feud. Symptoms of Cameron's independence become more manifest in 1850, when because of his activities at the Williamsport Democratic Convention he was accused of bribing delegates called to select a candidate for canal commissioner.[11] This was only the second of a long series of instances in which with monotonous regularity he was accused of using questionable methods to accomplish his designs.

Selection of a Democratic majority to the state legisla-

[11] Mueller, *Whig Party in Pennsylvania*, f.n., 174.

ture in 1850 indicated the election in early 1851 of a
Democrat to the United States Senatorial vacancy created
by the expiration of Daniel Sturgeon's term. The race
for the caucus nomination was considered wide open
until near election time; consequently Cameron actually
had visions of capturing it. Shortly before the election one
observer reported Cameron's presence among the legislators, his energetic efforts on his own behalf, and the confidence expressed by his friends. If Cameron were to
secure the nomination it certainly must be accomplished
through the medium of "friends." He showed surprising
strength but not enough to secure him the nomination,
which went to Richard Brodhead. Keeping his candidacy
before the public eye served the useful purpose of serving
notice of his intention to remain in the public life and of
retaining the loyalty of the many who had already attached their fortunes to his.

Following Brodhead's election, Cameron further demonstrated his determination to weaken the Buchanan leadership. When the state convention met at Reading June 4,
1851, to choose the Democracy's candidate for governor,
Buchanan, who expected obedience from the convention,
was jolted to discover rebellion in the air. Cameron, it was
ascertained, had, previously to the time of the convention,
tampered with several county delegations in an effort to
seat unpledged delegates. Moreover, some delegates from
Lehigh were reputedly anti-Buchanan. It was part of
Cameron's strategy to force William A. Bigler, who expected to receive the nomination on a platter from Buchanan, to deal directly with him for convention votes.
The effect would be to lower Buchanan's leadership and
prestige.

That Cameron's strategy achieved a measure of success

is proven by Bigler's secret communication through his uncle, William Dock. Although Dock made no pretense of speaking for Bigler, Cameron was well enough versed in political chicanery to penetrate Bigler's thinly veiled subterfuge. Bigler's appeal for aid was doubtless highly pleasing to Cameron, who in a patronizing manner pledged his support accompanied with a guarantee of several counties which he could personally deliver. At the convention, Samuel W. Black, obstensibly the Cameron candidate, suddenly withdrew, leaving the field to Bigler.[12] Thus Cameron, who had no reason to oppose Bigler, secured direct recognition for his faction from the Commonwealth's next governor.

Bigler went on to defeat the Whig incumbent Johnston by a majority of 8,500 in the October election. One interesting sidelight of that year's state election was the loss of Democratic votes in David Wilmot's district; the other was the defeat of a prominent Democratic candidate for supreme judge, James Campbell. The judge's defeat was a reflection of the strong anti-Catholic sentiment prevailing during the 1850's. Cameron was accused of participating in this so called anti-papacy campaign.

As Buchanan developed plans for his Presidential drive of 1852, Cameron appeared as a thorn in his side. Name-calling between the two in 1850 received press comment. Cameron went to the length of presenting a newspaper of 1820 vintage to Jefferson Davis, thereby offering proof of Buchanan's opposition to the spread of slavery. Through 1851, local Democratic conventions within Pennsylvania reported resolutions supporting Cass for the Presidency. One example of these anti-Buchanan resolutions is found

[12] Crippen, *Simon Cameron*, 119-20.

in Cameron's own county of Dauphin where Cass was "nominated" for the Presidency by a vote of 53 to 3. When John W. Forney failed to publish such scandalous resolutions in his *Pennsylvanian* and followed with attacks on Cameron, the latter labeled them Buchanan-inspired. The fued between the pair attained such proportions as to attract the attention of both the New York *Times* and the New York *Tribune*. Although Buchanan's friends urged him to seek a *rapprochement* with Cameron before 1852, he spurned such proposals on the grounds that the injury imposed upon him by Cameron had been performed without cause.[13] To Buchanan, who was skilled in the art of political parrying, any proposal to deal with Cameron appeared a move to force his, the legitimate Democratic organization, to recognize the rebel one of Cameron's which sought to supplant Buchanan's. Cameron's strategy was identical to that used successfully against Bigler.

Not the least of Cameron's victories in his feud with Buchanan was his capture of the newly elected United States Senator Richard Brodhead, who was resentful because some Buchanan men had opposed his election. Buchanan, according to his own version, had not knowingly opposed Brodhead,[14] but his admission that his right hand didn't know what his left was doing proved unacceptable to Brodhead.

The first open battle between the two factions took place at Philadelphia in early February, 1852, where an attempt to name instructed delegates to the coming Baltimore Democratic Convention ended in bedlam and the

[13] Myers, "Rise of the Republican Party," 67.
[14] Roy F. Nichols, *The Democratic Machine, 1850-54* (New York, 1923), 61.

loss of a portion of chairman Peter Rambo's coat. Using steamroller tactics the Buchanan men had no difficulty in controlling the Harrisburg state Democratic Convention. The minority led by the able John Scott of Huntingdon registered a strong protest against the use of undemocratic method. The Buchanan strategy, although successful, boomeranged when the impression was given by papers outside the Commonwealth that the state's Democracy was not united in its support of Buchanan, and that consequently the candidate's machine would collapse quickly were it not bound by force.

At Washington on the eve of the Democratic Convention the Cass-Cameron forces were exerting themselves in a last minute effort to weaken Buchanan, with John L. Dawson, a western Pennsylvania Cameron man, attacking Buchanan's tariff views. Reputedly the Cameron men were offering a $10,000 wager on Buchanan's inability to carry his own state. Failure of the Cameronians to "put up" when Buchanan money confronted them still failed to silence them; it was the Buchananites, they contended, who had failed to cover the wager.[15] At any rate, a solid bloc of Buchanan supporters was sent to the National Convention.

The Democratic National Convention of 1852 met June 1, in Baltimore. Cameron was one of the three Cass lieutenants entrusted with the assignment of bringing about his nomination, a task which at the beginning of the convention did not appear too formidable. For over thirty ballots the results deadlock around Buchanan, Cass, and Douglas. On the thirty-fifth ballot the Cass vote of 131 was considerably greater than Buchanan's. At this juncture

[15] *Ibid.*, 77.

the Buchanan forces, having no stomach for a Cameron-led Cass victory, were now prepared to change their strategy, which led to Pierce's nomination on the forty-ninth ballot.[16] If Cameron had little to show for his pains on behalf of Cass, neither did the defeated Buchanan. Both returned home sworn enemies. Cameron had no intention of lessening his drive to gain control of the state's Democracy, while Buchanan on his part could not afford to drop his guard or vigilance momentarily, for fear of finding himself dispossessed of his crown.

In the Presidential election Franklin Pierce experienced no difficulty in carrying the Keystone State over the Whig candidate, General Winfield Scott. When the President-Elect sought advice from Buchanan on the matter of Pennsylvania appointments, former Governor David Porter and Judge James Campbell, Cameron's enemy, received favorable comment. Buchanan evidently added gratis one category of names to be avoided in the matter of appointments, that of the Cameron coterie, whom he described as promoters of party chaos when personal interests conflicted with party success. Cameron's worst shortcomings, wrote Buchanan, consisted of unorthodox tactics for purposes of personal gain and of party irregularity.[17] But the Cass lieutenant, experiencing no embarrassment from his questionable party status, boldly called upon the President-Elect before his inauguration but received little satisfaction from Pierce. Cameron's next step was to extend unsolicited advice to Pierce and, what is even more astonishing, he actually scored some successes.

[16] Nevins, *Ordeal of the Union*, II, 19.
[17] Crippen, *Simon Cameron*, 132.

With his hopes already centered upon the coming Senatorial election of 1855, Cameron set to work slowly building upon a personal following which would serve as a nucleus for his future machine. Some newspaper men supporting him were E. B. Chase of the Montrose *Democrat*, Reah Frazer of the Lancaster *Lancastrian*, editor Rosenthal of a Philadelphia German organ, and Barrett of the Harrisburg *Keystone*. Chase was formerly speaker of the State House while Colonel Frazer was conveniently located in the Buchanan stronghold, Lancaster county. Other leading Cameron partisans were Judge George Rahn of Philadelphia, Judge Luther Kidder of Wilkes-Barre, Henry A. Muhlenberg, Jr., and two western Pennsylvanians, John L. Dawson and J. K. Moorhead, the latter soon to prove himself a strong political figure in the Pittsburgh area. A native of Dauphin county, Cameron had known him when he secured contracts on the Pennsylvania state works and occupied the post of adjutant-general of the Commonwealth under Porter.[18]

The Cameron group mended political fences with several leading political figures in the state and audaciously attempted to wean Buchanan's leading lieutenant, Jehu Glancy Jones of Reading, away from him. Jones had supplanted the jealous Forney as Buchanan's leading confidant and later managed the forces which nominated him for the Presidency.[19] By early 1854 David Wilmot had lost his enmity toward Cameron and was awaiting an opportunity to repay him for past favors.[20] Even that intellectual giant from Somerset County, Jeremiah S. Black, a

[18] McNair & Robson, *Biographical Encyclopaedia*, 572-73.

[19] Roy F. Nichols, *Disruption of American Democracy* (New York, 1948), 13, 15.

[20] Wilmot to Cameron, quoted in Crippen, *op. cit.*, 135.

Buchanan supporter, was not above observing and noting
how people were requesting Cameron's views on various
questions. Black was among the first to characterize
Cameron a "boss politician." [21] Now that the incumbent
governor, Bigler, was seeking Cameron's aid in his race
for re-election for governor, it is not much wonder that
the latter was sanguine over his chances of success the
following January.

It is difficult to describe adequately the results of the
Pennsylvania state elections of 1854. On the surface the
results of these elections seem to defy logical analysis. A
decaying Whig party had elected James Pollock governor
by a handsome majority over the strong Democratic
leader William Bigler. On the other hand, the Democratic
candidate for canal commissioner had received an un-
heard majority of 190,000 votes over George Darsie, the
Whig candidate. For Supreme Judge, Jeremiah Black, a
Democrat, had received a plurality over separate Whig
and American candidates.

The answer to this electoral riddle lies in the spectacular
rise of a secret order known to its initiates as the Order
of the Star Spangled Banner. Its political organization,
formally titled the American Party, was popularly dubbed
the Know-Nothing. The party was looked upon as the
resurrection of a species of Nativism with pronounced
anti-Catholic sentiments. Heavy Irish-Catholic immigra-
tion, scars left by the decade-old Philadelphia religious
riots, appointment of a Philadelphia Catholic to the Pierce
cabinet, and the national tour of Cardinal Bedini, the
papal legate, all were factors contributing to the unrest.
In addition, rumors of Catholic plans to transplant the

[21] Black to Cameron, February 20, 1854, quoted in *ibid.*, 135.

Vatican to the United States must actually have shocked a strongly Protestant group well acquainted with the harrowing details of Fox's *Book of Martyrs*.

Besides those discontented because of social, economic, and religious factors named, a new dissatisfied political bloc was added when proposals were made to open to slavery territory north of the old 36°30' line. The ingredients of this new antislavery political cauldron consisted of Free Soil Democrats, Tariff Democrats, Free Soilers, Conscience Whigs, Anti-Nebraska men, and Know-Nothings, with a dash of protectionism for seasoning. The Free Soil Whigs were just as uncomfortable as the Free Soil Democrats because their party had accepted the truce of 1850.

Because of the methods used by the Americans in selecting candidates within the secret confines of their lodges, it was possible for candidates of the various parties to secure Know-Nothing backing if they professed adherence to American principles. A Know-Nothing especially in local elections, might be elected without public knowledge of his candidacy. Alexander K. McClure cited Chambersburg as an interesting example where an entire secret slate was elected over a publicly unopposed Whig ticket.

It was because of secret Know-Nothing help that James Pollock, who was probably a Know-Nothing himself,[22] was easily elected the Whig governor of Pennsylvania in conjunction with the Free Soil element of the state. Re-

[22] In his *Notes*, I, 217, McClure stated that Pollock was not a Know Nothing initiate, but immediately after the election McClure wrote: "But huzza for Pollock. Of course Judge [Pollock] is a Know Nothing, and I aint." McClure to Slifer, Oct. 12 [1854]. Slifer-Dill Papers, Dickinson College.

putedly, Andrew G. Curtin, Chairman of the Whig State Central Committee had consumated a deal with the Know-Nothings.[23] The election to the General Assembly in 1854 of 61 men calling themselves Whigs presaged a victory in the coming Senatorial election for their party. Forty-nine Democrats, including 24 Pierce men, and a motley group of 20 which included avowed Americans, Free Soilers, Independents, and Nativists made up the remainder. But it was soon ascertained via grapevine channels that the American caucus would constitute over half the total membership of the legislature and therefore would be in position to elect its candidate for Senator.

The appearance of the Americans with their undefined party lines came as a great boon to the notorious opportunist, Simon Cameron, who felt that he could not afford to wait any longer. Certainly there were few indeed who knew better how to play such a role and his followers would encounter no difficulty in finding seats in the American caucus. In fact, the heavy invasion of pseudo-Americans at the last hour into the Know-Nothing ranks resulted in the "bona fide" members losing control of their own caucus.

During the campaign of 1854, Cameron, a factional Democrat, had worked for his party, delivering a speech in Governor Bigler's behalf on the last day of the campaign. At the same time, he worked primarily to secure the election of legislators favorable to his Senatorial candidacy. In view of the chaotic condition of state politics and disintegrating party lines, personal loyalty could be achieved. Cameron's strong financial standing led to a flood of petitions from legislative candidates

[23] McClure, *Old Time Notes*, I, 214-15.

pledging their adherence to him but doubtful of their ability to win without financial aid. A perusal of Cameron's papers shows that such petitions, which he often considered on the same level as blackmail, greatly angered him; but nevertheless he did pay. During this particular campaign none of the petitioners estimated their "expenses" at more than $1,000. Cameron's ability to grant financial aid to pledged candidates when often his opponents were unable to do so helps to explain the bitterness of charges directed against him during and after the heat of a political battle. Financial assistance awarded to adherents during the contests followed by the spoils of patronage after a victory was an important rung in the politico's rise to power.

Cameron's success in creating a strong political following based on personal loyalty made it possible to work as he chose either within the Democratic or American caucus. His lieutenants were actively at work in every section of the state. A few of these supporters were Francis J. Grund, Reading; Colonel Reah Frazer, Lancaster; J. P. Anderson, Huntingdon; Thomas McDowell, Hollidaysburg; D. Purviance, Greensburg; J. B. Packer, Sunbury; Edward J. Fox, Easton; D. C. Boal, Bellefonte; J. W. Killinger, Lebanon; John Crouse, Johnstown; H. C. Longenecker, Allentown; R. DeFrance, Mercer; O. Watson, Williamsport; John Purviance, Butler; E. B. Chase, Montrose; W. A. Ponley, Waynesburg; Col. A. Cummings, Philadelphia; and D. L. Smith, a prominent leader of the Know-Nothing Council in Pittsburgh, which was pledging its support for Cameron as early as February, 1854.[24]

[24] Correspondence, 1853-1854, Simon Cameron Papers, Dauphin County Collection, Harrisburg, Pa. Hereafter cited as Cameron MSS, DDC.

Prominent leaders like Senator James Cooper and Richard Brodhead were tolerant of Cameron's activities while J. Glancy Jones covertly promised to "venture as far as I dare." [25]

Cameron's determination to try for the Senatorship brought his chickens home to roost. Enemies emphasized his refusal to accept the decision of a Democratic nominating caucus in 1849 and, even worse, the spectre of the Old Winnebago scandal rose to haunt him. Prospects for victory on the Democratic ticket were practically nil for Cameron. The party constituted a minority in the legislature and the Buchanan-Pierce men were strong enough to defeat his nomination in the Democratic caucus. Even so, the "old Buck and his hounds" were very suspicious of his movements. [26]

Apparently there was a good chance for election if he could capture the American caucus. For Simon Cameron to appear in the guise of an American was not difficult. His strong protest against the appointment of a Catholic, Judge James Campbell, to the Pierce cabinet had been well received in the Protestant ranks. Actually, Cameron had protested against Campbell because the judge had worked to prevent him from becoming a Democratic caucus candidate in 1849. At the propitious moment, a Know-Nothing emissary presented Cameron in public with a series of questions bearing on important phases of public policy. Cameron's answers appear to consist of a list of pre-arranged propositions to which he merely affixed his signature; how otherwise could one explain his request for alien residence of twenty-one years as a prerequisite for citizenship. Cameron's already-declared

[25] J. Glancy Jones to Cameron, August 28, 1854, *ibid.*
[26] Reah Frazer to Cameron, Sept. 8, 1854, *ibid.*

approval for continued application of the principles of the Wilmot Proviso and of the protective tariff were acceptable to the Commonwealth's Americans. Lastly, Cameron could not understand why any President could veto appropriations for rivers or harbors. In other words he was in complete agreement with the principles of what a later generation aptly termed pork barrel legislation. A last minute maneuver on Cameron's part was his advocacy of a Whig for the Treasurership, thereby making it easier for a Democrat to receive the Senatorial nomination.[27]

When the American legislative caucus met on February 9, 1855, to organize, the Whigs appeared almost in a body, while less than half the Democrats appeared. The appearance of any Democrats in the Know-Nothing caucus must have been very painful to the old line leaders of the Democracy who were exceedingly anxious to retain the accustomed Catholic vote. The Cameron men did not chose to reveal their strength during the organization of the American caucus and consequently only eight votes were registered for a "Democratic" chairman. With a total of 91 legislators seated in the American caucus it looked as if the Know-Nothings would be able to elect their Senatorial candidate with 25 votes to spare.

Simon Cameron's vote of 27 on the first Know-Nothing ballot revealed him a leading contender. First glance at the results of the fifth ballot indicated his election to Senatorial candidacy by a majority of one with 46 votes to 37 for Andrew G. Curtin, the dashing new secretary of the Commonwealth. Great excitement prevailed when the total vote was shown to exceed the number present. Refusing to accept the results of this particular ballot as

[27] Philadelphia *North American and United States Gazette*, Jan. 10, 1855.

a possible mistake in tallying of votes, 29 members most of whom claimed to be original Americans and who were supporters of Curtin, walked out of the caucus declaring they "were not to be bought." [28] An over enthusiastic Know-Nothing editor attributed the following quotation to the righteous American bolters:

But what we say unto one we say unto all, invite us not in to partake of a buzzard's feast. Ask us not to support a nomination brought about, as we believe, by the concentrated and cohesive power of public plunder, and the superadded element of shameless and wholesale private bribery.[29]

This withdrawal greatly simplified matters for the Cameron rump, which nominated its candidate on the next ballot; but that emasculated American group now constituted less than one half of the legislative membership.

The Know-Nothing bolters, regarding themselves the bona fide representatives of the American Party, immediately, under the leadership of Francis Jordan of Bedford, drew up an "American Petition" directed to the public. This circular, issued in the form of a broadside, charged that enemies of their organization having found their way into their caucus had seized control of it, consequently bringing about the "nomination of one of the most intriguing, if not the most corrupt politician in the state." [30] According to the petitioners, these Cameron intruders had first successfully resisted attempts to force their withdrawal and then maintained their right to a secret caucus vote. Fewer than 20 of them had openly ad-

[28] Philadelphia *Public Ledger*, Feb. 10, 1855.
[29] Harrisburg *Pennsylvania Telegraph*, Feb. 21, 1855.
[30] "American Petition" of Feb. 12, 1855, against Simon Cameron, Society Miscellaneous Collection, HSP.

mitted their intention of supporting Cameron, thereby deceiving the caucus body.

Three minority groups then met to nominate candidates. The thirty-three members of the American seceding caucus failed to agree on a candidate. On the same day eight lonely Whigs nominated Thomas Williams and 26 Pierce Democrats chose Charles Buckalew.[31] The following day, February 13, a joint session of the Pennsylvania legislature convened for the purpose of electing a United States Senator to succeed the incumbent, James Cooper. Although Cameron, with 58 votes led a field of a dozen aspirants, and came within five votes of snatching the prize, he could not break the deadlock, whereupon the legislature adjourned for a two week period.[32]

The interlude, besides furnishing the opportunity for candidates to marshall additional strength while denouncing their opponents in the strongest terms, gave birth to a new host of hopeful Senatorial aspirants, some of whom, wrote Alexander McClure, went home with greatly depleted bank accounts.[33] Of the many meetings held throughout the state offering resolutions on the Senatorial crisis, the great majority reported by the press were denunciatory of Cameron and his methods. Here was a political leader, chorused Cameron's enemies, who for years had masqueraded as a true Democrat, only to be remembered by posterity for his insidious treachery.

A special committee of the state legislature took testi-

[31] Philadelphia *North American and United States Gazette*, Feb. 13, 1855.

[32] Crippen, *Simon Cameron*, 142-43.

[33] *Old Time Notes*, I, 199. In his Chambersburg *Repository and Whig*, Jan. 10, 1855, McClure charged that Cameron had opposed the Americans until he perceived their strength. See Russell, "Alexander K. McClure," 63.

mony relative to charges of bribery during the past election period. To the disgust of the American bolters, the testimony pinpointed the guilt on no one, the most desirable witnesses were reported *in absentia*, and the Jordan investigating committee, sans the signature of its chairman and one other member, reported imperfect and unsatisfactory evidence. Part of the report read: "However much certain outside parties may be implicated, your committee has been unable to discover anything of importance . . . which should justify the general suspicion of corruption and charges of bribery." [34] The majority report, testifying to the "vindication of the character of the Legislature" seemed not to have been believed by the legislative members in view of a new statute compelling witnesses to testify to them if a law had been violated.

The second session of the two houses, reassembled on February 27 for the purpose of electing a United States Senator, followed the same course as the preceding one. At one time or another approximately one-third of the legislative members considered themselves candidates for the high office. At the end of five ballots Cameron's 55 votes led the Democratic candidate, Buckalew, by 32, but he lacked the 10 additional votes needed to give him victory. Cameron's friends had selected the third ballot for the coup which was to bring him the nomination. At this juncture three Democrats bolted to him [35] but this surprise move did not initiate the hoped-for stampede. If Cameron had been a citizen of western

[34] *Report of the Joint Committee of the Legislature of Pennsylvania in Relation to Alleged Improper Influence in the Election of United States Senator*, PSL.

[35] Philadelphia *North American and United States Gazette*, March 1, 1855.

Pennsylvania it is likely he would have been elected.
The westerners disliked the idea of two eastern Senators.
Because of the deadlock the legislature voted adjournment until October; but the resolution actually placed the
matter in the hands of Governor Pollock. Cameron was
now willing to withdraw from the contest on condition
that the governor's friends would assist the Cameron
group in preventing the election of anyone who had
assailed him, which in this case consisted mostly of the
Andrew G. Curtin group. Pollock could hardly sponsor
such a proposal in view of his public office, his personal
friendship for Curtin, and his recent alliance with the
Americans. The legislature was not reassembled and
Cameron, with his hopes now pinned to a newly elected
legislature, remained a very active candidate for the
office.

Out of the contest between Andrew G. Curtin and
Simon Cameron in 1855 for the American Senatorial
caucus nomination there arose a *causi belli* of a personal
nature destined to color Pennsylvania political history for
a period of almost two decades. During the major portion
of this period, the state Republican Party, bearing various
titles, was rent by severe factional strife in the struggle
between these two men to achieve control of the party
organization within the Commonwealth. At times, for
example, during the Civil War era when Curtin was
governor of Pennsylvania and Cameron was concurrently
occupying the war office in Lincoln's cabinet, this enmity
may have influenced the course of national affairs. Both
contestants in this furious personal feud realized fully the
meaning of complete victory for either antagonist—the
choice of either complete political eclipse or exodus from
the party for the fallen warrior.

Documentary evidence relative to the cause of this enmity between the two men seems likely to remain buried with the past. Andrew G. Curtin's personal papers have disappeared and a perusal of the several Cameron manuscript collections sheds little light on the subject. A race between an avowed Whig and a pseudo-Democrat for nomination in a Know-Nothing caucus certainly does not provide the answer. In November, 1854, J. W. Killinger, after interviewing Pollock and Curtin, had reported to Cameron that he believed Curtin would not be a candidate for the Senatorship in view of his acceptance as secretary of the Commonwealth, and he was hopeful of an understanding being reached.[36] After the rump American caucus nominated Cameron, Curtin seemed to have taken no active part in the Jordan vilification, nor was he a candidate for the Senatorship at the time of the first balloting of the legislature.

Cameron supporters later spread a story concerning an understanding allegedly agreed upon between the pair in 1854 whereby Cameron would use his influence to have Curtin made secretary of the Commonwealth in return for which Curtin was to support Cameron for the Senatorship. But Curtin "basely betrayed Cameron and fought him with the knife to the hilt." [37] That this story was manufactured out of whole cloth is obvious. Simon Cameron, the ardent supporter of Democratic gubernatorial candidate William Bigler, could hardly be expected to have an influence over the selection of a secretary of Commonwealth for the victorious Whig-Americans, his

[36] J. W. Killinger to Cameron, Nov. 18, 1854, Cameron MSS, DCC.

[37] James W. Bristow to John Covode, Nov. 28, 1859, Papers of John Covode, HSWP.

political opponents. Pollock would certainly have needed little urging to select the man who had successfully managed his gubernatorial campaign.

A close confidant of Curtin, Alexander K. McClure certainly was in position to furnish a key to the riddle. This Chambersburg editor, who later wrote voluminously on the long political struggle between Curtin and Cameron, appeared peculiarly reticent to discuss at length this particular incident. His brief comment was:

They became intensely embittered against each other in the three month's struggle for the Senatorship . . . and reconciliation, or even the restoration of ordinary civilities of life, was made impossible by a personal reproach put upon Curtin by Cameron when he had several of his political friends about him in a convivial mood, during the heat of the Senatorial struggle.[38]

Because McClure chose to keep secret the "personal reproach" that the loose-lipped Cameron, while in his cups, cast upon his opponent, it may not be out of order to repeat a tale that at one time made its rounds in Curtin's home town of Bellefonte. Cameron's remarks, so went the story, were based on the doubtful paternity of an illegitimate child.[39] McClure's short commentary on the affair does lead one to believe that had this incident occured in the land of the *code duello*, satisfaction would have been sought and secured in a different manner.

Cameron's course of action resulting from the issues of his desperate struggle for the Senatorship in 1855 illustrates graphically the character of the man. At that time the presidency of the Bank of Northumberland was occupied by one John Taggart, who had secured a solicitor-

[38] McClure, *Notes*, I, 387.
[39] An elderly respected member of the Bellefonte bar to the writer, June, 1950.

ship for his son David. David Taggart, a member of the American Caucus of 1855, was a joint author and signatory of the scandalous anti-Cameron "American Petition." In November, following the episode, William Cameron replaced John Taggart as president of the Northumberland bank. With Simon Cameron's backing, his brother William had quietly bought controlling interest in the bank solely for the purpose of revenge, and to deprive the Taggarts of their means of sustenance. Cameron was completely successful; David Taggart knew he was whipped, asked forgiveness, was received into full Cameron communion, and subsequently embarked on a successful political career, ever harkening to his master's voice. It was David Taggart, president of the State Senate in 1857, who proudly announced the election of Simon Cameron to the Senate of the United States. He was further rewarded by Cameron in 1861 with the sinecure of paymaster in the United States army.[40] A vindictive Cameron knew full well how to forgive and forget after extracting his pound of flesh. On the back of his copy of the "American Petition" of 1855, Cameron noted many years later that the majority of its signers had lived "to express regret" and to furnish him aid.[41]

The Taggart episode illustrated two cardinal features of the rising Cameron political machine; namely, the use of a system of rewards and punishments. This juxtaposition of a political heaven and hell on earth squared nicely with the stern Calvinistic principles of Cameron. In 1855 the existence of a Cameron machine was recognized. In

[40] McClure, *Old Time Notes*, I, 270-71. From Easton, Nov. 21, 1855, E. J. Fox inquired of Cameron: "Is old Taggart turned out yet? Let me know when it is done." Cameron MSS, DCC.

[41] Cameron MSS, LC.

an open letter to the Bradford *Gazette*, printed February 24, 1855, David Wilmot, a Senatorial aspirant, wrote of the compact, organized, and disciplined Cameron forces.[42] During the long period of his candidacy from December of 1854 through the following fall elections of 1855, numerous correspondents, in the capacity of lieutenants or hopeful neophytes, wrote to Cameron asking for directions and advice. A Cameron client, Henry B. Hoffman, mentioned his machine in May, 1855.[43] The date makes such an allusion especially significant because in spite of the candidate's late failure, his support remained.

Having entered the Senatorial lists in 1855 under the banner of the American Party, Cameron could hardly have acted within the year in conjunction with any other party without complete loss of face. In April he attended a Lancaster Know-Nothing Convention which ended in bedlam. Dissension in the various Know-Nothing camps was symptomatic of an early demise for the party. In late September, Cameron represented the American Party at a conference held with Republicans and Whigs for the purpose of agreeing on a coalition candidate for Canal Commissioner.[44]

Results of the Commonwealth's fall elections augured hard times ahead for the Know-Nothings and the end of the road for the Whigs. Although no newly elected Whig would appear in the new Democratic controlled legislature of 1856,[45] a new species of political genera, the Republicans, would make their initial appearance. In

[42] Charles B. Going, *David Wilmot: Free-Soiler* (New York, 1924), 468.

[43] Crippen, *Simon Cameron*, note 60, 276.

[44] Myers, "Rise of the Republican Party," 70.

[45] Mueller, *Whig Party in Pennsylvania*, 223.

January, 1856, not even Simon Cameron possessed the temerity to stand for the Senatorial candidacy before the legislative caucus of the victorious Democrats, and an American-Republican fusion did not possess the power to elect him; consequently, he was not a candidate. Pennsylvania's long interim of only partial representation in the Senate ended with the election of William Bigler, Democratic nominee.

Twice Simon Cameron had turned his back on the party of his choice, the Democracy, but he would never do it again. And although for thirty years he was one of the recognized party pillars of the Commonwealth, strangely he had never been elected to any political office as a Democratic candidate, nor had he ever seen fit to submit his name before the electorate in a bid for public office.[46] His future political role was destined always to be that of a stout opponent of the party which had adopted and nurtured him.

[46] As already noted, Cameron in 1838 had withdrawn as a candidate for Congress after capturing the nomination. He wished to prove to his boastful enemies that he could have it if he desired it.

4
Recognition within the New Republicanism

PROPOSED CONGRESSIONAL LEGISLATION IN EARLY 1854, THE Kansas-Nebraska Bill, had the effect of coalescing thousands of Northerners possessing free soil sentiments. Regardless of past political affiliation, these antislavery groups were now prepared to oppose with votes any move to reopen the question of slavery extension north of the 36°30′ line. The bill providing for the organization of Kansas and Nebraska territories did not establish slavery in these regions, but neither did it prohibit its entrance; and it explicitly stated that the principles of the old Missouri Compromise must be void in light of its inconsistency with the new territorial legislation. Throughout the North, many local groups, mass meetings, or so-called conventions mushroomed into existence in protest against reopening the doors to slavery. By the fall of 1854 these "anti-Nebraska" groups were commonly known as Republicans.

In Pennsylvania the Congressional elections of 1854 produced no Republican slate, although 21 out of the 25

successful candidates professed anti-Nebraska sentiments.[1]
Rather appropriately these anti-Nebraska adherents
organized early in David Wilmot's district. In eastern
Pennsylvania, 32 representatives from ten counties sitting
at Reading issued a call for a mass meeting of Republicans
at Pittsburgh in September, 1855. This western city of the
Commonwealth was selected because of its strategic location near the center of Republican strength.[2] The radical
antislavery sentiments expressed by this convention had a
nauseating effect upon the conservative Free Soilers. This
convention, contrary to the wishes of prominent Whig
neophytes, nominated the notorious abolitionist Passmore
Williamson for canal commissioner at the very time he
was being held imprisoned for contempt of court arising
out of his failure to produce two escaped slaves.[3] Republican defeats in 1855 and 1856, stated the conservative
wing, were due to the antics of these radical crusaders
within the party.

Pennsylvania's commanding position in the new party
received recognition when, on invitation from Wilmot and
a few out-of-state chairmen, the Republican party was
organized on a national scale at Pittsburgh in February,
1856. Public interest in political conventions was shared
with the Americans, who were holding their national
nominating convention at the same time in Philadelphia.
Francis P. Blair, Sr., whom Cameron had assisted in
ousting from the editor's chair of the Washington *Globe* in
1849, presided over the convention.

As already indicated, Cameron had maintained his
Know-Nothing connections through the fall elections of

[1] Mueller, *Whig Party*, 215.
[2] Myers, "Rise of the Republican Party," 62.
[3] Mueller, *Whig Party*, 220-21.

1855. During the years 1854, 1855, and 1856 many voters were gravitating from one party to another. The call of crafty state Republican leaders for the formation of a "Union Party" to represent all groups opposed to Democratic support for the Kansas-Nebraska legislation brought response from old Free Soilers, Conscience Whigs, Anti-Masons, Independent Democrats, Wooley-Heads, Old Nativists, and Americans. Political mutation was simple and few questions were asked. For Simon Cameron, the opportunist, no season could be more opportune. An humiliating recantation at Buchanan's Canossa, where this particular pentitent would lose more than his shoes, was to Cameron unthinkable. Even the electorate of 1855 appeared to have taken summary vengeance upon the 58 legislative supporters of Cameron because only two of this group were returned.[4] But fortunately, Simon Cameron, like many another, found in the American Party a convenient political catalytic agent which rendered simple the transition from one major party to another.

Apparently Simon Cameron's appearance as a Republican would have greatly sapped the machine which he had labored patiently to weld, but its links had been forged with bonds of personal loyalty and showed few signs of weakening. Diehard old-line Democrats, it could be expected, would not follow him into the ranks of the hated Republicans. But his political correspondence reveals but slight disapproval from his numerous followers; only a few dared to reproach him while a surprisingly large number, although styling themselves Democrats, indicated that they preferred to support Cameron.[5] Most of

[4] Myers, "Rise of the Republican Party," 74.
[5] Cameron MSS, DCC; Cameron MSS, LC.

his American followers immediately graduated into the ranks of the new party. Even the dour Thaddeus Stevens condescended to request the company of Cameron during the proposed trip to attend the national committee's sessions in New York.[6] And from far away war-torn Kansas came a reassuring message from John White Geary, its disgruntled governor, protesting his friendship for Cameron and reminding him that Geary never forgets a friend.[7]

Recognition for Simon Cameron at the national levels within the new party necessitated fast work on his part. The coveted Senatorial prize would again be offered in January, 1857, and little time was left. Perhaps the Union coalition in conjunction with the personal following he had been able to maintain would suffice to enable him to capture what had narrowly eluded his grasp in 1855. Cameron's first appearance as a Republican was a complete success; he captured the chairmanship of a local Dauphin County meeting in August, 1856, and created some astonishment in the process.[8] Apparently there is no record of his attendance at the Pittsburgh National Republican Convention of February, 1856, but its President, E. D. Morgan, later invited Cameron to attend a meeting of the national committee.[9] That he received ready recognition as a national party leader there can be no doubt. In the absence of any Republican state organization, it was natural for national leaders to turn to ex-Senator Cameron, next to Wilmot the best known Republican in the state.

When the Republican delegates met in Philadelphia,

[6] Stevens to Cameron, August 16, 1856, Cameron MSS, DC.
[7] Geary to Cameron, September 25, 1856, *ibid.*
[8] Myers "Rise of the Republican Party," 78.
[9] Morgan to Cameron, August 14, 1856, Cameron MSS, DCC.

June 17, to select the first Republican choice for the Presidency, the question of John C. Frémont's candidacy, had in the minds of the leaders, Francis P. Blair, Thurlow Weed, and John Bigelow, already been determined. William Seward did not consider the time propitious for his own candidacy and Salmon P. Chase, the abolitionist, was unavailable.[10] This left Frémont practically unopposed except for Pennsylvania's choice, Justice John McLean, the perennial candidate. Accepted by the anti-Masons in 1831, considered by the Whigs in 1852, and now greatly favored by the bolting Know-Nothings calling themselves North Americans, McLean had on the eve of the national convention received Pennsylvania's endorsement largely through the vigorous efforts of doughty Thad Stevens.[11] He was also receiving the endorsement of Vice-Presidential aspirant, Lincoln of Illinois.[12] Only 23 of Pennsylvania's delegation backed McLean (to no avail) at the national convention, where Frémont achieved the nomination on the first formal ballot.[13]

Now came the question of the Vice-Presidency. In this particular case the wishes of the Presidential candidate bore no weight. Pennsylvania, the home of Democratic nominee James Buchanan, appeared to be the most crucial state in the coming election. It was Frémont's wish to have a Pennsylvania running mate to offset the Democratic advantage in that state. Neither the radical Free Soiler Wilmot nor the North American, William F. Johnston, was

[10] Nevins, *Ordeal of the Union*, II, 463-64.
[11] Myers, "Rise of the Republican Party", 100.
[12] Beveridge, *Abraham Lincoln* (4 vols., New York, 1928), IV, 34.
[13] John Tweedy, *History of the Republican Conventions* 1856-1908 (Danbury, 1910), 23.

acceptable. Only one prominent Pennsylvanian, Simon Cameron, appeared to have national stature. In addition, Cameron's well-known dislike for Buchanan would have induced him to marshal every possible resource in an all out effort to defeat the Democratic candidate. But at this juncture, Francis P. Blair, possibly with unpleasant memories of the Washington *Globe* episode still fresh in his mind, vetoed the suggestion of Cameron's candidacy.[14] The selection of William L. Dayton in lieu of Cameron, was, in the opinion of Thurlow Weed and Frémont, "an error of the first magnitude." [15]

The Republican party platform, a product of David Wilmot, appeared in the guise of a religious broadside against two cardinal sins; the polygamy of the downtrodden Mormons and human slavery in the American territories. Cameron's emphasis on the need for a protective tariff was ignored in the crusade against sin. Even the protectionist state of Pennsylvania forgot about tariff issues in the excitement over the Nebraska Bill. The Democratic State Convention showed little concern over the probability of a tariff issue while the strong protectionist Pottsville *Miners Journal* defined the issues as "free territory, free speech and Frémont." [16]

The evangelistic spirit manifested at the Republican convention maintained its fervor throughout the campaign in Pennsylvania. Here the Presidential question was more confusing than in most states because a wing claiming to represent the state Whigs endorsed Frémont instead of

[14] Allen Nevins, *Frémont, The West's Greatest Adventurer* (New York, 1928) II, 487-88.

[15] Nevins, *Ordeal of the Union*, II, 470.

[16] Malcolm R. Eiselen, *Rise of Pennsylvania Protectionism* (Philadelphia, 1932), 237.

Fillmore, the Whig-American candidate. All groups opposed to Buchanan and the Nebraska principles recognized the pivotal position of the Keystone State and the importance attached to its October elections. If the Democratic state slate could be beaten in the earlier election, the results would pave the way for a Frémont victory in November. With this goal in mind a state "Union" ticket, not withstanding the great difficulties suffered, was drawn up; but the Democrats beat the three top "Union" men by a slim majority of almost 3,000 votes out of an approximate total of 423,000.[17]

The Republican strategists on the national level recognized Pennsylvania's key position in the presidential struggle and in light of the state elections redoubled their efforts to carry the state. Even Francis P. Blair forgot his enmity toward Cameron in lieu of a greater one against Buchanan, whom he disparagingly referred to as "Old Buck,"[18] and late in the campaign urged Cameron to exert every effort to insure Buchanan's defeat. Thurlow Weed, taking for granted Cameron's state leadership, invited him to attend a national committee meeting in New York. Horace Greeley bemoaned the lack of campaign funds when he heard the report that a vast Democratic clientele had poured $500,000 into its Pennsylvania campaign coffers.[19] In a last desperate move, Cameron, Truman Smith, and S. P. Chase attempted to raise funds, but the effort was not enough. John W. Forney, the bibulous journalist, performed a masterful job in directing the Democracy's campaign, while his party's press

[17] Crippen, *Simon Cameron*, 155.
[18] Smith, *Blair Family in Politics*, I, 369.
[19] Nevins, *Ordeal of the Union*, II, 506.

presented the frightening specter of triumphant abolitionism under the regime of the "Freemonsters." [20]

Buchanan's meager state majority of 835 over the
Union and American ticket was even less than the Democratic majority in October, but it was enough to allow the
political veteran his own state and the requisite majority
in the electoral college. Cameron greatly lamented the
Democratic victory, especially because he had hoped to
secure federal patronage along with a Senatorial victory
in January, 1857. At the age of 57 he could derive little
comfort from Blair's prophecy of a victory four years
hence.[21] Privately he admitted his pessimism during the
past campaign, placing the blame for defeat in the state
upon Whig management.[22] In his own county of Dauphin,
boasted Cameron, the Union vote of November doubled
that of October.

In his criticism of Whig leadership, Cameron was
certainly directing his shafts at the Pollock-Curtin faction.
The former Whig, George Darsie, had led the Allegheny
section to victory and Cameron could not have had either
Wilmot or Johnston in mind; nor even Thaddeus Stevens,
the old "Wooly Head." Other former Whig leaders like
William B. Reed, Josiah Randall, and Isaac Hiester had
defected early in 1856. Certainly Andrew G. Curtin,
occupied with the duties of Secretary of the Commonwealth and ex-officio superintendent of the common
schools, must have found little time to campaign. Pollock,
whom Cameron labelled "our slow governor," [23] was
intimate with Curtin.

[20] Bellefonte *Democratic-Watchman*, Sept. 3, 1856.
[21] Smith, *Blair Family in Politics*, I, 398-99.
[22] Cameron to Weed, quoted in Nevins, *Ordeal of the Union*, II,
506n.
[23] *Ibid.*, 506.

Frémont, on his part, charged failure to award Cameron second place on the ticket a factor contributing to the Republican defeat.[24]

At his peaceful Wheatland, the tired warrior Buchanan had reason to relax in comfort. The next president's party would have a small majority in the state legislature and also of the Commonwealth's Congressional representatives. The Democracy's control of the Senate would allow him to dispense the federal loaves and fishes generously to his many hungry clients. Among these numerous patrons of Buchanan certainly none was more worthy than editor John W. Forney, who had directed the Buchanan forces at the Cincinnati nominating convention and finally secured, albeit by questionable methods, a slim victory for his man at the Pennsylvania polls in 1856. None could have pictured him the anti-Buchanan candidate for the House clerkship three years hence.

Rather paradoxically, it was Buchanan's supporters, the Southerners, who paved the way for his arch-enemy Cameron to return to the Senate, and for the eventual departure of his helpmeet, Forney. At first, Buchanan proposed to reward his manager with the editorship of the administrative organ, the Washington *Union*, which included lucrative printing contracts, but Southern opposition blocked it; again, when Buchanan placed feelers suggesting Forney for a cabinet post, a Southern storm rose to stop it;[25] and finally when Forney asked and received from Buchanan, pledged support for the United States Senatorship, the dogs of war were loosed within the ranks of the state Democracy. To Henry D. Foster, Buchanan's fiat on the Forney candidacy was especially galling. This

---

[24] *Ibid.*, 507.   [25] McClure, *Old Time Notes*, I, 257, 261.

popular ex-Congressman had returned to the state House with the expressed purposed and understanding of becoming the next Democratic choice for Senator.

Although Simon Cameron on his part had fought a vigorous campaign in 1856 with special interest focused on legislative returns as a determinant of the Senatorial outcome, one could see little hope of his success. At this time he had many enemies within the Unionist ranks and only its desperate position—a minority group in the legislature—could have made his candidacy acceptable.

Shortly after the November elections two very prominent Republican leaders, formerly his opponents, signified their intention to back Cameron for the Senatorship. David Wilmot, of Proviso fame, went to some length in explaining his former hostility to Cameron in the 1855 contest. His opposition at that time, explained the Free Soiler, was based not on personal enmity but rather upon the American platform. Wilmot was not willing to accept Cameron unconditionally: "The circumstances have changed, your position in the late contest . . . has placed you upon ground when our people recognize you as a co-worker in the cause of Freedom. You are identified with the Republican party." [26] Wilmot gave assurance of legislative support for Cameron from the members of his district.

Another prominent supporter appeared in the person of Thaddeus Stevens, once a mocker of Cameron before conventions. His yeoman service paved the way for Cameron's acceptance by the opposition within the Unionist ranks. Stevens personally contacted members of

[26] Wilmot to Cameron, Myers, "Rise of the Republican Party", 149.

the legislature, Governor Pollock, and finally Andrew G. Curtin, who, according to Stevens, consented to Cameron's candidacy. Curtin, in this instance, proved more gracious than his American caucus opponent of 1855 ever proved himself to be under like circumstances. Stevens further suggested what most Republican strategists must have already had in mind, a promise of enough Democratic bolters' votes to insure victory.[27] Four days later, Stevens clearly presented Republican chances to a Pittsburgh supporter:

It would be a great victory if we could send a Republican senator to the U. S. senate. If you tender the nomination to S. Cameron I have reason to believe that he can get enough of his old friends to elect him. . . . He is now a genuine Republican as his late acts have shown. It is clear that we can elect no one else, and I submit to you whether it would not be better to elect him than be defeated.[28]

To conceive in this case the near-diabolical plot of an archmanipulater, Cameron, who personally conceived and carried to successful execution the coup which gave him the Senatorship in 1857 is erroneous. There were doubtless many who realized the significance of Cameron's personal following among the Democrats. Following the October elections, Charles B. Penrose of Philadelphia had suggested Cameron's ability to procure three or four Democratic-American votes. A citizen of Uniontown believed a Democratic member of the Assembly from his county, one "of *easy virture* [,] . . . might be useful." [29]

---

[27] Stevens to Cameron, Nov. 30, 1856, Cameron MSS, LC.

[28] Stevens to E. D. Gazzam, Dec. 4, 1856, Edward McPherson Papers, Library of Congress.

[29] Penrose to Cameron, Oct. 25; A. Road to Cameron, Nov. 8, 1856; William Bailey to Cameron, Nov. 23, 1856, Cameron MSS, DCC.

On the last day of November, Stevens was wanting to know whether enough Democratic votes were forthcoming to secure Cameron's election. Although six days later he had reason to believe that these votes were available, only one person, Simon Cameron, was in possession of that particular information. Moreover, Cameron would not have dared to promise Stevens the votes without knowledge of their source. According to the logic of the circumstances, Cameron had lined up his Democratic votes one month prior to his election.

In spite of the Democratic majority in the legislature, John W. Forney expressed increased concern over the chances of his defeat. That Cameron was angling for the united support of the Union opposition was no secret; and Forney was not fool enough to suppose that Cameron's sole goal was to have himself designated Forney's fore-ordained victim. At the beginning of the year 1857 he considered his prospects good although he was not "sanguine." [30] Well might Forney fear the wrath of a united Republican-American coalition which attributed their recent party defeats largely to the venom spewed upon them by Forney's organ, the *Pennsylvanian*, and also to his machinations in the Philadelphia area during the recent elections. "Indeed, Forney virtually confessed the use of fradulent methods to Buchanan." [31]

Buchanan's forced nomination for Forney in the Democratic caucus of January 9 drew first blood for Cameron. The absence of eight Foster men and the Forney vote of only 35 out of the 60 present indicated great dissatisfaction in the Democratic camp, but not proof of any con-

[30] Myers, "Rise of the Republican Party," 150.
[31] Nevins, *Ordeal of the Union*, II, 508.

templated defection to the Union ranks. The Democrats had the advantage of a three-vote edge on a joint legislative vote besides a majority in the Senate which enabled the Forney men to use delaying tactics if necessary.

At a planned evening caucus of the Republican-American coalition, Charles B. Penrose, Cameron's liaison agent, suggested an avenue of victory for the minority coalition, the nomination of Simon Cameron for the Senatorship. Penrose, knowing that proof of proffered opposition support would be required in advance by the coalition, made arrangements to have a select committee meet the Democratic defectors in secret for the purpose of securing their individual pledges. Within the secret walls of Cameron's hotel room three renegade Democrats, in the presence of three Union committee members, solemnly swore to give their vote to Cameron in the forthcoming Senatorial election. In spite of the assurances there given, the Union caucus promised a united vote for Cameron only on the first ballot.

Alexander K. McClure has left in his *Notes* a most dramatic account of the election of Simon Cameron on January 13, 1857. At the beginning, wrote McClure, "the Democrats felt that there was a subtle miasma in the political atmosphere, but they were bewildered in attempting to locate it." As the vote proceeded alphabetically nothing unusual happened until representative William B. Lebo of Schuylkill, a Democrat, voted for Cameron. The bombshell made the suspense breathtaking, because all realized Lebo would unlikely bolt without allies. The feeble voice of Samuel B. Manear of York insured at least a tie and finally the third Democrat, G. A. Wagonseller from Schuylkill clinched Cameron's election, 67 votes to Forney's 58. Amidst pandemonium, the de-

voted Cameron Speaker David Taggart proudly announced Cameron's election to the Senate of the United
States. His son, J. Donald Cameron, making hasty exit
through a rear window, was the first to bear the welcome
tidings. Buchanan, the meddling autocrat, was discredited, chorused the Cameron bloc, and his man
Forney, now properly sobered, must needs go on his
travels once more.

Seldom has a Democratic press ever proved as re-
sourceful in heaping denunciations upon their own discredited party members as they did upon the three renegades, Lebo, Manear, and Wagonseller. Cries of corruption
and bribery were heard on every hand. The *Democratic-
Watchman* of Bellefonte announced "with regret and
mortification" the election of "that corrupt political
tactician, Simon Cameron to disgrace the state and make
himself ridiculous in the Senate." For the first time in
the history of Pennsylvania, observed the Pittsburgh
Gazette of January 15, a Senatorial nominee "had overcome a regular majority of the party opposed to him in
politics."; but the Pottsville *Miners Journal* sagely observed that the "Democratic 'traitors' had looked first to
the interests of the state." To cite all the editorial opinion
on this election would require many pages, usually either
monotonously condemnatory in tone or of benign indiffer-
ence to the results.

Suspicion of attempts at bribery began before the election. At that time Forney had written to Buchanan:
". . . at the moment Cameron's election seems almost
certain. The corruption here is frightful beyond certain.
Any amount is offered for a single vote." [32] This much is
certain, the Foster men did not prevent Forney's election.

[32] Myers, "Rise of the Republican Party," 150.

The renegade vote came from Cameron's old Democratic strongholds in eastern Pennsylvania. Few men of the time accepted the theory of three turncoats having accepted political martyrdom, risk of bodily injury, and public ostracism on the basis of purely personal loyalty. There is some incriminating evidence in Cameron's papers. Cameron's self-styled "agent" in York county had written: "Manaer [*sic*] . . . is a good subject, and under certain contingencies open to 'conviction.' He belonged to the old Cameron party in our county and is very much under the control of James M. Anderson." Exactly one month following Cameron's election, Anderson wrote that he had received Cameron's note and had missed seeeing him at the designated hotel. Anderson continued: ". . . if it is convenient to you to help me, please send me a check on any Bank you have confidence in, that I can draw the amount, *You Can Spare*, me, as the money might be miscarried however you can do as you chose for that, as no one can know our business." Anderson characterized himself a "true friend by God." [33]

That the Democrats firmly believed bribery was used on the occasion of Cameron's election is established by the precautionary measures they took during the election proceedings of 1863. The aged Henry Haines of Maytown, whose father was employed by Cameron, accepted the bribery story. According to Haines, one of the Democratic renegades, while engaged in a game of cards, related the great need of funds to educate his children and his

[33] D. F. Williams to Cameron, Jan. 2, 1857; James M. Anderson to Cameron, Feb. 13, 1857, Cameron MSS, DCC. On January 23, F. F. Kohler wrote Cameron that a William McAbee believed he was the one who had secured Manear and threatened to expose Cameron if he did not receive "that which was promised him."

acceptance of $10,000 for that purpose. One of the gamblers in turn recited the story to the father of Haines.[34]

Inquiry into the circumstances surrounding Cameron's election was not limited to the confines of the Commonwealth.[35] Immediately upon Cameron's entrance into the Senate, Pennsylvania's senior Senator, William Bigler, presented a petition of the Democratic members of Pennsylvania's legislature protesting the seating of Cameron and asking for an investigation of the affair. Cameron, expressing his eagerness for an early inquiry into the affair, volunteered to move the petition's acceptance by the Judiciary Committee.[36] The Committee in a prompt report quickly disposed of the technicalities listed in the petition and branded the remainder relating to corrupt methods too vague. The Committee saw no reason why the Pennsylvania legislature on its part should not produce the evidence; but in the meantime Cameron was entitled to his seat. A minority report of the same Judiciary Committee considered the matter one involving the honor of the Senate, in which case that body should make further inquiries. The Senate accepted the Committee report and the matter was dropped.

The election of Cameron to the Senate in 1857 signified more than a personal triumph or vindication; it elevated him to a recognized place of leadership over the powerful new Republican party within his state. The party, still in a state of flux, was yet to emerge from its mold with the distinctive features characteristic of the post-bellum years. Commanding a state passing through the throes

---

[34] Henry Haines to the writer, Maytown, Aug. 29, 1950.

[35] Hamilton J. Eckenrode, *Rutherford B. Hayes* (New York, 1930), 210.

[36] *Cong. Globe*, 34 Cong., 3 Sess., *Appendix*, 383.

of industrialization, Cameron was in position to establish Republican party precepts not solely negative in character —such as opposition to expansion of slavery—but rather affirmative progressive principles; *viz*, exploitation and development of America's seemingly unlimited resources, internal improvements, a tariff designed to protect America's growing industries (including safeguards for the livlihood of the American free laborer), and other goals which were to give the "new party of Lincoln" some aspects of Whigism reincarnated.

Simon Cameron, spokesman for the minority Union-Republican party of Pennsylvania, had achieved victory almost two years ahead of his state's Republican organization. The Democratic resurgence, which had placed Pennsylvania's son in the Presidential chair, reached flood-tide within the Commonwealth in 1857 when it elected William F. Packer governor and then receded, destined not to win another gubernatorial victory for a quarter of a century.

With one Senatorial seat now apparently lost for six years, the frustrated Democrats could do little beyond venting their wrath upon sacrificial scapegoats; one example in this case being that of a convention delegate from York who had openly boasted of his alleged control over the vote of Samuel B. Manear, one of the Democratic renegades captured by Cameron. After denying the York delegate his seat, the Democratic State Convention of 1857 inserted within its state party plank a clause deprecative of the means used to elect Cameron and manifesting its contempt for the three apostates of its party.[37] The convention finally completed the chief item on its agenda

[37] Myers, "Rise of the Republican Party," 163.

with the selection of William F. Packer, a native of
Centre County and one-time journeyman printer for Simon
Cameron,[38] for the gubernatorial candidacy.

The Republicans saw little hope for victory in 1858
without complete cooperation from the Americans, and
consequently included several prominent Know-Nothings
on their state ticket. Judge David Wilmot, the famous
"citizen of northern Pennsylvania with a doubtful [sic]
reputation for slovenliness of dress, intemperance in eat-
ing and drinking, and laziness,"[39] accepted the gubernatorial nomination and likely defeat for the purpose of
fallowing the ground for future political harvests.[40] In
June, the dissatisfied Americans chose their own candidate for governor, thereby weakening Wilmot's chances.

Wilmot, who on the basis of his past record could
hardly have posed as a protectionist, now made clear the
fact that he was at least not a free trader and received
the strong support of Cameron throughout the somewhat
sluggish, dignified campaign. This aid, largely in the form
of cash "judiciously placed" among Wilmot's "disinterested friends," sustained him during the last weeks of the
contest.[41] True to the pessimistic expectations of the Republicans, Packer, who discreetly had said little on the
controversial Kansas problem, was easily elected over
Wilmot in October.

The following year the Democrats paid the piper for
the violent business depression and President Buchanan's
endorsement of the proslave Lecompton Constitution for

---

[38] William C. Armor, *Lives of the Governors of Pennsylvania*
(Norwich, Conn., 1874), 434.

[39] "David Wilmot," *Dictionary of American Biography*, XX, 317.

[40] McClure, *Old Time Notes*, I, 299.

[41] Wilmot to Cameron, Sept. 1; Oct. 8, 1857, Cameron MSS, LC.

Kansas. Discontent was rife within the ranks of the state Democracy and Buchanan lost prestige following a revolt of the anti-Lecompton men at the Democratic State Convention. In October the state electorate would choose an entire Congressional slate which in turn would indicate its approval or disapproval of national administration policies; hence the importance to the Democracy of maintaining their lines intact within the state.

In 1858 the state Republicans appeared with a new title, the Peoples' Party. Although Cameron and Wilmot were the most prominent, Thaddeus Stevens, Andrew H. Reeder, Galusha Grow, former Governor Ritner, Andrew G. Curtin, William B. Mann, Alexander McClure, J. K. Moorhead, and Henry C. Carey were also accepted leaders. The name of Carey, a synonym for protection, indicated the reappearance of the tariff issue. The passage in 1857 of a tariff act enlarging the free list concurrently with a nationwide economic collapse of the same year made the arguments of the protectionists appear more than plausible. Extremely anxious to mold the new party into one devoted to protectionist principles, Cameron attended pro-tariff meetings, corresponded with businessmen on the subject of protection, and encouraged the nomination by the Peoples' Party of only those devoted to protectionist principles.

The politico's energy, money, and campaign strategy were not wasted in the Congressional and state elections of 1858. The wave against the Democracy allowed the People's Party to elect a canal commissioner and Supreme Judge. It captured the House of Representatives and reduced the Democratic majority in the Senate to one. In the new Congress, 20 Republican Congressmen from Pennsylvania, led by Thaddeus Stevens, would face only five Democrats, two of whom were anti-Lecompton.[42] The state's repudiation of President Buchanan's leadership made Cameron's claim to a new title—the Senatorial tribune of Pennsylvania's electorate—sound very convincing. Even the Democratic state administration leader, Packer, in his advocacy of popular sovereignty [43] was in the Douglas camp rather than Buchanan's.

Cameron's power over the new Peoples' controlled legislature and official party gatherings was reflected in the choice of presiding officers. Alexander K. McClure of Franklin County had expected the speakership of the lower house without opposition from his party, but after a conference with Cameron, in the course of which he failed to make any commitments satisfactory to Cameron and later (according to his account) refused to buy four critical votes at $200 each, found himself displaced by a Cameron man from Dauphin County.[44] Again, when the Peoples' Party Convention met the following June, Cameron's man, David Taggart, occupied the Speaker's chair. Continued victories for the Peoples' Party in the state elections of 1859 helped maintain Cameron's prestige in the state and augured well for the great year 1860 when the new party expected to exercise an important voice in Presidential politics.

The political medium of the Thirty-fifth Congress, to which Cameron returned in 1857, was one of the most exciting in American history. The Kansas question, a riddle of political dynamite, virtually rent the Democratic party of Buchanan in twain when the President recommended the admission of Kansas to the Union under a pro-slave

[42] Crippen, *Simon Cameron*, 189.
[43] Armor, *Lives of the Governors*, 444.
[44] McClure, *Old Time Notes*, I, 457-58.

constitution adopted by questionable methods. Under these circumstances, the friendly atmosphere and the congenial relationships which Pennsylvania's Senator had previously enjoyed with several Southern gentlemen now came to an end. Compensation for the loss of old ties was found by Cameron in the place of leadership which he gained among the Republicans in the Senate.

Many skirmishes occured in Congress during the heat of the controversy over Kansas. Although the politico participated in none approaching the theatrics exhibited in the House, by his fellow Pennsylvanian, Galusha Grow, he engaged in some sparring with Senator James S. Green of Missouri. Cameron was placed in an awkward position during the debates on the night of March 15, because of his promise to pair with an absent colleague from Virginia, in which case he wished not to be counted in the quorum. At the same time he was protesting against the gag tactics directed by Green, a member of the Committee on Territories.

The Democrats had stolen a march on the Republicans through an early caucus; the Republicans, not having had the opportunity to plan their latest strategy, desired delaying tactics. When a Senator from New Hampshire was forced to conclude a speech, though unable to go on, Cameron commented: "I though that all men aspire to be here because there was a degree of kindness, liberality, and generosity prevailing here, which could be found in no other body under heaven. I do not want to come here if it is to be changed from that rule." Green rose to a question of order while Cameron was asking for adjournment; whereupon the later responded, "I cannot be put down by that man." Later when Green called for a vote, Cameron's violent protest led to a verbal contest in the course of which each called the other a liar. Cameron ignored Green's suggestion that the question of veracity be settled, presumably by personal combat five minutes after Senate adjournment. As usually happened in such cases, both gentlemen later offered formal apologies before the Senate. Cameron on his part could not remember what offensive words he had used.[45]

Rather amusingly, Cameron teamed with two Republican colleagues in a compact of amity and mutual assistance to ward off the chronic insolence of a few Southern aggressors. The "Memorandum" of 1874 stated that "On one noted occasion, Robert Tombs indulged in such terrible and unjust denunciation of Seward and his followers that the undersigned felt themselves forced to do something to vindicate themselves and their constituents." The terms of this solemn compact required the three parties, Cameron, Zachariah Chandler, and Benjamin F. Wade to carry their quarrel, if required, into their graves.[46] With the passing of years the trio came to attach more and more sancity and reverence to an agreement regarded by them as a landmark in safeguarding the liberties of United States Senators. That Cameron was able and anxious to maintain old Southern friendships is illustrated by his willingness, in the face of severe criticism, to pair with Jefferson Davis on the critical Lecompton vote of March 23, 1858. This was an act of courtesy, worthy of the traditions of the old South itself,

[45] *Cong. Globe*, 35 Cong., 1 Sess., *Appendix*, 82, 94, 96, 109-10, 1131.

[46] "Copy," and "Memorandum," May 26, 1874, Cameron MSS. LC. The original compact was probably an oral understanding to come to one another's aid. Only the Cameron Papers has copies of the "memorandum" and "compact," but Albert Riddle saw Wade's copy.

which enabled the sick Mississippi senator to absent himself from the Senate chamber without endangering the results of the vote.[47]

The House would not agree with the Senate on the question of Kansas and had adopted an amendment proposed by an anti-Lecompton Democrat of Pennsylvania providing re-submission of the Lecompton constitution to the people of Kansas. The two houses of Congress followed with a compromise, the English Bill, which provided for a grant of land if the Lecompton constitution were accepted by the Kansas electorate. Douglas, it was believed by the compromising parties, could be persuaded to assist them because of the help he would need in Illinois where he faced a two-front war against Republicans and Buchanan Democrats in his fight to retain his Senatorial seat. Cameron and William Seward during the course of a luncheon had promised their full influence in persuading the Illinois Republicans to go easy on Douglas.[48] Douglas, after promising Robert J. Walker his support for the bill, suddenly reversed himself and rejoined the opposition, but he derived no comfort from the Illinois Republicans.

Although the land grant promised Kansas was analogous to that given other states, Cameron joined with his good friend Henry Wilson in calling the English Bill a bribe. He thus disapproved of the compromise more vigorously than he had the original bill because: "This to my mind is a trick to impose upon weak men, or to enable corrupt men to make the impression upon their constituents at

[47] Shortly before the departure of Davis from Washington in 1861, Cameron, on invitation from Mrs. Davis, was a breakfast guest.

[48] Nichols, *Disruption of American Democracy*, 166-67, 173.

home that they have been acting honestly." [49] The English Compromise became a law, but the Lecompton constitution was overwhelmingly rejected by the voters of Kansas. Four months of wrangling in United States legislative halls had for its fruits only deeper separation.

Of all public economic issues, the subject of the tariff was closest to the heart, and likely also to the purse, of Simon Cameron. If the Democratic platform of 1856 was a true harbinger of future legislation on this subject, the protectionists would be driven to the wall. The people of the United States, proclaimed this document, should "declare themselves in favor of free seas and progressive free trade throughout the world." [50] Secretary of the Treasury Guthrie, in his report of December, 1856, recommended reduction of the revenue by taking duties off raw materials, thus placing United States manufacturers on an international competitive basis. Using Cameron's pet product, iron, as an example, he cited the growth the country had made in that industry since 1840 and predicted fulfillment of domestic needs by 1860. The Tariff of 1857, enacted during the last days of the Pierce administration, was the first non-partisan legislation of that type passed in 40 years. Only one state, Pennsylvania, offered much opposition to the reduction in duties. Cameron had not yet taken his seat in the Senate; but his presence could hardly have made such difference in the end results. [51]

To Cameron, a sincere tribune of the worker, the interests of labor and capital were identical. As the effect of

[49] *Cong. Globe*, 35 Cong., 1 Sess., 1898.
[50] Stanwood, *History of the Presidency*, 268.
[51] Rhodes, *History of United States*, II, 500; Taussig, *History of the Tariff*, 115.

the Panic of 1857 spread, bringing unemployment to thousands of workers in the coal and iron industries, petitions praying for relief poured into the office of Senator Cameron. In the process of presenting these petitions before the Senate, Cameron extended his remarks to subjects usually foreign to that august body; namely, the question of responsibility which the government bears toward relieving its poverty-stricken citizenry in time of stress, and the future place the worker would occupy in the politics of the country. In this respect, like a prophetical Jeremiah a century ahead of his time, he predicted the common man's future control.

To bring about this supremacy, observed Cameron, the laboring man must elect members to Congress who will serve his interests; namely, pro-tariff men. With characteristic Cameronian political slant the speaker appealed to the laboring men of his own state, whom he now believed were "beginning to put their shoulders to the wheel," and whom he believed would "make such a noise in next October [1858], as will alarm the gentlemen all over the country who laugh at them. . . . Let them exercise the power wisely, and they will no longer be without plenty of work and good prices." [52] Thus the triumph of the laboring man must be accomplished through the medium of a protective Republican party.

Included in the numerous petitions for relief of the iron industry were some from Pittsburgh and the counties of Luzerne; Bedford, Blair, Montgomery, Centre, and Huntingdon. The petition from Huntingdon County, signed by the workmen, reported prostration of a two million dollar county industry "in consequence of the legislation [tariff of 1857] of the country." [53]

[52] *Cong. Globe*, 35 Cong., 1 Sess., 2563.   [53] *Ibid.*, 956.

Cameron blasted his senior colleague, William Bigler, before the Senate, labeling him a free trader and attributing the distress in Pennsylvania to the aftermath of Bigler's vote. The following year in a speech at Bellefonte, next door to Bigler's home domain, Cameron, in reply to Samuel Linn's welcoming address, reiterated the necessity for protecting labor: "Gentlemen when labor is shielded from unfair competition and fostered by liberal protection, you protect the whole community and prosperity must necessarily follow." [54] During the second session of Congress, Cameron, in response to a petition from the Pennsylvania legislature for a change to specific duties, again called the Senate's attention to the need for an amended tariff law.

With hasty rationalization and the urge to gain political capital wherewithal, the Keystone Republicans had attributed the Panic of 1857 to effects of the new tariff. Wilmot in his campaign for governor made those charges through the New York *Weekly Tribune* of October 10. In spite of Cameron's agitation no further steps were taken in the Congress to alter the tariff until shortly before Lincoln's election, when the House passed the Morrill Bill, more perhaps for its vote-catching possibilities in manufacturing areas than for its protective features. The bill, with amendments, did not become a law until March 2, three days before Lincoln appointed Cameron to his cabinet.

The Kansas question of the 1850's did not include all the territorial nightmares haunting the Democratic regime. In Utah Territory, the brilliant Brigham Young had succeeded, under nominal federal authority, in maintaining a patriarchial government over his thrifty Mormon

[54] Bellefonte *Central Press*, April 21, 1859.

flock. Opportunities in various fields of economic endeavor like building of railroads, land speculation, stage-coach operations, freight monopolies, telegraph communication, etc., led to great pressure from the gentiles of the various states for stricter supervision of these sinful Latter Day Saints. The Republicans, anxious to rid the continent of licentious polygamy, one of the remaining twin relics of barbarism, were prodding the legalist Buchanan to action. In the fall of 1857, when a military expedition unproperly prepared for the eventualities likely to confront it, was dispatched to the territory with unfortunate military and financial results, Congress was faced with a huge deficiency bill in addition to a request from Secretary of War Floyd for five additional regiments. The proposal to increase the size of the regular army led to extended debate, in the course of which the Republicans generally opposed Floyd's plan because it smacked of militarism and conceivably might later be used for nondesignated purposes.[55]

At first Cameron agreed upon the need for the use of troops in Utah, considering the emergency, and did not question closely the methods used to increase the size of the army. The anticipated clashes did not materialize and now, recognizing no emergency, he vehemently opposed a larger regular army because "all former republics have been destroyed by mercenary troops, and such will be the fate of this Government if the same course is pursued." The plan of Jefferson Davis to incorporate more men into the already organized companies likewise received unsympathetic treatment from him because West Point officers were opposed to promotions from ranks. If more troops were actually needed in Utah, General Simon

[55] Nichols, *Disruption of American Democracy*, 178-79.

Cameron, former adjutant-general of Pennsylvania, was prepared to raise and lead from his own state enough volunteers to cope with the crisis. In any case, the nation must not be denied the necessary troops. Congress finally passed a bill providing for volunteers who never saw service because Brigham Young came to terms with the gentile governor, Alfred Cumming.[56]

Consistent with his term of office in the Thirty-fifth Congress, it appeared that Cameron was championing the cause of economy in government. The Buchanan administration was pledged to carry into execution this same worthy service for the nation's benefit, but what with the national economic recession, the many deficits in the government services, the fall of the tariff revenue, the increased military expenditures wrought by costly western expeditions and a British war scare, rampant waste and corruption on the national level, and other deficiencies too numerous to mention, the party leaders found themselves unable to fulfill their promises and the public debt continued to increase by leaps and bounds.

Probably Cameron's early journalistic background led him to take a special interest in the problems pertaining to public printing, although a prominent Republican, Cornelius Wendell, was fast becoming the central target of the Democratic sleuths who accused him of reaping huge profits from the Treasury's coffers. In March, 1857, almost a year before the Senate took formal action, Cameron's resolution had called for an itemized statement from the Secretary of the Treasury covering the public printing bills of the past decade. In March, 1858, he again took the floor to discuss the problem, and over a year later he was urging that a special committee be as-

[56] *Cong. Globe*, 35 Cong., 1 Sess., 678, 875, 1426, 1443, 1564.

signed the duty of investigating alleged fraudulent printing for the Post Office Department. Specifically Cameron
pointed to the huge cost of printing only "a single dish
of strawberries"—$2000. In spite of its acknowledged de-
ficiencies, he favored a return to the old system of contracting the printing to the lowest bidder rather than
allowing directors to permit huge profits to favorite
clients. He continued his fight for economy in public
printing to near the end of his services in the ante-bellum
Senate.[57]

Although a spoilsman of the first order who would
fight vigorously to place his followers in positions of public
trust, Cameron did not ask that they be overpaid. He
insisted that $2000 was ample for a purser living in Phila-
delphia but perhaps one residing in Charleston or New
Orleans would require $2400. He deprecated the cut in
pay of clerks in the navy yards to salaries of only $600
and was pleased to see them restored.[58]

In the field of foreign relations, Cameron again inter-
posed the question of economy. Half-hearted efforts of
United States, contrary to treaty agreements, in curbing
the slave trade to the Americas, had let British naval units
operating in the Caribbean area to take matters into their
own hands, leading to a firing upon suspected Yankee
slavers. Buchanan, comprehending fully the realities of the
situation, contented himself with talk rather than action in
protesting against John Bull's insults to Old Glory. The
British action created a stir in Congress and increased
naval appropriations were requested to bolster the nation's defenses. Cameron delivered a long harangue on the
proposed appropriations. He was convinced, argued

[57] *Ibid.*, 330, 711, 1509; 2 Sess., 1658.
[58] *Ibid.*, 35 Cong., 1 Sess., 2749.

Cameron, that there was no danger of war because Britain could not afford it. "While I shall give everything to the defense of the country," concluded the Commonwealth's junior Senator, "I will not give one dollar for extravagance or waste." [59]

Many other questions were argued in the Senate during the years 1857-60, and Cameron expressed his opinion freely on them. He urged public improvements and government subsidies for projects he considered too mammoth for private enterprise; namely, a transcontinental railroad, a telegraph line westward to Utah, and mail for Europe, the latter a proposed gratuity exclusively for the Collins Line, for whose bankrupt founder Cameron displayed a deep personal interest.[60] He hoped to see enacted the Homestead Bill, which was fathered by his fellow Pennsylvanian, Galusha A. Grow, but President Buchanan's veto checked it.

When Simon Cameron left the Senate to enter Lincoln's cabinet, he chose to consider himself the Commonwealth's leading proponent for a protective tariff, which to his way of thinking promoted free enterprise in a growing industrial society and guaranteed a full dinner pail for the laborer.

[59] *Ibid.*, 2741.   [60] *Ibid.*, 2826.

5
Senate to Cabinet

TO TAKE THE POLITICAL AUSPICES OF SIMON CAMERON IN
1860 would be to discover few unfavorable omens. His
new adopted party was making rapid gains both within
the Commonwealth and the free states. His success in
being the first of his party to represent Pennsylvania in
the Senate of the United States, rather than David Wilmot or Thaddeus Stevens, had contributed greatly to his
prestige and leadership. Only the Curtin-McClure-Mann
faction barred his path to complete control of the Peoples'
Party within the state. And had a political seer been
able to predict the great schism about to rend the Democratic Party, Republican enthusiasts would have had more
cause to feel jubilant over their chances of capturing the
Presidency and control of the new Congress.

The transition from the Democracy to the ranks of the
Republicans via the Know-Nothing route apparently had
little effect on the personal following of Simon Cameron.
For each lieutenantcy created in key spots there stepped
forth numerous aspirants eager for the honor of being
designated his man. This strength became evident when
the time approached to chose state and presiding officers

elected by the state legislative bodies. In 1859 Cameron
had dumfounded and surprised the Curtin faction when
he forced the election of his neighbor, W. C. A. Lawrence,
over Alexander K. McClure to the House Speakership.[1]
The following year Lawrence was renominated without
opposition[2] and elected over Democratic candidate
Henry Dunlap. Although the state treasurership, a gift
of the General Assembly, was held by Eli Slifer, a Curtin
partisan, he wrote in a conciliatory manner to Cameron
and made the sage observation that common interests demanded friendship between the two.[3]

Cameron's capture of Russell Errett of the Pittsburgh
Gazette must be recognized as a victory of the first order.
No other man over a score of years served more faithfully
and efficiently in promoting Cameron's welfare through
the medium of the press. This native of New York City
apprenticed to a baker on Scotch Hill in Pittsburgh at
the age of thirteen, plied his trade in three states and returned to Allegheny County when the national recession
broke in 1837. After trying his hand at teaching and
clerking he became editor of two small organs, one of
which (Washington *Patriot*) was a strong abolitionist
sheet. At first a mercantile reporter with the Pittsburgh
Gazette in 1852, he became assistant editor under S.
Riddle and Company. In 1856 he assisted in perfecting
the organization of the Republican Party in the western
half of the state and in the following year was president
of the Pittsburgh Common Council.[4]

[1] Bedford *Gazette*, Jan. 7, 1859.
[2] Philadelphia *Press*, Jan. 4, 1860.
[3] Slifer to Cameron, Oct. 29, 1859, Cameron MSS, DCC.
[4] Pennsylvania Scrapbook, Vol. 4, 17, Pennsylvania State Library;
Thomas Cushing, *et al; History of Allegheny County* (Chicago,
1889), 244-45.

Two Pittsburgh men, D. F. Williams and J. K. Moorhead, called Cameron's attention to Errett's worth, the latter requesting Cameron to make Errett his personal guest when the editor attended the state convention in 1858. Williams, an associate of Errett, wrote: "Mr. Errett . . . will be at the Harrisburg convention. He is a valuable and influential man here—a man whose friendship every politician seeks. . . . I wish you could see him and be as agreeable as possible." [5] Cameron heeded his advice and Errett soon went to work paving the way for general acceptance of Cameron's Presidential candidacy. In October, 1859, he made a tour of midwestern cities laboring to build up favorable sentiment among party leaders for his chieftain.[6] Soon after the beginning of the new year, the enterprising editor was informing the Prairie State's favorite son, A. Lincoln, of the display of Cameron's strength upon organization of the state legislature.[7] Errett's election to the chief clerkship of the State Senate in 1860, was, according to the Democratic press, proof of Cameron's ability to reward his devoted followers.[8]

In addition to the powerful Pittsburgh *Gazette*, which soon absorbed the Pittsburgh *Commercial Journal*, Cameron had the backing of other leading papers. The official Republican state organ at Harrisburg, the *Telegraph*, was edited and partially owned by George Bergner, an unusually ardent supporter of Cameron. In Philadelphia, his one strong paper was the *Daily Evening Bulletin*,

[5] Moorhead to Cameron, May 30, 1858; Williams to Cameron, July 12, 1858, Cameron MSS, DCC.

[6] Errett to Cameron, Nov. 7, 1859, *ibid.*

[7] Errett to Lincoln, Jan. 2, 1860, Robert Todd Lincoln Collection, Library of Congress. Hereafter cited as Lincoln MSS.

[8] Erie *Observer*, Jan. 21, 1860.

but most of the other Republican sheets were tolerant. Elsewhere, the Greensburg *Herald,* the Conneautville *Courier,* the Lancaster *Examiner and Herald,* the Tamaqua *Anthracite Gazette,* the Mauch Chunk *Gazette,* the Erie *Dispatch,* the Connellsville *Patriot,* and the Huntingdon *Journal* furnished support in various strategic local areas.[9]

Simon Cameron's final determination to try for the Republican Presidential candidacy in 1860 was probably brought about through a persistent policy of "nagging" and suggestion carried on by his numerous followers, who were not unmindful of the benefits which might accrue to them should he succeed. In June, 1858, a Mercur County supporter wrote of his possible candidacy.[10] The following month an admirer in far away Keokuk, Iowa, was delighted to read of the New York *Herald's* endorsement of Cameron for President.[11] In November of the same year, D. F. Williams of the Pittsburgh *Gazette* presented his article, "Cameron and the Presidency."

First official party recognition came from his home county of Dauphin in late May, 1859, when Cameron was formally endorsed for the Presidential candidacy.[12] September 1859 found an active Cameron club in Chicago. When an Illinois paper printed an editorial of the Lancaster *Examiner* suggesting the team of Cameron and Lincoln for President, and, after one of Cameron's promoters had the temerity to urge Lincoln's early acceptance of second place on a Presidential ticket,[13] the crafty rail-

[9] Correspondence, 1858-1859, Cameron MSS, DCC.

[10] William S. Garvin to Cameron, June 23, 1858, *ibid.*

[11] R. M. McAllister to Cameron, July 20, 1858, *ibid.*

[12] William McHaffy to Cameron, June 6, 1859, *ibid.*

[13] Reinhard H. Luthin, "Pennsylvania and Lincoln," *Pennsylvania Magazine of History and Biography,* LXVIII (January, 1943), 63.

splitter promised to support such a ticket *after* it had been
"fairly nominated," and agreed that Pennsylvania's endorsement of the fitness of her favorite son "could scarcely
be deemed insufficient." [14] But in the preceding year
Cameron's own evaluation of his worth was that "the presidency is so very far above my ambition or qualifications
that it has not really entered my head." [15]

The first hurdle Cameron was forced to surmount in
his quest for the Presidency was the strong opposition of
McClure-Curtin faction at the Peoples' Party state convention, held February 22, 1860. The boastful followers
of Andrew G. Curtin, the leading gubernatorial candidate,
spoke of nominating their candidate, of giving a token
endorsement to Cameron, and of leaving the matter of
national convention delegates to the pleasure of the districts. But for Simon Cameron, simple endorsement would
not suffice; it must be followed by the creation of a state
delegation nominated and pledged by the state convention to vote solidly for him.

Cameron was well aware of the odds he faced. Two of
his lieutenants, Samuel Purviance of Pittsburgh and
Henry D. Moore of Philadelphia, could see no hope of
stopping Curtin, and the latter doubted the advisability
of pressing for a united delegation.[16] But the veteran
strategist determined to force a compromise from the
Curtin men. By encouraging several popular district
leaders to stand for the gubernatorial nomination

[14] Roy P. Basler, ed., *Collected Works of Abraham Lincoln* (9
vols., Washington, Sesquicentennial Edition, 1959), III, 491.

[15] Quoted in Thomas Howard to Cameron, Aug. 17, 1858,
Cameron MSS, DCC.

[16] Purviance to Cameron, Nov. 23, 1859, Cameron MSS, DCC;
Moore to Cameron, Feb. 20, 1860, Cameron MSS, LC.

Cameron drew more strength from Curtin than anticipated. This move, together with his success in using
methods known best by those concerned in weaning away
several Curtin men, enabled Cameron at the propitious
moment to endanger Curtin's nomination and consequently to demand compensation.

When the Peoples' Party convention in Harrisburg had
properly disposed of their preliminaries, and selected
former Governor James Pollock, obviously as an umpire
to occupy the chairman's post, the Cameron forces decided to press immediately for a showdown on the two
important propositions of convention endorsement for
their man and the selection of a convention-chosen delegation pledged to vote as a unit. These motions elicited
probably the two severest anti-Cameron denunciations
ever delivered against Cameron at a Republican state
convention. The first was delivered by boisterous Thomas
Marshall of Pittsburgh, the second by District-Attorney
William B. Mann of Philadelphia,[17] one of the craftiest
political bosses that unfortunate metropolis ever bore.
Nevertheless Cameron secured his endorsement easily
enough and forced the McClure-Curtin group into an
agreement providing for the power of the convention delegates to select the national convention representatives of
congressional districts, if they so desired. Cameron's apparent victory proved barren in its results because one-
half the convention Congressional delegates preferred to
refer the selection to their local political districts. Thus
Cameron was left with no assurance of a united delegation backing him.

[17] Philadelphia *Public Ledger* Feb. 23, 24, 1860; Bedford *Gazette*, March 2, 1860.

Cameron's part of the bargain provided for the release of the Curtin delegates he had "stolen." [18] Having carried out his promise, he washed his hands of the gubernatorial question, allowing two of his firm adherents, David Taggart and retiring state chairman Levi Kline to run their own races. The pair received a total of 23 votes on the same ballot which nominated Curtin.[19] Had Cameron proceeded with his plan to defeat Curtin, he would, at this juncture, have concentrated his forces behind John Covode, the second strongest candidate. Consequently, a few of Covode's backers, in ignorance of behind-the-scenes transactions, accused Cameron of bad faith in light of his lukewarm support for the Westmoreland leader, but Cameron told no lie when he affirmed that "under the circumstances," he had done his best for Covode.[20]

In addition to his formal endorsement, the state convention voted items which must have warmed the politico's heart. Three verbose resolutions were required to memorialize his nobility of character, leadership, superior statesmanship, and high quality of public service rendered. Inserted in the convention plank was a demand for adequate tariff protection—meaning the kind that would protect everyone.[21]

During the interlude of ninety days between the Republican state and national conventions, the Cameron managers were busy with the two-fold problem of bring-

[18] McClure Notes, I, 397. Apparently there is no other contemporary record of this deal.
[19] William Egle, ed., Andrew Gregg Curtin: His Life and Services (Philadelphia, 1895), 104.
[20] Samuel B. Lauffer to Cameron, April 5, 1860, Cameron MSS, DCC.
[21] Philadelphia Ledger, Feb. 24, 1860.

ing the anti-Cameron delegates into line so that the state could present a solid front at the national convention; and to convince the other states that Cameron was actually a bona fide candidate possessing all the attributes that spell availibility. Cameron's leading manager, J. P. Sanderson of Philadelphia, issued directives to the numerous men of his organization and Curtin's, requesting a letter bombardment of A. G. Curtin, warning him that he must support their candidate in order to save himself. Sanderson succeeded in eliciting opinions from Curtin and his manager Alexander K. McClure conceding Cameron's nomination to be a necessity to success in the states.[22] But not even lip service could be wrung from the independent Thaddeus Stevens or Cameron's Philadelphia nemesis, William Benson Mann, both of whom controlled a small coterie of followers. On the eve of the national convention Cameron lacked a united delegation—a prime requisite for success.

Little pro-Cameron sentiment existed outside the Commonwealth. Dr. Charles Leib of Chicago led the Cameron crusade in the mid-West, pointing out in several conversations with Lincoln the absolute necessity of carrying Pennsylvania—meaning this precluded the nomination of the Illinois favorite. Resurrection of the old Winnebago scandal by Chicago's *Tribune* and the *Press* is evidence that Leib was making some progress in the area.[23] Russell Errett, using the theme of urgency for Cameron's nomination, carried on a varied correspondence with Republican leaders of national stature including the potential candidates themselves. Letters like the one from Pennsyl-

[22] Sanderson to Cameron, March 7, 12, 1861, Cameron MSS, DCC.
[23] Leib to Cameron, March 2, April 2, 1861, *ibid.*

vanian Titian J. Coffey to Edward Bates, a Presidential hopeful, must have neutralized the efforts of Errett. Pennsylvania's endorsement of Cameron was to Coffey merely a "compliment." Later the delegation would go for Bates.[24]

At least a week prior to the opening of the Republican National Convention, scheduled for May 16 at Chicago, the Cameron men had established their headquarters at the Briggs House and were busy elaborating on their basic text—that only Cameron was able to carry Pennsylvania, the state needed to insure a Republican President. Among the strong Cameron men gathered there were Alexander Cummings, Samuel Purviance, John N. Purviance, Henry D. Moore, J. Donald Cameron, Joseph Casey, David Mumma, Morrow B. Lowry, and J. P. Sanderson, the latter acting as chief manager. The Cameron men were happy to learn of a "general impression" that William F. Seward, the leading contender, could not be elected President by the party.[25]

The convention which assembled in the Chicago Wigwam, it seemed to observers, was not an ordinary one. A political destiny was to be fulfilled and they were the privileged actors in the drama. "The whole mass was inspired with energy, and believed, without a shadow of doubt, that they had come to witness the nomination of the next President." [26] The recent split in the Demo-

[24] Howard K. Beale, ed., "Diary of Edward Bates, 1859-1866," *Annual Report*, American Historical Association, 1930, IV (Washington, 1933), 107.

[25] John N. Purviance to Cameron, May 14, 1861, Cameron MSS, DCC.

[26] James G. Blaine, *Twenty Years of Congress, 1861-1881* (2 vols., Norwich, Conn., 1884), I, 165.

cratic Party at the Charleston convention would lead
Presidential aspirants to seek the prize more eagerly.

Of Republican candidates there certainly was no
scarcity; and a motley group it was of mixed Democratic-
Whig-American-Free Soil antecedents. Serious objections
to their "availability" would soon reduce the field. William H. Seward of New York had embittered the Know-
Nothings and frightened the conservatives with his
"higher law" and "irrepressible conflict"; the old Free
Soiler and free trader, Salmon P. Chase of Ohio, appeared
shifty, with a following which could not be pin-pointed;
while the venerable conservative Edward Bates of
Missouri stood revealed in the new age like a political
anachronism of the past. Cameron, rather appropriately
dubbed the "Democratic Know-Nothing Republican Conservative" [27] was known nationally, it was true. But primarily his name was symbolic of high tariff proclivities,
in no way connotating superior statesmanship; and his
various past adventures in his own peculiar medium—
spoilmanship, opportunism, and political chicanery—had
left an obnoxious residue, the stench of which would not
down. Few took his pretensions seriously[28] but he commanded some votes, represented an indispensable state,
and could conceivably be presented as a compromise
candidate if a deadlock ensued. However, the Lincoln
managers soon showed that their candidate was, at the
same time, the least objectionable, possessing all the
essential ingredients of availability.

[27] New York *Herald*, June 28, 1858, quoted in James G. Randall,
Lincoln the President, I, 148.
[28] E. H. Bowen to E. B. Washburne, May 19, 1860, Elihu B.
Washburne Papers, Library of Congress.

The defection in the Pennsylvania delegation and the determined opposition of the Curtin faction to any support for Seward placed Cameron's managers in a distressing dilemma from which their chieftain emerged surprisingly well. In the spring of 1859, when Cameron did not consider himself a bona fide candidate for the Presidency, Seward visited Harrisburg, was feted together with the whole Assembly by Cameron, who assured the New Yorker that after the first ballot he would get Pennsylvania's vote.[29] Until near convention time in May, 1860, Cameron corresponded with Seward and made efforts to see Thurlow Weed, Seward's manager, in Washington or Philadelphia. Only six days before the Republicans met in Chicago, the Chicago *Herald* reported: "The friends of Mr. Seward rely upon Senator Cameron to assist them in putting him in nomination on Wednesday next."

Cameron had prematurely promised Seward something he had no assurance of delivering. Cameron's special forte was the handling of legislative bodies, but ephemeral conventions sometimes got out of control, a fact Cameron discovered a year later. Early in 1861 the crafty Cameron was keeping Lincoln and his man Leonard Swett informed of Seward's activities.[30] Cameron's political astuteness told him that he should maneuver himself into a position where he could bargain with either Seward or the new champion of the west, A. Lincoln. When the propitious time arrived Cameron was not in Chicago and Weed found he could make no deals with the Cameron

[29] Seward to Weed, April 29, 1859, Thurlow W. Barnes, *Life of Thurlow Weed: Memoir* (Boston, 1884), 256.

[30] Cameron to Lincoln, Jan. 2, 1860, Lincoln MSS.

managers,[31] although, according to Horace Greeley, only Curtin's powerful resistance checkmated Weed's gold.[32]

The first task of the Cameron men at Chicago was to establish a guarantee of a solid Pennsylvania vote for their favorite son not only on the first but on each succeeding ballot so long as any chance remained for him to benefit by a stalemate between two stronger candidates.

Not even the first item was successfully achieved. In spite of earnest entreaties by Morrow D. Lowry, Russell Errett, H. D. Moore, and others, over a period of several days, the morning for balloting (third day) dawned upon an almost evenly divided delegation. Only at an eleventh-hour caucus which terminated shortly before the balloting began was Cameron assured of the support of his own state on the first ballot, thereby rescuing him from public humiliation.[33] Only thirteen delegates, most of them Allegheny County men, representing a total of 6½ votes, did not cast their ballots for him.[34] The 47½ votes from his own state plus three from others placed Cameron next to Lincoln on the first ballot and stimulated the whisper: "The opposition to Cameron was mighty small after all." Two weeks after the convention adjourned, A. K. McClure informed Cameron that the "approach" to unanimity must be attributed to an "accident." [35] But more

[31] Glydon G. Van Deusen, *Thurlow Weed* (Boston, 1947), 249.

[32] Greeley to James S. Pike, May 2, 1861, James S. Pike, *First Blows of the Civil War* (New York, 1879), 520.

[33] Moore to Cameron, May 20, 1860, Cameron MSS, DCC. Forty-five years after the events took place McClure wrote that the decision to back Cameron on the first ballot was made the night before and prior to the "Bargain." *Old Time Notes,* I, 406-07.

[34] Samuel R. Purviance to Cameron, May 23, 1860, Cameron MSS, DCC.

[35] McClure to Cameron, June 6, 1860, *ibid.*

realistic is the proposition that the Curtin men realized that a token vote for Cameron could do no harm while at the same time it might prove to considerable value to their man in his race for the governorship.

The consummation of the first portion of the Lincoln-Cameron bargain, which was pre-arranged to occur on the second ballot (bringing the Keystone State's heavy vote to the Illinois candidate, thereby insuring his nomination), was the logical concomitant of the New England proposals. One the eve of the convention, Governor John A. Andrew of Massachusetts ascertained Seward's weakness in four doubtful states, one of which was Pennsylvania. Through committees and sub-committees Andrew worked for a concentration upon the candidate shown to be the strongest, which proved to be Lincoln. Samuel A. Purviance, one of Cameron's most trusted lieutenants, was one of three committee members from his delegation who promised in David Wilmot's room at 11:00 P.M. Thursday night to assist in swinging the Pennsylvanians to Lincoln after complimentary votes for Cameron and Justice John McLean.[36]

Concurrently with the parley in Wilmot's rooms, a weary Pennsylvania delegation was listening to the earnest pleadings of Russell Errett, David Mumma, and Henry D. Moore, praying its members to "stick" to Cameron and not go over to Lincoln on the morrow.[37] Midnight wit-

[36] Thomas A. Dudley, "Inside Facts of Lincoln's Nomination," *Century Magazine*, XL (XVIII, New Series, July, 1890), 477-78; Going, *David Wilmot*, 540; M. B. Lowry to Cameron, May 24, 1860, Cameron MSS, DCC.

[37] Errett to Cameron, May 29, 1860; Cameron MSS, LC; Moore to Cameron, May 20, 1860; Cameron MSS, DCC. Ida Tarbell in her *Lincoln*, I, 350, erroneously reported the Pennsylvania delegation in caucus all night.

nessed outright confusion in the Cameron camp and its right hand hardly knew what its left was doing, but this much was fairly certain; whether Cameron did or did not command a united vote on the first ballot, approximately half of the delegation's vote would go for Lincoln on the second ballot if the moment appeared propitious, and then Cameron's weakness in his own state would stand revealed.

The Cameron managers had to decide quickly whether their faction would turn to Seward, whom their leader preferred because of his pronounced tariff views, or to join the Curtin faction. The offer of the Lincoln managers, David Davis and Leonard Swett, later that same night offered a profitable face-saving escape from their dilemma. In writing of this incident "in the small hours of Friday morning" Swett noted that "our arguments prevailed and the Cameron men agreed to come to us on the second ballot. They did so right nobly and gave us forty-eight votes." [38] On the morrow Andrew Reeder withdrew Cameron's name before the results of the second ballot could be announced. Pennsylvania, whose voice came close to being lost because of her dilatory action, registered the vote which is credited with starting the stampede to Lincoln on the third ballot.[39]

Cameron's managers at Chicago understood that their man was assured of a place in Lincoln's cabinet—this idea was no invention of the much maligned A. K. McClure. Joseph Casey, after failing to extract a direct pledge from the managers of Lincoln, Leonard Swett and David

[38] Leonard Swett to the editor of the Chicago *Tribune*, July 13, 1880.

[39] For official proceedings see *Proceedings of the First Three Republican Conventions of 1856, 1860, 1864* (Minneapolis, n.d.).

Davis, received a promise of a place for "Pennsylvania." To argue that the post was promised not to Cameron, but some mythical politicial unknown yet to be conjured up is but to split straws. The pledge was made to two Cameron men, the Curtin faction not being represented. Only a Cameron man could get it (a fact Lincoln himself later admitted) and that man could be only Cameron. The later contention of the Honorable David Davis that he did not consider Lincoln bound by any pledge is very understandable—Lincoln had given instructions not to bind him.[40]

Judge Samuel Purviance, one of Cameron's managers, gave his chief the following report:

You could have been nominated for Vice-President but it would have cost you a fight & exposed you to the suspicion of having bargained for it with Mr. Lincoln's friends. They were prepared unanimously to present you whilit [sic] we didnt doubt our ability to carry you on a fight We thought it would only weaken you & therefore I [s]aid we would only advise you to take it upon a unanimous offering being made which New York would not allow. You were pretty generally designated for Secretary of the Treasury & it seemed to be conceded you could claim & Receive what you might desire. At your standpoint you cannot Realize the proud position assigned Penna & the Credit which was given to your friends for skillful management. . . .

Keep Cool & Shew [sic] no feeling & this Result will turn decidedly to your great advantage.[41]

Joseph Casey was one of the two Cameron men participating in the confidential talks with Swett and Davis. Part of his report read:

[40] Willard L. King, *Lincoln's Manager: David Davis* (Cambridge, 1960), 140-41. King considers the pledge true only in a "qualified sense."

[41] Purviance to Cameron, May 23, 1860, Cameron MSS, DCC.

We were all satisfied Mr S[eward] could not carry the State.
. . . It [the switch to Lincoln] was only done after everything
was arranged carefully & unconditionally in reference to
Yourself—to our satisfaction—and we *drove* the Anti-Cameron
men from this State into it—

Mr. Lincoln's Confidential friend Hon Leonard Sweat [*sic*],
will be here [Harrisburg] in a couple of weeks & will bring
with him assurance from Mr. Lincoln himself to you — &
— c —.[42]

Joseph Casey and Samuel Purviance would not have
dared to give a distorted report to Simon Cameron because J. Donald Cameron would have known it; in fact
Casey was surprised when he learned Cameron had not
already received J. Donald's report.

Few impartial observers at the convention believed
that Cameron stood any chance of winning the nomination but Cameron immediately contended that his delegation's lack of unity had cost him the prize and Russell
Errett, Joseph Casey, and M. B. Lowry agreed. Many
of Cameron's friends considered it fashionable to heap
the blame on Andrew G. Curtin but Morrow B. Lowry,
who in later years liked to think that he was one of the
principal connecting links in the "bargain" said not.
William B. Mann of Philadelphia and a few "radical"
delegates from Allegheny County were actually the chief
culprits. Mann had spread the word among the delegates
that he had enough on Cameron to send him to the
penitentiary.[43]

Cameron's first public appearance after Lincoln's nomination took place at the mammoth rally of the People's
Party held in Harrisburg, May 21, for the purpose of

[42] Joseph Casey to Cameron, May 24, 1860, *ibid.*
[43] Errett to Cameron, May 29, 1860; Lowry to Cameron, May
24, 1860, *ibid.*

"ratifying" the Chicago nominations and plank, where he combined the duties of chairman and main speaker. Cameron's good friend, George Bergner of the new Harrisburg *Pennsylvania Daily Telegraph,* used the occasion to magnify the importance of his patron. Cameron, in the guise of an apologist for the failure of Seward's candidacy, was seeking to pour oil on the troubled water created by the rumor of his reputed sell-out of the New Yorker at Chicago. Quickly he passed to wholehearted endorsement of Lincoln and Hamlin. There was little in the party's plank to arouse the enthusiasm of an ardent protectionist, although the Pennsylvania delegation at Chicago had pretended to believe so. Throughout his long harangue, the chairman had conveniently forgotten to mention the importance of electing the party's gubernatorial candidate, Andrew G. Curtin.[44]

To register a complete victory in 1860, the Peoples' Party of Pennsylvania would be required to win Presidential, Congressional, gubernatorial, and legislative elections. Two Democratic candidates, both claiming to represent the true party, opposed Lincoln. The followers of Stephen A. Douglas were often styled Northern Democrats while the adherents of John C. Breckenridge were generally called Southern Democrats. John Bell, the candidate of a new party, the Union Constitutional, had considerable strength in the Philadelphia area. Victory in Congressional elections would be needed to insure support for their President and likewise a victory in legislative elections would give backing to their new governor's program. Control of the new legislature would also allow the Peoples' Party to elect a new United States Senator

[44] Harrisburg *Telegraph,* May 21, 1861.

to replace the outgoing Democratic William Bigler and if
Simon Cameron should enter the cabinet another man
would be needed to complete his unexpired two years.

Because of the split in the Democratic ranks, the task
of carrying Lincoln was easier. On the other hand, the
state's early October elections were nationally regarded
as a political barometer of the forthcoming national returns in November, and the Democracy of Pennsylvania
was solidly united behind their gubernatorial candidate,
Henry D. Foster. This outlook made it imperative that
Curtin be elected in order to pave the way for Lincoln.

The campaign of 1860 had not yet gotten underway
before the antipathy between the Cameron and Curtin
men manifested itself. A. K. McClure, Chairman of his
party's state central committee, realizing that a majority
of the committee was hostile to him or pro-Cameron,
wrote some very conciliatory letters to Cameron accepting
his request that "protection must be the battle cry of the
campaign," and extending an invitation to attend a committee meeting at Cresson on July 10. Cameron in reply
complained bitterly of the injustice done him by Henry
C. Carey and William B. Mann (whom he had successfully excluded from the committee), and reported his inability to attend the Cresson meeting.[45]

In the meantime, Cameron's lieutenants worked on a
plan to unhorse McClure from his direct supervision of
the campaign by creating an executive committee empowered to act in that capacity. Russell Errett's report
emphasized that neither Lincoln nor Curtin could carry
the state if McClure remained in office, suggested his re-

[45] McClure to Cameron, June 6, July 2, 1860, Cameron MSS,
LC.

moval, and called for a strategy meeting on July 4. But
McClure, who knew what was coming, outgeneraled his
opponents and made them the laughing stock of the political season. At Cresson the sober Curtin men attended a
fifteen-minute morning session of the committee following an all night drinking orgy which most of the Cameronians failed to shake off, quickly accepted the proposed
resolutions and campaign plans, and adjourned to meet
only on call of the chairman. Truly, as J. K. Moorhead reported, it must have been a "hard party," the results of
which only aroused the Cameronians to greater efforts to
destroy the arrogant McClure.[46]

A meeting on July 26 between Cameron and Curtin,
which had been requested by the latter, had the effect
of intensifying the struggle between the two factions.
Curtin's attitude at the parley, according to Cameron's
notation, spurred the efforts of J. P. Sanderson in organizing a new state committee avowedly for the purpose of
furnishing supplementary financial aid in the campaign
but actually with the goal of preventing McClure from
securing badly needed funds. Russell Errett strengthened
Sanderson's move by writing to Lincoln forces that Mc-
Clure, in a previous political campaign, had kept for
himself most of $10,000 collected.[47]

Immediately McClure objected strongly to the usurping
of his prerogatives, regarded the creation of a new committee "as a personal reflection upon himself," reminded
Cameron of the latter's blessing when he accepted the

[46] Errett to Cameron, June 23, 1860, *ibid*. McClure related this
coup with evident glee in his *Notes*, I, 409-10. Moorhead to
Cameron, July 14, 1860, Cameron MSS, DCC.

[47] Curtin to Cameron, July 22, 1860 with Cameron's "notation,"
Cameron MSS, LC; King, *Lincoln's Manager*, 152.

chairmanship and hinted strongly that he would take
the matter to the Republican National Committee.
Cameron's reply well reveals the political sagacity of
Pennsylvania's leading politico. He had only been mis-
represented as usual, protested Cameron. Actually, he
had joined a "Republican Club" only on condition that
it not interfere with McClure's committee; but was the
rumor true that McClure's committee no longer existed? [48]

Lincoln was well aware of the struggle between the
factions and its accompanying dangers. Although the
affair appeared publicly in the press, William D. Kelley,
John Pomeroy, and Leonard Swett, who did not approve
of Cameron's "attitude," furnished Lincoln information on
the subject. Lincoln sent David Davis into Pennsylvania
to do some private investigating, secretly issued a warning to McClure, labelled the rift "local troubles," and expressed determination not to "expouse their quarrels on
either side." The Illinois Railsplitter, sagely preferring
votes to the reward usually accorded umpires, continued
to do business with both McClure's and Cameron's Auxili-
ary Committee.[49]

Davis' report to Lincoln of his visit to Cameron might
well, in view of past convention commitments, be indicative of the Judge's earnest desire to "soften up" Lincoln
on the subject of Cameron's questionable character. Davis
found Cameron possessed of a genial, pleasant, kind
personality. Many prejudices which the visitor had

[48] McClure to Cameron, July 31, 1860, "copy"; Cameron to
McClure, August 1, 1860, Cameron MSS, LC; Pomeroy to Lincoln,
August 27, 1860, Lincoln to Pomeroy, August 31, 1860, Lincoln
MSS.
[49] Davis to Lincoln, Aug. 5, 1860, Weed to Lincoln, Aug. 13,
1860, ibid.

formerly entertained were now removed. Cameron, on his part, acknowledged the pleasantries of the visit to Thurlow Weed and promised an industrious campaign.[50]

Because Cameron's oratorical talents were not of the best, he usually acted at political rallies in the capacity of chairman, but occasionally he delivered major addresses. His Erie talk on September 12, when he appeared with Andrew Reeder, Cassius M. Clay, and A. G. Curtin, received the most notice from the press. An over-imaginative reporter set the participants in the colorful Wide-Awake torch light parade at 3,500 and the audience at 25,000. In his speech Cameron scored Buchanan for his "slavish subservience to the supposed interests of a section," the South, called the apparent quarrel between Breckinridge, Bell, and Douglas, only a "sham" to "insure continuance in power." The puerile efforts of Cameron during the campaign led his critics to accuse him of political treason. One accuser wrote after the October elections: "His object is believed to have been to defeat Curtin by a small majority and to get Lincoln elected by a small majority" in order to maintain the balance of power in his state.[51]

Cameron was slow in reporting the progress of the campaign to Lincoln. In early June the Republican Presidential candidate could not remember having received any news from him.[52] Two months later Cameron apologized for not writing sooner, explained that he had been making a survey of the state, and could now predict

[50] King, *Lincoln's Manager*, 153.

[51] Joseph J. Lewis to Jesse W. Fell, October 21, 1860, Richardson ed., *Abraham Lincoln's Autobiography* (Boston, 1947), Appendix, 44.

[52] Lincoln to Lyman Trumbull, June 5, 1860, Basler, ed., *Works*, IV, 71.

Lincoln's coming victory in the state "beyond a shadow of a doubt." Curtin would also be elected but by a reduced majority, estimated between 15 and 20 thousand votes. The politico was finding, contrary to McClure's observations, no difficulty in raising sufficient funds for his state's campaign and had a surplus to send elsewhere. Cameron, divining Lincoln's pressing need for funds (the railsplitter was overdrawn at his bank), suggested a private loan, "cheerfully" provided, of a few thousand dollars.[53]

Results of the October and November elections brought to fruition the greatest expectations of the Peoples' Party. The day following the October elections Cameron telegraphed to his chieftain: "Pennsylvania comes greeting with 25,000 for Curtin." And the telegram in early November read: "Penna. seventy thousand for you. New York safe. Glory enough."[54] Official results showed Cameron had underestimated Curtin's figure by 7,000 and overstepped Lincoln's by 10,000 votes. In addition to many Congressional victories the party would possess overwhelming control of the next General Assembly and undoubtedly would send the next United States Senator to Washington.

The election of Lincoln to the Presidency moved South Carolina to take the initiative in leading a secession of Southern state from the Union. The gravity of the sectional crisis had already been recognized in the Congress

[53] Cameron to Lincoln, Aug. 1, 29, Sept. 21, Lincoln MSS; Cameron to Davis, Sept. 7, 1860, quoted in King, *Lincoln's Manager*, 155-56.

[54] Cameron to Lincoln, Oct. 10, Nov. 6, 1860, Lincoln MSS. For a full account of the 1860 campaign in Pennsylvania see Erwin S. Bradley, *The Triumph of Militant Republicanism* (Philadelphia, 1964), 77-96.

where the Kentucky sage, Senator John Crittenden, was proposing a compromise based upon restoration of the old Missouri Compromise line. Much time was consumed in debating counter proposals or amendments to Crittenden's proposals.

For a short period of time Simon Cameron stood out in sharp relief, much in contrast to his Republican colleagues, in expressing a conciliatory attitude toward the South. Certainly he did not condone the secessionist movement, but he believed Crittenden's solution would furnish a satisfactory basis for a peaceful settlement. However, he would have liked to see the thirty-six-thirty line restored but not extended into the territories.

In middle January, 1861, largely through the efforts of Senator William Bigler of Pennsylvania, the Senate decided to act on Crittenden's bill. But the day's labor ended on a vote to substitute the provisions found in the Constitution of the United States. Along with his Republican colleagues, Cameron voted for the substitution, which passed by a very narrow margin, and then surprisingly two days later he succeeded in having a motion passed which had the effect of restoring Crittenden's proposals to the calendar.[55]

The support accorded Senator Bigler by Cameron on January 21, creating a misunderstanding among his friends and foes, was actually provoked by the fact that only a dozen Senators had presented themselves to listen to Bigler, a representative of his own beloved and powerful state, Pennsylvania. His agreement with Bigler, he explained later, was in line with his colleague's spirit of conciliation and patriotic efforts to maintain peace. All

[55] John W. Burgess, *Civil War and the Constitution* (New York, 1901), 110-12.

reasonable concessions must be granted in order to serve the Union. He was glad Pennsylvania had not offended.[56]

All through the secession controversy Cameron had been receiving a steady stream of letters and their tempo increased when he publicly announced his desire for conciliation. His most valuable Western supporter, Russell Errett of the Pittsburgh *Gazette*, expressed much alarm over his chieftain's stand and warned him that the public mind of Western Pennsylvania was "inflamed against compromise." On the other hand, the many letters found in the Cameron manuscripts indicate Cameron, with the aid of his numerous lieutenants, had conducted a private poll throughout the Commonwealth, the results of which indicated most of the people desired conciliation. However, Cameron soon gravitated to the Republican Party "line" and when at last, on the eve of Lincoln's inauguration, a decisive vote on Crittenden's proposals was finally recorded, not a Republican voted for it.

In January, 1861, the victorious Peoples' Party expected to elect a junior colleague to serve with Simon Cameron. David Wilmot, it was believed by many party members, had easily earned the right to represent his party in the State. But there were many other aspirants for the prize, including Curtin's recent manager, A. K. McClure, who, upon receiving no encouragement from his chieftain and finding himself unable to make any bargain with Cameron, ostensibly dropped from the race but still kept himself alerted for promising deals.[57] Contrary to McClure's account in his *Notes*, Curtin very ardently backed

[56] *Cong. Globe*, 36 Cong., 2 Sess., 494-96; Harrisburg *Telegraph*, Feb. 7, 1861.

[57] Cameron to B. Rush Petriken, "copy" Dec. 11, 1860, Cameron MSS, LC.

Wilmot for the nomination, and advised his coterie that if they failed to elect him they would "all regret it when too late." [58]

The story of Simon Cameron's success in determining his next colleague in the United States Senate in 1861, while at the same time assuming the role of a disinterested spectator, is one of the most interesting of his career. It is true, as McClure related, that Cameron at first had no particular man in mind, but he was determined that it must be one whom he felt certain of being able to control and who was willing to allow all Senatorial patronage to be dispensed through other hands. In the course of his quest for the ideal puppet, one of Cameron's liaison men, B. Rush Petriken, presented Wilmot with his employer's terms. Wilmot expressed his willingness to support Cameron for the Treasury post, to "urge *no man*" for a benefice who was obnoxious to Cameron but he could "not go as far" as Cameron desired. Although no bargain was made—in fact Cameron regretted he had approached Wilmot—the Free Soiler, because of a prior "full understanding," confidently expected Cameron's support up to the hour of the caucus. [59]

The man whom Cameron decided to back was Edgar Cowan, recognized leader of the Westmoreland County bar. Cowan, a former Whig of very imposing appearance, had stumped effectively for the Peoples' Party in 1860 in those areas considered most radical. When Cowan approached the Curtin faction for support he received the cold shoulder, although McClure considered

[58] *Notes*, I, 443; Curtin to Eli Slifer, Dec. 31, 1860, Slifer-Dill MSS, DCL.

[59] Petriken to Cameron, Dec. 10, 1860; Cameron to Petriken, Dec. 11, 1860, Cameron MSS, LC; Wilmot to Cameron, Jan. 5, 1861, Cameron MSS, DCC.

him the most eligible of all the candidates [60]—except himself. Former Senator James Cooper preferred Cowan and the powerful John Covode would accept him in order to edge out J. K. Moorhead.

Cowan soon "struck pay dirt" when he contacted J. P. Sanderson, who quickly decided that the westerner was the answer to Cameron's prayer. Sanderson converted Cameron to his views, arranged for Cowan to meet many leaders of the party, whom Covode noticed were mainly Cameron men, and paved the way for a secret meeting at Cameron's residence before December 15, where apparently an agreement was reached.[61]

Cameron's public announcement of his neutrality only two days before the party caucus on January 7, 1861, caused his trusted lieutenants much concern. Although J. P. Sanderson and Andrew Reeder worked indefatigably to line up sufficient voters for Cowan, a small group of Cameron men stood by like lost sheep waiting for their master's voice. Reeder had seen little chance of effecting Cowan's nomination without the aid of a direct command from Cameron. A select group of Cameron men were called for a "conference" at the Cameron residence just before caucus time and at its end the eager newspaper men were encouraged to believe that Wilmot "was in." [62]

The result of the caucus vote, 58 to 38, gave the Peoples' nomination easily to Cowan and insured his election over Henry D. Foster, the Democratic nominee.

[60] McClure to Thaddeus Stevens, Nov. 7, 1861, McPherson MSS, LC.

[61] Sanderson to Cameron, Nov. 15, 1860, Cameron MSS, DCC; Cowan to Covode, Dec. 7, 1860, Covode MSS, LC; Cowan to Cameron, Dec. 15, 1860, Cameron MSS, LC.

[62] Reeder to Cameron, Jan. 2, 1861, *ibid.*; Philadelphia *Public Ledger*, Jan. 8, 1861.

By a curious trick of fate, Cameron's subterfuge probably worked more to his advantage then he had anticipated. A small Cameron coterie still believed that covertly their leader desired Wilmot elected and voted for him, while a few McClure men ignored Curtin's plea and voted for Cowan. To the badly duped Wilmot it may have looked as if McClure's "treachery" rather than Cameron's "neutrality" had effected his defeat.[63]

Wilmot's leading biographer introduced an interesting deduction which to him was "obvious." He believed that Cameron, shocked by the humiliating news which he had just received (probably January 7) from Lincoln recalling his proffer of a cabinet post, had led him to strike immediately at Wilmot whom he believed had aided in bringing about Lincoln's action.[64] But the correspondence in the Cameron manuscripts do not bear out this deduction. Cameron had made up his mind to support Cowan prior to December 15. Apparently, Lincoln sent a telegram on January 3 preparing Cameron for the shock.

Immediately following Cowan's election, Sanderson had a two-hour conference with the new tool for purposes of instruction. "He is highly pleased with your behavior," reported Sanderson to Cameron, "and will cordially and fully cooperate with you." Under Sanderson's direction Cowan would write to Lincoln stressing Cameron's fitness for the office of Secretary of the Treasury and, if the need should arise, would see Lincoln personally. "You have a man in the Senate," concluded Sanderson, "who will be right and is anxious to work with you." [65]

[63] Petriken to Cameron, Jan. 11, 1861; Cameron MSS, LC.

[64] Going, *David Wilmot*, 552.

[65] Sanderson to Cameron, Jan. 8, 1861, Cameron MSS, LC. Evidently Cameron had not informed Sanderson of Lincoln's recall of his cabinet offer.

During the period of the campaign of 1860 little correspondence had passed between Lincoln and Cameron. In late May the Republican standard-bearer had remembered to send special respects to the Pennsylvanian and before the summer had ended Cameron condescended to congratulate the victor and became particularly interested in certain aspects of Lincoln's Whiggish past in hope of gleaning scraps of protectionism to bolster Old Abe in the leading pro-tariff state.[66]

Possibly a portion of Cameron's stimulus for more active participation in the campaign had stemmed from renewed interest in the Chicago agreement. About August 20, David Davis, Leonard Swett, Thurlow Weed, Cameron and some Rhode Island men rendezvoused at Saratoga. Some historians, by patching together scraps of evidence, believe that the powerful Seward-Weed faction agreed to push Cameron for the Treasury post with the idea of checkmating the cabinet aspiration of Salmon P. Chase of Ohio.[67] Cameron's alleged treachery to Seward at Chicago was easily explained by the bitter opposition of Curtin to Seward's candidacy. Thus the Seward faction could secure double satisfaction through placement of Curtin's most powerful enemy into the Presidential family.[68]

The concerted drive of the Cameron faction to place

[66] Basler, *Works*, IV, 91-92; Cameron to Lincoln, Aug. 1, 1860, Cameron MSS, LC.

[67] H. J. Carman and R. H. Luthin, *Lincoln and the Patronage* (New York, 1943), 21-22; Harry E. Pratt, "Simon Cameron's Fight for a Place in Lincoln's Cabinet," Abraham Lincoln Association *Bulletin*, No. 49 (1937), 3-11.

[68] Note, however, Weed's alleged lukewarm endorsement (the account of which was written many years later) of Cameron when questioned by Lincoln. He though Cameron should not be given the Treasury post. *Memoir*, 293.

their man in Lincoln's cabinet began during the latter
half of November. A week before Lincoln's election, Davis
questioned Cameron's leading confidant in Chicago, Dr.
Charles Leib, concerning his leader's willingness to accept
a cabinet post. Leib in turn requested Cameron to send
J. P. Sanderson and Joseph Casey to Chicago soon after
election.[69] Casey was a state supreme court reporter who
had received his legal training in the office of Charles B.
Penrose, the political go-between largely responsible for
Cameron's Senatorial victory over Forney in 1857.

In a week's time the deluge of letters in Cameron's
support reached such proportions that Lincoln related
to his future Vice-President: ". . . also find letters here
from very strong and unexpected quarters in Pennsylvania, urging appointment of General Cameron to a place
in the cabinet." [70] Testimonials included the well known
names of Andrew Reeder, Russell Errett, Isaac Hazlehurst, J. K. Moorhead, J. P. Sanderson, and James Pollock.
The "unexpected quarters" likely pointed to former
governor Pollock, a close friend of Curtin, and John W.
Forney, who had lately completed his masquerade of a
Douglas Democratic editor in order to sabotage the Little
Giant's Presidential aspirations. Forney was pleased—
surely with tongue in cheek—to pay tribute to Cameron's
"integrity, sincerity and ability." Naturally, Lincoln could
hardly be expected to recognize one of the periodic
Forney-Cameron rapproachments. Sanderson added the
names of David Wilmot and Thaddeus Stevens. Then
followed letters from Henry D. Moore and W. B. Thomas,
prominent Philadelphians.[71] Unquestionably the list was

[69] Leib to Cameron, Nov. 4, 1860, Cameron MSS, DCC. King,
Lincoln's Manager, page 163, fails to note that the "rush" of Casey
and Sanderson to Chicago was brought about by Davis himself.
[70] Lincoln to Hamlin, Nov. 27, 1860, Basler, *Works*, IV, 145.
[71] Letters cited, dated Nov. 21-27, in Lincoln MSS.

impressive but also without exception the group was strongly "Cameronized" by visions of morsels to be offered via the public trough.

Joseph Casey, on the basis of his recent visit to Lincoln, realized that the Presidential candidate had not been informed of the Chicago bargain. Casey, a party to the affair, wrote Leonard Swett concerning the urgency to fulfill the "understanding" exchanged the night before Lincoln's nomination and Swett, probably realizing that the information could no longer be withheld, passed the letter on to Lincoln.[72] Swett advised Lincoln what the President-Elect already knew—he was not bound by any pledges made by himself or Davis.

If, as assumed, Cameron greatly desired a cabinet post, his reactions to such suggestions could be described only as coy. Several times his devoted followers learned of his desire to remain in the Senate where he could best serve his state. Even after Andrew Reeder reported Lincoln's desire to see him, Cameron would not go to Springfield except on direct invitation.[73] It was incomprehensible to to him, who was always the lord with suppliants eagerly grasping for the crumbs from his table, to picture himself a solicitor at the feet of the mighty Lincoln whom, secretly, it was believed, he held very much in contempt.

But the expected visitation was not long delayed. Ten days after Reeder's report, Leonard Swett at Lincoln's request paid a visit to Cameron's lovely estate, Lochiel, enjoyed his host's rare wines and liquors, extended on

[72] Casey to Swett, Nov. 27, 1860, Swett to Lincoln, Nov. 30, 1860, Lincoln MSS.
[73] Reeder to Lincoln, Dec. 12, 18, 1860; *ibid.* In October his enemies believed Cameron was working hard to enter the cabinet. See Joseph L. Lewis to Jesse Fell, Nobert D. Richardson, ed., *Abraham Lincoln's Autobiography*, Appendix, 42-43.

Lincoln's behalf an invitation to visit Springfield as soon as convenient, and wrote Cameron a letter of introduction.[74] In the meantime Lincoln received additional arguments and learned of powerful new forces supporting Cameron's candidacy. According to Joseph Medill, the entire Pennsylvania delegation in Washington had joined in claiming a place in the cabinet. That Lincoln considered Pennsylvania's support imperative to the coming success of his administration was commonly known. On December 24, Lincoln visited with a strong Cameron man, Senator Edward D. Baker, who exerted a strong influence over his old Springfield friend. After Christmas, Cameron, in company with J. P. Sanderson, left for Springfield.

Lincoln's last two days of the year 1860 were occupied largely with the question of Cameron's cabinet candidacy. On Sunday, December 30, from his hotel suite in Springfield, Cameron dispatched a brief message to Lincoln naming Swett's notes as his reason for coming, and that same afternoon paid his respects to the President-Elect. At night Lincoln reciprocated with a call on Cameron at his hotel. Edward Bates, another cabinet prospect, paid a surprise visit to the suite and the group engaged in a "conversation" of two hours duration. Apparently the entire time was consumed in pleasantries, no mention being made of the cabinet. Cameron, certainly no stranger to the game of social repartee, may have impressed his visitor quite favorably.[75]

To assist him in arriving at a decision, Lincoln had

[74] Account of G. G. Fogg to Wells, December 3, 1865, Welles, *Diary*, II, 390. Swett to Cameron, Dec. 26-28, 1860; Cameron to Lincoln, Dec. 30, 1860; Jan. 11, 1862, Cameron MSS, LC.

[75] New York *Herald*, Jan. 7, 1861; Cameron to Lincoln, Dec. 30, 1860; Lincoln MSS, Bates, *Diary*, 171. Fogg's account of Lincoln's "surprise" is in error. See Welles, *Diary*, II, 390.

prepared two memorandums listing names and arguments pro and con. Approximately sixty persons almost all from Pennsylvania had signified their approval of Cameron. Seven had seen service in Congress, a dozen were delegates to the Chicago Party convention, and a sprinkling were journalists of repute. Former Governor James Pollock, David Wilmot, A. H. Reeder, Isaac Hazlehurst, William B. Thomas, J. W. Killinger, J. K. Moorhead, and J. S. Haldeman were among the most prominent names. At first sight the list of petitioners resembled an expression of public opinion, but with few exceptions these supporters were either well known henchmen or were seekers of high office via the Cameronian portal.

The memorandum against Cameron resurrected the Winnebago claims scandal, charged bribing or its attempt in the Democratic State Convention of 1849 and during the Senatorial election of 1857. Two bitter enemies of Cameron, J. M. Bomberger and W. B. Mann, were, respectively, the chief witnesses and the holders of damaging evidence. At this date Lincoln had received few letters of testimonials against Cameron's fitness because the opposition was not organized, few took his candidacy seriously, and a lesser number believed that Lincoln would not actually offer him a post.

Lincoln's communication of December 31, 1860, delivered to Cameron in Springfield before his departure, must have greatly inflated the recipient's ego. Lincoln wrote that at the promised time and with Cameron's permission he would nominate him for either Secretary of the Treasury or of War.[76] Instead of discreetly maintaining public silence over his good fortune, Cameron ex-

[76] Basler, *Works*, IV, 165-67.

hibited Lincoln's tender wherever he went not unlike an exuberant school boy.[77]

Immediately press announcement of Lincoln's proffer together with the loud and boastful rejoicing emanating from the Cameron coterie over their victory created a minor bombshell even in national political circles and led to the registering of a strong protest against consummation of the invitation. True, leadership of the movement appeared to be assumed by A. K. McClure, one of Cameron's inveterate enemies, but a good proportion of the protests came from civic-minded public leaders interested in bringing good government to the incoming administration.

Only three days after making his commitment, Lincoln changed his mind regarding Cameron's fitness. During the interlude he interviewed Alexander K. McClure, who reputedly was acquainted with the complete history of Cameron's villainy, and Salmon P. Chase, a prospect for the Treasury post who opposed the Weed-Seward combine. Although he did not present documentary evidence, McClure emphasized Cameron's moral unfitness for high office. He argued that the appointment would be a "misfortune" to the state's party and Lincoln, and pointed out that the seemingly wide public support given Cameron consisted only of his own followers. Unquestionably, some type of evidence against Cameron was collected, because Charles Ogden of Philadelphia telegraphed McClure upon his arrival in Springfield asking whether he should bring the "documents." Both Curtin and his new Secretary of the Commonwealth, Eli Slifer, affirmed McClure, were

[77] Lincoln to Cameron, Dec. 31, 1860, *ibid.*, Philadelphia *Press*, Jan. 5, 1861; E. B. Washburne to Lincoln, Jan. 10, 1861, Lincoln MSS.

content to see no cabinet appointment go to Pennsylvania rather than accept Cameron.[78]

On January 3, 1861, Lincoln dispatched the following brusque note to Cameron:

Since seeing you things have developed which make it impossible for me to take you into the cabinet. You will say this comes of an interview with McClure; and this is partly, but not wholly true. The more potent matter is wholly outside of Pennsylvania; and yet I am not at liberty to specify it. Enough that it appears to me to be sufficient. And now I suggest that you write me declining the appointment, in which case I do not object to its being known that it was tendered you. Better do this at once, before things so change, that you can not honorably decline, and I be compelled to openly recall the tender. No person living knows or has an intimation that I write this letter. Your truly

A. Lincoln

PS. Telegraph, me instantly, on receipt of this, saying "All right"

A. L.[79]

Only a week later, McClure wrote Thaddeus Stevens that "pressure" had compelled Lincoln to reconsider.[80]

The "more potent matter" according to Lincoln lay "wholly outside" Pennsylvania. A complete list of these objectors is a matter of conjecture but to Hannibal Hamlin's way of thinking Cameron "would not do"; Lyman Trumbull found Lincoln's "truest friends" in the Senate opposed to Cameron; and James H. Van Alen recognized the candidate as "Corruption Cameron." Very likely Horace Greeley, S. C. Fessenden, George Julian, Francis P. Blair, and the two influential Illinois factional leaders,

[78] McClure to Lincoln, Jan. 3, 1861; Ogden to McClure, Jan. 2, 1861, Lincoln MSS; McClure, *Lincoln and Men of War Times*, 140.

[79] Basler, *Works*, IV, 169-70.

[80] McClure to Stevens, Jan. 10 [1861], McPherson, MSS, LC.

Gustave Koerner and Norman K. Judd, likewise registered strong dissent to Lincoln.[81]

Some of the strongest letters against Cameron's appointment arrived in Springfield after Lincoln changed his mind. A "certain class of jobbers and speculators," advised J. R. Doolittle, should be barred from the Treasury; Cameron's name, W. C. Bryant had discovered, suggested to every honest Republican in New York "no other than disgusting associations"; and according to Henry C. Carey, the best citizens regarded Cameron as the "very incarnation of corruption." His appointment would herald a descent of "all the vultures of the Union" upon the Treasury.[82]

Succeeding events brought only distressing dilemmas to both Cameron and Lincoln. A. K. McClure, who expressed his willingness to retire if only he could get some credit for overthrowing the "arch-scoundrel" of the state, had publicly announced in Pittsburgh on January 4 that Lincoln "positively had decided" on no cabinet appointment for Cameron.[83] On the other hand, Cameron had asserted that Lincoln had positively promised him a post. To reveal Lincoln's withdrawal meant unbearable loss of face and as the situation then looked to the public, McClure had impeached Cameron's integrity. At this juncture Cameron instituted the policy which he con-

[81] Hamlin to Lincoln, Dec. 27, 1860; Trumbull to Lincoln, Dec. 31, 1860. Van Alen to Lincoln, Jan. 11, 1861, Lincoln MSS. The cry for a man of "Democratic" antecedents was a hangover from his feud with Polk.

[82] Carey to Lincoln, Jan. 7, 1861, "copy", Henry C. Cary Papers, HSP.

[83] McClure to Stevens, Jan. 10, [1861], McPherson MSS, LC; Philadelphia *Press*, Jan. 5, 1861.

sistently pursued the following tortuous months—public silence including the President-Elect.

Lincoln made the first move to cushion the blow Cameron had sustained. Having decided that Salmon P. Chase should have the Treasury post, he took steps to appease Cameron, whom he considered spokesman for the powerful protectionists of Pennsylvania and to persuade him if possible to remain in the Senate with the assurance of patronage for his followers. That Cameron would gladly settle for the War Department Lincoln fully understood, but he dreaded the "fierce opposition" that was bound to come.[84] Following a visit from J. P. Sanderson and Edgar Cowan, Cameron's newly acquired helpmeet, Lincoln wrote Cameron two letters on January 13, one of which he antedated January 3, asking for relief from great embarrassment springing from "an unexpected complication" by allowing him to recall the offer of a cabinet post. Lincoln had not changed his views regarding Cameron's ability or faithfulness. The other letter offered an apology for any offense (unintentional) suffered by the communication of January 3, requesting its return, and assured Cameron that no cabinet appointment should be made from his state without first taking into consideration his wishes.[85]

Then followed a period of wild rumors, denials, and uncertainty. The crestfallen candidate signified to at least three prominent men, Preston King, Leonard Swett, and Thaddeus Stevens, that he would not enter Lincoln's cabinet. Following his confidential declaration to Stevens that no earthly contingency would induce him to accept

[84] Lincoln to Trumbull, Jan. 7, 1861, Basler, *Works*, IV, 171.
[85] Lincoln to Cameron, Jan. 13, 1861, enclosure dated Jan. 3, 1861. Lincoln MSS.

a cabinet post, the Commoner, with Cameron's blessing, began to think of himself as a cabinet prospect. Cameron's final decision, as he saw it, probably rose from the boasting of the McClure-Curtin faction, the numerous letters received from his disappointed clientele, the necessity for maintaining his prestige at all costs, and finally the advice from "insiders," including David Davis, who advised him to hold on.[86]

The unanswered question of Cameron's entrance into the cabinet dragged into the second half of February. McClure, contrary to promises given Lincoln, declined to appear in the role of prosecutor in presenting Cameron's "alleged political and personal delinquencies," although Lincoln was expecting him to do so; consequently the allegations now seem to constitute only rumor. Following the visit of two of Cameron's supporters, Alexander Cummings and J. K. Moorhead, to Springfield on January 21, Lincoln invited him to come to Illinois if he wished. The President-Elect's address of January 24 to a Pennsylvania delegation gave him renewed hope. Lincoln felt a "disposition" and a "strong desire" to appoint him, but any cabinet member, like Caesar's wife, must be above suspicion.

With time running out it looked as if Pennsylvania might not find representation in the executive family. The Commonwealth's powerful business interests moved to heal the factional break in order to insure themselves a spokesman at the highest level. Andrew G. Curtin, the man who had vowed he would personally invervene if necessary in order to debar Cameron from the cabinet,

[86] Stevens to Washburne, Jan. 19, 1861, *ibid*; Elias Wampole to Cameron, Jan. 10, 1861, David Davis to Cameron, Feb. 8, 1861, Cameron MSS, LC.

capitulated under the urgings of James Milliken, the intermediary, who guaranteed the McClure-Curtin factions a
share of the patronage.[87]

The way was now open for a fresh reappraisal of
Cameron's claims to a cabinet post when Lincoln appeared
in Philadelphia en route to the capital. On February 22,
Simon Cameron received personal or proxy endorsements
from A. K. McClure, A. G. Curtin, Eli Slifer, Morton
McMichael, Henry C. Carey, and James Milliken,
speaking for the powerful coal and iron interests of Penn-
sylvania. Senators James Dixon, Edward D. Baker, and
Zachariah Chandler sent endorsements to the capital.
Capitulation of the anti-Cameron faction, believed the
New York Times, had removed the last barrier to
Cameron's entrance into the cabinet.[88] At Washington, on
February 28 and March 1, talks took place between
Lincoln and Cameron. Since S. P. Chase was definitely
slated for the Treasury, only the War Department was
available. According to the pro-Cameron sheet in Harrisburg, the *Telegraph*, Lincoln urged the War Department
upon him. Lincoln nominated Cameron for the post the
day following his inauguration.[89].

The view that a "bargain" determined Cameron's entrance into the cabinet is unacceptable, although the
strong influence of Leonard Swett and David Davis cannot be discounted. The logic of developments pointed to

[87] Basler, *Works*, IV, 179-80; A. K. McClure to Thaddeus
Stevens, Jan. 7, [1861]. Edward McPherson Papers, LC; Milliken
to Cameron, Feb. 18, 1861; Cameron MSS, LC; McClure, *Lincoln
and Men of War Times*, 143; Nicolay and Hay.

[88] Milliken to Cameron, Feb. 22, 1861; Purviance to Cameron,
Feb. 23, 1861, Cameron MSS, LC; Crippen, *Simon Cameron*,
241-42; Basler, *Works*, IV, 248.

[89] *Ibid.*, 242; Harrisburg *Telegraph*, March 2, 1861.

his appointment. Lincoln was morally bound to accept him if the opposition did not furnish proof of his unfitness. Lincoln was practically obsessed with the idea that success of his incoming administration was dependent upon representation of powerful Pennsylvania's interests in his cabinet. But if he rejected Cameron he could take no other. He asked: "Who is stronger or better than General Cameron?" [90] The trump card, it seemed, was possessed by Cameron; he would consent to no other Pennsylvania appointment except his own. The appointment, it should be remembered, was in line with the policy used by Lincoln in forming his cabinet—to recruit from regional leaders of the party.

[90] McCormack, ed., *Memoirs of Gustave Koerner*, II, 114; J. K. Moorhead to H. Lamon, April 29, 1871, Jeremiah Black Papers, LC; Weed, ed., *Autobiography of Thurlow Weed*, 608.

6
Secretary of War

THE RESOURCES OF THE OFFICE TO WHICH SIMON CAMERON succeeded had proved inadequate even for peacetime needs. The state of total unpreparedness for the exegencies of 1861 has unfairly been blamed upon the Buchanan Administration and more specifically upon the irresponsible Secretary John B. Floyd. But its roots were traceable to the foundations of our nation, resting upon a philosophy which taught that military preparedness was incompatible with freedom and the democratic way of life. A patriotic militia, it was urged, would overnight spring forth in overwhelming numbers to rescue its beloved republic from any danger. General Winfield Scott had urged increases in an armed force which he considered inadequate to cope even with the Indian problems, but his pleas fell upon the deaf ears of a complacent Congress. The strength of the regular army in 1860, including a considerable proportion of Southerners, numbered fewer than 17,000 men.

In 1860, the War Department, with its eight bureaus, was staffed with approximately 90 employees, using antiquated systems of bookkeeping and hostile to any

changes. Perhaps a third of its members could not be relied upon to uphold the North if war came. The bureaus
were officered by personnel whose service records dated
back forty years.[1] The short tenure of Joseph Holt, dating
from January 18, 1861, produced few changes. To expect
such an office to meet adequately, on a few days notice,
a national crisis on an unprecendented military scale
seems preposterous, but to an unthinking public, which
included many responsible leaders, a half century of national neglect offered no excuse for the sorry performance
which followed.

When the great civil strife began in 1861, Simon
Cameron, confronted with a Herculean task that no human
being could have accomplished properly, proved to be the
"weakest cog in the federal machine."[2] Certainly,
judged by his past accomplishments, a better than
mediocre performance could have been expected. Possessed of keen business acumen, energy, affability, and
a good measure of common sense, Cameron had demonstrated his ability to meet successfully new situations, to
amass a fortune in a highly competitive medium, and to
handle large groups of men. But his organizational procedures of the world of business and politics were not
applicable to the direction of a chaotic War Office, mushrooming with maddening rapidity—and it was in organization that his greatest weakness lay.

Following Lincoln's call for troops, Cameron's performance was that of a nervous, confused, embarrassed executive who had completely lost control of the situation.
Frequently dispensing with the services of a clerk, he de-

---

[1] A. Howard Meneely, *The War Department,* 1861 108.
[2] Fred A. Shannon *Organization of the Union Army* 1861-1865
(2 vols., Cleveland, 1928), I, 26.

pended upon the petitioner for a proper explanation of the proposed transaction, and apparently kept the records in his head or pockets.[3] Hordes of office seekers, local political hacks, potential contractors, "go-betweens," and impatient pompous men of the government beseiged him day and night, accusing the Secretary of devoting too much time to other less important affairs. With the coming of Thomas A. Scott, the genius of the Pennsylvania Railroad, into the War Office, efficiency greatly improved but Scott could never overcome the contempt which West Point bureau-heads held for civilian management.[4]

Cameron, realizing his many shortcomings, sought guidance from his old friend, Secretary Seward, who apparently intended to dominate the cabinet anyway. The proud Cameron could accept advice but not domination. This fact Seward soon discovered when he presented a solution of the Pensacola problem to General Scott. Cameron "flew into a passion at once and said . . . 'I supposed you do! You are always meddling with that which don't concern you.' " According to Secretary Caleb B. Smith, Lincoln enjoyed immensely the spectacle of seeing Seward cowed by Cameron. Secretary Gideon Welles also recorded Cameron's anger at Seward's attempts to run his department.[5] Cameron soon found Secretary Chase's discreet omission of condescending methods of assistance much more to his taste and by the end of

[3] Albert G. Riddle, *Recollections of War Times* (New York 1895), 180; Frederick W. Seward, *Reminiscences of A War Time Statesman and Diplomat, 1830-1915* (New York, 1916), 163.

[4] L[ucius] E. Chittenden, *Recollections of President Lincoln and His Administration* (New York, 1891), 169-70. Scott did not receive his commission as Assistant Secretary of War until Congress authorized it in August, 1861.

[5] Frederick Bancroft, *The Life of W. H. Seward* (2 vols., New

May, 1861, was asking the Treasury chief to assume full responsibility for his office during absences from Washington.[6] A close personal relationship soon developed between the two which continued unabated to the close of Chase's life, although one would have guessed otherwise when Cameron later played a leading role in scotching Chase's Presidential aspiration.

Cameron cared little for the trappings and flair of military reviews and seldom visited theaters of operations. However, shortly before the Battle of Bull Run he visited General Irvin McDowell's headquarters, then enveloped in an atmosphere of joviality and boastful confidence, but he revealed vis-a-vis only a countenance "apprehensive of evil."[7] In November, Cameron assisted Lincoln in a review of a portion of McClellan's grand new army. The War Secretary, very likely feeling ill at ease on a charger, quietly dropped out of the party. At the end of the year he joined General George G. Meade in a review of Pennsylvania troops at Camp Pierpont.

Cameron's reputation as a master spoilsman doubtless encouraged many to seek his patronage. It must be kept in mind that the numerous other offices in Washington, during the early war days, were likewise crowded with office seekers, not least of which was Lincoln's. The Secretary of War, in view of the proposed gigantic military ex-

---

York, 1900), II, 350; John P. Usher, *President Lincoln's Cabinet* (Omaha 1925), 21; Howard K. Beale, ed., *Diary of Gideon Welles* (3 vols. New York, 1960), I, 25. Welles wrote his account several years after the event.

[6] Cameron to [Chase], May 25, 1861, Salmon P. Chase Papers, Historical Society of Pennsylvania.

[7] James B. Fry, "McDowell's Advance to Bull Run," *Battles and Leaders of the Civil War*, new introduction by Roy F. Nichols (4 vols., New York, 1956), I, 183.

pansion program, was peculiarly prepared to pay off
en masse, his numerous political debts and to add considerable numbers to his already sizable clientele. Unquestionably his department received the most thorough
"house-cleaning." [8]

Petitioners seeking to become lower grade army officers,
military storekeepers in ordnance, clerks, paymasters, assistant paymasters, or sutlers were generally channeled
through the War Office. A sutlership was highly prized
because it permitted the recipient to operate, privately,
what today's soldier would call a PX or post exchange.[9]
Paymasters were supposed to have tenure. In practice,
Cameron did not exercise a free hand in dispensing these
positions, usually accepting the advice of a prominent
leader from the petitioner's district. Lincoln repeatedly
requested or commanded the appointments of his friends;
and not infrequently sinecures for henchmen or relatives
of his friends. For example, John W. Forney, whose
former Democratic *Press* was now defending administration policies, saw his two sons receive commissions as
lieutenants although the younger was only eighteen years
of age.

The War Secretary suffered sharp criticism for using
personal friendship only as a basis for appointments and
for allegedly alloting Pennsylvania more than its quota.
It is true that paymasterships were granted to David

[8] Carl R. Fish, "Lincoln and the Patronage," *American Historical
Review* (October 1902), VIII, 57.

[9] General Orders, No. 38, June 27, 1861, ruled that all sutlers
be appointed by the Secretary of War. See *War of the Rebellion
. . . Official Records of the Union and Confederate Armies* (128
vols. 1880-1801), Series III, I, 299. Cited hereafter as *Official
Records.*

Taggart, Russell Errett, Francis Jordan, and Andrew Sallade, all political lieutenants.[10] Two acts of nepotism which made his brother, James, a colonel and his son, Brua, a paymaster, brought him only grief; James Cameron fell at Bull Run and Brua Cameron died in 1864. The recklessness of some appointments is illustrated in the case of Edward Smith, who modestly requested a lieutenantcy; the War Secretary replied this was not enough for a relative of George Smith, who had voted for him thirty years ago—he should be made a major.[11] J. P. Sanderson, one of the first three in his political hierarchy, secured the first clerkship in the War Department.

There was no favoritism shown Pennsylvania on an early list of military commissions and assistant quartermastership totaling 247. Pennsylvania received 38, less than the one-sixth to which she was entitled (border states excluded), but Illinois and Ohio were favored over New York.[12] In Washington, however, 27 Pennsylvanians were soon at work in the War Department, which in early March had a total of only 90 employees.[13]

Although holding no United States Senatorial office through which civil patronage is usually dispersed, Simon Cameron still exercised major control over his state's appointments. The postmastership of Philadelphia went to his man, C. A. Walborn. In turn Walborn found positions for the "small fry." [14] George Bergner, editor of Cameron's mouthpiece, the Harrisburg *Pennsylvania Telegraph*, be-

---

[10] Cameron's records of War Department, Cameron MSS, LC.
[11] Usher, *Lincoln's Cabinet*, 20.
[12] Cameron's records, Cameron MSS, LC.
[13] Meneely, *War Department*, 107.
[14] Cameron to Walborn, April 23, 28, 1861, Society Autograph Collection, HSP.

came postmaster at the capital, and two Philadelphia
Evening Bulletin men were installed in the Philadelphia
customs. Joseph Casey's "many letters" to Lincoln on
Cameron's behalf finally brought its rewards, a judgeship
on the Court of Claims. S. Newton Pettis, of Crawford
County went to Colorado Territory as associate justice.[15]
A. K. McClure's statement that Cameron controlled
foreign appointments has little meaning. Pennsylvania received none of the first class missions although Cameron
secured minor posts for E. Joy Morris and Jacob Haldeman. Consulships and clerkships were used for district
patronage.[16]

The new Secretary of War, along with a majority of
Lincoln's cabinet, exhibited meager comprehension of the
larger aspects of the Fort Sumter crisis. Abandonment of
the Federal fort except under direct military duress could
easily be interpreted as de facto recognition of the new
Confederacy and an unwarranted, unconstitutional surrender of sovereign territory of the United States.
Cameron, having entered the cabinet late, had not
listened to the cabinet discussion of March 9, nor had he
examined General Scott's memorandum, originally prepared for interim Secretary Joseph Holt, on Fort Sumter.
Perhaps he assumed, along with others, that Lincoln was
not actually the final arbiter of national policy and intended to follow in the train of William Seward. The
deluded Secretary of State, at the time beguiled by Confederate emissaries, was misleading the Confederacy with

[15] Basler, *Works*, IV, 84-note, 166, 294.
[16] McClure, *Notes*, I, 455. From Stockholm, Haldeman sent
$1,200 and notes for $4,500 toward payment of Northern Central
Railroad stock "which he was to take" from Simon Cameron. See
the many Lincoln letters on the subject in Basler, *Works*, IV.

unauthorizd assurances of a policy of appeasement including the abandonment of Sumter.[17]

On March 15, Lincoln addressed the same question to all cabinet members: assuming that Sumter could possibly be "provisioned," asked the President, was it now feasible? Cameron's reply of March 17 confessed inadequate study of the problem, confirmed the findings of Scott that abandonment seemed an "inevitable necessity" (Scott said "sure necessity"), and predicted that the plan of Gustavus Fox, Montgomery Blair's man, "would initiate a bloody and protracted conflict." There was "no doubt," stated Cameron, that Sumter could have been easily supplied a month earlier. This inferred that earlier relief would have changed Confederate determination to possess the fort by an act of war if necessary. Cameron was in agreement with Seward's suggestions, as was the majority of the cabinet.[18]

The final decision on the Sumter crisis was deferred. On March 29, cabinet members again returned written statements on policy, but Cameron was absent and returned no opinion. Evidently the Secretary of War exercised no influence on Lincoln's thinking and was actually in ignorance of some expeditions being projected at the moment. Cameron, according to George Harrington's account, later changed his mind and argued, "upon the final disposition of the subject by the cabinet," for Sumter's relief. Apparently Lincoln's final decision was made at a White House "kitchen-cabinet" session with both Cameron and Seward absent.[19]

[17] For an illuminating discussion on Seward's part in the Sumter affair see W. A. Swanberg, *First Blood* (New York, 1957), 226-41.
[18] *Official Records*, Series I, I, 196-201.
[19] Samuel Wylie Crawford, *Genesis of the Civil War* (New York,

Stressing the peaceful nature of the expedition for provisioning Fort Sumter, Secretary Cameron dispatched a messenger to Governor Pickens of South Carolina, informing him of it and Major Robert Anderson was authorized to capitulate if he deemed it necessary.[20] But a week later the Confederates, impatient about maintaining any longer a status quo, intolerable to a "sovereign state," used military might to secure possession.

In accordance with Lincoln's proclamation calling for 75,000 volunteers to serve for three months, the War Office issued specific quotas for each state. Cameron received defiant refusals from six states; Missouri's chief executive labelling the requisition "unconstitutional . . . inhuman and diabolical. . . ." But loyal states (including Missouri) furnished 91,000 men under this call.[21]

The determination to call for only 75,000 ninety-day militiamen, for which Cameron later suffered much abuse, was not his. In agreement with the opinion of Chase, the Secretary of War recommended a minimum of 500,000 volunteers. Instead, Seward's figure of 75,000 was adopted because his reconciliation policy was still partially in vogue.[22]

To discuss in detail the work of the War Office in 1861 is beyond the scope of this political biography, but a listing of a few of the many difficulties and problems of the first few weeks of the war crisis will bear evidence

---

1887), 367-68, quoting "Harrington's Reminiscences." Harrington, Assistant Secretary of the Treasury, was present at the informal White House meeting.

[20] *Official Records*, Series I, I, 235, 245.   [21] *Ibid.*, 69, 303.

[22] Cameron to special reporter, *New York Times*, June 3, 1878; Lurton D. Ingersoll, *History of the War Department* (Washington, 1879), 328.

of the magnitude of Cameron's task. The capital, surrounded by militant southern sympathizers, isolated, rail and telegraph communications severed, infested with disloyal elements, devoid of military protection under a decrepit military chieftain, must be saved for the Union. New competent military leaders must be selected, relief troops re-routed, communications re-established, and provision made for the care of the thousands expected to pour into the city. Authorization must be made quickly to provide the many necessities required of a field soldier. All this—enough to engage the energy of a dozen men— and not an iota of preparation behind it.

After an interlude of seventeen years, recollections of that frightening specter of 1861 remained fresh in Cameron's mind:

> . . . it was almost impossible to find a man who had any intelligent idea of the magnitude of the struggle. . . . Oh it was a terrible time. . . . We were entirely unprepared . . . to engage in war. We had no guns, and even if we had, they would have been of little use, for we had no ammunition. . . no powder, no saltpetre. I did the best I could under the circumstances, working day and night . . . there were very few persons who believed that the war would last for more than a few weeks. . . . At first having no means at my command; then laughed at for predicting that the war would be a long and bloody one; and all the time harassed by contractors and others . . . I was certainly not in a place to be envied.[23]

At first the War Office was particularly embarrassed at the outpouring of troops far beyond requested quotas. Time after time, governors or important political leaders, fearing the cooling of public ardor, protested the rejections. Although Lincoln's proclamation had limited the quotas, the President occasionally requested Cameron to

[23] *New York Times*, June 3, 1878.

accept additional troops. The nefarious practice of authorizing the acceptance of units raised by private individuals (Cameron authorized 58 in Pennsylvania) bent on securing high ranking military commissions, added to the confusion. Lincoln and Cameron, although under tremendous pressure from powerful political leaders, must accept blame.[24] Often the Secretary of War directed the suppliant to direct his proffers to the governor of his state. Pennsylvania took the lead in solving this problem with a law of May 15, prohibiting any volunteers from leaving the state unless they had been accepted by the governor.[25]

The excessive troop problem remained until after the July debacle of Bull Run. In retrospect it is hard to question the wisdom of the early policy of rejecting many unequipped ninety-day volunteers, capable only of consuming huge quantities of food—at that time a very scarce item—and then free later to walk home at the moment they might be of some use. Cavalry units were often rejected because of the elaborate equipment required and the question of their usefulness in wooded areas.[26] Lincoln's call of May 3 for an additional 83,000 service men somewhat relieved the pressure.[27] General Scott, vis-a-vis the Secretary of War, did not accept the theory that partially equipped troops were useless.[28] On the day of the defeat at Bull Run, Cameron wrote Chase

[24] Basler, Works, IV, records Lincoln's request. *Official Records,* Series III, I, 440.

[25] *Laws of Pennsylvania,* 1861, 753.

[26] William H. Ganse, *History of the United States Army* (New York, 1936), 250.

[27] *Official Records,* Series III, I, 146.

[28] Meneely, *War Department,* 159.

that good would emerge from the defeat, that Congress would now cooperate unselfishly and that he had "no fear of the ultimate result." [29]

The Secretary of War was innocent of any knowledge of military science in spite of his title of "General," which he had borne for thirty-five years. Like Lincoln, he believed that following an intensive brief study of military works, he could join the growing corps of civilian "generals" and participate intelligently in their conversations; but through his tenure of office he showed very little interest in military movements or their planning. The only aspect of the military arts which occupied much of his time was the one he could not avoid, logistics—supervising the supplying, quartering, and transportation of troops. However, at the first War Council of April 14, Cameron, following the ideas of James R. Gilmore, a wealthy New York busybody, presented a grand plan of victory. First having secured the coastal cities, he would hermetically seal the Confederacy.[30] General Scott's "Anaconda" would bring pressure from without in contrast to Cameron's idea of allowing the germs of rebellion to consume itself from within. No cabinet member agreed on the feasibility of his plan.

When Cameron presented the first report of his department to Lincoln on July 1, 1861, no crushing military defeats had been suffered, the nation's morale was high, and an over-confident public was clamoring for the move on Richmond which was to end the Confederacy. Complaints against the War Department had not yet reached serious proportions.

[29] Cameron to Chase, July 21, 1861, Chase MSS, HSP.
[30] James R. Gilmore, *Personal Recollections of Abraham Lincoln and the Civil War* (Boston, 1898), 25-27.

The War Secretary's report tracing briefly the unconstitutional growth of the Confederacy, emphasized the illegal nature of its seizures and the multiple acts of treason accompanying them. He called for continuation of the volunteer system, "actual facts" having proved its worth; but henceforth only three-year men must be accepted. A cash bonus of $100 upon discharge would aid in recognizing their meritorious services. All regimental commanders were either graduates of West Point or had "served with distinction in the field." To date the total of 310,000 men available had cost the quartermastership bureau only 70 million dollars.

To suppress the rebellion, continued the report, an overwhelming force must be brought to bear, as in the case of the defiant Mormons, on the disloyal secessionists. Additional Congressional legislation was needed to carry out these objectives, the commissariat lacking powers to provide adequate camp equipage and transportation facilities. The Department had no official assistant secretary and a large increase in the force of clerical workers was needed badly. Cameron praised the work of Miss D. L. Dix, General Scott, with whom he had differences, and the bureau heads in his department. His interest in American industry was reflected in his wish to see domestic producers encouraged to produce all needed military equipment.[31]

Fortunately for the War Secretary he never suffered the pain of undergoing close scrutiny at the hands of the notorious Committee on Conduct of the War. Yet it was the position which he, a member of the executive branch, took against encroachment from the legislative division which led to its creation.

[31] *Official Records*, Series III, I, 301-10.

Its genesis is traceable to the crushing defeat in September of a small body of Federals, personally directed by Colonel Edward Baker, one of Lincoln's closest friends. Baker, who lost his life, exhibited rashness, failed to take proper precautions, and disregarded orders of his superior, General Charles P. Stone.[32]

In early December, the Radicals pushed through a Congressional resolution requesting Cameron ("if not incompatible with the public service") to report whether measures had been taken to pinpoint responsibility for the defeat. It was General McClellan's opinion, replied Cameron, "that an inquiry . . . would at this time be injurious to the public service." In answer, Senator Roscoe Conkling, author of the original resolution, secured a second one this time demanding what he deemed a satisfactory answer. The shrewd Secretary, now operating in the medium in which he particularly excelled, replied that "measures have been taken to ascertain" responsibility but as yet it was not "deemed compatible with the public interest to make known these measures." [33]

Not to be thwarted, the newly born Committee on the Conduct of the War went to work on the case and aided largely by the evil genius Edwin Stanton, finally conjured up the scapegoat, General Charles P. Stone. Cameron later became the special target of another specially created nemesis, the Committee on Contracts.

The "problem" generals of Cameron's administration were Scott, McClellan, Benjamin F. Butler, William T. Sherman, and John C. Frémont. He had dealings with

[32] Stone's "Report," Oct. 29, 1861, *Official Records*, Series I, V, 293-99.

[33] Quotations from *Cong. Globe*, 37 Cong., 2 Sess., 6, 274, in Meneely, *War Department*, 320-21.

many others but the ones named command special consideration.

At first proper deference was shown the ailing Scott because of his rank and enormous prestige. With the emergence of the self-publicized new "Napoleon of the West," George B. McClellan, and failure to bring a quick end to the rebellion, administrative, military, and public dissatisfaction mounted rapidly. Even before Bull Run, Montgomery Blair, expressing no confidence in Scott, was urging Cameron to take charge of "matters," he being the one who would have to accept responsibility.[34] But Cameron, well aware of his limitations in matters of army strategy, wisely refrained from following Blair's suggestions.

After July 27, when McClellan, now in active command of the Union Army, undertook to instruct his chief and to deal directly with the War Department, Scott complained to the Secretary of McClellan's insubordination.[35] Cameron, seeing in McClellan the coming man, and relying on his keen political astuteness in such matters, remained aloof from the controversy. On October 31, 1861, the day of his resignation, Scott, acknowledging his many obligations to the War Secretary, praised him for the "high considerations" shown him. Cameron returned a highly laudatory communication to the old soldier whose personal friendship he had enjoyed over a period of thirty years.[36] Happily, this problem had found its own solution.

[34] M. Blair to Cameron, June 22, 1861, (Mrs) Jessie A. Marshall, ed., *Private and Official Correspondence of General Benjamin F. Butler*. . . . (5 vols., Norwood, 1917), I, 155.

[35] Charles W. Elliott, *Winfield Scott* (New York, 1937), 735.

[36] *Official Records*, Series III, I, 611-12, 614.

Granted the advantage of twenty years of reflection, the new general-in-chief much preferred Cameron in the War Office to his successor Stanton. Never had he interfered in military affairs, always giving McClellan "full support." Occasionally the general became vexed with the Secretary's refusal to allow the former (whose appetite was insatiable) to allow supplies to be distributed in accordance with his desires. In his memoirs McClellan flattered himself that only his influence over Lincoln prevented Cameron's earlier departure from the cabinet. However, in November, 1861, a thoroughly frustrated McClellan, able to pour out his soul only to his trusted wife, spewed his venom on all members of the cabinet except Blair, and branded Cameron a rascal.[37]

Benjamin F. Butler actually caused Cameron little trouble, but his persistent attempts to persuade the War Department to accept his views on the status of fugitive slaves, or slaves within union lines, and his repeated acts of doubtful constitutionality, gave the Secretary a few headaches. He overwhelmed Scott with his seizure of the Annapolis Railroad, his conception of Baltimore as conquered enemy territory, and his "instructions" to his superior at Washington.[38]

Immediately upon hearing of Lincoln's call for troops, the cunning Butler, through Senator Henry Wilson and Cameron, practically promoted himself to the ranking volunteer brigadiership in the army. Cameron's quick request to Massachusetts for a brigadier laid the foundation for a long feud between Butler and Governor John

[37] *Battles & Leaders*, II, 163; George B. McClellan, *McClellan's Own Story* (New York, 1887), 152-53; McClellan to his wife, Nov. (?), 1861, quoted in Meneely, *War Department*, 314.

[38] *Official Records*, Series I, II, 28.

A. Andrew which continued unabated into Edwin Stanton's Administration.[39]

As early as May 24, Butler was forming male labor details composed of fugitive (contraband) slaves. The women and children he retained for humanitarian reasons. Upon his request to the Secretary of War for a ruling on procedures (actually he had already established them) Cameron approved Butler's actions, instructing him not to surrender fugitives to "alleged masters" but at the same time not to interfere with the slaves "held to service" in the state. Final disposition of the fugitives, constituting precedents in national policy, was not Cameron's to give; yet his unwarranted instruction anticipated the provisions of the Confiscation Act of Congress, August 6, which legalized Butler's Act.[40]

General William T. Sherman, commanding the Department of the Cumberland, undoubtedly suffered from the looseness of Cameron's tongue. In September, accompanied by his Adjutant-General, the Secretary of War toured the western theater of operation, chiefly for the purpose of checking the activities of General Frémont. He diverted his return route in order to visit Sherman, who was extremely anxious to see him.

In Sherman's hotel room at Louisville, the tired and ailing Secretary reclined on the general's bed while his host, with the use of a map, explained fully the military situation, which he deemed very serious. Surprisingly, a half-dozen newspapermen, for whom Cameron personally vouched, were admitted to the room. When Sherman remarked that for his 300-miles line, 200,000 troops would be needed for offensive operations, the astonished Secre-

[39] Butler's *Correspondence*, I, 12; *ibid.*, Series III, I, 810-11, 818.
[40] Butler's *Correspondence*, I, 112-13, 119, 185-88, 195, 201-02.

tary shouted, "Great God! Where are they to come from?"[41]

Sherman's lecture, at the time, certainly made some impression on Cameron because he wired Lincoln the same day that conditions in Kentucky were "much worse" than he anticipated. The next day he ordered a Pennsylvania brigade sent to Sherman "at once" together with a consignment of muskets.[42] His other orders reinforced Sherman for a total of 10,000 men.

The stories surrounding Sherman's "insanity" comprise truths, half-truths, distortions, and falsifications. Cameron's "memorandum" of the trip, stated Sherman, mentioned his "insane request." This must have been the embellished newspaper accounts, because the original version of October 21 did not include the phrase.[43] William Foulke stated that when Cameron paid his Indianapolis visit to Governor Morton and Senator Chandler, he laughed heartily at Sherman's crazy idea of 200,000 men. This account is obviously false because Cameron did not visit Sherman until the following day. But at Harrisburg, according to A. K. McClure, Cameron reported Sherman "absolutely crazy." Probably Cameron had dropped the same remark to his party of newspaper reporters. An enraged member whom Sherman had threatened to hang reported the story with great embellishment in a New York paper.[44]

[41] William T. Sherman, *Memoirs, Written by Himself* (2 vols., New York, 1890), I, 228-32.

[42] *Official Records*, Series I, IV 308-09.

[43] Sherman, *Memoirs*, I, 332; *ibid.*, Series I, III, 548; Series I, IV, 313.

[44] William D. Foulke, *Life of Oliver P. Morton* (2 vols., Indianapolis, 1899), I, 147; McClure, *Recollections*, 333; B. H. Liddell Hart, *Sherman-Soldier-Realist-American* (New York, 1929), 108.

Sherman had no way of fighting back. His war was hopeless with an enemy he could not see. Newspapers all over the nation carried distorted accounts, wagging tongues circulated wild rumors, and wits tapped their heads significantly when his name was mentioned. Sherman always felt that Cameron should have denied or affirmed the contents of the "memorandum" when rumors were rife. Soon after Sherman was relieved of his command, his brother, Senator John Sherman, determined to bring the Secretary of War to account. Cameron's reply netted Sherman nothing. Sherman's recall had taken place in Cameron's absence and his new appointment (under Halleck) was "evidence of the confidence reposed in him." [45] Sherman finally found his place with the man who believed in him—U. S. Grant.

John C. Frémont, yet a popular figure, had, largely through the influence of the influential Blair family, been assigned jurisdiction over a great western expanse of territory lacking commensurate resources in men and supplies. Frémont, who would have preferred a foreign mission, stayed closeted in his headquarters, working day and night but accomplishing little. After Captain Lyon was killed at the defeat of Wilson's Creek, the younger Francis P. Blair, reversing his stand, demanded Frémont's removal.

The action for which Frémont gained special notoriety was his military proclamation of August 30, freeing the slaves of Confederates within his department. This order reflected his association with the notorious abolitionist, Owen Lovejoy, one of his civilian aides. The proclamation

[45] Sherman, *Memoirs*, I, 233; John Sherman, *Recollections* (2 vols., Chicago, 1895), I, 267.

received wide acclaim over the North. From his home Cameron responded with an immediate congratulatory message. The Secretary's snap judgment indicated that he had not grasped the wider implications of the proclamation; but Lincoln, realizing its impact upon the slave-owning border element, ordered Frémont to rescind his order.[46]

Largely as a result of Blair's charges against Frémont, his case was discussed in a cabinet meeting. Cameron and Chase supported Frémont and Lincoln was doubtful. The President delegated Cameron to conduct an on-the-spot investigation. Although Cameron carried orders for Frémont's dismissal, delivery was discretionary on his part.

Cameron arrived at Frémont's headquarters in Tipton, Missouri, on September 13. During the time Frémont was entertaining his guest, Adjutant-General Thomas was "snooping," acquiring much hearsay, and listening to a tale of woe from Frémont's second-in-command, General David Hunter, who termed his superior "utterly incompetent." Other "gentlemen" in Missouri (Blair was one) had found Frémont's mind "incapable" of concentration. Frémont, upon discovering the nature of the Secretary's visit, wailed pitifully, promising a victory in the near future. The sympathetic Secretary returned to Washington with the dismissal order—in fact he still had it a quarter of a century later.[47]

Colonel Blair recorded a private conclusion on the secre-

[46] For a full discussion of the Frémont affair see Allen Nevins, *Fremont,* or *War for the Union,* I.

[47] Bates, *Diary,* 198; "Memorandum", *Official Records,* Series I, III, 544-45; Cameron to Lincoln, Oct. 14, 1861, Lincoln MSS; Cameron to Fremont (copy), Aug. 27, 1885, Cameron MSS, LC.

tary's visit: "Cameron had *flummuxed* on the Frémont business." In fact, Blair fumed against Lincoln and his cabinet "apes" who had allowed Frémont to remain. Frémont's dismissal, charged Blair, had been promised by Cameron as soon as he returned to Washington; now, "Who can believe him?" [48]

Frémont finally received his dismissal order by special messenger in early November. In spite of the many difficulties confronting Frémont, his competent biographer agreed that he cannot be "exonerated from blame" in spite of his lack of executive competence and poor judgment in selecting men.[49]

When mention is made by writers of Simon Cameron's work in the War Department, it will almost invariably include a clause commenting on the public abuses suffered under his administration. During this period of national stress, not only its leaders, but all patriotic citizens were bound to put aside their greed for personal profit at their country's expense. In 1861 the perpetrators of wholesale graft were more at fault than the executive who had not the time to scan individual contracts and who took no gain for himself. Men like Governor Edwin Morgan, Thurlow Weed, and J. P. Morgan of New York—all reputable citizens—and Simon Stevens, a protegé of Thaddeus Stevens' from Pennsylvania, have their names linked to these unsavory deals. Nor can General John C. Frémont be excused.

In April of 1861 a utopia for corrupt profiteers had been created by the exigencies of the situation. There was a law requiring open purchase or by sealed bids, if

[48] W. E. Smith, *Blair Family*, II, 83-84.
[49] Nevins, *Fremont*, 495-96.

advertised, but the immediate demands of 100,000 unequipped volunteers would not brook delay. Bidding by
some states began before Fort Sumter's surrender and
soon there appeared the ridiculous spectacle of the Federal government bidding against the several states. For
example, Governor Curtin of Pennsylvania, only five days
after Lincoln's call, had let a contract for clothing 10,000
militiamen.[50] If the Federal government had started buying early and forbidden the states to do so, this might
have been avoided. Strongly competitive bids, the law
of necessity, and compulsive haste forced the acceptance
of inferior goods at exorbitant rates.

At a cabinet meeting on April 21, the members agreed
with Lincoln that under the conditions of the crisis, with
communications severed, that extra-legal steps were necessary to save the Union. Thus it came to pass that three
New Yorkers were given authority to disburse two million
dollars to "authorized agents" of the government. The two
leading agents named in New York were its governor,
Edwin D. Morgan, and Alexander Cummings, lately a
Philadelphia lieutenant of Cameron. The agents were
given this authority by Cameron only until such time as
communications could be "completely re-established" between the capital and New York.[51]

Cummings, more than any other man, contributed to
the unsavory reputation of Cameron's regime. Surely the
Secretary of War expected something better when he
wrote Cummings earlier: "The Department needs . . . an
intelligent, experienced, and energetic man on whom it

---

[50] Fred A. Shannon, *Union Army*, I, 85.
[51] Meneely, *War Department*, 119; *Official Records*, Series III, I,
104, 136.

can rely, to assist in pushing forward troops, munitions, and supplies." Cummings began his operations with the modest sum of $160,000. At $15 each he hastily purchased worthless carbines which the government had sold at $2. The government rejected them and they were sold at $3.50 to private speculators.

The sequel to this story is even more interesting. After alterations which had allegedly made them trustworthy, Simon Stevens, on a loan backed by J. P. Morgan bought the carbines at $12.50 each and contracted them to General John C. Frémont, government agent, for $22 each. When Cameron visited Frémont in October, he gave him orders not to operate through "irresponsible agents." Charles Van Wyck, speaking for the House Committee which succeeded in blocking final payment, stated that Simon Stevens, a law partner of Thaddeus, expected to make $50,000 in one day. In the meantime, Governor Edwin Morgan delegated his agency to his business partner, George D. Morgan.[52]

Cummings expanded into various spheres of operations— the acquisition of citizen apparel, sea food, liquid refreshments, and ships. Total purchases costing $250,000 included straw hats, linen pantaloons, herring, pickles, ale, and porter. Cummings never did account for an additional $140,000 which passed into his hands. His transport, the Cataline, cost $18,000 with rental pledged at $10,000 per month. When questioned about his transactions, Cummings replied that he left "details" to his clerk, a nominee of Thurlow Weed.[53]

[52] H. White, *Trumbull*, 185; Shannon, *Union Army*, I, 61; *House Reports*, 37 Cong., 2nd Sess. No. 2, 78, 1088.

[53] Shannon, *Union Army*, I, 61-62; White, Trumbull, 179-80; Robinson, *Public Press of Philadelphia*, 107.

It is strange indeed that a man whose fantastic purchases and apparent dishonesty were so widely publicized should later emerge a colonel under Secretary Edwin Stanton, a territorial governor under President Johnson, and gain endorsement "as a capital man" by William Seward for the Office of Commissioner of Internal Revenue.[54]

Other "scandals" centered on the purchase of horses, mules, and beef cattle. Quartermaster Montgomery Meigs, under Cameron's orders, let two Pennsylvania contracts for the delivery of 1,000 cavalry horses to be corralled at Huntingdon at a maximum price of $117 per head. Critics said that the horses averaged 30 to 40 dollars in value —the government had been "taken" for $50,000. The local Huntingdon papers reported, however, that an inspector at the town rejected about three-fourths of the horses for sale. When the horses arrived at Louisville, 485 of the lot were judged worthless and Henry L. Dawes stated that transporting the animals had cost $10,000. If all these statements are true it would seem that potential cavalry horses did not exist in central Pennsylvania. The mules were bought in Kentucky at the fancy price of $125 per head wholly for political effect. This was in line with Lincoln's policy of maintaining strong Union sentiment in the area and at the same time milking Confederate sources.[55]

The "celebrated beef contract" was let early in the war when Union soldiers were isolated in the capital with meat supplies exhausted. Four men proposed to supply the needs at once at 8 cents per pound, considerably

---

[54] Welles *Diary*, IV, 414-15.
[55] H. White, *Trumbull*, 182-83; Meneely, *War Department*, 264-65; *Official Records*, Series I, IV, 277-78.

above the usual market price. The best defense for this action was given by Cameron himself: "When we expected large arrivals of soldiers . . . and there was nothing to feed them with, the Acting Commissary General . . . said 'I can now buy two thousand beeves if I pay three cents more than they should be worth.' Well I replies . . . pay a dollar per pound rather than have a soldier should suffer. . . ." [56] Critics had charged that the beef contract was an act of favoritism but the leading contractor, George M. Lauman, was Cameron's political enemy.

One of the most shameful aspects of war contracting was the fact that bidders were often forced to pay middlemen a percentage of the profits in order to secure contracts. Evidence before an investigating committee showed that a United States Senator bargained for a stipend of 5 per cent amounting to $50,000 for securing a million dollar contract. In another case, a $100,000 contract for a type of pistol considered unfit by the Chief of Ordnance was accepted upon payment to an "agent" of a fee of $10,000. Contractors found that bids were more likely to be procured if processed through certain channels. Again, contractors sometimes paid blackmail in order to secure a favorable audit—a necessary procedure before payment was authorized. [57]

Cameron was not without his defenders. Under existing conditions, contended Alexander McClure, a bitter political enemy of Cameron, no man could have administered the office "without flagrant abuses." Horace Greeley spoke for him in his New York *Tribune*. Cameron's best defense

[56] Philadelphia *Inquirer*, May 25, 1861; Harrisburg *Pennsylvania Telegraph*, May 5, 1862.
[57] *Official Records*, Series III, II, 193; Allen Nevins, *Abram S. Hewitt* (New York, 1935), 205.

for his act of investing Cummings with control of public monies came from the President after the House's censure of the Secretary. Reviewing the emergency of April, 1861, Lincoln said he "directed" Cameron to make the authorization to Cummings and that he was not aware (May 2, 1862) that a dollar of public funds "thus confided . . . was lost or wasted." In his opinion these extraordinary measures had saved the nation. If censure was due, then Lincoln, along with the other cabinet members, must share Cameron's responsibility.[58]

Like Lincoln, the Secretary of War was accused of unconstitutional measures in respect to the rights of citizens. Cameron, in anticipation of an act of secession when the Maryland legislature met in September, determined to checkmate it by force. Area commanders were ordered to arrest, if necessary, part or all of the members; and to do the work effectively. Under these orders a total of 19 members, together with the mayor of Baltimore, a Congressman, and two editors, added for good measure, were incarcerated in Northern military prisons. No charges were preferred.[59]

The case of Pierce Butler was of unusual interest because of its developments. Cameron, suspecting that Butler had received a Confederate commission, had him thrown in jail where he remained a month. After Cameron's retirement from office, Butler sued him for assault and battery and false imprisonment. Lincoln assumed responsibility for the act, ordering Federal

[58] A. K. McClure, *Abraham Lincoln and Men of Wartimes*, 147; *Official Records*, Series III, II, 73-75.

[59] *Ibid.*, Series I, V, 193-94; James F. Rhodes, *History of United States from the Compromise of 1850* (7 vols., New York, 1893-1906), III, 554.

attorneys to defend Cameron—consequently, the case was dropped.[60]

On December 1, the Secretary of War was required to file a report which together with those of other cabinet members would be used as a basis by Lincoln for his annual report. The first portion dealt with the raising of troops, their number in the different branches, and even cited measures taken by Napoleon. If necessary, the nation was capable of putting three million men into the field. Next followed a discussion on the scope of the "conspiracy," activities in border states, and the procurement of arms. He recommended the expansion of West Point and the integration of volunteers with members of the regular army.

Evidently in rebuttal against the criticism he had suffered in connection with troop movements, Cameron noted that at first it had cost $6 to transport a soldier from New York to Baltimore. By re-routing them through Harrisburg at a cost of only $4, he had saved one-third on transportation. This re-routing, it is to be noted, added tremendously to the income of the Northern Central Railroad, commonly called the Cameron road. The Secretary did not disclose that the gross earnings of his railroad had increased 44 per cent in the past year.[61]

One paragraph of the report dealt with peculation in contracts. Errors had occasionally been made by subordinates, and "extravagant prices" paid because of the need for "haste and the pressure of rapid events." Notwithstanding, never had such a well equipped force been

[60] James G. Randall, *Constitutional Problems Under Lincoln* (New York, 1926), 188-89.

[61] Thomas Weber, *The Northern Railroads in the Civil War*, 1861-65 (New York, 1952), 49.

provided in such a short time "at so small an expense." Cameron was gratified with the "economical administration" of the various branches of the services.

The portion of the report relating to the future status of slaves created somewhat of a bombshell. "The law of self preservation," argued the Secretary of War, demanded that former slaves be used in the best way to assist in quelling the rebellion. ". . . it is the right, and may become the duty . . . of the government to employ their services against the rebels under proper military regulation, discipline and command." [62]

Departing from customary procedure, the cunning Cameron had copies mailed to strategic post offices with orders for their release simultaneously with Lincoln's. This report, as Cameron surely realized, would be accepted by the public as the President's policies. Luckily, the printer, noting the unusual significance of the slave clause, hurried to the White House with a copy. In anger, the President reputedly said: "This will never do! General Cameron must take no such responsibility. This is a question that belongs exclusively to me." Support for the clause from Secretary Chase did not suffice. Lincoln had the report altered and ordered the mailed copies reclaimed, but the original version found its way into the New York newspapers by January 3, 1862. [63]

Cameron's advocacy of armed slaves poses an inter-

[62] The altered, or official version of the report is found in *Official Records*, Series III, I, 698-708.

[63] For the unaltered version see McPherson, *History of the Rebellion* (Washington, 1865), 249; F. B. Carpenter quoted in Burton J. Hendrick, *Lincoln's War Cabinet*, 231; Ben: Perley Poore, *Reminiscences*, II, 97. Cameron wrote Chase (Aug. 18, 1862), that Lincoln had agreed privately with him on the arming of the slaves and promised to put it into writing.

esting question—his motives. By the fall of 1861, perhaps influenced by the powerful logic of Chase, the War Secretary was passing over to the Radical abolitionist camp. He gave open approbation when Colonel John Cochrane, in an address to his regiment, advocated the arming of slaves. Cameron had mounted the "nigger hobby," argued Montgomery Blair, because he thought it would advance his Presidential aspirations. To others the Secretary's actions constituted a device to divert attention from the charges of corruption directed toward him. To the secretary this proposal was an added powerful weapon to be used in crushing the rebellion. Developments a year later proclaimed him a "prophet without honor in his own land." By middle November he was arguing in cabinet sessions for the arming of Southern slaves.[64]

During the progress of a dinner party given by John W. Forney, Cameron invited the selected circle to pass judgment on the questionable part of his proposed report. His host warned: "It will never do, Mr. Secretary," and implored Cameron, "For God's sake," not to insist upon inserting it. "Put it in sir!" shouted David Wilmot, "By God sir, it is right!" When Caleb Smith attacked Cameron for his view, Edwin M. Stanton stood silent; yet it was this controversial figure who penned for Cameron the most obnoxious phrases of the report.[65]

Apparently the Secretary of War had assumed an atti-

[64] Charles Sumner's *Memoirs*, IV, 46; Welles, *Diary*, I, 127; Carman and Luthin, *Lincoln and the Patronage*, 131; Bates, *Diary*, 203.

[65] M. H. Cobb, "Reminiscences of Washington in 1861", Cameron MSS, LC; Forney, *Anecdotes*, I, 76; W. W. H. Davis to Cameron, June 5, 1877, Cameron MSS, LC; Frank A. Flower, *Edwin McMasters Stanton* (New York, 1905), 116.

tude of defiance when ordered to expunge the objectionable portion. His proposition was not unusual he insisted,
and he supposed it had the approval of the cabinet and
the President. Not until a second cabinet meeting did
Lincoln force Cameron's capitulation. ". . . But the copies
I have sent out," Cameron reminded the President, "will
stand." Accordingly the public in some cases read one
version while Congress received the official altered
account.[66] At this juncture began the final deterioration of
relations between the two, the finale of which marked
Cameron's departure from the cabinet.

All the details leading to Cameron's resignation do not
seem clear, but by January, 1862, Lincoln's cup was running over. His contemporaries agreed largely on total
factors but differed on the major determinants. Following
Bull Run, opposition newspapers began a propaganda
campaign to bring about his removal. In early October
John Nicolay's memorandum of Lincoln's oral medita-
tions read: "Cameron utterly ignorant and regardless of
the course of things, and the probable result. Selfish and
openly discourteous to the President. Obnoxious to the
country. Incapable either of organizing details conceiving
and executing general plans." [67] Seven weeks later the
President expressed his wish to see Joseph Holt back in
the War office. And finally there appeared the straw that
broke the camel's back—his December "Report."

It is therefore evident that Lincoln over a period of
time was contemplating on how he might rid himself
gracefully of a man who had proven to be a liability.

[66] *Ibid.*, 116.
[67] Meneely, *War Department*, 232-33, 365; Helen Nicolay,
Lincoln's Secretary: A Biography of John G. Nicolay (New York,
1949); 125.

A direct removal would result in unpleasant repercussions, the powerful state of Pennsylvania (of which Lincoln always stood in awe) would suffer great offense, and in the process he would create a martyr. Cassius Clay's wish to resign his Russian mission opened the spot for which Lincoln was watching. At least two men, Thurlow Weed and Salmon P. Chase, on request of the President, discussed in advance the subject of the Russian mission to Cameron and communicated his favorable reaction to Lincoln. Weed wrote: "[Cameron] allowed me to ascertain from the president whether the suggested change could be made." [68]

In spite of his strained relations with Lincoln following his December report and the hints given him by Weed and Chase, Lincoln's short curt note of January 11 delivered Sunday, the following day, completely unnerved the Secretary of War. The president merely informed him that the chief executive was now in a position to gratify Cameron's expressed desire for a change—he was to be nominated for the Russian mission. The letter included neither an acknowledgement of the worth of the War Secretary's past services nor regret for his departure. Cameron visited Secretary Seward's quarters where he also found (probably by prearrangement with Chase, who had delivered Lincoln's note) the Secretary of the Treasury. The War Secretary "was quite offended supposing the letter intended as a dismissal, and therefore discourteous." Lincoln did not so intend it, assured Seward and Chase. Before midnight Cameron found his assistant, Thomas A. Scott, and there in the presence of Alexander

[68] Thurlow Weed, "Reply to Ex-Senator Cameron", New York *Tribune*, July 5, 1878; July 4, 1870, Crippen note from J. M. Cameron Papers.

K. McClure "wept bitterly" over the President's personal affront which to him meant "personal degradation." But both gentlemen contended that Lincoln intended no personal offense.[69]

Once again the President chose to use the device of an antedated letter to facilitate his proposals. Lincoln, having no desire to wound needlessly the feelings of his powerful War Secretary, agreed to write another letter intended for public consumption which could be substituted for the original of January 11:

Though I have said nothing hitherto in response to your wish, expressed long since, to resign your seat in the cabinet, I have not been unmindful of it. I have been only unwilling to consent to a change at a time, and under circumstances which might give occasion to misconstruction, and unable till now to see how such misconstruction could be avoided.

But the desire of Mr. Clay to return home and to offer his services to his country in the field enables me now to gratify your wish, and at the same time evince my personal regard for you, and my confidence in your ability, patriotism, and fidelity to public trust.

I therefore tender to your acceptance, if you still desire to resign your present position, the post of Minister to Russia. Should you accept it, you will bear with you the assurance of my undiminished confidence, of my affectionate esteem, and of my sure expectation that near the great sovereign whose personal and hereditary friendship, for the United States, so much endears him to Americans, you will be able to render services to your country, not less important you could render at home.

Very sincerely your friend
A. Lincoln[70]

[69] Lincoln to Cameron, Jan. 11, 1862, Cameron MSS, LC; David Donald, ed., *Inside Lincoln's Cabinet: The Civil War Diaries of Salmon P. Chase* (New York, 1954), 60-62; A. K. McClure, *Men of Wartime*, 150-51.

[70] Lincoln to Cameron, Jan. 11 [*sic*], 1862, Crippen note from J. M. Cameron Papers. Lincoln erroneously dated his letter 1863.

The tone of Lincoln's second letter, it must be noted, suggested the move as voluntary on the Secretary's part. If Cameron chose to "accept" the new post the President would continue his "undiminished confidence."

Cameron's response likewise antedated, January 11, is as follows:

I have the honor to acknowledge your favor of this date, and to thank you, with profound respect, for its kind and generous tone. When you were elected President a result of which I contributed my best exertions, I had no thought of leaving the Senate of the U. S. or of accepting any position in your gift. But when you invited me to Springfield, Ill., and presented me the choice of two named places in the list of your constitutional advisers, I could not, for grave public reasons, and after great reflection, refuse a trust so trying and laborious. My life has been one of constant labor and excitement. I looked to the Senate as the best field after such a life, in which to serve my country and my State. It was only when I realized that I might be of service to the general cause in the darkly foreshadowed, future, that I ventured to undertake the manifold and various responsibilities of the War Dept. I felt when I saw the traitors leaving their seats in Congress and when the Star of the West was fired upon in Charleston Harbor, that a bloody conflict was inevitable.

I have devoted myself without intermission to my official duties. I have given to them all my energies, I have done my best. It is impossible, in the direction of operations so extensive, but that some mistakes happen and some complications and complaints arise. In view of these recollections, I thank you from a full heart for the expression of your confidence in my ability, patriotism, and fidelity to public trust. Thus, my own conscientious sense of doing my duty by the Executive and by my country is approved by the acknowledged head of the government itself.

When I became a member of your administration I avowed my purpose to retire from the Cabinet, as soon as my duty to my country would allow me to do so. In your letter of this day's date, so illustrative of your just and upright character, you revive the fact that sometime ago I expressed the same purpose to you; and, in reminding me of this you profer for my acceptance one of the highest diplomatic positions in your gift; an additional mark of your confidence and esteem.

In retiring from the War Dept. I feel that the mighty army of the U. S. is ready to do battle for the Constitution; that it is marshalled by gallant and experienced leaders; that it is fired with the greatest enthusiasm for the good cause, and also that my successor in this dept. is my personal friend, who unites to wonderful intellect and vigor, the grand essentials of being in earnest in the present struggle, and of being resolved upon a speedy and overwhelming triumph of our arms. I therefore gratefully accept the new distinction you have conferred upon me and as soon as important and long neglected private business has been arranged I will enter upon the important duties of the Mission to which you have called me.

> I have the honor to be my dear sir,
> Your obedient and humble servant,
> Simon Cameron[71]

Whether or not Cameron's resignation was forced, it proved to be, publicly at least, a debatable question. At first the public accepted the act as a voluntary change. According to his mouthpiece, the Harrisburg *Telegraph*, he had "long" determined to retire. Four years later Alexander McClure's *Repository* was revealing its secret history, the story of Chase delivering Lincoln's sudden notice of the Russian appointment. The major moving force, contended McClure, had been a group of powerful New York financiers, who were frightened by the nation's financial plight and looked upon the War Secretary's removal as a means toward restoring public confidence.[72]

Although Cameron sometimes contradicted himself on the question of a voluntary resignation, he consistently insisted to his dying day that his proposal to arm Negroes

---

[71] Cameron to Lincoln (copy) Jan. 11 [*sic*], 1862, Cameron MSS, LC.

[72] Chambersburg *Franklin Repository*, July 19, 1865.

prepared the way for his departure. In 1870 a controversy raged over contradictory articles by Jeremiah Black in the *Galaxy* and by Henry Wilson in the *Atlantic Monthly* concerning Secretary Stanton's appointment. The debate came to include the question of Cameron's resignation. In rebuttal to Black's contention of Cameron's dismissal by Lincoln, Wilson massed evidence to show the Secretary of War had voluntarily resigned and named his successor. An interesting round of letters by Simon Cameron, Montgomery Blair, Salmon P. Chase, and Benjamin F. Wade, found in the James M. Cameron collection, center around this controversy.

Chase, who supposed himself well informed on the case, "certainly never imagined that there was anything like removal" and vouched for the correctness of Wilson's views. Benjamin Wade had heard Cameron, in the presence of Chandler and Stanton, state his "determination to resign" and remembered Stanton's willingness to accept the post if it were offered. Montgomery Blair likewise recalled Cameron's expressed wish to resign in favor of a foreign mission. Lincoln's chief dissatisfaction with his Secretary of War, believed Blair, was the ascendancy which Chase exercised over him. Cameron, confessing little personal interest in the debate, was very anxious to see the history of the period "vindicated." [73]

Jeremiah Black in conjunction with his ally, Alexander McClure, could muster only two cabinet members, Welles and Bates, who believed Lincoln forced the resignation.

[73] Chase to Wilson, May 25, 1870; Chase to Cameron, July 4, 1870; B. F. Wade to Wilson, June 18, 1870; M. Blair to A. K. McClure (copy), Sept. 29, 1870; M. Blair to Cameron, Sept. 29, 1870; Cameron to Chase (copy) June 23, 1870; Crippen notes from the J. M. Cameron Papers.

Bates, while not considering Cameron strong, did "believe him an honest and faithful man." [74]

Shortly after his return from Russia, when Cameron believed that Seward would soon leave Lincoln's official family, he reminded Chase: "*I* needed no second whisper to induce me to give place to another." In 1862, upon Lincoln's pronouncement of his preliminary Emancipation Proclamation, the jubilant Cameron wrote: "Well hurrah for Lincoln and the Emancipation Proclamation with the use of Black troops after the War Minister was deposed for the recommendation." [75]

In company with Seward, McClellan, and Chase, the retiring War Secretary claimed the distinction of having determined his successor, Edwin M. Stanton. At any rate the public generally agreed with Lincoln's secretary, J. G. Nicolay, that a change in the direction of the War Department was needed. To date, concluded Nicolay, the department had "substantially taken care of itself." [76]

[74] Bates, *Diary*, 227; Welles, *Diary*, I, 58.
[75] Cameron to Chase, Dec. 24, 1862, Sept. [?] 1862, Chase MSS, HSP.
[76] M. Blair to A. K. McClure (copy), Sept. 29, 1870, Crippen note from J. M. Cameron Papers; J. G. Nicolay to Therena [Bates], Jan. 14, 1862, Nicolay MSS, LC.

7
The Way Back

THE YEARS 1862, 1863, AND 1864 CONSTITUTE A PERIOD OF shameful censure, "exile," a political defeat, and, finally, rehabilitation for Simon Cameron. He would need to fight his way back during an era when control of the state administration lay in the hands of the Curtin-McClure faction and when the Democratic opposition was registering suprising gains. Wisely, Simon Cameron chose the Lincoln way and so well did he succeed that by 1864 no one contested his right to call himself the "President's man" in Pennsylvania. To aid him in his quest for recovery of his lost prestige, two factors played an important role; the magic of his name as a dispenser of patronage retained its effectiveness and his alleged martyrdom for the cause of emancipation and the armed freedmen transformed him into a darling of the Radicals.

The advantages of Simon Cameron's promotion to the Radical vanguard were apparent the same day Lincoln nominated him for the Russian mission. Charles Sumner, grieved by Lincoln's personal confirmation of his order to delete a portion of the secretary of war's December "Report," rose in the Senate to move unanimous confirmation without committee action—thereby provoking a bitter three-day struggle. Republican Lyman Trumbull, leader of the opposition, branding the nomination a whitewash to disguise the true character of an unworthy servant, argued that the ultimate purpose was intended to assist Cameron's Senatorial ambitions. The charges leveled at the ex-Secretary, contended the Radicals, Henry Wilson, Charles Sumner, Benjamin Wade, Zachariah Chandler, and W. P. Fessenden, were "without just foundation." Although the nomination was confirmed behind barred doors on January 17, 28 to 14, seven Republican dissenters (granted permission to do so in the secret executive session of the Senate) proudly and publicly announced their stand. The true source of the unusual debate over a confirmation, suggested the Philadelphia *Evening Bulletin*, was Cameron's "unpardonable sin" of advocating the use of armed blacks and emancipation.[1]

Doubtless, following his withdrawal from the cabinet, Cameron had hoped that the charges of corruption associated with his regime would wither away and die, but the worst was yet to come. While the Senate was pondering over the Russian mission, the House was listening to a tirade of Henry L. Dawes, charging the former secretary with corruption in recent army contracts. In response to Sumner's prodding, Cameron sent the Senate a note explaining that bureau heads had negotiated for all contracts; he had made none. Dawes countered with

---

[1] Sumner, *Memoirs*, IV, 63; Browning, *Diary*, I, 524-25; White, *Trumbull*, 187-89; Philadephia *Bulletin*, Jan. 20, 1862; Senate *Executive Journal*, XII, 87.

official records showing Cameron contracts for almost two million muskets, while the chief of ordnance had contracted for only 64,000. Moreover, the War Secretary had overruled an ordnance rejection of a contract and authorized it after his notice of resignation.

Verily, Cameron's chickens had come home to roost. Early in his capacity as Secretary of War, he had written: ". . . after having tried to serve every one, I shall probably go home as much cursed as poor miserable Buchanan . . . such is patronage." [2]

Simon Cameron's departure to Russia was delayed until May. The future minister was busy putting many business affairs in order, in arranging for staff personnel, in defending his recent cabinet record against an increasing tempo of criticism, engaging in litigation with Pierce Butler, and angling for a political maneuver which would allow him to remain in the country.

When Cameron had left the Senate to enter Lincoln's Cabinet he had offered no opposition to David Wilmot's succession, although earlier he had shelved Wilmot for Edgar Cowan. In February, 1862, encouraged by friends, he made inquiries, hoping to have Wilmot sent on a mission to Russia or Spain thereby making it possible for him to re-enter the senate. Such a move, contended Cameron, would have the effect of bolstering the Peoples' Party—which he considered in "a bad condition"—in the coming fall elections. Although under Cameron's urging, Wilmot apparently "warmed up" to the idea, the switch received no encouragement from Republican members of the state legislature. In addition, rumor had it that

[2] White, *Trumbull*, 188-89; Cameron to B. H. Brewster, Savidge, *Life of Brewster*, 97.

Lincoln opposed the move. By March 1, Cameron was resigned to the idea of going to Russia.[3]

The suit of secessionist sympathizer Pierce Butler of
South Carolinian birth caused the former War Secretary
much embarrassment. When Cameron visited Philadelphia on April 15, Butler arrested him for alleged false
imprisonment occurring in August, 1861. Cameron's
counsel, Benjamin H. Brewster, immediately petitioned
Seward for federal remedies. State attorney-general William Meredith and Governor Curtin studied the constitutional aspects of the case to see if the proceedings could
be suppressed. Meredith's recommendation of a federal
"Act of Indemity" was transmitted to two powerful friends
of Cameron, Secretary Chase and Benjamin Wade.
Lincoln promptly presented the case to Congress. Butler
dropped the proceedings in May.[4]

Cameron's successful confirmation to the Russian mission engendered renewed efforts by his enemies to
discredit his past secretarial administration. Two commissioners appointed by Secretary Stanton to "audit and
adjust" certain types of pending claims on the War Department began work on March 17 but not until July 1,
1862, was the results of its labor, the damaging Holt-
Owens "Report," made public. But a Congressional Committee on Contracts, working overtime, soon completed
its inquiry, including a clause condemning the regime of

[3] Cameron to S. P. Chase, Feb. 11, 1862, Salmon P. Chase
Papers, HSP; Cameron to Judge Harris, Feb. 6, 1862, S. Gratz
Autograph Collection, HSP; Stanton L. Davis, *Pennsylvania Politics*
(Cleveland, 1935), 227.

[4] Frank Moore, ed., *The Rebellion Record* (11 vols., New York,
1861-63), IV, 89; Meredith to Cameron, April 20, 1862, Meredith
to Seward, May 2, 1862, Chase MSS, HSP; Richardson, *Messages*,
VI, 1899.

Cameron. On the same day, April 30, the House promptly accepted the report and passed a resolution of censure against Simon Cameron, scoring his past administration of the War Department. Two of his acts, "highly injurious to the public service," were noted: the authority granted Alexander Cummings to handle huge sums of money for military purchasing without proper guaranties; and the granting of contracts to persons not "legitimately" engaged in such business. The censure contained no charge that the former secretary had overstepped his authority or that he had profited personally through fraudulent transactions.[5]

Only two days following his censure, Cameron found the opportunity, in a public declamation, to answer the charges, and he made the most of it. Before 150 guests seated at an extremely elaborate farewell dinner given in his honor at the Jones House in Harrisburg, the former Secretary of War, during the course of a lengthy harangue broken by frequent responses, defended himself, by the aid of germane documents, ably and vigorously. The moment in question had been one of national emergency, requiring immediate action and brooking no delay. The purchasing authority granted Alexander Cummings and his colleagues had been terminated at the end of two weeks. He had given no one authority to draw money— that request had been properly referred to the treasury department. And the *cause célèbre* of the Congressional charges, the Herman Boker transaction, had first been initiated by Lincoln and accompanied with the President's personal endorsement.

[5] *Official Records,* Series III, Vol. II, 188-95; *Cong. Globe,* 37 Cong., 2 Sess., 1888.

Before concluding, Cameron directed blasts against his leading Congressional tormentors, including Henry L. Dawes and Charles Van Wyck, the revengeful souls, who were "ever besieging" his doors and who had waited patiently for hours for an opportunity to "catch a part of the drippings of the War Department." Dawes represented the Wilmington and Baltimore Railroad interests whose exorbitant transportation rates for soldiers he had scotched. The vindictive Van Wyck had been foiled in his effort to outfit a regiment early in the war.[6]

Simon Cameron, greatly pained at the injustice, as he saw it, suffered from the House censure, and embarrassed by rumors that Lincoln's administration had endorsed it, turned to his close friend Salmon P. Chase, requesting only the "simple truth from anyone in authority." Chase's response, indicating that he was proposing a public paper from Lincoln, furnished much comfort. Such an "act of justice" from the President, answered Cameron on the eve of his departure for Europe, "would silence the whole herd." [7]

Following a waiting period of three weeks, Secretary Seward, under Lincoln's direction and with cabinet approval, prepared a public apology in Cameron's defense. The message, addressed to both houses of Congress, reviewed in detail the emergency following the fall of Ft. Sumter. Lincoln had directed Cameron to grant the authorizations to Cummings and others without requiring financial guarantees and he had acted similarly with respect to the advance of public monies. If censure of the

---

[6] "Banquet to the Honorable Simon Cameron," Cameron MSS, LC; Harrisburg *Telegraph*, May 3, 5, 1862.

[7] Cameron to Chase, May 2, 7, 1862, Chase MSS, HSP.

former Secretary of War was in order, asserted the President, then Lincoln, together with all members of the cabinet, "were at least equally responsible." Although Lincoln did not contend that his Secretary of War had exercised his unusual authority wisely and efficiently, he did believe that the "effort to save" the Union being paramount, emergency measures were justified. Only three years later, William H. Seward could publicly "bear witness" that Cameron's administration had been "honest, correct, zealous, and patriotic." [8]

This humiliating nadir of Cameron's political career was not without its compensating factors. Many supporters, grateful for his past favors, sent expressions of loyalty and asserted their belief that he still retained the confidence of the Lincoln administration. Although numerous members of the People's Party openly rejoiced at his discomfiture, proclaiming his political demise, neither A. G. Curtin or A. K. McClure sought to humiliate him further. The governor invited him to attend a reception he was giving to members of the legislature and McClure expressed hope of enjoying "an hour's chat" with him before his departure.[9]

Following several delays, Cameron, accompanied by his wife and legation secretary, Bayard Taylor, sailed on the "Persia" for Liverpool on May 7. *Harper's Weekly*, *Leslie's Weekly*, and *Vanity Fair* joined in lampooning his "exile" to Russia. "In no good humor with many people,"

[8] Seward to Cameron, May 28, 1862, Cameron MSS, LC; Basler, *Works*, V, 240-41; Frederick W. Seward, *Seward at Washington, as Senator and Secreatry of State* (2 vols., New York, 1891), II, 298-99.

[9] Curtin to Cameron, April 10, 1862, McClure to Cameron, April 24, 1862, Cameron MSS, LC.

resulting from the verbal assaults and House censure, the former war secretary would have preferred to remain in the country to defend himself, but not wishing to forfeit his passage fares, he sailed with prophetic "faith in the right." [10]

Cameron's ten days in Britain were occupied with business affairs, shopping, attending social functions, and in a hasty study in genealogical research. Diplomatic protocol and the dread of the coming Russian winter necessitated the purchase of a brigadier-general's frock coat, a silk dress coat with matching trousers, and a great beaver coat totaling about £20. Henry Adams, son of his dinner host, Charles Francis Adams, desired to see his father's guest, "the whited sepulchre," disappear into the vastness of Russia, there to "wander for eternity." [11]

Cameron had hoped to establish his descent from Donald Cameron, the "Gentle Lochiel," chief of the highlander Clan Cameron—staunch supporter of the Stuart cause. His resemblance to the heroic family, remarked a London expert on Scottish clans, was "obvious." Such identification moved John Bigelow to remark: "Poor Lochiel." [12]

The serpentine route to Russia via England, France, Belgium, Holland, and Germany afforded the new minister much pleasant sight-seeing and some opportunity to gauge public opinion abroad. At Paris he particularly

[10] Cameron to Chase, May 3, 1862, Chase MSS, HSP; Cameron to Lincoln, May 5, 1862, Lincoln MSS; Philadelphia *Evening Bulletin*, May 7, 1862.

[11] Items of expenditure, May, 1862, Cameron MSS, LC; Worthington C. Ford, ed., *A Cycle of Adams Letters* (2 vols., Boston, 1920), I, 153.

[12] John Bigelow, *Retrospections of An Active Life* (5 vols., New York, 1909-13), I, 493.

enjoyed seeing the emperor's 230 horses stabled at the Tuileries. In Western Europe apparently only a few men of "distinction" favored the Union cause, but in Berlin it was different. The last leg of the journey, a rail ride from Konigsberg, East Prussia, to St. Petersburg, ended on June 15.[13]

The first ten days of Cameron's stay in Russia were occupied in getting settled, reading the accumulated mail, writing accounts of his trip, sightseeing, and in preparation for his Court presentation. Reluctantly he occupied the house vacated by Cassius M. Clay. The annual rent of $3,000 he found in line with other prices in Russia—much too expensive. In spite of the fact that his first mail told him of Lincoln's defense in the Cummings case, he expressed his determination to secure an early furlough in order to defend himself at home. Prince Alexander Gorchakov, the Czar's leading statesman, received him graciously and explained the cause of the emperor's prolonged absence from the capital.[14]

On June 25, Clay, the retiring diplomat, presented the new minister to Alexander II. The interview proved to be most gratifying. After congratulating the emperor on his efforts in behalf of Russia's serfs, Cameron thanked him for his "prompt and cordial sympathy" to the United States in its efforts to end the rebellion. He believed that his country and Russia constituted the only great powers whose friendship "could never be disturbed by rival interests." His sympathies, responded the Czar, were "always" with United States because the interests of the

[13] Cameron to J. D. Cameron, June 2, 1862, Cameron MSS, LC; Cameron to Chase, June 20, 1862, Chase MSS, HSP.

[14] Cameron to Chase, June 20, 1862, *ibid.*; Cameron to B. F. Butler, June 23, 1862, Butler, *Correspondence*, I, 631-32.

two nations were in many respects identical. A half
hour's pleasant conversation followed formalities. In
Clay's opinion, the new minister's performance was a sorry
one. Not only had he interrupted Alexander's recognition
address; he had exhibited coarseness hardly tolerable in
the house of a Pennsylvania backwoods "Dutchman." [15]

Bayard Taylor, the legation secretary, was in a jovial
mood. The noted author and journalist had accepted the
subordinate position only because he expected to succeed
shortly to the important ministerial post. His facile pen
gave needed literary forte to Cameron's official communications and served (so he believed) to establish his
capabilities with the Secretary of State. By the end of
June, Taylor had enjoyed a round of receptions, dinners,
and tours complete with all the trappings of royalty, carriages, footmen, fine liqueurs and cigars.[16]

Diplomatically, the period of Cameron's mission to
Russia was one of the most crucial in our history.
Napoleon III, Emperor of the French, was waiting only
for Britain to take the first step toward full recognition of
the Confederacy and eventual intervention, before following in her train. The restraining influence of a powerful Russia in such a crisis counted for much. Certainly
Lincoln recognized the importance of a firm stand by the
Czar's government and there is evidence that Cameron
conveyed a special personal message from the President

[15] Cameron to Seward, June 26, 1862, *Papers Relating to Foreign Affairs, Executive Documents*, 37 Cong., 3 Sess., Vol. I, 447-
48; Cassius M. Clay, *Life, Memoirs, Writings, and Speeches* (Cincinnati, 1886), I, 300.

[16] Taylor to R. H. Stoddard, July 1, 1862, Horace E. Scudder,
The Life and Letters of Bayard Taylor (2 vols., Boston, 1884), I,
387-88.

on the subject. Reputedly, Alexander replied that in case of European interference, "the friendship of Russia for United States will be known in a decisive manner, which no other nation will be able to mistake." [17]

Several weeks later, when rumors of coming French intervention were current on the continent, the minister sought reassurances from Prince Gorchacov. His answer was emphatic; Russian sentiments had not changed. The proposed Berlin Conference of Sovereigns would find United States with a friend in attendance.[18]

Cameron had waited impatiently for two weeks following his arrival at St. Petersburg for the moment when he could, with propriety, apply for a leave of absence. On June 26, the day following his official acceptance at the czar's court, he wrote his first letters to Seward and the President. Both dispatches included a request for an immediate furlough. Appropriately, the minister began his letter to Lincoln with a note of thanks for the President's apology in his defense: "It was a good act, bravely done . . . very many men, in your situation, would have permitted an innocent man to suffer rather than incur responsibility." Cameron's final phrase on the subject was prophetic: "At all events, I can assure you that I will never cease to be grateful for it." [19]

The chief reason for the new minister's anxiety to leave Russia at once is not difficult for a student of his political career to fathom. Allegedly he desired to return because

---

[17] A. S. Draper in James M. Callahan, *Russo-American Relations During the Civil War*, West Virginia University *Studies in American History*, Series I, Vol. I (Morgantown, 1908), 4.

[18] Cameron to Seward, Aug. 19, 1862, *Executive Documents*, Vol. I, 37 Cong., 3 Sess., 445.

[19] *Ibid.*, 454; Cameron to Lincoln, June 26, 1862, Lincoln MSS.

of the coming rigorous Russian winter, his wife's poor health, his desire to seek vindication, and finally the hope that his appearance in Pennsylvania might not be too late to assist in stemming the Democratic tide currently engulfing the state prior to the state elections.

To a master politico who had only recently succeeded in welding a powerful political machine through the loyalty of hundreds of clients, it was unthinkable that such a headless hierarchy could long survive his absence. His future political career, to a large extent, depended largely upon his ability to salvage the deteriorating machine in the near future.

Upon receipt of Cameron's first dispatch Secretary Seward had not felt at "liberty" to grant the furlough. The minister determined, if there were no strong objections, to accompany his ailing wife the whole way to America. Upon arrival he would resign. In the meantime he renewed his plea for a leave and urged his son and Secretary Chase to use their influence in his behalf. The news of the furlough granted on September 6 did not reach him until his arrival in Geneva on October 10. His tortuous path to Liverpool led him through Vienna, Geneva, Rome, Paris, London, and Edinburgh. The minister's travels over a period of three months had cost £3000, a sum in excess of his annual salary of $12,000.[20]

In the Cameron collection of the Library of Congress there is an interesting "Diary," probably the work of Mrs. Cameron, recording the family trip from St. Petersburg to Liverpool. In Paris, it notes, her husband, a devout

[20] Cameron to J. Donald Cameron, Aug. 16, 1862, Cameron MSS, LC; Cameron to Chase, Aug. 16, 18, Oct. 11, 1862, Chase MSS, HSP; *Executive Documents*, Vol. I, 37 Cong., 3 Sess., 454-55, 459; Baring Brothers, "Statement of Credit," Cameron MSS, LC.

Presbyterian, visited the grave of John Calvin, and plucked a few roses from it to be pressed and preserved. A significant note testifying to the minister's character is the statement of Mrs. William E. Wright, granddaughter of Simon Cameron, that her grandfather had refused many valuable gifts while in St. Petersburg, saying "it would not be honorable for a minister to accept gifts under the circumstances."[21]

Immediate acceptance of the lately ostracized Russian minister by powerful party men was a most encouraging omen. A reception committee had been organized to meet him in New York and letters from many supporters including greetings from James G. Blaine, John W. Forney, and Salmon P. Chase poured in shortly after his arrival at his country estate, Lochiel, on November 8, 1862. His future, he wrote to Clay, would be determined after a visit to Washington.

Although a candidate for the Senate in January, 1863, the minister to Russia could see no impropriety in retaining his post. In Washington, enemies of Cassius Clay, fearful of his entrance into the Lincoln Cabinet, were pressing for Cameron's resignation in order to rid themselves of Clay. At Lincoln's request he visited the White House on December 14 and had two Presidential interviews during January, 1863, but the matter dragged on for two months until Lincoln peremptorily demanded a decision. On February 23, 1863, in the midst of the embarrassing inquiry of the Pennsylvania House of Representatives into the methods of his Senatorial candidacy, Cameron tendered his resignation to Lincoln. Not only

[21] Mrs. William E. Wright to Lee F. Crippen, Nov. 29, 1940, in possession of writer.

was concern for his family's health a compelling factor in his decision; he was also "activated by a strong desire once more to mingle with his countrymen," and to use all his energy "in every measure essential to the overthrow of a conspiracy." He gave assurances of continued support for the Lincoln administration. If given the power to do so, he would not recall one recommendation offered during his cabinet tenure. This last remark, clearly a slap at the President, referred to his altered report on arming of the slaves.[22]

Selection of his successor was one patronage package Cameron could not deliver. When Bayard Taylor was offered the position of legation secretary the proffer included a bonus: "if I should not return I can manage to give you my place." However when Cassius M. Clay left Russia, Lincoln promised him that if Cameron voluntarily resigned his new post, Clay, if he so desired, could return. Now the erratic Clay, as early as September 6, was heckling Cameron to carry out his promise of an early resignation so he might return to Russia. Immediately following Cameron's resignation, Lincoln nominated Clay for his place. Bayard Taylor expressed his wrath with a political sonnet, "A Statesman," starring chief eunuch William H. Seward.[23]

In order to attain complete political rehabilitation,

[22] Lincoln to Cameron, Dec. 14, 1862, Cameron MSS, DCC, Feb. 13, 1863, Cameron MSS, LC; Cameron to Lincoln, Feb. 23, 1863, Lincoln MSS, LC.

[23] Taylor & Scudder, *Life and Letters*, 384; Clay to Cameron, Sept. 6, 1862, Cameron MSS, LC; Judge Casey to J. D. Cameron, Nov. 3, 1862, Cameron MSS, DCC; Lincoln to Clay, Aug. 12, 1862, Lincoln Collection, Lincoln Memorial University; Basler, *Works*, VI, 103-04. Bayard Taylor's parents of Maytown were well acquainted with the Cameron family.

Simon Cameron.

Margaretta Brua Cameron.

Virginia Cameron MacVeagh.

Rachel Cameron Burnside.

James Donald Cameron.

The Donegal Mansion.

Cameron Memorial, Maytown Reformed Church.

Simon Cameron would need to acquire high office, preferably on the national level, to maintain an imposing patronage, and to secure control of the state Republican organization within the state. Pennsylvania would select a United States Senator in January, 1863, to succeed David Wilmot, but a Democratic majority of one vote in the state legislature apparently barred him from that office. Governor Andrew G. Curtin, his strongest opponent within the party, was likely to seek a renomination in 1863, and his supporters argued that only he could stem the Democratic resurgence of 1862.

Lincoln, well aware of Cameron's ability to execute well-nigh impossible political coups, hoped to maintain friendly relations with the strategist, but could not afford the risk of readmitting him into his official family. The December of 1862, in spite of warm seasonal greetings from numerous adherents, portended only a bleak outlook for the fallen warrior.

While in Russia, the minister had written that in "no event" would he compete with David Wilmot for the Senate if the incumbent wished to succeed himself. For him, "his course was run." Ample time for reflection had lessened his desire to return to public life; he had plans only for a comfortable life at Lochiel while at the same time giving his country his "ardent support in all its efforts to crush out the rebellion." But the hopelessness of Wilmot's candidacy against a Democratic legislative majority, the necessity for his speedy rehabilitation, a genuine desire to serve his country, urgent appeals for actions from numerous followers, and encouragement from powerful leaders of his party contributed to his decision, made only a few days after his return home, to try for the Senatorship in the hope of appeasing Wilmot with a judgeship.[24]

Lincoln's Emancipation Proclamation had changed Cameron's status from an obnoxious radical to that of a prophetic seer. "At length the President and Governor Seward have come to the position," Chase reminded Cameron, that "we occupied a year ago." James G. Blaine believed that Pennsylvania would again call the fallen Secretary of War to a "position of high honor." John W. Forney took the initiative in secretly promoting his senatorial candidacy. "Honest John" Covode invited 40 Pennsylvanians to a dinner in Cameron's honor. "We want to hear from Simon Cameron, our old war horse," cried the uncouth host. A long harangue enumerating the virtues of the Republican party constituted the response. On December 15, he gave another address before the Soldiers Relief Association.

The Cameron forces followed the strategy of pretending that Wilmot was certain to be the party's candidate while, at the same time, Democratic votes were being solicited secretly for their man. There was no argument for substituting Cameron for Wilmot at the eleventh hour unless party leaders were satisfied that he could win. At a secret meeting of a select caucus committee, Cameron gave assurances, if all Republican members supported him, that he could secure the needed Democratic votes. There was a chance that a member of the Curtin-McClure faction or a disgruntled Wilmot disciple might bolt his nomination.

[24] Cameron to Chase, Aug. 16, 18, 1862, Chase MSS, HSP; B. H. Brewster to Cameron, Nov. 12, 1862, Cameron MSS, DCC; Savidge, *Brewster*, 97, 99.

Several of Cameron's friends sent him advice on procedures for capturing Democratic votes and listed legislators they considered amenable to pressure. One of his early moves was to request Stanton through Chase to hold up several pending appointments slated for Pennsylvania "for the reason that two or more men, who have votes, are seeking such places for friends; and . . . it is believed that the gratitude of politicians is prospective."[25]

A seasoned veteran of political strategy, Cameron would not have gambled his political future on the promise of only *one* Democratic vote. One Democrat, without a doubt, selected for bargaining was Dr. T. Jefferson Boyer, a state representative from Clearfield. Cameron requested J. Laurence Rightmeyer, treasurer of the North Central Railroad, to contact John C. Myers of Kensington, a close personal friend of Boyer. After completing work on his ship, replied Colonel Myers to Rightmeyer, he would "go to work for Simon—God bless him," and see Boyer when he visited Reading. Rightmeyer also promised to assist in securing Boyer's vote. Under oath Boyer later testified that the bargain included $10,000 in cash and a paymastership in the army. Later the alleged offer was raised to $20,000. Democratic Representative Nelson of Wayne County, reported C. S. Minor, had promised his vote to Cameron. To insure Cameron's election, however, Minor recommended "two strings in the bow." Privately Cameron considered his election doubtful without the backing of Wilmot because his "democratic friends"

[25] Chase to Cameron, Nov. 16, 1862; Forney to Cameron, Nov. 2, 15, 1862; Blaine to Cameron, Nov. 24, 1862, Cameron MSS, DCC; Usher, *Lincoln's Cabinet*, 18; Philadelphia *Bulletin*, Dec. 18, 1862; Cameron to Chase, Dec. 4, 1862, Chase MSS, HSP.

would be afraid to risk themselves if apparently the Republicans were not harmonious.[26]

On January 12, each party held its nominating caucus. The Democrats chose James Buckalew but the Republicans (Unionists), having decided to shelve Wilmot, purposely delayed the nomination until the next morning so they could present a surprise candidate. Two Cameron organs, the Philadelphia *Press* and Pittsburgh *Gazette*, predicted Wilmot's nomination.

The Democrats were not fooled. For some time they had anticipated Cameron's nomination and were busy making preparations for any exigency. A gang of hoodlums, armed with pistols and knives, were transported from Philadelphia for the purpose of keeping all Democratic members in line. No traitor to the Democratic Party, predicted its leaders, would leave the House alive. There would be no repeat performances of the elections of 1845 and 1857 when Cameron had snatched the Senatorial prize from majority party candidates. Cameron's pleas to the Curtin administration for protection from intimidation fell on deaf ears.

The Senatorial election of January 13, 1863, according to many witnesses, was breathtaking. The Senatorial roll was called first. When the first Republican, Senator Boughter, voted for Cameron, excitement mounted. This first intimation of his candidacy signified pledged Democratic support for the Republicans. However, every member of the legislature except Bartholomew Laporte, a

---

[26] John C. Meyers to Dear Larry [Rightmeyer], Nov. 24, 1862, J. Laurence Rightmeyer to Cameron, Nov. 26, 1862, C. S. Minor to Cameron, Jan. 3, 1863, Cameron MSS, DCC; Cameron to S. P. Chase, Jan. 7, 1863, Chase MSS, HSP; "Report of the Committee on Frauds," 1863, PSL.

Republican, voted for his party's candidate. Albert Schofield, a Democrat, announced that a vote for Buckalew, and the preservation of electoral integrity, was worth more than the enormous sum of $100,000—the amount he hinted had been offered him. The final vote tallied 67 for Buckalew, 65 for Cameron and one for William D. Kelley. "For once," quipped the prejudiced Meadville *Crawford Democrat*, Cameron's money had failed.[27]

The true reasons for Cameron's defeat are not easy to fathom. The public believed that the potential Democratic defectors, fearful for their lives, dared not to bolt their party's nomination. Cameron, writing immediately to both Lincoln and Chase placed the onus of failure upon David Wilmot: ". . . my election *was certain* but Mr. La Part [*sic*], the friend of Wilmost . . . voted for Judge Kelly [*sic*] and thereby alarmed the gentlemen of the democratic party whose names [Nelson?] comes after his." Apparently Cameron had not really expected Boyer to vote for him. On the other hand he had assured the secret caucus committee that a House Democratic vote would come within the first half dozen. Boyer was number five. Both Colonel Myers and Rightmeyer were "overwhelmed" by the "drama of treachery" dealt their chieftain. "Our man [Boyer]," stated Myers, "was overawed by threats for his life." [28]

[27] Pittsburgh *Gazette*, Jan. 13, 14, 16, 1863; Philadelphia *Press*, Jan. 13, 14, 1863; McClure, *Notes*, II, 30-34; Penna. *Legislative Record*, 1863, 26-27; *Journal of the Senate*, 1863, 50.

[28] Cameron to Lincoln, Jan. 13, 1863, Lincoln MSS, LC; Cameron to S. P. Chase, Jan. 12, 1863, Chase MSS, HSP; Myers to Larry [Rightmeyer], Jan. 19, 1863, Rightmeyer to Cameron, Jan. 21, 1863, Cameron MSS, DCC.

Two interesting sequels are attached to the drama of treachery. Cameron asked his man, C. A. Walborn, postmaster of Philadelphia, the following question: "Can you tell me why it was that our friend Milward [sic] was not in the House that day, as you said he would be. From that came all the blunder." William Millward was the United States marshal for the eastern district of the state with headquarters in Philadelphia. According to A. K. McClure, Cameron never stood a chance to win. Four Unionists had secretly pledged themselves, if necessary, to vote against him, in order to prevent the "stain of a corrupt election." Laporte was one of the four. If this is true, Wilmot was innocent as charged.[29]

To add to the bitterness of defeat, Simon Cameron soon found himself the central target of a political scandal involving the charge of bribery, the end result of which could mean his personal destruction. A Democratic House majority appointed a special committee to investigate the recent Senatorial election. The committee began work without delay. According to the testimony of four witnesses, Boyer met Cameron at the State Capitol Bank; others agreed that Cameron visited Boyer in his hotel room. William Brobst, the liaison man, confirmed the interviews but claimed no money was involved. There was no intention, testified Jefferson Boyer, of accepting a bribe; he pretended his willingness in order to prevent the debauching of other Democrats. Cameron's statement

[29] Cameron to Walborn, Jan. 30, 1863, Society Autograph Collection, HSP; McClure, *Notes*, II, 32. In 1870 Millward confessed to having accepted a sizeable sum from a candidate's father in 1862 for having secured a West Point appointment. See Harrisburg *Telegraph*, March 9, 1870.

that Boyer approached him first conflicts with the evidence of the Myers-Rightmeyer letters.

The committee completed its work in less than three months. During the 43 sessions, 36 witnesses were heard. The Democratic majority report definitely concluded "that unlawful means were employed to secure the election of Simon Cameron." The three Unionist-Republican committee members scored Boyer and Buckalew for "leading Cameron on." The House of Representatives accepted the committee's resolution and directed the state's attorney-general to prosecute Cameron, Boyer, and others for bribery.[30]

In his hour of distress, the accused politico turned to the despised Curtin-McClure faction of the party for aid. With the Democrats in the ascendancy and a critical gubernatorial election on the horizon, the Unionist Party dared not risk the condemnation of any of its outstanding political figures. That men of all parties were frequently guilty of engaging in questionable political bargaining no one doubted. To the Democrats, reasoned the Unionist-Republicans, the Cameronian sacrificial goat which they so freely offered up upon the altar of electoral sanctity, was only a partisan device to seize control of the Commonwealth and to hinder the war effort.

A. K. McClure claimed he urged Attorney-General William M. Meredith, whose respected name had strengthened the ailing Curtin administration, not to prosecute Cameron "if he could do so consistently." Omitting comment on McClure's plea, Meredith replied: "I wonder that it did not occur to you to say to General Cameron

[30] "Report of the Committee on Frauds," 1863, PSL; Pittsburgh *Gazette*, April 15, 1863.

that the attorney general of the state had vastly more important duties to perform than to prosecute cases in quarter sessions." [31] No legal action followed and the directive remains on the *Journal* of the House only as a memorial to a notorious political scandal.

The way back for Cameron during the Lincoln years was not simply one of leading the Unionists to victory over the Democrats. Even his Senatorial defeat in 1863 was attributed to members of his own party. The chief contest was between factions of the Republican Party, neither of which could afford to be satisfied with anything less than complete victory. Only a rising Democratic tide could temporarily force the Cameronian camp to work harmoniously with the Curtin-McClure faction. Personal animosities which had their beginnings in 1855 engendered the ferocity of the struggle. Each faction, ever distrustful of opposition members, were loathe to be associated with them in public office. The danger of such a course was strikingly illustrated in the case of Curtin's first attorney-general, Samuel Purviance, the outcome of which almost torpedoed the new governor's administration.

As a concession to the Cameron faction for its contribution to his gubernatorial victory, Andrew Curtin had consented to accept temporarily Samuel Purviance, a leading Western Pennsylvania Cameron lieutenant, into his cabinet. At the end of 1861, it was understood, Purviance would resign the office of attorney-general in favor of Senator Darwin A. Finney. At first Purviance believed he could prevail upon Curtin to retain him but by May he was convinced he would be forced from his post. The

[31] McClure, *Notes*, I, 523-24.

revengeful Purviance chose to resign abruptly, successfully convincing a large part of the public that his resignation was in protest against the corruption of the Curtin
administration, at that time under fire because of the
shoddy equipment furnished Pennsylvania's volunteers.
Purviance's resignation, which the governor first learned
from the Harrisburg *Telegraph,* mentioned reasons which
appealed to his "self respect." The account was widely
circulated in the Cameron and Democratic organs. Even
the neutral Philadelphia *Inquirer* swallowed the story. In
desperation the Curtin men appealed to the highly respected William M. Meredith, former Secretary of the
Treasury under Taylor, to bolster the wobbly state administration. Although in poor health, Meredith was persuaded to accept the vacancy created by Purviance, and
soon restored confidence.[32]

In the spring of 1863 Cameron had visions of being
able to name the next gubernatorial candidate of the
Unionists. Early in the year he had expressed his determination to block Curtin's renomination—now suddenly
it looked as if fate had granted him victory without a
struggle. The governor's extremely poor health, it was
believed, would make it suicidal for him to accept another
strenuous term. A. K. McClure, John W. Forney, and
Cameron joined in making it possible for Curtin to retire
gracefully. Following a visit from the trio, Lincoln on
April 13, 1863 promised in writing, if he were still in
office, to tender Curtin a first-class diplomatic post at the
conclusion of the governor's term. Curtin thanked the
President, transmitted the news to the legislature, and

[32] *Ibid.,* 514-19; Purviance to Cameron, Feb. 7, 1861, Cameron
MSS, DCC; Philadelphia *Inquirer,* May 25, 1861.

announced the withdrawal of his gubernatorial candidacy.[33]

Much to Cameron's chagrin, popular demand for Curtin's renomination continued to pour in from all parts of the state, and even his own lieutenants privately conceded the governor's strength. In the meantime the Democrats rejected the nomination of General William B. Franklin, a gallant Democratic soldier whom Curtin felt that all loyal men would support. Postponement of the Unionist state convention, Curtin's frequent public appearances, the governor's known popularity with the soldiers, and finally, popular conviction that only the governor could defeat the Democratic candidate, George W. Woodward, convinced Cameron (weeks before Curtin himself had made a decision) that the governor would consent to a renomination.

Early in June Cameron made plans to block Curtin's candidacy. To C. A. Walborn he wrote: ". . . Curtin is in his true character of cheating. You and others of the delegates can *check mate* him." Knowing the animosity existing between Secretary of War Stanton and Curtin, he believed that the Lincoln administration would "not meddle" in his favor. He surmised correctly; the President, not wishing to become involved in the factional disputes, had decided to leave the Union men of Pennsylvania to their "own good judgment." [34]

When the Union State Convention met at Pittsburgh on August 5, the Cameron forces, led by G. V. Lawrence, Walborn, and the notorious Alexander Cummings, in con-

[33] S. Fuller to Covode, Jan. 18, 1863, Covode MSS, WPHS; McClure, *Lincoln and Men of Wartimes*, 242-45; Basler, *Works*, VI, 170.

[34] Cameron to C. A. Walborn, June 2, 1863, Society Autograph Collection, HSP; Chase to B. H. Brewster, June 9, 1863, Cameron MSS, LC.

junction with the Pittsburgh group, which was hostile to
Curtin because of his railroad policies, planned to defeat
the governor's renomination by first supporting the radical John Covode and then to withdraw his name in the
interest of party harmony, hoping thereby to coalesce
enough sentiment to force Curtin's withdrawal. This
would clear the way for the nomination of H. D. Moore,
the Cameron candidate, or possibly a Pittsburgh man.
After Covode withdrew, Cummings delivered a powerful
anti-Curtin address contending that the governor could
not secure the support of his own party or the office
holders. But the conviction of many lukewarm delegates
that only Curtin could lead the party to victory gave him
the nomination easily on the first ballot. Neither McClure
in his voluminous writings nor Wayne MacVeagh in his
article, "Curtin Re-elected Governor," reveals the determined fight of the anti-Curtin group. A total of 36 delegates voted against him.[35]

During the gubernatorial campaign of 1863, Cameron
appeared publicly several times in support of his ancient
enemy. At Harrisburg, September 19, before introducing
the speaker, General B. F. Butler, he appealed for the
electorate's support of Curtin. The following day he wrote
in a sarcastic mood: "Hurrah! I presided at a Curtin meeting last night. Hurrah! . . . well hurrah for Lincoln and
the Emancipation Proclamation with the use of Black
troops after the War Minister was desposed for the recommendation! Hurrah! Hurrah!" Curtin defeated Woodward by 15,000 votes.[36]

Before the end of 1863, behind the scenes, political

[35] Harrisburg *Patriot*, Aug. 6, 1863; Pittsburgh *Gazette*, Aug. 6,
1863.
[36] McClure, *Notes*, II, 120; Cameron to Chase [Sept. 20, 1863],
Chase MSS, HSP.

circles were buzzing and speculating on the Presidential possibilities for 1864. That Lincoln faced defeat, if re-nominated, was a belief of many prominent Unionist leaders. Cameron's position was such that he could not afford to bet on the wrong horse in 1864 and, as it happened, his final decision was to become the most important factor in his successful comeback.

The radicalism of General Benjamin F. Butler together with the rigorous treatment he meted out to "traitors" during his New Orleans regime had caught the public's fancy, including many politicians. Butler, confided Cameron to a friend, belonged in Washington. When Cameron visited Lincoln on January 26, 1863, he protested on political grounds the suggestion of sending the general back to New Orleans. In the spring of 1863, he hinted to Butler of welcoming his candidacy because the next President would be a military man. The pompous general responded quickly; he was very desirous of exchanging views "on the subject" mentioned in Cameron's letter.[37] During the gubernatorial campaign of 1863, when Butler was performing yeoman's services for the Unionists of the state, Cameron took the opportunity to evaluate his vote-getting techniques, to observe public reaction to his addresses, and to judge him as potential Presidential timber. The end of the gubernatorial campaign saw also the end of his private Butler-for-President boom.

Cameron now began in the most calculating manner to gauge Lincoln's chances for re-election. Few men, it must be admitted, could match him in this difficult technique in a day when public polls were non-existents and "public opinion" often constituted the whims of scheming poli-

[37] Butler, *Correspondence*, II, 590; III, 58, 65.

ticians. Before the end of October he was observing reactions in public discussions to suggestions of Lincoln's renomination. By early December, 1863, reports from his lieutenants, added to his keen political perceptions, told him that although radical leadership might consider Lincoln's election destructive both to the party and its goals, there existed at the grassroots a great mass of loyal people who still believed in their President.

It was the master politician's determination to initiate very early a powerful movement designed to insure Lincoln's nomination, thereby gaining for himself much credit for having defeated the anti-Lincoln radicals, and later to place the President in an apologetic position. The Blairs of Silver Spring—Francis P. Blair, Sr., and sons— leading confidants and supporters of Lincoln, were likely to encourage such a plan and to them Cameron turned for advice and aid. Lincoln was "very pleased," reported Montgomery Blair, with Cameron's letter, and Blair agreed that since a decision had been made "we must not let the traitors beat Old Abe." The elder Blair, an old Jacksonian warrior, compared the situation with that existing at the end of Old Hickory's first term and stressed the danger of "changing the front in the face of the enemy." [38]

Although apparently Simon Cameron never acknowledged it, Francis P. Blair, Senior, planned the procedures allowing the President to "Suggest the course" which the Blairs and Cameron had previously agreed upon. When Lincoln spoke in fear of the powerful forces of S. P. Chase and Benjamin Wade arrayed against his renomination,

[38] E. C. Wilson to Cameron, Oct. 28, 1863, John Purviance to Cameron, Dec. 4, 23, 1863, M. Blair to Cameron, Dec. 17, 1863, F. P. Blair to Cameron, Dec. 31, 1863, Cameron MSS, DCC.

Cameron related the story of how Jackson, after having pledged himself to one term, found the way opened to a second term by his manager, William B. Lewis, who manipulated a petition from 68 Democratic members of the Pennsylvania legislature requesting the President to run again. "Cameron," asked Lincoln, "could you get me a letter like that?" "Yes I think I might," was the reply. By the end of the first week in January all attending Union members of the state legislature had subscribed to a "legislative memorial" congratulating the President on the success of his administration and stating their "unshaken preference" for Lincoln's re-election. While yet in Russia, Cameron had assured Lincoln that he would never cease to be grateful for the President's acceptance of a share of the blame heaped upon him by the House censure. Exultantly he boasted of having kept his promise.[39]

Over an anxious period of four months, Lincoln's man in Pennsylvania periodically sent reassuring messages to his chief. The first, of January 9, concluded: "Providence has decreed your re-election and no combination of wicked can prevent it." Following the appearance of the Pomeroy Circular, a broadside designed to negate the movements initiated for Lincoln and to promote S. P. Chase, Cameron thundered: "I can tell you . . . the Devil and all his imps cannot take Pa from you." The next move of Stevens' radicals and A. K. McClure was to promote postponement of the national convention in order to gain more time in

[39] Dennett, *Letters*, 152-53; "Simon Cameron at Home," *New York Times*, June 3, 1878. The paper erroneously cited Thurlow Weed's name instead of Wade. Weed protested in "Reply to Ex-Senator Cameron," New York *Tribune*, July 5, 1878. Cameron then explained the error. The memorial is printed in Pittsburgh *Gazette*, Jan. 18, 1864.

selection of a candidate. McClure was pondering on the probability of defeating Lincoln's nomination by drafting Grant.[40]

The McClure-Stevens factions were thwarted in their delaying tactics both in the Union State Central Committee and at the state convention. It was one of Cameron's most trusted lieutenants, George Bergner, who directed the Lincoln men at the state convention, who moved unit support of the delegates for him and whose resolution nullified all efforts at postponements. The Presidential nomination in early June emerged as a tame affair, the formidable opposition to Lincoln having evaporated.[41]

The seat which Lincoln had lately assigned to Cameron in his inner circle was first discernible to the public eye when, on March 8, 1864, he was spotted escorting a newly christened lieutenant general of United States, U. S. Grant, to the presidential reception.

There was much speculation over the choice of a running mate for Lincoln. The wily president, publicly naming no choice, kept even his private secretaries in ignorance of his behind-the-scenes campaign. Cameron, secretly coveting the spot for himself, allowed his lieutenants to put out feelers in his behalf, but no boom materialized. It is quite likely therefore that Pennsyl-

[40] Donald V. Smith, *Chase and Civil War Politics* (Columbus, 1831), 49, 108; Nicolay and Hay, *Lincoln*, IX, 53; McClure to Stevens, March 9, [1864], McPherson MSS, LC. This letter refutes McClure's later statements (*Notes*, II, 134) of his strong support (friends of Curtin) for Lincoln's renomination.

[41] S. A. Purviance to Cameron, April 30, Cameron MSS, DCC; Hay *Diaries and Letters*, 177. According to Montgomery Blair both Curtin and Forney wished to postpone the national convention. See M. Blair to Cameron, April 12, 1864, Cameron MSS, LC.

vania's political artist did not feel highly flattered when
Lincoln named him the liaison to contact his choice for
Vice-President.

Lincoln had selected, obviously for political reasons,
General Benjamin F. Butler, a prominent war Democrat
from New England. Cameron's mission to visit Butler at
Fortress Monroe was assigned February 24, but he and
his companion William H. Armstrong did not go until a
month later. Jokingly, the "beast of New Orleans" agreed
to accept the honor only on condition of being assured of
Lincoln's death or resignation soon after his inauguration.
Had it been given to man to vision the future, the Prince
of Radicals would have succeeded to the Presidential
office in May, 1865. Butler's judgment was sound, conceded the messenger, who promised to relay some unsolicited observations on the character of the President's
cabinet. Lincoln received his emissary's report about ten
days after his return from Virginia on March 28. On
April 11 Lincoln postponed his visit to Butler.[42]

The question of Lincoln's expressed choice of Andrew
Johnson for the Vice-Presidency in 1864 has become controversial among historians. The revisionist school admits
that three men from Pennsylvania, Simon Cameron, A. K.
McClure, and S. Newton Pettis, testified that Lincoln had
asked them privately to support Johnson; but all three
leaders, presumably worried over the verdict of posterity,

---

[42] The pass written on White House Stationery was signed by
Lincoln on February 24. See also Benjamin F. Butler, "Vice-Presidential Politics in 64," *North American Review*, CXLI (Oct.
1885), 331-34; Cameron to Lincoln, March 29, 1864; Lincoln MSS;
Lincoln to Cameron, April 7, 1864, Cameron MSS, LC; Earl S.
Miers, editor-in-chief, *Lincoln Day by Day* (3 vols., Washington,
1960), III, 252.

deliberately lied and thereby cast the onus of Johnson's nomination upon Lincoln.

The limited scope of this work precludes a detailed presentation of the facts in the case but basically it is morally wrong to accuse three political leaders of having lied when only they and Lincoln were in position to know the truth. The question first became controversial in 1891 immediately after Hannibal Hamlin's death. Over a decade had passed since Johnson's impeachment, and the "disgrace" attached to his supporters of 1864 counted for little. Before Hamlin's death, Pettis had inadvertently revealed to him Lincoln's choice of Johnson.

One historian has called Judge Pettis a "publicity seeker," but he disclosed his information privately two years before the beginning of the controversy. It is due to Pettis to say that early in 1861 he carried confidential messages for the President. To Lincoln, Pettis was no ordinary delegate to a convention; he was an intimate, trusted, personal friend. Neither, as hinted, was Pettis in his dotage in 1889—he was 62 years of age.

There is considerable supporting testimony for Cameron, McClure, and Pettis. Charles Dana, a man close to Lincoln, said it was true; John W. Forney mentioned it in his *Anecdotes*, published in 1873; Marshal Lamon, the personal representative of Lincoln at the convention, wrote that Lincoln "expressed himself to prudent friends" for Johnson; and B. C. Truman, Johnson's secretary in 1864, said "I know it to be a fact that Mr. Lincoln desired the nomination of Johnson for Vice-President, and that Brownlow and Maynard went to Baltimore at the request of Lincoln and Johnson to promote the nominations."

Lincoln made a public declaration to the Baltimore delegation: "Wish not to interfere about V.-P." No serious student of American politics would become exercised over the statement. Obviously a political leader who wished to work behind the scenes would not publicly disclose it. One very strong argument against his alleged "hands off" policy was his secret attempt at first to procure Butler for his running mate. A repeat performance in another man's behalf was a logical concomitant.

The crux of the controversy is *not* whether Lincoln brought about Johnson's nomination—very likely he didn't —but whether he requested the Pennsylvania leaders to support Johnson: the following discussion is based upon the proposition that he did so.[43]

McClure, who because of well-founded rumors, had recently found it necessary to offer new pledges of loyalty to Lincoln, agreed readily to support Johnson—his Chambersburg *Franklin Repository* had already done so a month previously—but Cameron's detestation of the "low man" of the South brought from him grudging compliance.

Simon Cameron's tactics at the Baltimore National Union Convention may well be accepted as a model for political strategists. He successfully created the impression of moving in one direction while at the same moment he was actually piloting the proceedings 180 degrees off its assumed azimuth. At the secret caucus session where Johnson ranked third in an informal poll of the Pennsylvania delegates, it was arranged to cast a solid complimentary vote for Hannibal Hamlin, the incumbent, and then switch to Andrew Johnson. Only one person, Thaddeus Stevens, dared register his dissent.[44]

---

[43] For a full account of the controversial aspects of the question see McClure, *Lincoln and Men of War Times*, Appendix, 425-49, and James F. Glonek, "Lincoln, Johnson, and the Baltimore Ticket," *Abraham Lincoln Quarterly*, VI (March, 1951), 255-71.

[44] "Phonographic" copy of Address, Nov. 7, 1866, Andrew Johnson Papers, LC. In 1866, A. B. Sloanaker, a persistent office seeker

At the very beginning, Cameron's resolution for a roll call of each state's delegates, at a time when their credentials had not been accepted, became so entangled in amendments and counter motions that Henry J. Raymond had to rescue the floundering chairman. Later three delegates striving amidst riotous clamor to gain the honor of having presented Lincoln's name for a renomination were frustrated by the Pennsylvanian's trick of sending his written resolution to the clerk accompanied by a demand for an immediate reading; the bewildered functionary complied. His resolution calling for the package nomination of Lincoln and Hamlin created the effect desired. "Almost every delegate was on his feet objecting or hurrahing" wrote Noah Brooks, "and in the midst of it Cameron stood with arms folded, grimly smiling regarding with composure the storm that he had raised." [45] If it were in the "best interests" of the country, remarked the author of the impossible resolution, he was willing to withdraw it (with the understanding that Lincoln would be nominated by acclamation). Again the clear-headed Raymond steered the convention into an orderly roll call by states. One state voted against Lincoln.

On the roll call of states for the Vice-Presidency, again it was Cameron, on "instruction" from his state who presented Hamlin's name. On the first ballot Pennsylvania cast its unit vote for Hamlin, but its chairman remained on his feet to change the vote before results could be tallied. "I am directed by the Pennsylvania delegation," shouted Cameron, again in command of the floor, "to give

who had once been rejected by Johnson asserted himself to have been Johnson's lone supporter in the Pennsylvania delegation at Baltimore. Obviously such claims are to be taken *cum grano salis.* Sloanaker to [McCulloch], Feb. 26, 1866, Johnson MSS, LC.

[45] Brooks quoted in Sandburg, *The War Years,* III, 83.

her fifty-two votes for Andrew Johnson." If Cameron at
the end of the first ballot (New York *Herald,* June 9,
1864) did offer to throw his delegation to Dickinson, he
did so in the knowledge the Weed faction would not
accept it. Hamlin, not perceiving the legerdemain per-
petrated upon him, wrote to its artificer, praising the
noble state of Pennsylvania for its performance.[46]

Lincoln's nomination problems did not end with adjournment at Baltimore. Not until middle September did
diehards like Thaddeus Stevens acknowledge the futility
of running a radical Unionist candidate.

The burden of the Lincoln campaign in Pennsylvania
fell upon its state chairman, Cameron. Some of his special
problems were to secure the soldier's vote in the field, to
compensate for unpopularity of the draft, to collect campaign assessments, and to overcome the popularity of
General George McClellan, a native of Pennsylvania.
Over one hundred men on special assignment assisted in
procuring the vote in the field; thousands of other soldiers
under furlough voted at home. After the discouraging
October elections, the chairman pleaded with Lincoln to
suspend enforcement of the draft. Assessment of federal
office-holders was left to the national chairman except in
the post offices of Philadelphia and Harrisburg, the do-
mains of two Cameron men, C. A. Walborn and George
Bergner.

During the summer of 1864 the Lincoln movement fell
to a low ebb in the Keystone State. Its director, exhibiting
a surprising aversion to political activity, succumbed, it
would seem, to a state of defeatism, a mood prevailing

[46] Johnson, *Proceedings;* Randall and Current, *Last Full Measure,*
125-37; Hamlin to Cameron, June 18, 1864, Cameron MSS, LC.

among many of the President's supporters, not excepting the chief executive himself. Accompanied by two of the Blairs, Cameron retreated into the wilds of northern Pennsylvania on fishing and hunting excursions. In August he disclosed his fears of defeat to national chairman Henry J. Raymond, but September saw some improvement in his outlook. He arranged speaking tours for energetic Unionists and sought campaign orators of national stature. He now envisioned, he confided to S. P. Chase, victory in the October state elections. To Lincoln he reported: "All looks well here in Philadelphia." But the October election returns failed to attain the majorities predicted by John W. Forney and Cameron.[47]

Lincoln, particularly concerned over Pennsylvania because of its size and immense prestige, and angered over reports of bungling campaign methods, determined to arouse its Unionist chairman from his lethargy. Cameron, "greatly distressed" by the election results, acquiesced in the President's request to accept A. K. McClure's assistance during the closing weeks of the campaign. A new appeal to the electorate, mostly the work of Wayne MacVeagh, was released and both "chairmen" kept Lincoln informed of the campaign's progress. By November, a Lincoln victory in the state was assured.[48]

The Lincoln victory of 20,000 votes in the state over McClellan on November 8 and the Unionist victories in

[47] Smith, *Blair Family*, II, 272; Cameron to Nicolay, Sept. 11, 13 25, Nicolay MSS, LC; Cameron to Chase, Sept. 19, 1864, Chase MSS, HSP; Cameron to Raymond, Aug. 19, 1864; Cameron to Lincoln, Sept. 6, 1864, Lincoln MSS.

[48] Dennett, *Letters*, 232; A. K. McClure, *Notes*, II, 152-53. For a complete account of the political history of Pennsylvania in 1864 see Bradley, *The Triumph of Militant Republicanism*.

the legislative contests were great boons to Simon Cameron. In both official and social circles he was again accepted at the highest levels. His appearance in the Lincoln box during a performance of John Wilkes Booth in "The Marble Heart" contributed rumors for Washington patter. The First Lady was well impressed with the gentleman who had brought her "a very charming affair" —a watch from Europe.

Henry J. Raymond, under Lincoln's direction, had prepared a campaign book for 1864. The original manuscript had included in the President's personal platform "an endorsement of the honesty and integrity of Simon Cameron." The entire work was suppressed but news of it leaked out. Years later Raymond published an altered version with additions.[49]

By 1865 Union party leaders were recognizing the powerful influence exerted upon the President by the former disgraced Secretary of War. Wayne MacVeagh, former chairman of the Union State Central Committee and member of the Curtin faction, saw the trend and deserted to the opposite camp. To his new chieftain he wrote: "Mr. Lincoln listens to nobody else from Pennsylvania as he does to you."[50]

All successful personal political machines must dispense patronage. On the national level, federal appointments within a state are usually channeled through the senior United States Senator if he is a bona fide member of the President's party. During the war period, cabinet officers commanded thousands of appointments. Although such appointments were theoretically doled proportionately

---

[49] W. Frank Gorrecht, "Lincoln, Stevens and Cameron," A paper read before the Lancaster Historical Society, 1938.

[50] W. MacVeagh to Cameron, Jan. 2, 1865, Cameron MSS, LC.

among the several states, in practice this seldom happened. Cameron's favoritism for Pennsylvanians was one of the scandals of his regime in the war office. His favorites seemed endowed with the perspicacity to remain in office long after their patron had fallen from grace.

Ostensibly, from 1862 through 1866, when he occupied no domestic public office, Simon Cameron was powerless to nurture his numerous clientele; but his proven ability to do so seems almost unique in his profession. When Edgar Cowan accepted the caucus nomination in 1861, he did so with the understanding of remaining aloof from patronage problems. In spite of the full strength of the Curtin administration against him, the seasoned manipulator kept his old appointees in office and persuaded Chase, Stanton, and Lincoln to add new ones. Actually, the master was in the process of welding the machine which was destined to defeat Governor Curtin early in 1867.

Every one of the leading Cameron lieutenants occupied important posts, some of them highly lucrative, during the "lean" years through 1864. Henry C. Johnson, Speaker of the House of Representatives, had charge of the stores in the medical department of the army. A.W. Benedict procured the appointment of chief clerk of the Pennsylvania House. George Bergner, editor of Cameron's voice, the Harrisburg *Telegraph*, received a double reward. His shop charged $7.00 for each page it printed of the *Legislative Record*. At the same time he was the capital's postmaster. When Governor Curtin rid himself of Samuel Purviance, the ex-attorney general moved his law office to Pittsburgh—the anti-Curtin capital—and for no explained reason was selected to represent Pennsylvania on the 1864 Union National Committee. George V. Lawrence, a per-

ennial Cameron candidate for presiding offices, wielded
the gavel in the state senate. Henry D. Moore, one of the
Philadelphia faithful, held for three years, the office of
state treasurer, a gift channeled through a majority vote
of the state legislature. Cornelius A. Walborn, who "sna-
fued" the 1863 Senatorial election for his chieftain, was
postmaster of Philadelphia. General John N. Purviance
accepted a collectorship from Chase. Starting as chief
clerk in the war department, John P. Sanderson in two
years became colonel of a regiment. The next year, shortly
before Sanderson's death, Cameron prevailed upon Stanton to assign him the post of Provost-Marshal-General in
the Department of Missouri.

The firm support given Cameron by the Pittsburgh
Gazette in the early 1860's led to a close personal tie between editor Russell Errett and the politico which never
relaxed over a period of almost thirty years. The first
reward was the chief clerkship of the Senate in 1861; the
second, a paymastership; but the editor was unhappy with
army quarters—"a house without windows or a fireplace."
By 1864 he was comfortably "stationed" in his home city
of Pittsburgh. Errett's golden years lay ahead under the
Grant administration.

Alexander Cummings was the best known of the Cameronian henchmen because of his notoriety in connection
with war contracts. In 1863, while serving on the state
Board of Revenue Commissioners, Stanton allowed him a
colonelcy in the cavalry, from which he emerged a general. Although slated for a governorship of Montana in
1864, he had to wait until the following year when he
went to Colorado.

Recognized Republican leaders not in the Curtin camp
were given assistance. W. W. Ketcham, the strong Union-

ist leader from Luzerne, renewed his periodic ties with Cameron at the Baltimore Convention, and soon afterwards, upon the recommendation of the latter and Chase, became solicitor of the United States Court of Claims. William B. Thomas, recipient of the most lucrative post in the state—the collectorship of the Port of Philadelphia —had, on behalf of the Republican Club of Philadelphia, endorsed Cameron for Lincoln's cabinet in 1861, the same year he received his reward. Enemies of Chase clamored for his removal in 1864, but upon Cameron's intervention Lincoln retained Thomas.

Occasionally, for "old times sake," advancement for the relatives of old associates was solicited. Examples of these were William Ingham, Frederick E. Brewster, and Charles P. Muhlenberg. The ailing commandant at Camp Chase, former Senator James Cooper, requested "something better." Death within six weeks came quicker than the material relief he sought.[51]

The Curtin faction controlled hundreds of state appointments, most of them for the "small fry," but when it came to procuring Federal appointments for supporters, the governor's efforts were nil. Nor did he succeed in opening the impasse of 1861 that his cunning enemy, Simon Cameron, had contrived. In 1862 the frustrated state executive could no longer contain his ire. Not *one* important appointment from Pennsylvania, he reminded Lincoln, had been made on his recommendation since the beginning of his administration. A year later the situation remained unchanged. "The Lincoln government," wailed A. K. McClure, "has not met anything like reasonable

[51] The material on patronage is taken from the two Cameron collections, the Chase manuscripts and the R. T. Lincoln collection.

expectation." He followed his note with a telegram asking if "something could be done." [52]

Certainly another factor which enabled Lincoln's man to retain a large following was fear. His past political career testified to his power to punish defectors. Disbarment, double in nature, was the punishment. The renegade could not share in the spoils nor could he hope to seek public office within the ranks of the Republican Party. Apparently only one important personage, William B. Mann of Philadelphia, was able permanently to oppose Cameron within the party. The politico's reputation to stage seemingly impossible comebacks was never lost upon those who wavered in their loyalty. Cameron's insistence on the dismissal of David Taggart of Northumberland, whom he had once forgiven and rewarded with a paymastership, illustrates his persistent vindictive policies. [53]

Only a reader of the letters addressed to Simon Cameron during the period 1861-1865 can fully realize the awe and fear in which he was held in state political circles. Some craven souls, in protesting their continued loyalty, apologized for being seen in public places alongside members of the Curtin-McClure faction. Local caucus committees were likely to seek his "advice" in advance of nominations.

A shallow public, possessing little depth of discernment, remained unaware of the true public status of Simon Cameron during the late years of the Lincoln regime.

[52] Curtin to Lincoln, July 6, 1862; [McClure] to Lincoln, Sept. 11, 29, 1863, Lincoln MSS.

[53] Cameron to Lincoln, Sept. 12, 1864, Lincoln MSS. William Cameron, Simon's brother, had crushed Taggart's family by buying controlling interest in their bank.

8
The Great Triumph

THE SPRING OF 1865 FOUND TIME FAST RUNNING OUT FOR THE Confederacy. In late March, the Union high command completed plans for the final phase of the conflict and two weeks later, Lee, accepting the desperate realities of the situation, agreed to Grant's terms.

Unionist political leaders were already beginning to enjoy the fruits of their conquest. The radical Senator Benjamin Wade planned with Simon Cameron a pleasant spring sea voyage taking them as far south as Savannah.[1] Secretary Edwin Stanton graciously granted transportation and subsistence at public expense to Cameron and his entourage for a round-trip junket.

A month later an assassin's crime had elevated Lincoln to national martyrdom and his successor, Andrew Johnson, was already undergoing close political surveillance from all factions and parties.

Even in death Lincoln brought honor to Simon Cameron, a man devoid of any public office or trust. Although named one of the nation's four honorary civilian pall

[1] Wade to Cameron, March 6, 1865, Cameron MSS, LC.

bearers, he was not present for the state funeral in Washington.[2]

The sudden death of a friendly chief executive with almost four years of his term yet uncompleted could easily bring changes jeopardizing Cameron's political career. He must wait almost two years before a Senatorial vacancy would occur, during which time the full strength of the hostile Curtin-McClure faction was certain to be exerted against him. Many of the Republican state legislators elected during this period would undoubtedly be occupying seats in the General Assembly of 1867. It was therefore imperative that he tap his only possible source of strength—the Federal patronage. Execution of such a feat by one not occupying Senatorial office could not fail to impress prospective legislators or incumbents—a group notoriously sensitive to such matters. Another potential source of strength lay in the election in the fall of 1866 of a Republican governor whose candidacy was a gift of Simon Cameron.

Republican leaders of the Commonwealth along with others of the nation were prompt in assuring President Johnson of cooperation in a program which they assumed would be sterner than Lincoln's. To John W. Forney, Lincoln's assassination was a fulfillment of God's purpose to place the reins of government in less gentle hands.[3] A hurriedly-called unofficial convention of Union Republicans met at Harrisburg, adopted resolutions of confidence in the new President, and dispatched Simon

[2] O. Browning, *Diary*, II, 23.

[3] Philadelphia *Press*, April 17, 1865. A. K. McClure, it should be noted, had called for Vice-President Johnson's resignation following his sorry drunken performance at Lincoln's second inauguration. See his *Repository*, March 15, 1865.

Cameron with a delegation to Washington. Traitors must be punished for their crimes, declared Johnson to the delegation. This reassuring declaration was not likely to conflict with the view held by a majority of Pennsylvania's Republicans.

Within a few months the President had reversed his prospective radical attitude to that of benevolence toward the prostrate South, although he possessed neither the prestige nor the political acumen of Lincoln to carry such an unpopular program to a successful conclusion. At this juncture Cameron found himself confronted with a dilemma from which he emerged practically unscathed.

Following an interview with Johnson on June 14, Cameron decided to give his support to the President and, by modifying the opposition at that time rapidly gaining momentum under the leadership of Thaddeus Stevens and A. K. McClure, gain precious time for a final decision.

At the Union State Convention of 1864, George V. Lawrence, in the face of a petition for McClure's appointment signed by a majority of the delegates, had made Cameron chairman of the State Central Committee after adjournment. Now, predicted McClure with righteous indignation, his enemy would seek public recognition for his past services in the presidential campaign of 1864.[4]

McClure divined correctly. When the Union State Central Committee met at Harrisburg to complete final plans for its state convention, the Philadelphia donors' representative, after delivering the laudatory oration demanded for such an occasion, presented Cameron with his own portrait as a "fitting testimonial" of appreciation for his

[4] Cameron to Johnson, telegram, May 2, 1865, Andrew Johnson Papers, LC, cited hereafter as Johnson MSS; Blaine, *Twenty Years*, II, 12-13.

campaign services. The recipient's reply included a statement of his "reluctance" to accept the heavy responsibility in 1864.[5] The critical Beaver *Argus* discerned subtle satire in the character of the gift—a recognition of service to oneself.[6]

A week later the honored chairman of the Central Committee received a diploma to hang alongside his portrait. The University at Lewisburg (Bucknell) conferred upon him the exalted degree of Doctor of Laws, a distinction "eminently appropriate," declared President J. R. Loomis, "in view of his long experience in . . . legislative councils and . . . invaluable public services at home and abroad." At the termination of a respectable lapse of time, Doctor Simon Cameron presented his alma mater with bond number 834 of the Southern Central Railroad, a gift valued at $1,000.[7]

The enemies of Simon Cameron within the party boasted he had suffered a "crushing defeat" at the Union State Convention of August 17.[8] The correctness of this view depends upon his main objective at the convention; whether it was John Hiestand's nomination for a state office or whether it was an expression of support for President Johnson. His known efforts in the President's behalf at the convention, regardless of their adoption, were bound to bring him favor in the chief executive's eyes.

[5] Beaver *Argus*, Aug. 2, 1865; McClure to Slifer, June 10, 1865, Dill-Slifer MSS, Dickinson College Library.

[6] August 2, 1865.

[7] J. R. Loomis to Cameron, Aug. 3, Sept. 8, 1865, Cameron MSS, LC; *Bucknell University Alumni Catalogue*, 1851-1926 (Lewisburg, 1926), 19.

[8] Chambersburg *Franklin Repository*, August 23, 1865.

The temper of the convention was that of Thaddeus Stevens, who had already predicted destruction of the Union Party if the Southern states were restored to their former position in the Union. The convention's resolution that the rebellious states "be held in subjugation," subject to the will of Congress, might well have been written by the radical Commoner himself. On the other hand, the resolution to show honor to Lincoln by lending "generous support to his fellow patriot and successor, Andrew Johnson," was a victory for Cameron because, to the public, it appeared Johnson's policies had been endorsed.[9]

Cameron could have had his candidate for auditor general, John A. Hiestand, a genial newspaper editor, if he had not connived behind the scenes to have one of his men elected permanent chairman of the convention in the place of John Cessna, a former Speaker. The purpose of this maneuver was to have his obedient permanent chairman appoint him or one of his lieutenants chairman of the Union State Central Committee for the ensuing year, a favor George V. Lawrence had executed for Cameron the preceding year.

This time the manipulation failed. Malcontents led by the Curtin and Stevens factions allowed Cameron's candidate for permanent chairman, Henry C. Johnson, to assume his chair and then nominated John F. Hartranft for auditor-general instead of Hiestand. Cameron suffered further humiliation when the convention deprived Johnson of the customary right to appoint the next state chairman, and selected John Cessna for the spot. However it is doubtful whether the triumphant anti-Cameronians knew

<hr />

[9] Stevens to Johnson, July 6, 1865, Johnson MSS, LC; *Tribune Almanac*, 1866, 44.

that Hartranft had earlier signified his willingness to become a Cameron man if an understanding could be reached.[10]

Shortly before the Union State Convention, a feud between Cameron and Congressman W. D. Kelley of Philadelphia became so widely featured in the press that public interest in it eclipsed the more prosaic political convention news.

William Darrah Kelley, Cameron's antagonist, was certainly one of America's most unusual men. A dispenser of justice and student of political economy in the antebellum days, Judge Kelley had proclaimed the blessings of free trade. He was one of the first to gain the confidence of Lincoln, pushed his way to the vanguard of the radicals, and embarrassed the President by hailing him wisest of the lot. In the post-bellum era he called for inflation, claiming it did not stimulate a rise in prices; and so ardently did he push the interests of the arch-protectionists that he was dubbed "Pig Iron" Kelley, although innocent of any material interest in the metal. In 1868 he reascended the seat of judgment (in spirit) and pronounced Andrew Johnson the greatest criminal of his age. A Puritan who considered dram drinkers guilty of mortal sin, Kelley may have suffered some pangs of conscience himself when a Congressional investigation disclosed a profit of $329 on a Credit Mobilier investment costing him nothing.[11]

Apparently the feud had its origin in the period after

---

[10] A. K. McClure, *Notes*, II, 186-88; Altoona *Tribune*, Aug. 18, 1865; James Wood to Cameron, June 29, 1865, Cameron MSS, LC.

[11] James McCabe, *Behind the Scenes in Washington* (n.p., 1873), 270; James F. Rhodes, *History of United States*, VI, 87; David M. DeWitt, *Impeachment and Trial of Andrew Johnson* (New York, 1903), 361.

Cameron's return from Russia when he began a drive to have the House of Representatives expunge its resolution of censure against him. His close friend Cornelius Walborn, postmaster of Philadelphia, approached Congressman Kelley on the subject of using his influence on Cameron's behalf. Newspaper patter had it that Kelley replied: "To stir foul matter would be to produce a stench." In 1864, it came to Lincoln's ears that every post office employee in Philadelphia was opposed to Kelley's renomination to Congress. That Simon Cameron was behind postmaster Walborn's efforts to defeat Kelley's renomination there could be no doubt. Lincoln intervened to save Kelley from Walborn and Cameron.

The feud attained its zenith during the summer of 1865 when Kelley, taking the offensive, failed to bring about Walborn's dismissal but did succeed in persuading Johnson to "fire" a United States marshal, one of Cameron's most ardent partisans, and replace him with his own candidate. In an address at the Girard House in Philadelphia on August 10, Cameron made pointed references to Kelley's nefarious activities, reproaching him for sinking below his Congressional status in seeking jobs for friends.

Kelley, whose unusual forensic abilities were fully recognized by his colleagues, responded with a terrific broadside against his tormentor. Citing the Senatorial elections of 1857 and 1863 as prime examples, he asserted that not once had Cameron proved false to his criminal instincts; moreover, in succeeding decades Kelley's children could vindicate the vilification heaped upon him by Cameron simply by naming who was responsible for it.[12]

[12] Philadelphia *Age*, Aug. 16, 18, 1865; Lancaster *Intelligencer*, Aug. 16, 23, 1865; Chambersburg *Franklin Repository*, Aug. 16, 23, 1865.

Although in a few instances his clients were removed from office, Cameron easily outdistanced his competitors in maintaining federal patronage through 1865. He succeeded in keeping his men in key posts in Philadelphia and Harrisburg and even added one with important connections like B. F. Hancock (the general's father), and C. B. Penrose to his clientele. Both John W. Forney, who had been working to procure his son the collectorship of Philadelphia, and Governor Curtin, who was insisting upon Walborn's removal, failed.[13]

In his desperate quest for patronage it was Cameron's policy to "nag" both the President and members of his cabinet. For example, one recipient thanked him for a lieutenant-colonelcy and another for a naval commission. The observation of Secretary Gideon Welles testifies to the politico's persistence and success:

Cameron called on me with his friends for the twentieth time at least, in relation to two appointments in the Philadelphia Navy Yard. He does not conceal from me, nor probably from any one, that he intends to be a candidate for the Senate. Hence his vigilance in regard to certain appointments, and he has prevailed in the Treasury and in the Post Office, against the combined efforts of all the Members of Congress. In sustaining the policy of the President he shows sagacity.[14]

Cameron's enemy McClure likewise testified to his success in dispensing patronage within the Commonwealth.

Three weeks prior to the fall state elections, Cameron made a promise to Johnson which he repudiated within a

[13] Cameron to Gen. Hancock, July 17, 1865, Johnson MSS, LC; C. B. Penrose to Cameron, June 25, 1865, Cameron MSS, DCC; Curtin to Johnson, June 22, 1865; Johnson MSS, LC. The prominent Democratic leader, Samuel J. Randall, was working through Montgomery Blair to keep Walborn in office.

[14] Beale, ed., *Diary*, II, 349.

year. First he called the President's attention to the fact that George Bergner, postmaster at Harrisburg and editor of the influential Republican *Telegraph,* was endorsing the President's policies in his columns and should not be removed from his postmastership to make way for a "certain general Knipe" bent on capturing a lucrative position for himself. After we "carry the state" in the fall elections, pledged Cameron, "we will sustain your policy be what it may." [15]

The results of the October elections were most gratifying to the Unionists. Their candidates for state offices were easily elected and in the new legislature of 1866, the focus of Cameron's interest, the Unionists would possess a majority of 43 on joint ballot. Only a tremendous reverse in the fall of 1866 could prevent the election of a Republican Senator in January, 1867.[16]

The late autumn political lull allowed Cameron the opportunity to observe the feverish activities brought about by a new oil boom centering around Pithole City in the northwestern part of the state. There a farm had metamorphosed into an ephemeral city boasting fifty hotels and a post office business exceeded only by Philadelphia and Pittsburgh. But to the *Crawford Democrat,* which noted the presence of prominent politicians in his entourage, the tour took on the aspect of visitations at strategic spots to insure the excursionist votes in his drive for the Senatorship.[17]

On the eve of the Union State Central Committee's session, an elaborate dinner for lovers of shad—a delicacy

[15] Cameron to Johnson, Sept. 20, 1865, Johnson MSS, LC.

[16] *Tribune Almanac,* 1866, 54-55.

[17] John J. McLaurin, *Sketches in Crude Oil* (Harrisburg, 1896), 158-60; Meadville *Crawford Democrat,* Oct. 28, 1865.

of the era—was held at Harrisburg. Actually, the primary purpose of the meeting was to stimulate public sentiment for a fish bypass around the proposed Susquehanna dam; but because Simon Cameron presided over the gourmets' ceremonies, his enemies tried to make him appear ridiculous as one who had "wormed" his way to a commanding spot in the world of fish. But Cameron's few remarks on the occasion disclosed his humorous appraisal of his position: "not [just] anybody could preside over a fish convention."

When the Union State Convention met in early March, 1866, Cameron had two main objectives in view; first to name the party's gubernatorial candidate and secondly to carry out his pre-election pledge to Johnson by securing an endorsement of the President's reconstruction policies from the delegates.

The man whom Cameron had settled upon was General John White Geary of Westmoreland County, the candidate of John Covode, western Pennsylvania's leading radical. In correspondence with Geary as early as April, 1865, Covode by late fall was actively campaigning for the general and was his chief advisor in planning pre-convention strategy.[18] Before leaving the Harrisburg "Shad Convention" Cameron had announced his endorsement of Geary and J. W. Forney's powerful Philadelphia *Press* followed suit. Thaddeus Stevens, high priest of radicalism in Congress, satisfied of Geary's orthodoxy, instructed his delegation to support the general.[19]

During the critical pre-convention period, efforts of the Curtin men to unite and to work energetically for an anti-

[18] Geary to Covode, April 23, 1865, Jan. 18, Feb. 9, 1866; W. H. Painter to Covode [Feb.] 8, 1866; Covode MSS, HSWP.
[19] Philadelphia *Press*, Jan. 27, 1866.

Cameron candidate failed. Absence of the ailing governor in Cuba robbed the faction of badly needed leadership. He expected his lieutenants, A. K. McClure and Eli Slifer, to secure the selection of pledged delegates. Failure to do so, warned Curtin, would result in finding themselves confronted with a Cameronian packed convention.[20]

At first McClure had been hopeful of obtaining Pennsylvania's premier soldier, General Winfield S. Hancock, but at this time the hero of Gettysburg expressed no political aspirations. Also under consideration was Colonel Francis Jordan, head of the Pennsylvania State Agency at Washington through the good graces of Curtin. But Jordan, renown for his anti-Cameron leadership in 1855 was now petitioning Cameron on behalf of his own clientele. Another potential candidate, General Hartranft, was satisfied with his present office, auditor general.[21]

Winthrop W. Ketcham, an independent gubernatorial candidate from Luzerne County, received belated support from the Curtin faction. Ketcham had worked closely with Cameron during the Lincoln regime and had received his reward in a lucrative office, the solicitorship of a Federal court of claims.[22] Ketcham had failed to secure Cameron's backing in his efforts to secure the collectorship of Philadelphia and decided to strike out for himself.[23]

[20] Curtin to E. Slifer, Dec. 28, Slifer-Dill MSS, DCL.
[21] McClure to Slifer, June 10, 1865, *ibid*; G. V. Lawrence to Cameron, May 4, 1865; Jordan to Cameron, Feb. 4, 1865, Cameron MSS, DCC.
[22] Cameron to Lincoln, June 20, 1864, Lincoln MSS; Ketcham to Cameron, Jan. 13, 1865, Cameron MSS, DCC.
[23] W. W. Ketcham to Cameron, Jan. 13, 1865, Cameron MSS, DCC. McClure's observation that Ketcham was a Curtin man (*Notes*, II, 193) could better be stated by saying at this juncture that Curtin's followers were Ketcham men.

Curtin's fears were realized when the Union State Convention met on March 7. Delegates from the various counties had been polled previous to the convention and the Cameronians knew almost exactly how many votes they could command on the gubernatorial question. The thunderous oratory of Thomas Marshall and A. K. McClure against the acceptance of "a reconstructed Democrat" availed them nothing; Louis Hall manipulated the "strings" behind the scenes, while John Covode, exhibiting his ignorance of parliamentary procedures, sat in the chair. John White Geary won handily over the combined vote of three opponents with 29 votes to spare, or 7 more than Samuel Purviance, the Cameron pollster, had predicted. According to a Lancaster sheet, the conscience-stricken Geary had assured the radicals at the convention of his full conversion to all the dogmas of Thad Stevens except one—that former Chief Justice Taney, the one guilty of wrong to the colored man, was now undoubtedly receiving his just deserts in hell.[24]

If it was the master hand of Simon Cameron which guided the selection of a gubernatorial candidate, it was the titular spirit of Thaddeus Stevens which dominated the atmosphere of the convention. Radical fury in the North had attained a new high because of the President's recent veto of the revised bill authorizing continuation of the Freedmen's Bureau. In Washington the Commoner was busily engaged in a daily campaign of secret intrigues and bitter public invectives against Johnson who, on Washington's birthday, had tactlessly assigned Stevens to

[24] S. Purviance to Cameron, [Feb.] 24, 1866; Covode MSS, WPHS; Bellefonte *Central Press*, March 16, 1866; Lancaster *Intelligencer*, May 2, 1866.

a newly-arisen group of post-war traitors. Surely thousands
of proud Pennsylvanians were struck with resentment at
the absurd accusations leveled at their Congressional
leader. The floor of the state convention found itself bursting with a frenzied radical mob of 200 ruffians "who
cheered, yelled, and voted, and hissed everybody they did
not want to hear." Less than 15 per cent of the delegates,
according to a generous estimate given by the President's
lieutenant, favored his reconstruction policy.[25]

Under these circumstances, it is little wonder that
Cameron, heeding the warning given him by a group of
delegates that any attempt to cram pro-Johnson resolutions down the throat of the convention would bring about
a split in the Unionist State party, deviated from his prescribed course. One of Cameron's bitterest enemies, A. K.
McClure, had assumed leadership of the radical element
at the convention. He had been working in conjunction
with Stevens on methods designed to block Johnson's
policies and had already in the pages of his *Repository*
read the President out of the party.[26]

The convention, in a superlative tone of irony it would
seem, commended Johnson for something he had already
repudiated—his long past denunciation of Confederate
leaders guilty of the "crime of treason"—and pledged the
future support of "loyal masses" for measures "by which
treason shall be stigmatized." Other resolutions com-

[25] R. B. Carnahan to Johnson, March 16, 1866, Johnson MSS,
LC.

[26] Lancaster *Intelligencer*, March 7, 1866, quoting Chambersburg
Franklin Repository; McClure *Notes*, II, 194. There appears little
reason to doubt McClure's account of a threatened bolt discussed
behind barred doors; naturally, the President's man would not have
been invited to attend such a conclave.

mended Pennsylvania's Republicans for their radical stand in Congress, asserted the right of the legislative branch of government to reconstruct the rebel states, and demanded the "legitimate fruits of the war." Senator Cowan, because of his support for Johnson, was "earnestly requested to resign." Although Grant, Curtin, and Stanton received commendations, it was Thaddeus Stevens who was given three lusty cheers before adjournment. Cameron's voice, the Harrisburg *Telegraph*, "interpreted" the resolutions to mean that Johnson's policies had been endorsed.[27]

It is highly unlikely that Simon Cameron experienced any great disappointment over the outcome of the convention. In the light of later developments there is no reason to believe he could have given Johnson a conscientious endorsement. But his passion for patronage—one of the gateways to the coveted Senatorship—not his personal convictions, decreed his course. Until such time when he would be forced into a parting of the ways, he remained in the advantageous position of receiving Presidential favors. In Washington he took the opportunity to speak before a gathering of iron and steel men. There was no need of a hypocritical stand before this particular group; for years, although possessing little direct material interest in the subject, Cameron had worked fervently to bring favorable tariff legislation for the industry.

[27] Phila. *Press*, March 8, 1866; Beaver *Argus*, March 14, 1866; Bellefonte *Central Press*, March 16, 1866. For a different interpretation of this convention see article by Brooks Kelley in Pennsylvania *Magazine of History and Biography* for October, 1963. Kelley used the curious argument that *if* Stevens' recent anti-Johnson antics had actually produced radical fervor at the convention, there would not have been a hot contest for the gubernatorial nomination.

Political developments during the summer of 1866 forced Cameron into a break with the President. Senator Edgar Cowan, the man Cameron had selected for the long term in 1861, had determined to support the President against all odds, and in conjunction with a few minor state Republican leaders assisted in organizing a Johnson-Republican movement within the Commonwealth.

During the August days in Philadelphia, a mammoth "arm-in-arm" convention, composed of all elements endorsing Johnson's lenient reconstruction policy, attracted far more prominent Democrats than it did Republicans. According to the dogmas of this motley group, likened by contemptuous radicals to that of beasts, clean and unclean, assembled in Noah's Ark, no state within the federal union was destructible; consequently the Southern states possessed the right of local government and equal representation in Congress.

Because the Johnson Republicans failed to establish a slate of candidates for state and Congressional offices, Republicans favoring Johnson's attempt to effect an immediate and complete restoration of the Union could voice their approval at the polls only by voting for Democratic Congressional and legislative candidates and for Hiester Clymer, gubernatorial choice of the Democracy. For many Johnson-Republicans, convinced of treasonable Democratic leadership during the late war, such a course was much too galling.[28]

The course was determined. Simon Cameron must give his unqualified support to his radical choice for governor,

[28] For a full discussion of the Johnson movement in Pennsylvania see Erwin S. Bradley, "Post-bellum Politics in Pennsylvania, 1866-1872" (unpublished doctoral dissertation, Pennsylvania State University, 1952), 55-94.

who now represented a party which had repudiated the President's leadership. Moreover Johnson had entered into a coalition with the Union Party's enemies. Seized with a sudden fit of enthusiasm, the politico asserted Geary's election paramount over his own to the Senate because the "safety of the country" depended upon a Union Party victory in the coming state elections.[29]

The Unionists were fortunate in possessing a sizeable group of first class orators, mostly Curtin men, to conduct their anti-Johnson-Democratic campaign. Cameron's lack of forensic talents coupled with his weak voice limited open air stumping, but he could not afford to allow Governor Curtin to steal the whole show in the campaign. Consequently, he appeared frequently at public gatherings in the guise of presiding chairman, usually content to confine himself to opening remarks; but occasionally he delivered long addresses.

There were numerous foreign and domestic happenings of the day to divert public interest from an "off year" political contest. Napoleon still had troops in Mexico, General Meade was engaged in tracking down Fenian military adventurers along the Canadian border, and Queen Emma, a most unusual attraction from the heathen Sandwich Islands, had just made her initial American appearance. Nevertheless, great enthusiasm was demonstrated from the opening of the campaign on August 1, at York. Here Curtin delivered a severe attack upon Johnson, hoping no doubt to popularize himself with the radicals of his party—a wing very likely to dominate the next Union Senatorial caucus.

Although not to be classed with Thaddeus Stevens—

[29] Cameron to Charles A. Dana, Aug. 12, 1866, Cameron MSS, LC.

monarch of ridicule, irony, sarcasm, and repartee—the seasoned warrior, Simon Cameron, excelled most men in the art of delivering destructive political broadsides against his opponents. Beginning with his first public appearance, he left no doubt of his position at the anti-Johnson vanguard.

Cameron began his campaign appearances in the East. At Williamsport he presided for the main speaker, Louis Hall, his chief liaison at the late convention. In Philadelphia, where, much to the embarrassment of Thad Stevens, Loyalist-Unionist (South-North) conventions were staged to neutralize the one held for Johnson, Cameron, a delegate-at-large, was spotted, ferreted out of his seat, and escorted to the platform in company with Geary, Curtin, and General Burnside. The two Unionist enemies suffered further close contact at Harrisburg. While state senator John Scott was delivering an exposition of the problems of reconstruction within a crowded court room, Cameron propped himself against the witness stand, presumably under the piercing glare of Curtin stationed by the jury box. Once more, at Erie, the pair made a joint appearance, but spoke from different points of the compass. The present disturbances and crises concerning Reconstruction, asserted Cameron, existed merely because of the North's lenient policy; the solution was an end to such leniency. The following day at Warren he predicted another Southern rebellion if the people failed to elect a Radical-dominated Congress.[30]

The Soldiers and Sailors Convention at Pittsburgh highlighted the Unionist state campaign. Several months had passed since Cameron had requested General Benja-

[30] Harrisburg *Patriot*, Aug. 28, Sept. 10, 1866; Phila. *Press*, Sept. 4, 5, 13, 1866.

min F. Butler, of Massachusetts, to assist in the campaign. Although engaged in his own Congressional race, Butler complied, and the politico found himself in the congenial company of the radical general and Geary at the iron city convention of veterans.[31]

Throughout the campaign the Unionists used with telling effect a newly-discovered propaganda device, the "Bloody Shirt." Victory for the Union Party, it was argued, was imperative to maintain the gains achieved through a bloody sacrifice of Northern manhood; defeat would bring, through a coalition of Johnson-Republicans and Democrats, a return to the political conditions of ante-bellum days with the Negro in a state of virtual slavery. Thaddeus Stevens, with remarkable candor, demanded support for Radical policies in order to insure continued supremacy of the party.

The Democracy, asking for immediate restoration of the Union, supported Johnson against the Unionist radicals. Its gubernatorial candidate, Heister Clymer, lacking the confidence of the Johnson wing, conducted practically a oneman campaign. To Clymer, who called himself the white man's candiate, the Unionist fight for Negro civil rights was only the first step toward political equality for the race.[32]

All phases of the Commonwealth's elections were gratifying to the Unionists. Geary crushed Clymer by 17,000 votes and although the Republican Congressional candidates polled only 51 per cent of the total vote it sufficed to give them 18 of the 24 seats allotted to Pennsylvania, thus assuring Stevens of strong Radical support from his state. In the new General Assembly of 1867, the Unionist

---

[31] *Ibid.*, Sept. 25, 26, 1866.   [32] *Ibid.*, Oct. 6, 1866.

majority of over 30 votes would insure the election of a
Republican to the Senate of the United States to replace
the party's renegade, Edgar Cowan.[33]

On November 8, at Harrisburg, a huge victory dinner
was celebrated by the "Boys in Blue" in honor of Major
General John W. Geary, the governor-elect. Both Curtin
and Cameron served as after-dinner speakers but it was
the latter's address which captured most of the publicity.
At least two copies of this anti-Johnson philippic were
forwarded to the chief executive. He had not believed,
asserted Cameron, that a "low white," which a century
of education could not rehabilitate, was fit for the Presidency. It was he and Thaddeus Stevens, he reminded his
hearers, who had warned against Johnson's nomination at
the 1864 national convention. Because the Civil War was
truly not at an end, the Congress—a group composed of
disinterested and impartial men—was within its rights to
determine the future destiny of the unrepentant South
and ought to impeach the President. Although not a
lawyer, concluded Cameron, if he were a member of
Congress, he would be the first to impeach and remove
Johnson.[34]

Before the year of decision, 1866, was concluded,
Cameron's federal patronage suffered, but curiously this
reversal did not aid his opponents within the Union Party
who were also seeking the Senatorial nomination. All
bona fide members of the Union Party from Pennsylvania,

[33] Protectionism was a minor issue to Pennsylvanians. For a detailed account of the campaigns of 1866 in Pennsylvania see Bradley, *Triumph of Militant Republicanism*, 236-51, 260-74.

[34] Enclosures with L. Strong to Johnson, Nov. 9, 1866, J. Knipe
to Johnson, Nov. 9, 1866, Johnson MSS, LC. Cameron, it should be
noted, concealed his behind-the-scenes activity on behalf of Johnson
at the 1864 convention.

thanks to Edgar Cowan's screenings, were debarred; consequently the followers of Curtin, John W. Forney, and Thaddeus Stevens also found themselves outside the Johnsonian pale. Cowan and the president found it impossible to reconcile the claims of the Johnson-Republicans and the cooperating Democrats in their unseemly scramble for "bread and butter." Cameron's greatest losses were the postmastership at Philadelphia and Harrisburg, the offices of United States marshal in the eastern and western divisions, and many assessorships and collectorships in the 25 revenue districts.[35]

The constitutional stipulation of a two-thirds approval by the Senate of Presidential appointments proved a godsend to the Republican radicals. Until March, 1867, when Cameron re-entered the Senate, Pennsylvania, lacking a spokesman for the group, turned to Senator Benjamin F. Wade of Ohio for aid in checkmating Johnson's Pennsylvania appointments. These circuitous methods of the radicals, contributing to the rejection of presidential nominees, resulted in a stalemate—appointments were left "hanging."

Following Cameron's election to the Senate in 1867, he sought a solution to the patronage stalemate through Secretary Hugh McCulloch. The proposed compromise—really a division of spoils between Democrats and Cameron men,—provoked the wrath of William D. Kelley and Thaddeus Stevens when they found Democratic assessors slated for their districts. After blocking a Cameron appointment to his own district, Stevens penned a sharply worded letter requesting to know why he should

[35] An exception to the rule was the procurement by Curtin of several army appointments for his friends.

be made to suffer torment from W. W. Wiley, the persistent creature of Simon Cameron.[36] Pennsylvania's leading Democratic Congressman, Samuel J. Randall, advised Johnson to reject all compromises and especially not to consider the appointment of John Hiestand, a journalistic proponent of Cameron, to a Philadelphia naval sinecure.

Nevertheless, by May 1, Henry A. Bingham, a man acceptable to Cameron, "had assumed control" of the United States Court House building and post office in Philadelphia.[37] Bingham formerly resided in Hollidaysburg as a neighbor of Louis Hall, a man who expected and received rewards for his services to the Cameron machine.

Following the triumph of the Commonwealth's radicals in the fall of 1866, political circles focused their attention upon the selection of a Republican to replace the discredited Senator Edgar Cowan. Not even the most optimistic organ of the Democracy dared to conjure up a magical plan of victory in the Republican-dominated legislature and therefore assumed the prerogative of publicly reflecting upon the list of candidates, their merits, and their chances of election.

The Senatorial hopefuls represented wings, factions, geographical areas, political philosophies of the moment, and personal ambitions with little following. The Pittsburgh area, where Curtin had not been popular, was represented by the hardy perennial J. K. Moorhead and the rising radical Thomas Williams. Galusha A. Grow, from a

[36] W. W. Wiley to McCulloch, April 5, 1867; Stevens to Cameron, April 11, 1867, Cameron MSS, LC.

[37] H. H. Bingham to C. Gilpin, May 3, 1867, Gilpin Papers, Gratz Collection, HSP. On the Johnson patronage see Bradley, "Post-Bellum Politics," 169-72.

Northern county, coveted the spot, and John W. Forney, following a spectacular entrance into the lists, withdrew in favor of Thaddeus Stevens.

That the Commoner, because of his spectacular tactics in Congress, was capturing the imagination of the state's masses, there was little doubt; but his candidacy was punctuated with a multiplicity of "ifs." "If he had been younger, if he had built up a state machine, if he were not considered indispensable in his present position, and if only his candidacy could be taken seriously," [38] he could have emerged as the compromise candidate. Cameron, it is to be noted, in a letter to New York journalist Charles A. Dana, cleverly rationalized his own candidacy in the place of Stevens, whom he admitted deserved it, partially on the great need for Stevens' direction of the radical program in the Congress.[39]

The chief contestants, the public agreed, were Curtin and Cameron. But this was no ordinary struggle for the Senatorship; the stakes were control of the state's Unionist Party. Neither antagonist expected any quarter to be granted and the defeated warrior, finding all positions of power and trust denied him by the triumphant faction, must eventually sink into political obscurity. Over a decade had passed since Andrew Curtin and Simon Cameron had battled for the Senatorial nomination in the Know-Nothing (American) caucus of 1855. Cameron won (but failed to secure election) and in the process the two became bitter personal enemies. When the pair emerged as leaders of the new Republican Party, the old

[38] *Ibid.*, 138.
[39] Cameron to Dana, Aug. 12, 1866, Cameron MSS, LC. Cameron and Dana had become confidants during 1863-64, when the latter was Stanton's assistant in the war department.

Whig coterie supported Curtin while Cameron depended largely upon a personal following drawn from the Democracy.

Now in 1866, Curtin, the "Soldier's Friend," was receiving plaudits for having energetically led his state through the critical war years. On the other hand, his opponent, leaving the security of the Senate for cabinet service, had accepted an awkward escape from the embarrassments of the War Department through "exile" to Russia and, finally, skillfully rehabilitated himself the Lincoln way. Both sought ardently the highest radical recognition; but ironically, Cameron, who had enjoyed the Johnson patronage, was the one selected for admittance to full radical communion.

Reflecting the governor's popularity, a majority of his party's journals, consisting mostly of county weeklies, favored the predicted Curtin's election. Significantly, none of three giant dailies, the Pittsburgh *Gazette*, the Harrisburg *Telegraph* or the Philadelphia *Press* supported him. The first two were actually Cameronian mouthpieces, and the last was the sole voice of J. W. Forney. The strong Democratic Harrisburg *Patriot*, harboring less enmity against Curtin than Cameron, believed the former stronger. Former President James Buchanan, retaining vivid memories of "impossible" victories by Cameron, believed his chances best.[40]

No one can fully grasp the realities of the political situation in 1867 unless he understands the circumstances under which a United States Senator might be elected.

[40] Moore, ed., *Works*, XI, 422. McClure's *Franklin Repository* listed 46 for Curtin, 12 for Cameron, and five for Stevens. At first the Pottsville *Miners Journal* vouched for the accuracy of McClure's figures, but later upped Curtin's number to 60.

The process, not a democratic one, was accomplished by the combined votes, numbering 133, of the two houses of the General Assembly. If, for example, one party could command 84 votes (the case in 1867), easily more than a majority, then theoretically it was possible for 43 members, a majority of its caucus vote, to name a United States Senator. Not often did a member bolt his party's nomination unless he could secure enough support from others to change the results. This conceivably could have happened in 1867 if Curtin had received the nomination. In December, 1866, Cameron was assured that Democratic votes from three counties were his if he needed them.[41] Through local emissaries a candidate could canvass and solicit votes in person far in advance of elections. An undiscerning public often confused the meaning of the word "pledged." Legislative members were usually instructed or requested by a local caucus to vote for a specified Senatorial candidate; but secretly he may have pledged his vote to another. To which candidate a member was actually "pledged" is a moot question. Theoretically, in the caucus, he had freedom of choice.

Simon Cameron was master of this gigantic game of politics—a game which according to the records possessed no rules; in fact the politico had played a leading role in developing the ruleless "rules." During his long career he never cared to participate in the type of political maneuvering which would subject his name to popular vote; his was a personal, man-to-man relationship with every "voter." To some extent in 1864 and increasingly in 1865 he laid the groundwork for his future success. It was, in

[41] H. P. Ross to Cameron, Dec. 17, 1866, G. H. Gonndie to Cameron, Dec. 26, 1866, Cameron MSS, LC.

every legislative and senatorial district, his policy to promote a Union Party candidate favorable to his interest.
Few men possessed the patience or necessary financial resources to pursue such a methodical and meticulous
course.[42]

Such was Cameron's already established "reputation,"
if one may term it such, that Republican potential legislative candidates would think twice before refusing
Cameron's "backing," although acceptance was equivalent
to selling his body and soul politically. If he assented, he
could look forward, if Cameron emerged the victor, to becoming king of his own little demesne with the prestige
that accompanied petty patronage; on the other hand, if
he refused, he could expect persistent hounding until he
was defeated, became repentant, or retired from politics.
If this statement appears fantastic to the reader he should
keep in mind that by 1873 almost every Republican in the
General Assembly was a "Cameron man." Reward and
punishment was the theme and soul of the Cameronian
system. A pragmatist of the first order, Cameron knew
his system was good because it worked.

One of the first testimonials one can find of the fruits
of this technique is contained in a very confidential letter
addressed to his friend Charles Dana two months prior
to the state elections. There was a possibility that Curtin
would be elected; but Cameron at that time did not see
how he could be defeated and confidently predicted a
victory unless the way "greatly" changed. He was telling
Dana that unless the Democrats succeeded in defeating a
considerably larger proportion of his legislative candi-

[42] In the two main Cameron collections, 1864 through 1866,
numerous letters testify to this policy.

dates than that of his opponents within his own party, he would win. Such an event was only a remote possibility. One week following the state elections he wrote with increased confidence to MacVeagh: ". . . I say Gov C[urtin] cannot succeed." [43]

Perhaps it was Curtin's continued state of ill health or a premonition of defeat, or both, which contributed to his lack of will to direct an energetic fight. At Atlantic City in late July his conference with his eastern backers led him to conclude that if he could find stronger financial backing, Philadelphia was his. He hoped Cameron's conflict with railroad interests working for outside connections from the Philadelphia area would hurt his opponent's chances. Actually, Cameron's feud with the Baltimore and Ohio (a road commandeered by his order) dated from 1861 when his Northern Central Railroad became a favored channel for the transportation of troops and materiel of war. Curtin could have better spent his time checking on the position of Thomas Scott and his cohorts in the Philadelphia area who had established virtually a monopoly of the state's transportation system. His "heart" was not in the Senatorial office, admitted Curtin to Eli Slifer, and if it were not for his "real friends" he would drop from the race. Actually, Curtin, who was thinking in terms of popular elections, could not make himself accept the realities of Senatorial election methods. To radical John Covode, whose neutrality he was seeking, he wrote: ". . . let all aspirants . . . submit their claims to the people." [44]

[43] Cameron to Dana (confidential), Aug. 12, 1866, Cameron MSS, LC.; Cameron to MacVeagh, October 16, 1866, MacVeagh MSS, HSP.

[44] Curtin to Slifer, July 28, 1866, Slifer-Dill MSS, DCL; Curtin to Covode, Nov. 17, 1866, Covode MSS, LC.

In the meantime the press was busily engaged in printing mythical statistics on the respective strength of the candidates. For instance, if the Pittsburgh *Gazette* reported in mid-October that Cameron could muster only 19 votes in the coming caucus,[45] it is evident that the "information" was leaked in order to lull the Curtin group into a false sense of security. There is no other reason why Russell Errett, Cameron's most loyal journalist, who had returned to the *Gazette* after an absence of five years, would make such a statement.

The Yuletide festivities of the Cameron family at Harrisburg in 1866 were merrier because of a new member, Isaac Wayne MacVeagh, recently wed to Virginia Rolette, Simon's youngest daughter, following a summer courtship at the romantic Bedford Springs spa. A past captain of emergency infantry, chairman of the Union State Central Committee in 1863, and recent migrant from Chester County to Dauphin, MacVeagh was formerly a substantial pillar of the Curtin faction. Although the artifices of Cupid may have hastened his transition to the enemy camp, it is likely he would have gone anyway. Two years earlier Cameron had declined an invitation to attend a dinner in MacVeagh's honor although he admitted the honored guest was a "nice fellow." In early 1865, MacVeagh was flattering Cameron and making overtures for his support. His course was comparable to that of a rat of extraordinary perspicuity which sought escape from a ship before it began sinking and stumbled upon a golden cheese in the operation.

[45] Brooks M. Kelley, "Simon Cameron and the Senatorial Nomination of 1867," *Pennsylvania Magazine of History and Biography*, LXXXVII (Oct. 1963), 383. Kelley dated it "mid-October," and footnoted it Jan. 15, 1867.

On Christmas day, evidently in a jocular frame of mind, Cameron penned his greeting of the season to the Benjamin F. Butler family, inviting the General to visit and assist in making him Senator. The note ended: "I expect and intend to win." [46]

Apparently the first public test of factional strength would take place on January 1 of the new year when the two houses of the General Assembly organized and elected speakers. If neither the Curtin nor Cameron group commanded a majority, then, conceivably, a compromise candidate from the Stevens or Grow faction would secure election. Because such a test did not occur one will never know the exact pre-organizational strength of the contestants.

If Thaddeus Stevens, absent in Washington, actually possessed any degree of political acumen or sagacity in such matters, he failed miserably to exercise it. The leaderless Stevens men dribbled leisurely into the capital. Before all arrived J. Donald Cameron, in a brilliant coup executed three days prior to the speakership caucus, pledged four Stevens men to support his candidate for Speaker, John P. Glass.

Assuming that Stevens was actually a Senatorial candidate, which he claimed he was, Don Cameron could have used only one argument—that allegedly the Curtin group was the strongest and could be checkmated only by a coalition of all opponents. The gullible Stevens men and a few other swallowed the bait and William B. Waddell

[46] Butler, *Private and Official Correspondence*, V, 717. In the autumn of 1866, Curtin lost another prominent supporter, Darwin A. Finney. See Titusville *Morning Herald*, Sept. 20, 1866. Mac-Veagh's span of public service extended from the Civil War to World War I, which he wanted the United States to enter in 1915.

of Chester County, upon arriving late on the scene in expectation of standing for the Speakingship on behalf of Stevens, found his candidacy for the Speakership already withdrawn by his friends. Confusion became worse confounded when Matthew Quay, the Curtin candidate for the Speakership, offered to withdraw and throw his strength to Waddell.

Without further ado, Don Cameron solved Waddell's dilemma for him. In the late afternoon of December 31, he visited the latter in his hotel room for the purpose of divorcing him from further unseemly conduct. As a result of this "conference," patterned truly after the velvet-fisted persuasive style of father Simon, Waddell emerged no longer a candidate. Conscience-stricken by Don Cameron's moral sophistries, he felt honor-bound to respect the previous actions of his comrades.[47]

Revelation of the scandalous pact to sell out the Commoner's candidate without his knowledge or consent kept the telegraph lines hot for three days between Washington and Harrisburg. The final decision of Stevens to make certain a Curtin man should not be made speaker brought no modification of a *fait accompli*; but it did reveal his belief along with that of his helpmeet, Thomas Williams, and Stanton that Curtin could never rise above the level of a pseudo-radical.

The effect of the Speakership race on the naming of Geary's cabinet is a moot question. All members of the legislature knew Geary was Cameron's candidate for governor and his election in October should have set at rest any doubts that some member of his cabinet was

[47] R. W. Shenke to Stevens, Dec. 29, 1866, Edward Reilly to Stevens, Dec. 31, 1866, Stevens MSS, LC.

bound to bear the Cameronian trademark. Geary, himself, was to blame for creating the impression he intended to appoint a factionless cabinet. On March 19, 1866, Geary and Cameron had sealed a bargain in a Lochiel hotel room. Geary promised, if elected, to name H. C. Johnson of Meadville Secretary of the Commonwealth; instead he yielded to strong pressure brought by Louis Hall, and appointed the husband of his sister Mary, (a bride of one year) Francis Jordan of Bedford. In compensation for the rejection of Johnson, Cameron was pleased to have one of his best friends, Benjamin H. Brewster, appointed attorney general.[48]

It is important to examine the import of Francis Jordan's appointment to the Geary cabinet. In 1855 he had taken the lead in preparing the "American Petition" declaring Cameron to be "one of the most intriguing, if not the most corrupt politician in the state." He followed with a refusal to sign an investigation committee's report pointing no finger of accusation at Cameron. This was a factor in preventing Cameron from becoming Senator that year. For a decade he had been considered a Curtin man, although the governor failed to give him a cabinet post. Curtin subsequently appeased Jordan by making him Pennsylvania agent at Washington with the rank of colonel. In 1865 McClure's *Repository* was advancing Jordan for governor, and George V. Lawrence, Cameron's man, reported him a Curtin gubernatorial candidate. According to John B. Warfel, Jordan in October, 1866, was "openly" exulting at the prospect of seeing Curtin elected Senator. In November, F. C. Brewster heard that Mann,

[48] Notation by Cameron, March 19, 1866, Cameron MSS, LC.; H. C. Johnson to Cameron, Jan. 1, 1867.

Curtin's man in Philadelphia, was backing Jordan for a cabinet post. At the time Jordan's appointment was announced it could have been interpreted publicly as anti-Cameron.[49]

In spite of all the pre-caucus commotion, the nomination of a Union speaker proved to be a tame affair; John P. Glass was elected without opposition. No candidate from the Stevens or Curtin faction was presented. Glass was elected easily over the Democratic minority candidate, as was Louis Hall in the Senate.

During the intervening days before the Senatorial nomination a spirit of pessimism pervaded the Curtin faction, many of the group considering the governor's cause hopeless. The governor's expression of radicalism in his annual message was checkmated by the Cameronian editors of the Harrisburg *Telegraph* and Pittsburgh *Gazette*. His late conversion to extreme radicalism, charged the journalists, was transparent—he sought only to secure radical Senatorial votes.

In retrospect, one of the amusing features of the contest was the excitement produced, especially among the Stevens' group, by rumors that Cameron's gold was in circulation. One supporter knew well the disposition in the "legislature" to elect Cameron, but revolted "at the means used to accomplish it"; the situation was analogous to the purchase of oxen and asses. Another commented on the presence of Cameron, "the most consumate scoundrel in Pennsylvania," for the purpose of buying the members. Stevens, admitting the corrupt nature of past legislatures, was convinced of the purity of the present one. After his

[49] John B. Warfel to Stevens, Oct. 17, 1866, Stevens MSS, LC; F. C. Brewster to Cameron, Nov. 26, 1866, Cameron MSS, LC.

tardy arrival in Harrisburg, he decided to remain a candidate although according to *his* information, Cameron could command whatever number of votes were required to elect him.[50]

Only four days prior to the Union Senatorial caucus, Cameron expressed privately to a friend his appraisal of the situation.

> I am I think going to win. Indeed, I do not see how I can be defeated . . . Forney and Stevens and Grow all believed the fight would be so violent and so evenly divided between Curtin and me, that one of them would get the prize—and each believed himself the fortunate expectant, but my strength was developed so early that they found Curtin was beaten—and now they are combining against me. I feel certain they will be disappointed again. They are all to be here, in person, and for the next 4 days I will be the best abused man in 'there parts'. I like a fight, and if I don't whip them, they will have more luck than they merit.[51]

A last-minute conference of all opposed to Cameron, including Curtin, Stevens, Grow, and John W. Forney, was held in the latter's hotel suite. The leaders of the factions could not agree on a plan of action or discover any methods of defeating Cameron except by bolting the caucus nomination and proposing a deal with the Democrats. Curtin would not agree to a party split.[52]

That same evening, on January 11, 1867, the caucus drama came to an end. The rabid Democratic Lancaster *Intelligencer* could not resist the temptation to picture a mythical scene presenting the Great Winnebago Chief,

[50] L. Kauffman to Stevens, Jan. 4, 1867, S. L. Kanfelt to Kelly [*sic*] and Stevens, Jan. 4, 1867, Stevens MSS, LC.; Philadelphia *North American*, Jan. 5, 1867; Huntingdon *Globe*, Jan. 16, 1867.

[51] Cameron to S. P. Chase, Jan. 7, 1867, Chase MSS, HSP.

[52] Huntingdon *Globe*, Jan. 16, 1867. Two absent members from Lancaster County were pledged Stevens men.

Simon Cameron, his chief sachem, George Bergner of the Harrisburg *Telegraph*, and his forty "odd" Indians, properly equipped with moccasins, all marching stealthily in single file to the state hall. The first ballot gave Cameron 46, Curtin 23, Stevens 7, and Grow 5 votes, respectively. The master politico won handily with 11 votes to spare; a coalition had no chance of stopping him.

Announcement of the result produced much excitement in the state capital. One of the governor's devotees, staging a mock auction, disposed of Curtin's lost votes to the highest bidder.

In the General Assembly, Cameron defeated Edgar Cowan, the Democratic Senatorial candidate by a straight party vote, 81 to 47.

At a congratulatory meeting held in the Lochiel Hotel dining room after his election, the victor revealed the emotional stress under which he had labored. He termed President Johnson a traitor, called for continued military rule of the South, and digressed to extol his favorite theme of thirty years, the protective tariff. He thanked God that, in spite of two decades of slander, his fellow citizens, who bore witness to his life, had aided him in winning "this last political struggle" of his life. In anticipation of the final outcome Geary had written: *"Victory—Congratulations. May Heavens choicest blessing rest upon the evening of your well-spent life."* [53]

Considering the publicity and interest shown during the caucus stage there was little press comment on the final result. The Democratic *Bedford Gazette* regarded Cameron the best of the radicals. Two other leading organs of the Democracy, the Harrisburg *Patriot* and the

[53] Huntingdon *Journal*, Jan. 23, 1867; Geary to Cameron, Jan. 11, 1867, Cameron MSS, LC.

Lancaster *Intelligencer* agreed with McClure's *Repository*
that Curtin's nomination had been bartered for a price.
After a lapse of six months Thaddeus Stevens remembered
the election as a time when "Cameron had his men with
their handfulls of greenbacks working in the legislature
for his election." The conservative Gideon Welles considered Cameron greatly preferable to the evil Stevens
or Curtin, a man "limber, deceptive, and unreliable." [54]

Although according to A. K. McClure 21 members
pledged for Curtin had voted for Cameron, he named
only "three monuments of perfidy," and actually two of
these (F. S. Stumbaugh and David McConaughy) were
renegade Stevens men. A good example of how rashly
the Curtin faction had "counted" its vote is the case of
Jacob Ridgeway of Philadelphia, who met Curtin at
Atlantic City in late July. It is quite apparent Ridgeway
did not definitely pledge his vote because Curtin reported
he "seemed right." Later his vote for Cameron was
branded perfidious. W. C. Harrison of Lawrence County,
according to the Beaver *Argus*, "should have" voted for
Curtin. Although M. B. Lowry of Crawford had declared
himself independent of any faction, the Curtin men insisted he belonged to them. The observation of the neutral
Philadelphia *Telegraph*, that Philadelphia "made"
Cameron, is worthy of note. The great city had formerly
been a Curtin stronghold, but in the caucus ten of the
city's 15 members supported Cameron.[55]

The writer has found no evidence to show Cameron
bought his election. His victory was a superlative example
of the triumph of a hierarchial political organization over
mass popularity. Foolish or unseasoned warriors might

[54] New York *Herald*, July 8, 1867; *Diary*, III, 16.
[55] Philadelphia *Evening Telegraph*, Jan. 11, 1867.

pay for a victory netting a wide margin, but Cameron was not such a man. Indirectly, he contributed financially to his victory, but not in the corrupt sense. Over the years Cameron had given cash to assist in the election of assemblymen favorable to his cause; he had made loans with the tacit understanding of tardy collection; and he procured jobs for friends and needy relatives of legislators. He exhibited extraordinary pains to execute one simple favor. In the game of politics rich men obviously had the advantage over the poor.[56]

Although Simon Cameron had just won his third Senatorial contest, the victory of 1867 was no ordinary one. It marked the end of a decade of bitter struggle with the Curtin-McClure faction for control of the Commonwealth's Republican Party's organization, which had emerged from the Know-Nothing political catalyst of 1855. A faithful following dating from the days when he was only a renegade Democrat assisted in making the victory possible. The temporary anti-Cameron sentiment exhibited within the new popularly elected state House early in 1868 was a grass roots reaction engendered by Curtin's defeat for Senator. True, Cameron would again engage in a titanic struggle with only a skeleton of his old Union antagonists, but this time they would be as aliens, no longer faithful members of the party fold and in alliance with the war-disgraced Democracy. His victorious faction had taken on many trappings of old Whiggery and there was little to distinguish it from its beaten opponents.

The day of exciting contests in the Republican Sena-

[56] In 1866 the listed income of Simon Cameron, J. Donald Cameron, and Don's father-in-law, James McCormick, totaled $101,460. That of A. G. Curtin was $3,205. See "Income List," Harrisburg *Patriot*, Oct. 25, 1866.

torial nomination caucus was ended. One faction was to exercise mastery of the Republican legislators of Pennsylvania for decades to come. The great war governor was transformed into a political ghost destined to haunt Cameronism for almost another decade. After Curtin belonged to the ages it was remembered that he had engaged in two contests of "intense bitterness," the first in 1855, the second in 1867, both of them with Simon Cameron; and they "left political scars which never healed until the conflicts of ambition were ended." [57]

For the victor, in spite of his approach to the Biblical limit of three score years and ten, there yet remained new worlds to conquer; and with a son of proven political aptitude to succeed him, the paternalistic urge was strong to seek establishment of a political dynasty bearing the name Cameron.

[57] A. K. McClure, "Life and Services of Andrew G. Curtin" (Harrisburg, 1895), 22. For a detailed account of the Senatorial election of 1867 see Bradley, *Triumph of Militant Republicanism*, 210-19, and Kelley, *loc. cit.*

9
New Worlds
to Conquer

THE FORTIETH CONGRESS, TO WHICH SIMON CAMERON HAD been elected, normally would have convened in December, 1867; but a radically inspired Congress, in an act of doubtful constitutionality begotten by fear of Presidential leadership, provided for the first session to begin immediately following the termination of the old Congress on March 4.

An absence of five years produced no marked effect upon Pennsylvania's junior Senator's ability to move freely in the circle he considered peculiarly his own. His presentation of several petitions praying for "such an adjustment of the tariff on imports as will give protection to American manufacturers and industry" reminded the Senate that Pennsylvania, the ultra-protectionist state, was once again represented by the leading exponent of its benefits. A member of the relatively insignificant Committee on Agriculture, Cameron, out-debating the able Senator William Pitt Fessenden, persuaded his colleagues to transfer $50,000 from the funds of the Freedmen's Bureau to provide for free distribution of seeds to the Southern people.[1]

An amusing feature of the March days in the Senate was the politico's feat in securing passage of one of his bills without the formality of steering it through a committee. By unanimous consent of the Senate he was allowed to introduce a bill providing for the port of Chester to be included in the Philadelphia collection district. Twice, Senator Lyman Trumbull moved to have the bill referred to a committee, but the persistent arguments of its proponent won. All members of the Committee on Commerce and the head of the Treasury Department, argued Cameron, had already signified their approval and a precious day could be gained with immediate approval; his state had asked for nothing that year, he did not generally "disturb the other gentlemen," and he trusted his colleagues' indulgence in his request. The bill passed without benefit of committee action.[2]

The character of Simon Cameron was well illustrated in his vigorous defense of Senator J. R. Doolittle, an untouchable of the detested Johnson-Republican group, against outrageous allegations from a House committee. Admitting the relationship of a kindred spirit in the controversy, because of the recent calumniations against him, he exclaimed: "Every man who is at all in public life is constantly subjected to attacks by bad men, and the more successful he is the more frequently he is attacked, abused and villified."[3]

The new member used his Senatorial prerogatives to

[1] Cong. Globe, 40 Cong., 1 Sess, 34, 330, 372-73, 429.
[2] Ibid., 250-51.   [3] Ibid., 297.

continue an old feud with the Baltimore and Ohio Railroad, revived in the Philadelphia area during his recent Senatorial campaign. His resolution required the Secretary of War to give the Senate a complete account of business transacted by the road during the war years, and if it were shown that the railroad received higher rates than others, why was it so. When his enemies countered with an amendment to include the Northern Central, his road at the time, and the Pennsylvania, Cameron readily agreed.[4]

During the Congressional recess of two months, the Commonwealth's new Senator enjoyed an excursion into Kansas, a center of railroad fever. At Leavenworth, Cameron entertained his audience with an account of his experiences in building the railroads of Pennsylvania and of his efforts to arouse public interest in them.[5]

Two problems especially interested Cameron after the Senate resumed its labors. The first was the effort of the radicals to plug the loopholes of their Reconstruction law with supplementary acts. Cameron, indicating his approval of such legislation, could not see how the South, after its effort to destroy the government, could expect the clemency Congress was extending. If the people of the South showed they were "not content" with present legislation, he would give them "something else [more unpalatable]." [6]

The other question was the final fate of the treaty for the purchase of Alaska, then hanging precariously in the balance. The Senate, largely through the strenuous efforts of Secretary Seward and Senator Sumner, had approved

[4] *Ibid.*, 430, 456.   [5] Altoona *Tribune*, June 26, 1867.
[6] *Cong. Globe*, 40 Cong., 1 Sess., 628.

the treaty, it had been formally ratified and the territory transferred; but now a stubborn House seemed unlikely to appropriate the purchase price. The former minister to Russia could testify to the strong ties of friendship existing between the two nations during the most critical period of the Civil War and exerted his influence to bring about House approval. "It was generally stated . . . that since America had solicited Alaska from Russia, the great territory could not honorably be thrown back into her face." Many felt with Senator Cameron "that the purchase was 'an act of recompense to a tried friend.'" The appropriations were carried in July, 1868.[7]

At home the politico read and mused over a voluminous mail reflecting his recent Senatorial victory. The many congratulatory notes were matched by others requesting positions or recommendations. Even his Democratic colleague Charles Buckalew was now forced to submit names he hoped might be acceptable to the new master.

But Cameron's position could not long be maintained without a continuation of his party's victories. The election of a Democratic judge to the state's supreme court in 1867 reactivated the depressed Democracy of Pennsylvania. Although the victor's personal popularity contributed largely to his election, Democratic successes in five other "Republican" states pointed to a trend disconcerting to moderate Republicans who, although deprecating radical leadership, preferred it to the Democracy. James Buchanan attributed Democratic state gains to a reaction against Negro suffrage, while the embittered Curtin lieutenant, A. K. McClure, ascribed it to the listless-

---

[7] Thomas Bailey, *Diplomatic History of the American People* (New York, 5th ed., 1955), 403.

ness of Republicans disappointed at Curtin's failure to win a Senate seat.[8]

One man, U. S. Grant, all factions agreed, could stop the Democratic trend in 1868 and carry concurrently on his coattails many doubtful Republican Congressional candidates in the process. The radicals succeeded in rescuing the nation's top military hero from his former Democratic and Johnsonian affiliations and without opposition nominated him for the Presidency at the Chicago national convention.

The Curtin faction, led by A. K. McClure, realizing the desperate plight into which the former governor and his followers were thrown by Cameron's Senatorial victory, sought to rehabilitate him on the national level by securing his selection as Grant's running mate. The delegates at the Republican state convention were willing to see Curtin compensated for his Senatorial defeat, and McClure's use of steam-roller methods enabled him to take a state delegation to Chicago pledged to vote as a unit for Curtin, although 22 adamant Cameron men under Russell Errett's leadership had voted for Benjamin L. Wade.[9] In March, 1868, many people believed Wade was about to assume the Presidential office soon to be vacated by the disgraced Johnson.

The national nominating convention became the next theater of operations between the two factions. One of the

[8] Bradley, "Post-bellum Politics," 173-86. Rhodes (*History of United States*, VI, 204) noted dissatisfaction caused by unsatisfactory business conditions.

[9] *Raftsman's Journal*, March 18, 1868; McClure, *Notes*, II, 217-18. McClure erred in stating that the anti-Curtin men supported Grow. Geary had withdrawn his candidacy. See also McQuaide to Covode, March 16, [1868], Covode MSS, HSWP.

resolutions engineered by McClure disbarred J. Donald Cameron, a Congressional district delegate, from taking his seat. Cameron, along with a half dozen other unhorsed delegates, took their cases to the convention and were awarded compensation with seats on the floor. Simon's son, it will be recalled, had served his father well at the 1860 Chicago convention and had played a very prominent role in the late Senatorial election. The new Senatorial duties of his tiring father, together with his own political aspirations, impelled Donald to accept a junior partnership in the management of the Cameron machine.

Immediately following the boisterous behavior accompanying Grant's nomination, a huge portrait of the hero along with the motto "Match Him" was unveiled on the stage. In retrospect one can see that Curtin stood little chance of representing that motto. Curtin's availability rested upon the fame of a war governorship representing a doubtful eastern state to match the western Presidential nominee.

On the other hand, radicalism was rampant in the spring of 1868 and the former governor could convince none of his orthodoxy; his state was not as doubtful as some others, especially Indiana, and Cameron, with personal Senatorial connections, could work through powerful midwest leaders like Wade and Chandler. At the end of three ballots it was apparent Curtin possessed no potential strength and his name was withdrawn. On the fifth ballot the delegates stampeded from Wade to Schuyler Colfax, the "good tempered, chirping, warbling, real canary bird of a speaker." The Old Winnebago Chief, commented the Reading *Eagle*, had taken Curtin's scalp at Chicago. His ancient enemy Cameron had prevented him from getting the Vice-Presidency, insisted Curtin shortly before his conqueror's death over two decades later.[10]

A month following the Chicago nominations, George Bergner, recipient of public printing contracts and the voice of Cameron as expressed in the pages of the Harrisburg *Telegraph,* presided at a special mass meeting called for the purpose of endorsing the choice of Grant and Colfax. Among a group of resolutions was one commending the Honorable Simon Cameron, United States Senator, for adding dignity to the great office which he held.

This decorum, suggestive of inner nobility or worth, was earned by the honoree during the impeachment of President Johnson. The politico's personal bonds with presiding officer S. P. Chase must have suffered excessive straining when the persistent Cameron, exhibiting inclinations to carry on unauthorized debate on several occasions, was declared out of order. On May 6, a demonstration of spectators staged to intimidate the pro-Johnson Senators prompted the Chief Justice to order the galleries cleared. Ignoring a call to order from his colleagues, the calm Cameron rose to remind the "court" that "such outbursts will occasionally take place," and expressed hope for no action against the disorderly populace. Again Chase declared him out of order and the galleries were cleared. Cameron's pronouncement of Johnson's guilt, before the presiding officer was half way through the question, provoked tittering laughter in the body. The requisite number for conviction having failed by one vote, the Senate, on a motion by Cameron, recessed

[10] New York *Tribune,* Jan. 6, 1868; Washington *Post,* Jan. 6, 1889.

until May 26 when the process was repeated with identical results.[11]

In a prepared speech never delivered before the Senate, Cameron expressed his views on the trial. In order to secure conviction it was not necessary to assert or prove Johnson guilty of "deliberate intention to violate the law or constitution." Acquittal would leave the "military power of the nation in the hands of a lawless ruler," whereas conviction would "confirm the principles and secure the blood-bought fruits of the mighty convulsion."[12]

Thaddeus Stevens did not long survive failure of his one remaining earthly goal—removal of Johnson from office. News of the Commoner's death was announced in Harrisburg concurrently with the arrival of the New York political boss, Roscoe Conkling, on a visit to the Cameron home. An apocryphal tale widely circulated after the death of Stevens related how in 1861, when Lincoln was faced with the cabinet dilemma, he asked Stevens his opinion of Cameron's honesty. "I do not believe he would steal a red hot stove," replied Stevens. Lincoln's sense of humor impelled him to relate the incident. Cameron, furious, demanded Stevens' retraction of the slanderous remark. With cheerful promptitude, the sardonic Stevens complied, because after all he might be mistaken; perhaps Cameron *would* steal the stove. Although the story

[11] *Cong. Globe, Supplement*, 40 Cong., 2 Sess., 209, 406, 411; David M. Dewitt, *Impeachment and Trial of Andrew Johnson* (New York, 1903), 551. In the opinion of Oberholtzer (*United States*, II, 124) Cameron was among a dozen Senators who, by openly exhibiting their bias against the President, had proven unworthy to sit as judges.

[12] Copy filed in collections of April, 1868, Cameron MSS, LC.

is not authentic, no account could better illustrate the nature of Thaddeus Stevens. Before the year had ended, Chief Justice James Thompson congratulated Cameron on his eulogy of Stevens.[13]

Both Curtin and Cameron, refreshed by vacations at Bedford Springs threw themselves vigorously into the campaign to carry the state for Grant against the man editor Forney labelled "a Democrat disguised as a gentleman"—Horatio Seymour. But it was the master politico who conducted the state campaign of the newly christened National Union Republican Party, including the disagreeable but necessary levying and collecting of party funds. Captains of industry and finance like Jay Cooke of Philadelphia, eager to secure advance guarantees of future administrative favors, allowed themselves to be "milked" to the limit.[14]

The climax of the party's national campaign was attained in Philadelphia by the use of "conventions" of soldiers, sailors, self-appointed delegates, mass meetings, and a reunion of the "loyal" war governors sponsored by former Governor Curtin.

The Republicans squeezed through the early state elections by approximately 9,000 votes and gained 12 seats in the General Assembly. The strength of Grant's name with the state's electorate was evidenced by his majority of 29,000 votes over Seymour in November.

At once, speculation was rife over the probable make-up of the hero's cabinet. Members of the Curtin coterie,

[13] J. Thompson to Cameron, Dec. 28, 1868, *ibid.*

[14] Lycoming *Gazette*, Sept. 3, 1868; E. P. Oberholtzer, *Jay Cooke, Financier of the Civil War* (2 vols., Philadelphia, 1907), II, 69-71.

desperate over the dim political future of the faction, were advancing their chieftain for a cabinet post, which, according to McClure, the former governor did not particularly desire because the office would entail a feud with Cameron over dispensing of the patronage. Grant kept his cabinet nominations a secret even from his wife, but some close friends did extract a hint of a Philadelphia appointment. This information Simon Cameron must have accepted with great relief. His candidate for a post, George H. Stuart of Philadelphia, whom he had urged upon Grant, was offered a place, without a pledge, by the President, but did not accept. The Philadelphia appointee, correctly prognosticated by Don Cameron, proved to be the darkest horse in cabinet history, Adolph Borie.[15]

Although publicly Curtin gave no hint of disappointment over his failure to attain Grant's cabinet, sources close to him claimed otherwise; and privately he acknowledged his willingness to accept compensation in the form of a foreign mission—a move contributing to the healing of "political discords" within the state. Certainly the unseemly conduct of his supporters, especially of McClure, in pushing his cabinet candidacy had contributed to his humiliation.[16]

Both Elihu B. Washburne and Adolph Borie, men very close to the President, wished to see Curtin rewarded for his services to the party. Apparently his nomination by

[15] *Ibid.*, 79; William B. Hesseltine, *Ulysses S. Grant* (New York, Republished 1957), 142; MacVeagh to Cameron, received Feb. 24, 1869, MacVeagh MSS, HSP. For an account of the presidential election in Pennsylvania and the cabinet question see Bradley, *Triumph of Militant Republicanism*, 288-99, 301-04.

[16] George H. Boker to Cameron, Feb. 27, 1869, Cameron MSS, DCC.

Grant for the Russian mission encountered no opposition in the Senate Foreign Relations Committee. Simon Cameron's action on the war governor's nomination in executive session behind barred doors is controversial. According to the Philadelphia *Press* and Reading *Eagle*, his remarks, abounding in acrimonious invectives against Curtin, were delivered in hope of defeating Senate confirmation. The newspaper account, declared Cameron, was incorrect. His "authorized" version, appearing in the Beaver *Argus*, was moderate in tone. Curtin, the senior Senator reminded his colleagues, was *not* the choice of his state's Republicans, nor was he the choice of Pennsylvania's Congressmen; however, in deference to the wishes of the new President, Cameron would not oppose him, although he could not vote for him. "I *could have rejected him*," boasted Cameron to Wayne MacVeagh. The *Senate Executive Journal* recorded no roll call; only agreement on the nomination following a period of debate. By exercising time-honored Senatorial prerogatives, the knowledge of which Grant was obviously innocent, the junior Senator could very likely have blocked the nomination. In any case, the nomination was carried with only oral protests, and in June Curtin was on his way to "Siberian exile." [17]

Cameron's wish to keep Curtin at home in 1869, contrasted with his eagerness to get the governor out of the country on a mission in 1863, is of special significance, because he knew well that his enemy's political influence soon would wane in Russia. Now feeling his own position secure with nothing to fear from Curtin, he would labor

[17] *Ibid.*, Bradley, *Triumph of Militant Republicanism*, 309-12; Cameron to MacVeagh, [April] 18, 1869, MacVeagh MSS, HSP.

to debar his old nemesis from political office at all levels of government and relegate him to the practice of law in the obscure village of Bellefonte.

The extension of Simon Cameron's political empire began properly with the year 1869. His immediate objectives were to secure the election of a Republican colleague to the Senate who would prove amenable in matters of patronage; to organize his legislative following in such a fashion as to control the annual election of the extremely coveted office of state treasurer; to solve the dilemma of support for Governor Geary's re-election in the face of increasing signs of independence from the incumbent; and especially to gain some measure of ascendancy over President Grant, the new dispenser of the juiciest political plum obtainable—federal patronage. In the meantime the politico would pursue liquidation of the remaining Curtin coterie while at the same time maintaining constant vigilance against any attempt of the former governor to seek rehabilitation at home.

The strategy of Simon Cameron in 1869 for the procurement of his Senatorial candidate paralleled that of 1861 when he managed the nomination of Edgar Cowan. Assuming an air of disinterested dignity—a position quite proper for a senior statesman disdaining to step down from his Senatorial pedestal—the politico went quietly to work wrecking a newly arisen coalition which threatened control of both the Senatorship and the continued manipulation of the state's treasury funds.

A combination commonly called the "Ring" because of its treasury connections had for its principal leaders William H. Kemble, a rich banker of Philadelphia and three-term occupant of the state treasurership, and Matthew S. Quay of Beaver. Kemble's prominence in the campaign of 1868 had markedly inflated the consciousness of his own political worth. He was treasurer of the state central committee and a national committeeman of the Republican Party. In his quest for desperately needed campaign funds he had made personal solicitations for aid from W. E. Chandler, the party's national secretary. Reputedly, the Philadelphia factional leader had realized a fortune from his manipulation of state funds and was now earnestly seeking the Republican Senatorial caucus nomination for 1869. By late October, 1868, J. K. Moorhead, leader of the Pittsburgh Republicans representing mostly manufacturing and commercial interests, conceded that because Kemble's combination had "so effectively occupied the ground" only the united efforts of all opposed to his nomination could bring about his defeat. The Democratic press likewise conceded his pre-eminence over other candidates.

Cameron, anxious to bring his son into prominence at every opportuniy and to have him share honors for bringing victories to his machine, depended mainly upon J. Donald Cameron's intrigues to checkmate the "Ring." Within two months the task had been accomplished and Kemble remained only a nominal candidate.

The Philadelphia connoisseur of fine laces and satins now found himself free to join James McManes, a rising municipal luminary, and William B. Mann in forcing their corrupt administration upon the unfortunate city. In 1868, Cameron had used Philadelphia's old Know-Nothing chieftain, Isaac Hazlehurst, to force Mann's temporary retirement from the district attorney's office. Although not crushed, Mann never regained all his old power and prestige.

The emergence of Matthew S. Quay as a Cameron

lieutenant almost coincidental with the liquidation of the combination of which he was an integral part provokes interesting questions. The path of Quay to Cameronianism had its origin during the furious Senatorial battle of 1867 when Quay stood for the House speakership nomination on behalf of the Curtin faction. Cameron's personal intervention at the time was doubly significant; it was an acknowledgement of Quay's worth and also a hint of a possible rapprochement based upon future benefits for both. Quay's eagerness at the caucus to move unanimous nomination of Cameron's candidate for the speakership was looked upon askance by other members of the Curtin faction. Following words of goodwill to Quay from Cameron's Harrisburg *Telegraph*, the former Curtin lieutenant succeeded in getting a neighbor from his town of Beaver elected state treasurer in 1868. A. K. McClure, who certainly was in position to know, stated Quay and Cameron had terminated their hostility by the end of 1867.

During the Christmas season of 1868, Matthew Quay utilized his new paper, the Beaver *Radical*, to review recent political trends he had observed in Harrisburg. Quay displayed remarkable clairvoyant qualities following a visit to J. Donald Cameron's office—an ostentatious center of operations crowded with fawning politicians. The younger Cameron would "have as much to do with the election of a U. S. Senator . . . as any man in the state, the editor of the *Radical* not excepted." Quay's prophecy, it seemed to the Beaver *Argus*, was actually a boast of his recently acquired recognition by the Camerons. Apparently, Quay, by using his powerful Kemble connections for bartering purposes, had sold out his Philadelphia partner in exchange for a political life insurance policy.

Surely Quay's overnight acceptance into full Cameronianism communion constituted the founding of the Cameron-
Quay political dynasty—a hierarchy destined to last into
the twentieth century.[18]

At the moment, in spite of tearful supplications from
close friends, especially Benjamin H. Brewster, promotion
of a Senatorial candidate based upon personal relationships played no part in the careful planning of Simon
Cameron, obsessed with the desire to attain permanent
intrenchment in power. A step toward this fulfillment, he
perceived, could be the cementing of alliances not only
with individuals as such, but also with concentrated group
interests as illustrated in the corporation. The interest very
closely paralleling that of his own and also exercising an
extraordinary political influence within the Commonwealth was that of the Pennsylvania Railroad. Under the
leadership of the dynamic Thomas Scott, the road was on
the threshold of exercising a stranglehold on the state's
transportation system—an accomplished fact within two
years.[19] Wisely Cameron chose to ally himself with this
new leviathan of transportation.

One must agree with A. K. McClure's contention that
the Senatorship in 1869 was "irrevocably disposed of before the legislature met," but surely it was *not* "very early
discovered by all." Up until the very eve of the nomi-

[18] Beaver *Radical* quoted in Beaver *Argus*, Dec. 23, 1868. Simon
Cameron and J. Donald Cameron were each elected four times to
the Senate. Quay was elected three times. The Senatorial service
of the trio totaled over half a century. The elder Cameron lived
to see his son and Quay serving concurrently.

[19] For a detailed account of this interesting story see Rolland H.
Maybee, *Railroad Competition and the Oil Trade, 1855-1873*
(Mount Pleasant, 1940).

nating caucus some of Cameron's closest confidants were not aware of it, nor was Governor Geary. Only one Cameronian journalist, E. B. Moore of West Chester, was able to conjure up the result.[20]

The man selected to represent the liaison in the Senate of the United States in the place of Democratic Charles Buckalew was John Scott of Huntingdon—Geary's first choice for the post of attorney-general in his cabinet.[21]

There was little question of his availability to the interested parties: a former counsel of marked ability for the railroads, he could be counted upon to understand and foster their interests; his personal integrity was not questioned even by his political opponents; and, because in the past he had shown little interest in political entanglements, was likely to prove tractable to Cameron's exercise of Pennsylvania's federal patronage.

Outward pretense of Cameron's disinterestness was scrupulously maintained when the state House, meeting for purposes of organization on January 4, 1869, elected John Clark, a man of only one year's service, to the Speaker's chair. Although ostensibly pledged to no one, Clark's past services in the construction of the Central and Northern Railroads, and his emergence as a lieutenant-colonel in the Civil War, should have raised speculative eyebrows. The peculiarity of no opposition to Clark's caucus nomination disappears when one notes the heavy list of callers Don Cameron entertained throughout the preceding night at his Lochiel Hotel suite.

John Scott's nomination in the caucus by acclamation on

[20] McClure, Notes, II, 224; West Chester Republican, Jan. 5, 1869.
[21] L. Kauffman to Stevens, Jan. 4, 1867, Stevens MSS, LC.

January 6 consumed only 15 minutes of time.[22] All candidates except the rebellious B. H. Brewster had withdrawn their names. The Republican Party's heavy majority in the General Assembly made Scott's election over William Wallace, the Democratic nominee, a foregone conclusion.

G. Eyster, a gentleman apparently closely related to Ann Eyster Scott, the candidate's wife, gave an account of what had happened behind the scenes:

> . . . Schofield and Grow were convinced that their case was hopeless, and both withdrew; I think that an interview was had during the night [of January 5] between these gentlemen, Mr. Scott and the Messrs. Cameron. . . . The real caucus in this matter was held in a room in Phila., not far from the Penna. RR. Office, this night one week. Mr. S[cott] was present by request. He had an important interview in Harrisburg with one of its citizens [J. Donald Cameron] by *request* three weeks ago in which he refused to assist in the organization that was proposed. His independence there gained him support that subserviency might have repelled.[23]

Quite naturally, John Scott, like any normal human being, would have been loathe to admit being party to a bargain which specified his sub-serviency, but surely no one can believe that Simon Cameron and Thomas Scott decided to make John Scott Senator because of his declaration of independence. If a combination had brought about his nomination, declared the Philadelphia *Telegraph*, even John Scott could not make the position of Senator meritorious. Commented the dour Gideon Welles: . . . "the railroad controls Pennsylvania, and Cameron has had the adroitness to secure it." Only two weeks after his election,

[22] Philadelphia *Evening Telegraph*, Jan. 5, 1869; Huntingdon *Register*, Jan. 13, 1869.

[23] [G. Eyster] to McPherson, Jan. 8, 1869, McPherson MSS, LC.

Senator John Scott, claimed the Pittsburgh *Gazette,* was working to seat Donald Cameron in Grant's cabinet.[24]

The same Republican caucus which surprised both Democrats and Republicans by pulling John Scott from the proverbial magician's hat performed equally well when it adopted Quay's candidate for state treasurer, Robert W. Mackey, a banker and political leader of Allegheny County. Possibly, if Quay had not suffered a breach with the incumbent, W. W. Irwin, and had a liberal portion of the state's funds been deposited in the pet banks of the Camerons, the man who was destined to share equal honors with Quay in the Cameron hierarchy for a decade would not have emerged.[25]

The disease-ridden Mackey was no stranger to the Camerons. He was supported by Cameron's journalist, Russell Errett, in the Allegheny factional fight against the extraordinary extrovert, Thomas Marshall; and during the Johnson patronage fiasco of 1868 he had suggested to Cameron a plan of compromise for a division of spoils in the Pittsburgh area. At that time, Errett assured Cameron, Mackey was in a position to help him; that he would not do "anything" to injure him, and had expressed a wish to "serve him." [26] Although temporarily unhorsed in 1870 through a combination of Irwin's friends with the Democrats, Mackey never relinquished his iron grip on the most coveted of (speaking financially) state offices. So

[24] Philadelphia *Telegraph,* Jan. 18, 1869; Welles, *Diary,* III, 505; Pittsburgh *Gazette,* Jan. 21, 1869.

[25] Lancaster *Intelligencer* quoted by Bellefonte *Democratic Watchman,* Jan. 15, 1869; McClure *Notes,* II, 255-68. General Cass received credit for furnishing the funds needed to persuade legislative Republican caucus members to vote for Mackey.

[26] Errett to Cameron, Feb. 6, 1868, Cameron MSS, DCC.

great was Cameron's faith in his new lieutenant's ability and judgment, asserted A. K. McClure, that he allowed Mackey a free hand to determine the machine's policies.

Simon Cameron had reason to feel gratified over the progress achieved during the first quarter of 1869; neither Curtin nor any of his clique had secured a place in Grant's cabinet; two new able lieutenants, Quay and Mackey, had been added to the Cameron stables, and the alliance with powerful corporate interests had produced a United States Senator favorably disposed to both parties.

But already a major dilemma—the question of Geary's renomination—was pressing for a solution. Although a proven Radical of the first order, the governor had adopted a progressive program calculated to woo the Commonwealth's political, moral, and social reformers. The liquor men were apprehensive of his temperance proclivities; employers disliked his pro-labor utterances; irreconcilables detested his philosophy of equal rights; and corporate interests feared future anti-monopolistic vetoes. But worst of all, from the politico's viewpoint, was the governor's efforts to secure a renomination in his own right, thereby in effect declaring his independence of Cameron's faction in addition to the outlawed Curtin men.

Some of Cameron's close supporters took for granted their chieftain's support of Geary's renomination if for no reason than his anti-Curtin sentiments. But to Cameron, who divined Geary's high political ambitions, this was not enough. Made aware by his lieutenants of Geary's grassroots strength, he decided very wisely to actually maintain a hands off policy thereby avoiding the ignominy of having suffered a defeat by Geary at the nominating convention. His most important task would be to maintain control of the Republicans in the state legislature, the spot where any future Senatorial ambitions of Geary could be checked. Two weeks before the convention date, Quay's *Radical* propounded the compromising position of the Cameron camp; Geary would receive the faction's support unless he was considered too weak to be elected over the Democratic nominee for governor.

Geary was renominated easily in a convention marked chiefly by Quay's ostentatious display of his new commanding position in the Cameron hierarchy. To the exuberant proud governor it seemed that he had achieved the "Lookout Mountain" of his political life against the combined efforts of the Curtin and Cameron factions. Geary's acceptance address before the convention included a declaration of no recognition for party factions. Its significance was easily determined—he purposed to unite the Republican state party under *his* leadership.[27]

Geary's lone-wolf campaign for re-election against the wealthy Democratic choice, Asa Packer, lacked vigor and interest. State Chairman John Covode, fearful of Geary's defeat, advised direct appeals to the Cameron faction for special assistance. After Geary and Cameron conferred in Reading in middle September, the elder Francis P. Blair wrote of his pleasure in hearing of supplications for aid from the Geary camp. Although provoked at Geary's eleventh-hour capitulation, Cameron conceded privately the desirability of Geary's re-election; but publicly, he exhibited no special efforts in the governor's behalf.

John Covode, convinced of the odds against victory,

[27] Geary to Edward Geary, Jan. 7, 1870, Geary Letters, Oregon Historical Society, on loan to PHMC. The writer has found no evidence to support McClure's contention of Cameron's support for Geary's renomination. See Bradley, *Triumph of Militant Republicanism*, 342-45.

turned to William B. Mann for assistance in manipulating the Philadelphia election returns in Geary's favor. According to McClure, who claimed a share in the scandalous bargaining, Geary, after considerable haggling, agreed to dismiss Benjamin H. Brewster, who had proven especially obnoxious to the Curtin men, from his cabinet and to replace him with an unrecognized half-brother of the attorney general, F. Carroll Brewster.

Geary's pseudo-victory in October by a majority of less than 5,000 votes, 90 per cent of which originated in Philadelphia, brought consummation of the agreement against the bitter protests of the victim.

Cameron had no reason to feel sympathetic toward Brewster, formerly one of the most servile of his creatures. When the politico had turned a deaf ear to his Senatorial supplications in January, Brewster publicly expressed his disgust of Cameron's support for special interests. In August, when Brewster sought a rapprochement, his former ideal merely concurred in expressing regrets over the "separation" of their long friendship; but again Brewster expressed his desire to resume pleasant relations. As a face-saving device Cameron entered a strong personal protest against the rumored dismissal to Geary. What was truly disturbing to Cameron was the entrance of F. Carroll Brewster into Geary's cabinet. His appointment, he conceded, would be very bad because of the new attorney general's close association with William B. Mann and his band. Later, Cameron did seek compensation for Brewster by asking Grant to take him into the cabinet when it seemed E. Rockwood Hoar would move to the Supreme Court.[28]

[28] *Ibid.*, 350-54; Cameron to MacVeagh, Oct. 29, Dec. 9, 1869, MacVeagh MSS, HSP.

Quite likely, to the politico's way of thinking the coming of Grant into office presented him with the most crucial and delicate task of the year. His goal was to secure more than the ordinary courtesies prescribed for the senior Senator whose party had elected the chief executive of the nation; he aspired to be admitted to the inner council of advisors usually found surrounding a President suspectible of being fashioned by persuasive sophistries, and which often succeed in exerting a pronounced influence on the politics of the nation.

Cameron's labors were made easier in some respects by the character of the President. With incredible naïveté, Grant would allow wealthy men to load him with very expensive gifts, to fête him, and to pay him unusual esteem solely on the basis of their desire, or so he believed, to do honor to the nation's savior and hero.

On the other hand Grant's inclination to run the nation like an army, and his ignorance or contempt of the time-honored civilities accorded senior Senators of the administration's party in respect to patronage, augured a clash against one who, President Polk had learned, would not countenance any disrespect for Senatorial prerogatives. This was first illustrated in the case of Curtin's former adjutant general, Alexander L. Russell, Grant's nominee for minister to Ecuador. This "straw" which broke the camel's back impelled Cameron to fight the nomination and Grant withdrew it. Concurrently, in executive session Cameron also blocked the consular appointment of Ferdinand Cox whom he labelled a "constitutional thief" from Philadelphia. These two examples should have taught the President the wisdom of seeking advice in advance of appointments.[29]

[29] Huntingdon *Globe*, April 29, 1869; Cameron to MacVeagh, [April] 19, 1869, McVeagh MSS, HSP.

While the politico was staging the battle for recognition of his privileges in Senatorial priority, wealthy Senator William Sprague, a gentleman not sharing the same opinion of Cameron as his father-in-law, Chief Justice Chase, was delivering a series of Senate speeches, attacking the grip of capitalists and industrialists upon government policies. The publicity resulting from his addresses netted him a special interview by a correspondent of the New York *Herald*. Sprague, because he believed Cameron was planning a rebuttal, entered into a short tirade against him:

I used to meet him a good deal sometime ago. He would take me down to his agricultural committee room, and set out champagne and ask me to drink. Finally I said to him, "Cameron, you are a vicious old fellow. I am a young man and you are an old sinner, and you are always putting temptation in my way. Now I don't intend coming to your committee room anymore." Since that time I have had little to do with Cameron.[30]

The summer months brought a period of relief from Congressional wrangling and allowed the elderly Senator pleasure in association with his patriarchial domain, now expanding by virtue of a rapidly growing brood of grandchildren. In early June, Jennie (Virginia) MacVeagh was blessed with a son and a month later his son Don reported the birth of his fourth daughter.

The recent bout with Grant over diplomatic appointments ordinarily would have proved a barrier to the development of a friendly personal relationship between the two men, but fortunately for Cameron he found a valuable intermediary in the person of General Thomas L. Kane, McKean County's most distinguished citizen. This creator of Pennsylvania's famous Bucktail Rifle Regiment

[30] New York *Herald*, April 24, 1869.

had erected a fine mansion in the great northern wood at Kane Summit near the Philadelphia and Erie Railroad of which he was a leading promoter. When Grant accepted Kane's invitation to visit him in June, the general, because he was Cameron's special friend, pronounced him the only other guest. The proposed visit, having come to the ears of John Scott, led the senator into arriving at some premature conclusions: ". . . the president has either captured you or you have captured him."

Following several delays Grant finally arrived at the Kane rendezvous in August in a special Northern Central car made available by Donald Cameron. In Kane's judgment, Cameron had made a very favorable impression upon the President and it was evident that he now "had it in his power to exert a *commanding* influence at Washington." With unaffected simplicity, it would seem, the general was hoping to see Cameron exercise his new power over Grant in matters of national interest rather than patronage.[31]

The most highly publicized fishing trip of the pair—the one allegedly taking place in the wilds of Cameron County on the banks of the Sumemahoning River where angler Simon, emulating the example patterned by the apostolic father of old, emerged not a fisher of finny aquatics, but one of men—never occurred. The trip was duly planned but Grant, greatly exercised over the Dominican problem in June, 1870, postponed it. The New York *World*, not wishing to see such a human interest story go by the board, related the tale anyway, and caught gullible historians in the process.

[31] T. Kane to Cameron, June 15, 23, July 6, 1869, Cameron MSS, LC; Scott to Cameron, June 4, 1869, Kane to Judge Gordon, Aug. 29, 1869, MacVeagh MSS, HSP.

In the fall of 1869 the President enjoyed another trip through Pennsylvania. This time his entourage included J. Donald Cameron. The party remained overnight at the Logan House in Altoona, site of the notable war Governors' Conference, and proceeded to Pittsburgh. Early the next year J. Donald Cameron was Grant's guest at the White House.[32]

That son Don was at the head of Cameron's patronage list there could be no doubt. It became the politico's ever-present passion to see his son represent Pennsylvania in the President's cabinet, but such a desire could not be fulfilled with an obtrusive suggestion to Grant. He could request positions of the chief executive for other men's sons but not his own. He must work with patience and persistence—qualities peculiarly his own—until Grant realized for himself the need for taking Don into his cabinet. Not until the expiration of seven long exasperating years did Cameron see the accomplishment of this primary goal.

Although in 1871 Cameron complained of Grant's habit of not consulting him in matters of Pennsylvania appointments and asserted his belief that his "supposed influence" over the President actually weakened his position,[33] his patronage justified the public's view of his commanding position.

Apparently, no anti-Cameron man, except Curtin, received appointments from Grant. The list included the names of Russell Errett, James Kerns, Dr. H. E. Muhlenberg, Wayne MacVeagh, George H. Boker, Henry D.

[32] Harrisburg *Patriot*, Sept. 15, 1869; Lancaster *Intelligencer*, Feb. 23, 1870.
[33] Cameron to MacVeagh, March 19, 1871, MacVeagh MSS, HSP.

Moore, William Strong, George Bergner, John Hiestand, and John W. Forney.

Henry D. Moore, a Cameron lieutenant dating from ante-bellum days, received the lucrative post of the collectorship of the Port of Philadelphia. A cooling off of his relationship with Cameron is indicated by his failure to seek his patron's bond for the position. When Moore resigned in March, 1871, because Cameron insisted upon the dismissal of one of his employees in the customs house, the "Ring," led by Kemble, Quay, and the chairman of the Republican State Central Committee, pushed William E. Elliott for the position.[34]

But Grant wisely chose the editor of the Philadelphia *Press*, J. W. Forney. The exuberant alcoholic's last periodic feud with Cameron, dating from the Senatorial contest of 1867, ended in December 1869, when the politico rose in the Senate to admit his error of accusing Forney of financial chicanery, and moved the closing of Forney's accounts. Instead of Forney, the "subject of wrong," it was his confidential officer who had improperly used federal funds. A few days later Forney responded with a series of articles reviewing Cameron's great services to his country. In March, 1871, Forney gave his former enemy credit for securing his confirmation to the collectorship and pledged himself to the "extent of his ability," to comply with any request or suggestion from his sponsor. This latest honeymoon lasted for one year.[35]

[34] A. Cummings to Cameron, March 20, 1871, Cameron MSS, LC.

[35] *Cong. Globe*, 41 Cong., 2 Sess., 164; Forney to Cameron, Dec. 29, 1869, March 26, 1871, Cameron MSS, LC. Forney had lost $40,000 through default of his "friends." According to Baron Stoeckl, Forney recovered $33,000 for pushing the Alaskan purchase. See Platt, *Russo-American Relations*, 159-61.

When an old personal friend of Buchanan, Justice Robert C. Grier, retired from the Supreme Court, Cameron, after playing a leading role in securing Hoar's rejection for the spot, succeeded in replacing him with another Pennsylvanian, William C. Strong. Concurrently, Joseph P. Bradley, a future father-in-law of Eliza Cameron, Simon's granddaughter, was also appointed to the court. Bergner was reappointed to the Harrisburg post office; Errett and Muhlenburg secured internal revenue sinecures; and "Jolly Jack" Hiestand, the Lancaster editor who had accompanied Grant on the mythical fishing excursion, went into the Philadelphia naval office.

A Washington letter to the Cincinnati *Times* reported, very likely with exaggeration, the employment of 200 persons in Washington who owed their jobs to Simon Cameron. "He is never a halfway friend to anybody," commented a Democratic organ, "and will make more personal exertions to oblige one than perhaps any man who has ever been in the U. S. Senate." [36]

The two leading disappointed candidates for sinecures were Alexander Cummings and Samuel Purviance. The former, failing to secure the Commissionership of Internal Revenue, became editor of *The Day*. Purviance tired of waiting for a judgeship and upon completion of his service at the Constitutional Convention of 1873 became an Independent Republican. Both Cameron and Senator Scott failed to secure a western judgeship for Henry C. Johnson, the man Geary had pledged to make Secretary of the Commonwealth.

If consensus of opinion is to be relied upon, there can be little doubt of the influence exerted by Simon Cameron

[36] Lewistown *Gazette*, Nov. 16, 1870.

upon the Grant administration. The press and respected political leaders, representative of both parties, named, with minor variations, a small cabal composed of Senators Cameron, Chandler, Conkling, Morton, and Representative B. F. Butler largely responsible for Grant's policies. Garfield, Hayes, Carl Schurz, and G. W. Julian acknowledged and regretted the influence exerted by these "friends" of the President.[37]

The members of this reactionary "kitchen cabinet" were czars of political machines within their respective states, maintaining their autocracy largely by the time-honored spoils system channeled through the Presidential office. Progressive programs and efforts of civil service reformers were anathema alike to the philosophy, power, and political life of these state bosses. A few reformers found their way into the Grant cabinet and Senator Cameron, acknowledged prince of the spoilsmen, willingly assisted the stalwart coterie in its drive to liquidate this growing menace.

Attorney General Hoar of Massachusetts, well known for his remarks about patronage hunters, political hacks, and demagogic Senators was their first victim. Grant sent to the Senate Hoar's list of nine eminently qualified judges to fill circuit court vacancies. The slighted Senators, although seething with wrath because none of them had been consulted in advance, dared not oppose the President and his worthy nominees. Their first opportunity to

[37] Springfield *Republican*, Nov. 24, 1871; Harrisburg *Patriot*, April 10, 1872; Rhodes, *United States*, VI, 390; Hesseltine, *Grant*, 254; Julian, *Recollections*, 334; Schurz, *Reminiscences*, III, 332-33. In 1875 Chandler entered Grant's cabinet. General Rawlins, until his death in September, 1869, exerted paramount influence over Grant.

humiliate Hoar presented itself in December, 1869, when Grant nominated him for the Supreme Court. The Senate promptly tabled the nomination. Never in his long career in the Senate, related Charles Sumner, had he seen such hostility exhibited to any nomination. Following the rejection, Cameron, who personally admired Hoar, asked him: "What could you expect for a man who had snubbed seventy senators?" B. F. Butler and a group of Senators led Hoar's forced resignation from the cabinet the following spring. It should be noted, however, other factors contributed to Hoar's departure.[38]

The resignation of Secretary Jacob D. Cox from the Grant cabinet was essentially the protest of a civil service reformer against the evils of the spoils system. Cox became especially obnoxious to Cameron following his refusal to allow financial assessment of his clerks for political campaigns. "Cameron . . . and Chandler," reported Forney to Sumner, "have got Cox out of the interior and got Delano in." [39]

The adventures of President Grant in the field of diplomacy furnished the background for attainment of the zenith of Cameron's power and prestige in the Senate— the chairmanship of the powerful and respected Foreign Relations Committee. The chief executive, probably embarrassed by domestic issues, sought diversion by personally advancing the interests of the United States in

[38] J. Forney to Cameron, Dec. 29, 1869, Cameron MSS, LC; Jacob Dolson Cox, "How Judge Hoar ceased to be Attorney General," *Atlantic Monthly*, LXXVI (Aug. 1895), 162-73; Charles Francis Adams quoted in Moorfield Storey and Edward Emerson, *Ebenezer Rockwood Hoar*, 197.

[39] Cox to Garfield, Oct. 24, 1870, quoted in Hesseltine, *Grant*, 217; Harrisburg *Patriot*, Nov. 7, 1870.

Caribbean waters. He bypassed channels ordinarily used for such transactions, ordered his private secretary to investigate and report, and without benefit of cabinet sanction presented a treaty for the annexation of Santo Domingo. The opposition to the treaty led by the able chairman of the Foreign Relations Committee, Charles Sumner, had the effect of translating the President's Santo Domingo scheme into a fetish. The bad feelings engendered by their differences and misunderstandings reached such a peak that the President raised his fist in defiance upon passing Sumner's residence.

The passing of a year brought no change. King Ahab had not yet secured Naboth's vineyard for his wicked Jezebel, but that minister of duplicity, Charles Sumner, who had prevented the foul deed, was now to suffer the consequences of his traitorous stewardship. If personal considerations were not enough—Sumner's proposal to impeach Grant—the administration could not harbor the anomaly of the chairman of the Senate Foreign Relations Committee completely out of accord with its policies.

What with the highly important Treaty of Washington in the making and a secretary of state no longer on speaking terms with Sumner, it is little wonder that at the beginning of the Forty-Second Congress in March, 1871, the Republican caucus, yielding to Presidential intimations, wielded the Grant axe and Sumner emerged shorn of his proudest prerogative. Awarding of the chairmanship of the trifling Committee on Privileges and Elections to the egocentric fallen Caesar was but to chafe salt into a mortal wound. Sumner's place was occupied by the second-ranking member of the committee, Simon Cameron.

By the expressed wish of Charles Sumner, when Cameron returned to the Senate in 1867 he became a member of the Foreign Relations Committee. He was always grateful to Sumner for the support given him when he was nominated for the Russian mission.

On March 15, 1870, Grant's Dominican Treaty had been reported out of the committee. Cameron was among the majority opposing ratification but, keeping in mind the probability of a change in the developments, he explained that he would have voted for annexation had different circumstances existed. The determination to enjoy a vacation prevailed over the urge to continue debate on the merits of the case and finally on the last day of June, 56 senators split their vote. The treaty, apparently, was lost. This time Cameron was on the President's side.[40]

Cameron was at his home in Harrisburg when news reached him by telegraph of the action to oust Sumner from the Committee. Not taking time to pack his bag, he left before daylight for Washington, resolving not to accept Sumner's place. As he was on the point of taking his seat in the Senate chamber he saw Senator Schurz on the floor and paused to get the trend of his address. He was surprised to find himself the target of Schurz's abuse, related with superlative sarcasm: "Nobody doubts, I presume that . . . [Cameron's] studies of international law have been profound, or that his long experience in the service of the country, especially as to our relations with foreign powers, eminently fits him for that place."

These "unjust remarks" by Schurz, Cameron explained

[40] Allen Nevins, *Hamilton Fish* (New York, 1937), 316; Harrisburg *Telegraph*, March 16, July 1, 1870.

to the Senate four years later, impelled him to leave the Senate chamber and to take no part in proceedings. It was imperative at the time, the apologist reminded his colleagues, for the chairman of the Committee to be "in perfect union" with the secretary of state. "My God, sir," concluded Cameron emphatically before his colleagues, "I did not rob him [Sumner] of anything. I would rather now, much rather, add to his reputation than detract from it in any way."

In later years, the politico explained how his "spirit of opposition to disparagement" had shaped the course of his career and cited the Sumner case as a prime example. He would show Schurz and the nation whether or not Simon Cameron "of all men was least fitted to fill the chair" of the distinguished Senator from Massachusetts.[41]

After Cameron retreated to his committee room, Senator T. O. Howe defended the proposed change and reiterated the importance of having a chairman on speaking terms with Grant and Secretary Fish. Cameron was not "especially fitted" for his proposed duties, conceded Henry Wilson, and he hoped there would be no changes. When Schurz entered into another philippic, Senator John Scott attempted to shame Schurz for his derogatory remarks against an absent Senator. Schurz's reply implied that *all* senators in favor of Sumner's deposition were influenced by the "propelling force" of Grant. Thomas Bayard's motion to change the committee's name to the Personal

[41] *Cong. Globe*, 42 Cong., 1 Sess., 35; *Cong. Record*, 43 Cong., 1 Sess., 3434; *New York Times*, June 3, 1878. In his interview with Frank Burr, April, 1882, Cameron erroneously stated that the Republican caucus unanimously voted to oust Sumner. The vote was actually 26 to 21.

Relations Committee stimulated shouts of laughter and the body (without a quorum) voted 39 to 9 to change the name.[42]

Fortunately for the new chairman, he was given assistance by his very able colleagues on the committee and unquestionably the change was a great relief to the harried Hamilton Fish, who now no longer needed to worry about having important treaties "pigeonholed or smothered in the Committee Room." Upon conclusion of the successful treaty with Britain, the grateful secretary of state tendered double thanks to the chairman for the "generous and very efficient aid and support" rendered the administration. Fish's evaluation of the abilities of the chairman differed from that of James A. Garfield, who heartily accepted the observation of a Philadelphia paper that it was at last understandable why the emperor Caligula made his horse a Roman consul.[43]

An amusing sequel, in light of the many disparaging remarks passed on Cameron's unfitness for his exalted position on the Foreign Relations Committee, occurred in 1873. During the Civil War, when the committee's room was remodeled, panels were constructed to accommodate the portraits of the four most eminent chairmen since the days of George Washington. In 1872, Cameron appealed to the Committee on Public Buildings to have the room "completely furnished." It was not revealed to the public just how it happened, but Cameron was one of the distinguished four; his portrait was assigned to the spot of greatest honor—the panel back of the chairman's

[42] *Cong. Globe*, 42 Cong., 1 Sess., 35-38, 53.
[43] Fish to Cameron, copy, May 30, 1871, Letter Books of Hamilton Fish, LC; Garfield quoted in Hesseltine, *Grant*, 254.

seat. His likeness, commented the Philadelphia *Weekly Press*, was fittingly portrayed in *brass*.[44]

The sequence of events suggests an interesting corollary to the Santo Domingo story. Shortly after Cameron's hesitating adverse vote on the Santo Domingo treaty on March 15, 1870, Wayne MacVeagh, his son-in-law (Margaretta's marriage in May gave him another one), whose health was poor, sought, primarily it would seem, an European mission to aid him in his program of physical rehabilitation. MacVeagh's first choice was The Hague. Senator Scott added his efforts to the worthy cause and what with Grant's determination not to accept defeat for his beloved treaty, Cameron was in an excellent bargaining position when he conferred with the President on April 18. Without a "moment's hesitation," Grant cast aside another candidate and agreed to MacVeagh's appointment to The Hague. Understandably, the visitor was "delighted with Grant's manner." A week later both J. Donald Cameron and father were back at the White House.[45]

The passing of another month witnessed no confirmation of Grant's promises and in late May, on the pretext of making final arrangements for the delayed fishing excursion, Cameron again saw the President. The persistent politico gave Grant exactly five days respite and the next time when he penetrated the chief executive's outer office, Presidential secretary Porter revealed MacVeagh's imminent nomination for the Turkish mission. Grant's hasty directive to the secretary of state would not have given incumbent E. Joy Morris an opportunity to

[44] Philadelphia *Weekly Press*, May 10, 1873.
[45] Cameron to MacVeagh, April 15, 19, 1870, MacVeagh MSS, LC.

resign. When Fish protested the unseemly haste, Grant allowed Morris time to telegraph his resignation from Constantinople.[46]

Before Fish or Cameron were notified of the appointment, a West Chester paper announced MacVeagh's plans of traveling in Europe to "restore his broken and shattered constitution." The Senate confirmed MacVeagh the day following his nomination and he sailed on schedule. Reputedly he was to receive $10,000 in gold plus the expense of his "outfit." In December, the Commissioner of Revenue announced no diplomat was being compensated for outfits. The minister's tortuous itinerary took him through Scotland, France, Germany, and Italy. Upon arrival at his destination in October, the nation's new representative in Turkey, exhibiting no desire to penetrate the mysteries of the seraglio or other adjuncts of the Porte, proposed to seek an immediate furlough from his arduous duties.

Although MacVeagh expressed his willingness to shoulder the public abuse he knew was sure to come following the completion of an uninterrupted junket taking him through Palestine, Egypt, and Greece on the way home, he heeded the admonitions of his father-in-law to remain. When he did return on furlough, advised Cameron, it was best to plan a route through Greece and Italy so he wouldn't have the urge to return.[47]

The era of the Forty-first and Forty-second Congresses was generally a sorry if not an exciting one. Ku Klux Klan

[46] Cameron to MacVeagh, May 26, June 1, 1870, *ibid.*, Nevins, *Fish*, 364.

[47] West Chester *American*, May 31, 1870; Harrisburg *Telegraph*, Dec. 9, 1870; MacVeagh to Cameron, Dec. 23, 26, 1870, Cameron MSS, LC; Cameron to MacVeagh, Nov. 27, 1870, MacVeagh MSS, HSP.

disturbances in the South, it was argued, justified a continued militant policy; solons of the financial world marveled at the Supreme Court's ruling of unconstitutional greenbacks and the prompt reversal of its own decision; financially interested Congressmen were freely giving away the citizen's public domain to mushrooming railroad companies; and social circles were buzzing with excitement over the visit of Victoria's Prince Arthur, the Duke of Connaught, to the Grants. Foreign "intelligence" proved not quite so humdrum: Fenians engaged in forays along the Canadian border; the Prussians toppled the dream castles of Napoleon III of France, and the first step toward fulfillment of one clause of the Treaty of Washington was revealed when the Geneva Tribunal convened for one day and stood adjourned for six months.

Less than two months after Cameron assumed the chairmanship of the Foreign Relations Committee, work on the Treaty of Washington was completed. He and Senator Morton discussed it with the cabinet and on May 9, the day following the signing of the treaty, another conference was held with cabinet members. Vexed at the suggestion of having Morton present the treaty, the chairman "declared that he would assume the responsibility of conducting the treaty to a successful conclusion." The treaty was approved with little opposition and ratifications were exchanged with Britain on the anniversary of Bunker Hill. Both nations were greatly relieved at finding a formula for solving the problems arising out of the Civil War conflict.[48]

Protectionist journals made much ado over the Pennsylvania Senator's presentation of a mammoth petition, 160

[48] Foulke, *Oliver P. Morton*, II, 175-76.

feet long, reputedly the second longest in the nation's history. Signed by thousands of laborers, mostly from the coal regions, the petition requested Congress to protect American labor and home manufacturers. Cameron's long speech, which gave evidence of considerable preparation, contained a mass of statistics on the anthracite industry and showed the negative effect on Pennsylvania's coal trade of foreign water-borne coal. A leading exponent of America's capitalistic system summarized his argument with a leaf from Karl Marx: "The capital of every nation is its labor. . . . When labor languishes all perish together in a common ruin." [49]

New worlds always remain to be subjugated by a conqueror, and so it was with Simon Cameron in 1871; but no one argued the pre-eminence of his position at both state and national levels. The influence of the Curtin-McClure faction was so inconsequential that the politico could now boast: ". . . the control of the [state] party organization is entirely in the hands of our friends." [50] He now enjoyed the most eminent chairmanship in the Senate and he sat on the inner council of Presidential advisors. Although holding no office of public trust, his son, J. Donald Cameron, moved freely in the highest political circles and was his father's recognized spokesman.

The Democratic Party had suffered a decline after its resurgence of 1870 and the Republican majority in the state legislature, holders of the key to the doors of the Senate, were largely "Cameron" men.

In the foreseeable future only the independent ambi-

[49] Pottsville *Miners' Journal*, March 12, 1870; *Cong. Globe*, 41 Cong. 2 Sess., 1725-27.

[50] Cameron to MacVeagh, March 19, 1871, MacVeagh MSS, HSP.

tious John White Geary might conceivably challenge the politico's position in the party. Simon Cameron sensed Geary's dream of succeeding him—"Like a fool as he is"— in the Senate and then of going on to the Presidency.[51] Unlike Cameron, who had only contempt for the might of his potential antagonist, Geary actually believed it possible for him to seize control of the Republican state organization.

[51] Cameron to MacVeagh, Sept. 5, 1870, *ibid.*

10
Defender
of the Fortress

THE YEARS FROM 1871 THROUGH 1874 CONSTITUTED A PERIOD
in which the master, in collaboration with J. Donald
Cameron, Mackey, Quay, and lesser lieutenants, maintained a wavering plateau in the struggle to ward off
threats to the supremacy of the machine. The epoch was
characterized by a final effort of the ostracized Curtin
faction, in an alliance with Republican reformers and the
Democratic Party, to overthrow, in the name of reform,
the Cameronian hierarchy within the state and Grantism
on the national level. Constitutional changes providing for
popular election of more state offices threatened to reduce
the machine's sphere of operations. A weakening of the
Grant-Cameron liaison menaced Cameron's control of the
patronage and adversely effected the politico's drive to
place his son in the Grant cabinet.

But it was the state Democratic triumph of 1874 which
offered Cameronism its greatest challenge. The party won
a majority of the Congressional seats, wrested control of
the General Assembly from the Republicans, and insured

itself the election of the next United States Senator. If the Democracy succeeded in maintaining its gains for two more years, Simon Cameron's machine would suffer a collapse and the historian would never have made reference to the Cameron political dynasty. As predicted by Cameron, the threat of John White Geary proved innocuous.

The need for reform in the Commonwealth's political circles was considered self-evident. The most publicized evil was the Treasury Ring, which allegedly used the state's money for private speculation. Governor Geary commented: "There is certainly some advantage to be gained . . . unknown to the public, by the holding of the position of State Treasurer, but which readily accounts for the disgraceful scramble, and for the political and moral debauchery which the people of this state seemed to be doomed annually to witness in the election of that officer."[1] Lesser rings dominated municipal government—the most notorious being the Philadelphia Gas Ring.

The legislative body of Pennsylvania vied with that of New York for the reputation of being the most corrupt in the nation. Venal legislators and brokers gave sponsors of legislation assurance of seeing things "put through" provided everything was "made right." Introduction of bills designed to inflict financial hardships on rich citizens or corporations provided legislative blackmail during the dull seasons. Selected friends of the Pennsylvania Railroad interests were allotted paid retainers and transportation passes at the end of the legislative session. Silver and gold rather than intrinsic value were used to measure the worth of prospective legislation. Philadelphia's large rep-

---

[1] *Papers of the Governors, 1857-1871*, 1009.

resentation in the General Assembly made logical the charge that the city was the leading beneficiary of graft.

According to Senator Morrow B. Lowry, a spokesman for the reformers, the Treasury Ring operated in the legislature through the Speakers of the two houses, who determined committee assignments, important chairmanships, and the clerkships. The Speakers in turn were the creatures of the majority party caucus. Cameron's leading lieutenant in the Harrisburg area, George Bergner, managed the Ring's interest in the legislature. The Bergner legislative bargaining did not involve financial transactions. Legislators were pleased to support his "legislation" in return for coveted posts and the opportunity to dispense petty patronage. Such was Bergner's power, asserted Lowry, that any bill he sponsored would pass.

It was not Lowry's contention that Republican legislators were any more corrupt than Democratic ones, but Republicans held the key offices and dominated the legislature. The operation of rings was not an integral part of machine politics but were adjuncts to enrich and maintain its members. Although Cameron himself did not direct the operation of rings, his leading lieutenants did so and he looked with tolerance upon their activities. The functions of the rings and of the machine could not easily be differentiated in the eyes of the public and it is logical that the overlord of these manipulators, who occupied positions of public trust, should become the prime target of the reformers.[2]

The voices of these reformers, including proponents of labor, temperance, and of women's rights, were first

[2] Lowry to correspondent of Erie *Observer*, Dec. 28, 1871. For a full discussion of the various aspects of state corruption see Bradley, *Triumph of Militant Republicanism*, 331-32, 362-64.

audible in 1870. A reform slate appeared in Allegheny County and the following year Pittsburgh elected a reform mayor. In Philadelphia, an Independent Republican supported by Democrats secured election to Congress.

Evidences of revolt within Republican ranks caused concern among its conservative leaders and they sought means of silencing them. One method was to remove leaders of reform from the scene by offering them attractive federal offices outside the state. These tactics were tried without success on A. K. McClure and M. B. Lowry.

The machine's temporary loss of control of Allegheny County in 1869 and of the state treasurership in 1870 must not be attributed to reform movements but to the dissatisfaction of powerful office-seekers. When Mackey unhorsed General W. W. Irwin from the state treasurership in 1869, the latter's friends led by M. B. Lowry sought revenge and secured enough votes from a few reformers in alliance with the Democrats to defeat Mackey in 1870.

Thomas Scott and J. Donald Cameron worked together to heal the Mackey-Irwin schism but found mutual antagonisms of a personal nature "make men to a degree unmanageable almost insane, to reasons from outside." [3] Don Cameron responded with some warmth against the suggestion to ditch Mackey before the next election for treasurer. He was willing to jeopardize the prestige of the organization by backing Mackey again;[4] to have done otherwise could have entailed the loss of the machine's ablest manager. Actually the risk was not great because the Democrats could not afford to continue their support of Republican candidates.

[3] Scott to Cameron, Jan. 11, 1870, Cameron MSS, LC.
[4] J. McAfee to Covode, Nov. 30, 1870, Covode MSS, HSWP.

The machine went to work methodically liquidating the fifteen Republican bolters from the party and in three years Mackey boasted that not one Republican who had voted against him in 1870 had been re-elected to the legislature. When he was a candidate again in 1871 only one Republican dared vote against him.

There was no evidence of a schism in the Republican State Convention of 1871—a body notorious for its composition of office holders. Matthew Quay directed from the floor while Mackey worked behind the scenes. The docile convention followed Quay's recommendation to allow the permanent chairman in conjunction with the two nominees for state office to appoint the chairman of the state central committee. Because the candidates, Colonel Robert Beath and Colonel David Stanton, were hand-picked by the machine, it meant the elevation of a Cameron lieutenant (in this case, Russell Errett) to succeed the late John Covode. Stanton was Quay's neighbor from Beaver County. Quay felt he was entitled to name another state officer when Irwin, his former protegé from Beaver, was excommunicated.

It was the state organization's plan to reverse the Democratic victories of 1870 by running soldier candidates, by calling for constitutional changes, and by giving lip service to civil service reforms. Continued use of the "bloody shirt" campaign technique together with the manipulation of election returns in Philadelphia provided the Republican candidates with liberal majorities. The electorate overwhelmingly endorsed the proposed convention for revision of the state's constitution. In Philadelphia, rather curiously, only 523 votes were cast against it, but the Democratic stronghold of Berks County recorded 11,000 negative votes.

Once again, the Republican state organization had set its house in order. Harmony had been restored, the party was again in possession of state offices, and it had won a working majority in both houses of the legislature. Apparently the party fathers could relax; but appearances were deceitful, this was the calm before the storm.

A movement, originating outside the Commonwealth, was soon to call for unified action against the evils of the era, the components of which, in popular parlance, were incorporated within the term "Grantism."

Responsible Republican leaders, viewing with alarm the poor record of the Grant administration, the abuses arising from the spoils system, and the general corruption emanating from Presidential circles (seemingly without any genuine note of protest from Grant), feared for the future of the party. There was no sign that Grant's renomination—a foregone conclusion—and his election would bring a change in policy. Moreover, except largely for political purposes, there seemed little reason for maintaining a militant policy in the South.

In 1871 Rutherford B. Hayes spoke for the reformers of his party: "I fear that such advisors as Chandler, Cameron, and Conkling are too influential with Grant. They are not safe counsellors. I hope that the disasters sure to follow this Sumner blunder [creation of a schism in party leadership], will make them pause and reflect. Otherwise a new candidate, or defeat,—perhaps, defeat in any event—awaits the Republican Party in 1872." [5]

The Liberal Republican movement in Missouri was designed primarily for the purpose of removing the political disabilities of Southern sympathizers and to rid the state's

[5] Charles R. Williams, ed., *Diary and Letters of Rutherford Birchard Hayes* (5 vols., Columbus, 1922-26), III, 136.

party of domination by Grant's manager, the director of the notorious Whiskey Ring. The crusade came to include national goals: "a movement to purge the Republican Party of the spoils system, political corruption, and vindictiveness toward the South." A contemporary wrote: "[Grant's] disgraceful conduct toward Sumner and alliance with Morton, Conkling, Cameron and their associates rendered it morally impossible for me any longer to fight under his banner." [6]

It would seem certain therefore that a struggle in Pennsylvania against Grantism must include, as one of its goals, the overthrow of its adjunct within the state, the political machine of Simon Cameron; and that his ostracized enemies within the party must be the first to respond to a call for action.

In January, 1872, the Missouri Liberal Republicans invited all Republicans throughout the nation opposed to Grant's renomination to unite in a national convention at Cincinnati on May 1.

In the meantime, A. K. McClure, notwithstanding active intervention of both Grant and Cameron, had succeeded through the assistance of Democratic votes in getting himself seated (following a post-election contest) in the state senate.[7] McClure's successful campaign of revenge against Grant and Cameron had been cleverly camouflaged under the banner of reform. The net result gained McClure recognition as the leading Republican reformer of the Commonwealth.

[6] James G. Randall and David Donald, *The Civil War and Reconstruction* (Boston, 2nd Edition, 1961), 658; Julian, *Recollections*, 334.

[7] In his *Notes*, II, 290-327, McClure devoted two chapters to the subject.

In response to the Liberal Republican invitation, Horace Greeley of New York called on A. K. McClure to enlist his aid. A survey satisfied Curtin's old lieutenant of "serious defection" in the Grant camp. Assuming leadership of the movement, McClure assisted in preparing the Commonwealth's Liberal Republican call to action signed by 41 men, not one of whom was a defector from the Cameron faction.

Pennsylvania's Liberal call was couched in general terms—"the party should have a nobler destiny than mere subordination to personal purposes"—but McClure's letter to the Philadelphia *Bulletin* branded Grant the "foe of every principle of reform," the shield of the dominion of kings, and lord of perpetrators of fraud. Although no reference was made directly to Cameron, no discerning reader could mistake the identity of "the bad men [who] had deceived" the President by their appeals for party organization.[8]

Pennsylvania's leading delegates to the Liberal Republican Convention were A. K. McClure, John Hickman, M. B. Lowry, and General Thomas L. Kane, the only close friend of Cameron to desert to ranks of the enemy. En route to Cincinnati, Kane had dispatched a pathetic farewell to the man he had guided to Grant.

The imposing A. K. McClure commanded much attention and comment at Cincinnati, but was powerless to determine the outcome of the convention. In full knowledge that Andrew G. Curtin, at that time absent in Europe, stood no chance of receiving the Liberal Republican nomination, McClure had Curtin's name presented before the convention, thereby irreparably damaging the

---

[8] *Bulletin* quoted in Bellefonte *Democratic Watchman*, April 26, 1872.

minister's status in the regular Republican organization. Pennsylvania's vote was pledged to David Davis following a complimentary vote for Curtin.

The convention's path to the choice of its Presidential nominee defied logic. The journalistic Quadrilateral, after having enjoyed its feat of breaking David Davis, failed in its efforts to initiate a stampede for Charles Francis Adams, and a political monstrosity, Horace Greeley, emerged victorious. McClure and his delegation returned home disappointed. The Liberal Republicans alone had not the strength to elect Greeley, and none could conjure up the picture of the Democracy bestowing the Presidential candidacy upon the despised New York editor.[9]

The delegates to the Democratic State Convention did not favor Greeley's nomination on the national ticket but they refrained from endorsing any candidate, thereby leaving the door open, as far as the Keystone State was concerned, to his acceptance.

Long before the Cincinnati Convention the politico showed his comprehension of the struggle that lay ahead. The Washington administration, he believed, would not prove equal to the crisis. In his own state he expected the battle to begin with an attack on him and then be carried to Grant. If it had been given to him to have a choice in the matter he would prefer not to participate, but he was not one to run from a fight. His country needed Grant's re-election and he would fight for his country.[10]

Both A. K. McClure and Cameron had emissaries at the Baltimore Democratic National Convention to repre-

[9] King, David Davis, 281; Henry Watterson, "Marse Henry" (2 vols., New York, 1919), I, 242-57.

[10] Cameron to MacVeagh, received Feb. 10, Feb. 14, 1872, MacVeagh MSS, HSP.

sent their political interests. McClure was working desperately to secure Greeley's nomination, while Cameron, believing the odds too great to hope for victory against a Democratic-Liberal Republican coalition, was fighting Greeley's nomination.

Cameron's agent was Amos L. Noyes a lumber merchant of long acquaintance formerly from Cameron County. In view of his own gubernatorial candidacy for the Democratic nomination, Noyes at first was reluctant to express opposition to Greeley. Later he agreed to help his friend but in his opinion Grant could best be elected by nominating Greeley. Only two states, Pennsylvania and Delaware, fought Greeley; he was nominated easily. Nothing except its obsession to triumph over Grantism could have induced the Democracy to swallow *in toto* the repulsive Liberal Republican candidate Greeley and its platform.

The Republicans met in national convention merely to ratify a Presidential nomination already conceded—that of Grant. The names of three Pennsylvanians, Simon Cameron, Donald Cameron, and Andrew Curtin, were mentioned for the Vice-Presidency. According to Forney, who was again at war with the Camerons, Simon pushed to have Pennsylvania present Don at the convention but he found so much resistance within the delegation that he dropped it. On the other hand the leading Democratic opposition paper claimed the delegation's willingness to back Donald. Under the circumstances one would think the Old Guard would have bolstered its ticket with a line Republican of liberal leanings. Andrew G. Curtin might have filled the requirement if unfounded rumors and the unauthorized action of McClure at Cincinnati had not killed his chances.

In any case Cameron got a man to his liking. He owed

Henry Wilson a debt and here was an opportunity to pay it. Wilson had defended him at the time of his nomination to Russia and again, in 1870, Wilson, in his article on Stanton, insisted that Lincoln's first Secretary of War had voluntarily resigned. The biographers of Schuyler Colfax and of Oliver P. Morton concede it was Cameron who played the leading role in bringing about the defeat of Colfax and the election of Wilson.[11]

With symptoms of the Liberal Republican revolt already in the air in early April, it looked as if the Republican State organization were actually courting defeat when it selected John Frederic Hartranft for gubernatorial honors. The auditor general's name was associated with the treasury ring and special state agent Oliver Evans, collector of war claims, who insisted upon retaining a 10 per cent fee ($291,000) for his successful collections. Investigation had revealed a loan of $7,000 from Evans to Hartranft. Moreover, allegedly, irregularities existed in Hartraft's accounts.[12]

According to Cameron's confidant, E. B. Moore, the politico questioned the wisdom of nominating Hartranft, but when he found the ring men, Mackey, Quay, Mann, W. H. Kemble, and his trusty Pittsburgh supporter Errett favoring Hartranft, he did not attempt to overrule them. Apparently Donald also approved the majority choice. This much is certain—Hartranft was the machine's candidate for governor and he had no hesitation in admitting it.

[11] Ovando J. Hollister, *Life of Schuyler Colfax* (New York, 1886), 373; Foulke, *Morton*, II, 257.

[12] Evans evidently shared his collection percentage with others because two years later he was unable to pay his counsel's fee. Evans to J. Black, July 19, 1874, Black MSS, LC.

The torrent of abuse following Hartranft's nomination was not unexpected, but it must have caused the Republican Old Guard considerable annoyance to find respectable Republican papers predicting defeat for the party. After the Democratic Party accepted the Liberal candidate Horace Greeley for its Presidential nominee, the state Democracy expected all reform-minded Republicans to reciprocate by supporting their gubernatorial candidate Charles Buckalew. Cameron well remembered this man who had defeated him for the Senatorial seat in 1863—"an artful fellow . . . with great bitterness hidden under a very meek manner." [13]

In addition to the handicap of running, in a reform-minded campaign year, a candidate accused of corruption, there was added the burden of attacks from J. W. Forney, the editor of the widely-read Philadelphia *Press.* During Forney's directorship of the Philadelphia customs, he resented Cameron's interference in distribution of the patronage. His resignation concurrently with McClure's struggle to obtain his legislative seat looked at first like a move to fight Grant and this was the interpretation Cameron gave to it.

True, the editor had expressed his disgust for the evil influences surrounding the President, his despair at seeing the Republican Party "going to the dogs," and predicted defeat in 1872 if there were no changes.

But Cameron was in error when he believed Forney was resigning for the purpose of gunning for Grant; it was he, his machine, and the Hartranft ticket that Forney intended to destroy. In February, 1872, the editor had requested a dinner conference for bargaining purposes and ended

[13] Cameron to J. A. J. Creswell, June 2, 1873, Crippen note from Creswell Papers.

his invitation with a laudable party slogan, "Let us have peace." Cameron saw no need for parleying and another periodic breach between the pair followed. In late April the Cameron men offered to appease Forney by withdrawing General Allen from the ticket, but the editor insisted upon an entire new state ticket including the delegation to the national convention.

Heedless of the logic of the process, Forney continued to support Grant, the fountainhead of the corruption he was seeking to destroy. He would cut off the body of the monster and preserve the head inviolate. Cameron and his ring men who nominated Hartranft, charged the editor, "thought by associating his name with Grant they could elect him and perpetuate their rule."

The combined attacks delivered by the Liberal Republicans, the Democrats, and Forney's organ shook the confidence of even the master strategists: "Things look bad in Pennsylvania," confided Cameron to his friend Henry Cooke. It was now clear, charged Forney, that because the Republican State Committee had failed to bring any modification of the state ticket, they were now "aiders and abettors of the conspiracy to continue the present rapacious state treasury ring." [14]

The grave situation and Forney's prodding brought some results. On July 26, the committee met in secret to consider the matter. The *Press* reported William B. Mann the only member in favor of a change, while the opposition Democratic *Patriot* reported Mann as promising to insure the ticket a large majority in Philadelphia. Allen and Hartranft did not volunteer to withdraw, the com-

[14] Philadelphia *Press*, June 15, July 26, 1872; H. Cooke to W. E. Chandler, July 10, 1872, Chandler MSS, LC.

mittee pleaded lack of jurisdiction, and no action followed.[15]

Cameron still sought a solution for his dilemma. A defeat for Hartranft in the October elections might bring not only Grant's defeat in November but also his own in January. He certainly hoped to see his son succeed him in the Senate and it was imperative to have himself elected once more. Even if the Republicans succeeded in carrying the legislative elections, a defeat for his gubernatorial candidate would result in a great loss of prestige and a weakening of confidence in his strength. Conceivably, a coalition of reform-minded Republicans and Democrats could elect a United States Senator in 1873.

Following a vacation at Bedford Springs with the families of his son and his daughter, Virginia, Cameron called another private conclave for the purpose of a final decision on Hartranft's candidacy. The Philadelphia municipal bosses, state treasurer Mackey, and his son Don were in attendance. The historian's chief source of information on the conference, A. K. McClure, certainly was not present, but he had close personal ties with Mann, a participant. McClure related: ". . . Hartranft's name would have been withdrawn from the ticket but for the heroic and defiant attitude assumed at that meeting by J. Donald Cameron. . . . He peremptorily declared that the party could save itself only by assuming the aggressive and standing by its State ticket." The outcome of the parley revealed J. Donald Cameron's pre-eminence in the party organization.[16]

Cameron tried to fight back at Forney by persuading

---

[15] Philadelphia *Press*, July 26, 1872; Harrisburg *Patriot*, July 26, 27, 1872.

[16] McClure, *Notes*, II, 346.

Grant to withdraw all patronage from him but this time
Grant knew which side of his bread was buttered and
through his secretary offered an apologetic refusal.[17]

Forney played his last trump card in late September.
He published figures from the auditor general's books
showing how since 1866 Hartranft had failed to collect
$460,000 in state taxes from the Cameron-controlled
Northern Central Railroad. Pennsylvania had received
annually $35,000 in taxes for 200 miles of the Northern
Central while Maryland was collecting three times as
much for 36 miles. Truly, Forney reminded his readers,
Hartranft deserved and earned his gubernatorial sponsor-
ship by the machine.[18]

In the meantime the state organization established
"proof" of Hartranft's innocence in the Evans Scandal.
Two Philadelphians in prison because of municipal frauds
bargained to retract their sworn oaths of Hartranft's
acceptance of profits in exchange for a pardon. Cameron,
Hartranft, Mackey, and Grant conferred in Philadelphia,
dispatched a special agent to Governor Geary for a
pardon, and received it the next day. State chairman
Russell Errett secured the affidavits of Hartranft's innocence. In defense of his action, Geary published the
list of 133 names attached to the petition of Charles
Yerkes, Jr., former broker for the city treasurer.

The Republican National Committee, well aware of the
necessity for carrying Pennsylvania, still the Keystone
State because of its early elections, exhausted its resources
to carry Hartranft. After receiving $75,000, Russell Errett
and William Kemble requested $10,000 more. Jay Cooke
and his associates, Henry Bingham, A. J. Drexel, and

[17] Babcock to Cameron, Aug. 16, 1872, Cameron MSS, LC.
[18] Philadelphia *Press*, Oct. 1, 1872.

George Childs, all of Philadelphia, were "milked" to the limit. The Democracy likewise found itself in financial straits. Samuel J. Randall, confessing his inability to conduct an efficient campaign, was pressing for additional assessments on the Democracy.[19]

An error accepted by the Liberal Republicans and the Cameron-Grant group alike was the hold former Governor Curtin exercised over the state's electorate. One would assume that Curtin could not afford to ignore an opportunity to assist in overthrowing his arch enemy Cameron.

In February 1872, Curtin resolved to return from Russia, mentioned the likelihood of his resignation, and later expressed his hope of arriving home in time to contribute to the success of his party in the fall. On April 8, taking offense at Secretary Fish's criticism of his handling (or mishandling) of a communication relating to the Catacazy affair which had the effect of embarrassing his government, he forwarded his resignation. Fish received it on April 25 and answered the communication the same day. Curtin arrived in London on July 15, made a trip to see E. B. Washburne, the American minister at Paris, and was back in London by August 6. His last letter to Washburne before leaving for home gave no hint of any intention of joining the Liberal Republican movement. The Harrisburg *State Journal* had already published a letter from Curtin's legation secretary berating the unauthorized use of Curtin's name at Cincinnati. Contrary to popular opinion Curtin did not resign the Russian mission for the purpose of fighting Cameronism.[20]

[19] Kemble to Chandler, Sept.—, Sept. 30, 1872, Bingham to Chandler, Oct. 2, 1872, Chandler MSS, LC; Oberholtzer, *Jay Cooke*, II, 355-56; Randall to Black, Aug. 1, 1872, Black MSS, LC.

[20] Curtin to Washburne, Feb. 23, March 4, April 8, June 21, July 15, Aug. 6, 1872, Washburne MSS, LC. Fish to Curtin, April 25, 1872, Letter Books of Hamilton Fish, LC.

During his campaign speeches, A. K. McClure stated (without contradiction from Grant or Fish) that an administration emissary (probably Washburne or McMichael) had offered Curtin another diplomatic post if he would remain in Europe. Having resigned his mission, Curtin was free to talk but he maintained silence for almost a month. Secretary Fish urged Grant to see Curtin and secure his request. Contrary to the opinion of W. E. Chandler, Grant believed Curtin's defection would cause the loss of Pennsylvania.

While Curtin was still in Europe, Cameron had expressed a conciliatory attitude toward his ancient enemy —"a pleasing, plausible speaker" with "a great many friends throughout the state." If Curtin should choose to oppose Grant (no mention was made of himself) the people would recognize the "sorehead" that he was and his influence would no longer exist. But after Curtin's return, Cameron expected Curtin to support Greeley because, having no longer any political status within the Republican Party, there was nothing else for him to do.[21]

Before leaving Saratoga Springs, where he had been convalescing, Curtin prepared a letter for public consumption assigning himself to the ranks of the Liberal Republicans. The letter, reflecting the bitterness and humiliation of his defeat in 1867, charged the power of Cameron with having, since the "dark days of the Civil War . . . struggled to gather advancements from the bitter sorrows of the people." [22] The primary purpose of the Liberal Republican movement in Pennsylvania was the overthrow of Simon Cameron, and Curtin chose to join it, in alliance with former enemies, because the Republican state organiza-

[21] New York *Herald*, July 19, 1872; Philadelphia *Press*, Aug. 31, 1872.
[22] Bellefonte *Democratic Watchman*, Sept. 27, 1872.

tion purposed to ostracize him permanently within the party he had help to build. But the defeat of Hartranft or Grant would not insure the defeat of Cameron; complete victory could be achieved only through the legislature.

The state organization soon absorbed the shock of Curtin's entry into the fray and both Camerons wrote letters expressing confidence in victory.

If rings and corruption were actually the issues in 1872, the people of Pennsylvania proved themselves more interested in military hereos, party regularity, and the shades of the Civil War than in reform, factional party warfare, and the restoration of former Confederates to full Union communion. It marked the triumph of a conservative militant Republicanism still deeply hued with the radicalism of the "bloody shirt."

To Simon Cameron, the master politician, the victory of 1872 provided a natural corollary to his Senatorial victory over Andrew G. Curtin in 1867. For the next five years, with Curtin in Russia, the faction withered until only a remnant remained. Matthew Quay, John F. Hartranft, and Francis Jordan gravitated to the opposite faction. Only one leader, William Mann, remained as a monument to a non-existent faction. Mann and Cameron hated one another, but the former's vote-getting techniques in Philadelphia saved the party on several occasions, and he had to be tolerated. He was accepted into the new rising Philadelphia hierarchy, an adjunct of the Cameron machine. His body was counted among the faithful but his soul was that of another.

In 1872 there was no longer any chance of victory for Andrew Curtin and his followers with the Republican Party—it could be achieved only in alliance with an alien party which retained the stigma cast upon it by the victorious Unionists. The state Republican Party for the first time since its inception was now factionless and purged of all anti-Cameron elements. Secretary Hamilton Fish pronounced the benediction on behalf of Grantism: "The expurgated Republican Party is stronger on account of those who have gone from it. Let the 'curtin fall.'"[23] Members of the former McClure-Curtin faction were now dead, retired from public life, converted into pro-Cameron men, or in the ranks of the Democracy. McClure after a time played the role of an independent journalistic political observer and Forney finally found his way back to his first love, the Democracy.

Andrew G. Curtin confided to a friend his reasons for bolting the party. The candidate Hartranft was not trustworthy, the state ticket represented a "dishonest ring," and he could not support it except by going back on his nature, his previous life and public history. Curtin truly wished to believe he had represented the forces of righteousness against that of evil. But he further bared the inner recesses of his soul when he wrote: "to have acted otherwise would have been *personal degradation.*"[24]

Almost concurrently with news of the victorious election returns, Cameron received anxious inquiries from his friends and journalists requesting information on his future political plans. Two years earlier in an interview with a New York correspondent he emphasized, in the characteristic vein of veteran political leaders, his disinterestedness in another candidacy. The reason for his

[23] Fish to Cameron, Oct. 9, 1872, Cameron MSS, LC. For a detailed account and analysis of the Liberal Republican movement in Pennsylvania see Bradley, "Post-bellum Politics," 334-43, 352-59, 376-94.

[24] Curtin to Washburne, Aug. 18, 1873, Washburne MSS, LC; Curtin to Carey, Oct. 15, 1872, Henry C. Carey Papers, HSP.

answer certainly was not the burden of his 72 years; he was unusually sound in body and mind, a blessing he enjoyed to the time of his mortal illness. In the fall of 1870 an erroneous Associated Press release reported a special car en route from Baltimore carrying the paralyzed person of Simon Cameron, victim of a "stroke." The following day the people of Harrisburg were astonished to see the subject walking down Market Street exhibiting nothing worse than the symptoms of a cold.

During the campaign, from the public's viewpoint, Hartranft's fight was also Cameron's; if the gubernatorial candidate were beaten, then the master would not again try for the Senatorship. The question is now solely academic, but if the study of a long political career is meaningful, he would not have retired without another struggle. He had already boasted that he could if he wished pass his power to his son; and who can doubt his wish. His vindication of the many charges against him, expressed by the electorate's response at the polls, suggested their consent to have him continue in office if he chose.

Having accomplished elimination of the Curtin faction, and with a working majority of Republicans in the legislature, Cameron anticipated no opposition to his nomination or election to the Senatorship; but he had not reckoned upon the venal character of many legislators unchanged by the preceding election.

It was the plan of a group led by an enterprising criminal lawyer, Lin Bartholomew, one-time personal secretary to Cameron in the War Department, to sponsor the candidacy of Charlemagne Tower, an "honest millionaire"—the implication being, under the circumstances, that the new man could be relied upon to pay for every vote for which he had bargained. It would also furnish an opportunity for the disappointed exponents of "reform" to defeat the high priest of corrupt Grantism.

The hoped-for race between the Republican gold-dust twins was well publicized, and from the anthracite region where the spectacle was first conceived came word that Captain Charlemagne Tower proposed to lift General Simon Cameron's scalp not with the conventional toma-hawk but with $200,000 in non-redeemable greenbacks. Probably the contest did not actually progress as far as the public assumed, because on January 3, Quay's paper announced the cautious Tower's withdrawal. In 1891 Mc-Clure recorded that Cameron showed enough concern in the matter to confer with him on the subject. The state Senator elected on a reform ticket gave assurance of not assisting in the blackmail. Cameron left for Washington and allowed his capable son, Don, and Matthew Quay to represent his interest.[25]

Quay's brilliant coup precluded any opportunity to arrange for a bargaining caucus. It was customary to call the party caucus in session just before the election, which in 1873 was scheduled for January 21. The Tower men were counting on two weeks of time to leisurely canvass all the Republican legislators. But only twenty-four hours after the scheduled arrival of the legislators with a work-able quorum Quay "dragged" the party faithful into caucus. Tower's managers were caught completely by surprise and did not present his name. Perhaps at that

[25] Scranton *Republican* and Lebanon *Courier* quoted in Harrisburg *Telegraph*, Jan. 7, 1873; Beaver *Radical*, Jan. 3, 1873; Frank B. Evans, "Pennsylvania Politics, 1872-1877: A Study in Leadership without Responsibility" (Ph.D. thesis, Pennsylvania State University, 1962), 60-61; McClure, *Men of Wartimes*, 153.

time they had no authority to do so. Quay excused his haste by explaining: "As it was understood Senator Cameron had no opposition, there was a general desire . . . to have it over." [26]

Their caucus having taken on the earmarks of a routine session with a predetermined outcome, the tired Republican legislators were disposed to hurry the proceedings. Senator James L. Graham of Allegheny County was granted the honor of presenting the name of Simon Cameron for United States Senator. Senator Elisha Davis of Philadelphia blocked a motion to nominate by acclamation with a nomination for his neighbor William D. Kelley. Six complimentary votes were cast for Kelley and J. K. Wickersham and then Cameron's nomination was made unanimous. This meant the nominee could count on 72 votes (not counting the absentee members), enough to elect him.

On January 20 when the houses met separately to vote for United States Senator, two Republicans and three Democrats were placed in nomination. The Liberal Republican Party, A. K. McClure announced, would not make a nomination because he had failed to sit in caucus with himself. The next day, when the official vote was announced, Cameron recorded 76 votes to 50 for the Democracy's candidate, William Wallace. Every Republican present voted for him. Cameron's fourth and last election was his only undisputed one. A. K. McClure cast his vote for Thomas Marshall, the convention delegate of 1860 who had claimed that the first man he could catch in a dark alley would surpass Simon Cameron's Presidential qualifications.[27]

[26] Beaver *Radical*, Jan. 7, 1873.
[27] *Journal of the Senate*, 133-34, Beaver *Radical*, Jan. 17, 24,

It is interesting to note press comment of the opposition newspapers on the victor. The Philadelphia *Age*, the most militant voice of the Democracy in 1865, now considerably mellowed, did not bother to devote an editorial on Cameron's election. The Democratic Erie *Observer*, pulled out one of its old files and reiterated "a bargain . . . formally consummated by the legislature." Editor Ezra Meek of Bellefonte predicted two eclipses for the year; one celestial, the other global—"a total eclipse of all that is creditable to a State, honorable to a people or right in a republican government"—an obscuration cast by the shadow of Simon Cameron. The Harrisburg *Patriot* was the voice of prophecy: "He is undisputed master of Pennsylvania. Every department of the State government is at his feet. He is the fountain of all political honors and preferments, and the signs are that he will be able to transmit his rule." [28]

The regime of Geary's successor began on January 22, 1873. The retiring governor expressed no bitterness over his failure to capture the Republican state organization or any anxiety over the special legislative investigation, of which he was the target, of collusion in the alleged frauds of Oliver Evans. "Alls well that ends well," he wrote to his brother in Oregon; but a week later he was dead. An autopsy revealed syncope (cerebral anemia), aggravated by nervous prostration, the cause of his death.

1873. *New York Times*, May 22, 1882. Both the Philadelphia *Age* and Harrisburg *Patriot* listed 48 votes for Wallace. Over two decades after Marshall delivered his famous philippic against Cameron, he claimed the Camerons were still awaiting an opportunity to "knife" him. A. K. McClure forgot he had voted for Marshall. See *Notes*, II, 350.

[28] Erie *Observer*, Jan. 23, 1873; Bellefonte *Democratic Watchman*, Jan. 24, 1873; Harrisburg *Patriot*, Jan. 29, 1873.

His heavy brain (56½ ounces) testified, according to scientific beliefs of his age, to his extraordinary superior intelligence.[29] Local gossips attributed his death to a poisonous preparation he used to maintain the color of his black luxuriant beard.

Matthew Quay's announcement of his candidacy in early January for the position of secretary of state was no surprise. The composition of Hartranft's cabinet and the legislative offices reflected complete control by the Cameron hierarchy. The speakerships were divided between Allegheny and Philadelphia Counties. Russell Errett received the clerkship of the senate.[30]

The Liberal Republican threat had not modified Cameron's conservative record in Congress. One could hardly expect him to support bills calling for merit qualifications of civil service workers—"new fangled notions"—designed to undermine patronage, the chief source of his power. In March, 1872, he supported an amendment to an appropriation bill which would repeal all laws or regulations establishing competitive examinations.[31] The politico received much criticism for taking under his wing one of the most discredited men in Washington, Senator John J. Patterson, a Pennsylvania carpetbagger who had secured his election from South Carolina by bribery. Patterson was former editor and part owner of the Harrisburg *Telegraph*. He had supported Cameron at Chicago in 1860.

Cameron's position on the "Salary Grab" bill was more commendable. The amended bill, providing for salary in-

---

[29] Philadelphia *Weekly Press*, Feb. 15, 1873.

[30] Beaver *Radical*, Jan. 3, 1873; Evans, "Pennsylvania Politics," 59.

[31] Rhodes, *United States*, VI, 388; Harris, *Chandler*, 117.

creases for top federal administrators, jurists, and legislators, had one discreditable feature—a retroactive clause for members of Congress. Two days before it passed he explained why he would vote for it "although he did not care a button about it [for] himself." The Presidential office deserved an increase. All public servants had a right to a living wage. When he first came to Washington at a salary of $8 per diem, explained Cameron, he ate the best food—canvasback duck for $10 a week. Now his cuisine expenses exceed his income, $100 every month. His position in the Senate was so pleasing to him, confided the politico, that he was willing to serve without pay rather than exchange his present position for another.[32] The following year the legislators, responding to negative public opinion, repealed the act.

The Pennsylvania legislature likewise was seized with the salary increase "bug." Treating Geary's final message with scant courtesy, it rushed a bill through to double the incoming governor's salary.

But the most notable event of the legislative session took place on the last day. The House members amused themselves by calling on incompetent members to preside and then bombarded them with ridiculous questions, motions, and amendments. Seeking diversion, one member suggested calling in A. K. McClure and the "balance of the Liberal Republicans" to address the House on the present condition of the political parties. A House "Committee" escorted him into the chamber amidst a chorus of huzzas and jeers, mingled with paper and cigar box missiles.

McClure was equal to the occasion and outwitted the

[32] Oberholtzer, *United States*, II, 330-31; III, 223; New York *World*, Dec. 12, 1872; *Cong. Globe*, 42 Cong., 3 Sess., 2046.

jokesters. He owed thanks to the legislators for the invitation because he knew of no body of men so badly in need of instruction on the necessity of public and private morality. It was his hope, McClure concluded, to find the deity determining the length of their lives by the measure of their virtues.[33]

Following adjournment of the Congress in early March, Cameron took an extended tour on his private railroad coach through the South to New Orleans, a city which revived memories of his stay 40 years previously when he supervised the Lake Ponchartrain canal project. This was the first of a series of annual visits into the gay French city where he found easier entrance into certain feminine circles than he did an exit. He returned to see the passing of his close friend, Chief Justice Chase. At first designated one of the official pallbearers, he chose to represent the United States Senate.

In 1873, the center of gravity for Republican state machine politics shifted from Hartranft to Robert W. Mackey, the state treasurer. Under the new constitutional amendment providing for popular election of state treasurer, the date for election had been set for October, 1873. Opponents of the "Treasury Ring" were outraged when a bill was steamrollered through the legislature allowing Mackey to remain in office until May, 1874, one year beyond the expiration of his term. The office of state treasurer being no longer the gift of the legislature, it was highly important to "vindicate" one of Cameron's leading lieutenants at the polls for a two-year term. He was nominated at the state convention with only token opposition.

The machine suffered difficulties of an internal nature

[33] Philadelphia *Age*, April 11, 1873.

in selecting a candidate for the state supreme court.
Cameron and Mackey were willing to accept a Philadelphia judge, the candidate of the Philadelphia Ring men
led by Mann; but the friends of a Chester County candidate put up such a strong fight that the nomination went
to Isaac Gordon of Jefferson County. Perhaps the
Cameron machine was not too anxious to expose two Ring
candidates concurrently to public scrutiny. The public
might assume that Mackey's running mate had accepted
his philosophy of "Addition and Division." [34]

With the failure of gigantic investment corporations
only a month away (the Panic of 1873) the party committed political hara-kiri. The Republicans were now in
control of the financial security of the nation and if the
people wished a guarantee of continued prosperity it
should support the party. By the use of such a platform
the Republican Party was forced to accept the responsibility for the coming recession. The party also reaffirmed
the tenets of militant Republicanism—meaning a continued Radical reconstruction policy supported by
bayonets.[35]

The Democrats, badly demoralized after the crushing
defeat of 1872, had to start from scratch. The party continued its crusade for reform with the warning: "The
greatest danger to free institutions is wide-spreading
corruption." It was the same song with no new notes.
Allegedly, treasurer Mackey had used two million dollars
of the people's money for private profits.

The campaign aroused little interest and only 30 per
cent of the electorate went to the polls. For the last time

[34] Evans, *op. cit.*, 166-67.
[35] *Ibid.*, 73, 77-78; Philadelphia *Age*, Aug. 13, 14, 1873.

in a state election Philadelphia Ring used the Registry Law to manipulate a much larger popular majority for Mackey than for his running mate Judge Gordon. Mackey's majority outside the city of Philadelphia was 59 but in the city it was over 25,000 votes. The returns, however, indicated a trend favorable to the Democrats. In the annually-elected House the Republican majority was reduced from 20 to 14.

In the meantime, some of the state's most respected and learned men had drafted a new constitution to replace the outmoded one of 1838. "From beginning to end," wrote A. G. Curtin, a participant, "there was not one political or partisan disunion note." [36] The new document featured more popularly-elected officers, longer terms, and a larger legislature. State officers could not succeed themselves. [37]

The machine, especially the Philadelphia Ring component, was unhappy over the prospect of having municipal salaries fixed. This would mean elimination of the notorious "Row Offices," where occupants of sinecures collected up to $100,000 in fees annually. The leading Cameron journals, the Harrisburg *Telegraph*, the Philadelphia *Inquirer*, and the Pittsburgh *Commercial*, an opposition organ bought by Mackey, all joined in opposing the new constitution. Adoption of the constitution led them to seek credit for a *fait accompli*. To the last, however, the Harrisburg *Telegraph* considered the document a "mountain of stupid blunders and contradictions." [38] Adoption of the constitution in spite of some geographic

[36] Curtin to Washburne, Feb. 2, 1874, Washburne MSS, LC.
[37] See Mahlon H. Hellerich, "The Pennsylvania Constitution of 1873" (Ph.D. thesis, University of Pennsylvania, 1956).
[38] Evans, *op. cit.*, 148.

patterns was due primarily to the consensus of a non-partisan electorate.

The year 1874 brought many personal sorrows to Simon Cameron. On March 11, Charles Sumner died. The beginning of spring saw the passing of J. Donald Cameron's wife, the former Mary McCormick, at the age of 40, leaving five daughters and one son.[39] The family received a large fortune when Mary's father, James McCormick, Senior, died in 1870. In late March, Cameron left for an excursion with Thomas Scott and three Senators into Mexico. Cameron spent some time in New Orleans, made the acquaintance of the "Widow" Oliver, and postponed the Mexican trip because of the yellow fever epidemic.

On his return to Harrisburg, Simon found an ailing wife. On June 19, Margaretta Brua Cameron, his consort of over half a century, died. Mrs. Cameron's funeral took place from the family mansion on Front Street overlooking the broad Susquehanna river. The funeral rites of the Lutheran Church were attended by Governor Hartranft and the leading officers of state. The Democratic Harrisburg *Patriot* deemed Mrs. Cameron "a most estimable lady" who would have "a mourner in every acquaintance." Many letters of condolences poured in upon the bereaved Senator.

In August, George Bergner, Cameron's chief pillar in the Harrisburg area, died. He edited the official Cameron mouthpiece, the *Telegraph*, and for years, because of his patron's influence, was the city's postmaster. He seemed

---

[39] Although James McCormick, the father of Mary, had a total of 21 grandchildren, the McCormick lineage of the powerful Harrisburg family came to an end in 1964 with the death of Miss Anne McCormick. See article by Paul Beers in Harisburg *Patriot News*, Jan. 26, 1964.

not to have any political ambitions for himself but "chose
to make himself useful and needful to his political associates." His son Charles maintained the same loyalty to the
Cameron cause.[40]

After Mrs. Cameron's death, Simon rested at Bedford
Springs in company with the Hartranfts and made plans,
probably with the idea of forgetting his troubles, for an
extensive western tour. Leland Stanford and other presidents of western lines took pains to make his trip pleasant
and to pass his private car wherever he chose to go. The
Pennsylvania Railroad contributed the services of Jerry,
its star porter. In late September, the traveler was enjoying the comforts of the Grand Hotel in San Francisco.
His trip to southern California took him to Santa Barbara
and by mid-October he was back at the Golden Gate
making plans for the return trip via the silver mines of
Carson City and through Utah.

Because of his advancing years, Senatorial duties, and
worldly cares the master politician was leaving the management of the machine more and more to the hands of
Donald, Matthew Quay, and Mackey. But the controversial issues of the day, especially the currency, on
which he took a prominent stand in Congress, brought
his name in conjunction with the declared policy of the
state's Republican organization. Business circles and
labor were in such distressed circumstances that
Cameron succumbed (his enemies said for political reasons) to the arguments of the inflationists. The bill providing for a maximum issuance of $400,000,000 worth of
national notes (greenbacks) would allow the authorization of an additional $44,000,000 worth. Under Grant's au-

[40] Harrisburg *Patriot* quoted in Huntingdon *Globe*, Aug. 11,
1874.

thority, $26,000,000 had already been issued, so actually only $18,000,000 in greenbacks were involved.

Carl Schurz, thoroughly prepared, delivered one of the best addresses of his career against the bill, practically demolishing the arguments of the inflationists. Cameron interrupted him with questions and retorts, which to the well-read of the era, probably did not sound very convincing. Pennsylvania's Senator did not have sufficient background to debate the question and it would have been best had he remained silent. To him it seemed the situation in the United States could not be judged by parallels drawn from history—our nation's case was different. The additional money, Cameron argued, would go west, because "money always goes where it is needed." He could not see any danger to investors caused by a fluctuating currency.[41] To the relief of the hard-money men, Grant vetoed the bill.

Publicly, Cameron had no hesitation in expressing his disagreement with the presidential veto—"a great mistake." The veto would alienate the western states, long the bulwark of the Republican Party; neither could it save the eastern states, where it was supposed to be approved. "I am not even sure about Pennsylvania," he admitted, "it will be harder work to carry that state than before." [42] The Democrats made political hay out of the disagreement in the camp of their enemy.

Their leader's stand in Congress presented the machine leaders with a dilemma. "Soft" money and inflation were anathema to most business men. The party fathers seized upon the best possible solution—a wide straddle on the

[41] *Cong. Record*, 43 Cong., 2 Sess., 1722-26; Hesseltine, *Grant*, 335-36.

[42] New York *Tribune*, April 23, 1874.

question. A legislative party resolution endorsing Cameron's stand in the Senate was changed to a "general endorsement of the state and national administration" [43] —or an adoption of opposite poles of thought.

The currency controversy had no effect on the machine's control of the party's state convention—a fact demonstrated by its slate of candidates.

The "hard times" from which the people of the Commonwealth were suffering in 1874 were attributed to the party in power—the Republicans. Millions of debtors, along with the millionaire creditor Simon Cameron, wanted more money in circulation to alleviate their ills. The state Democrats likewise straddled the currency issue, but not in such broad terms. The chief cry of the Democracy was for a *change*, a plea which attracted the desperate masses. The Old Guard relied upon the faded bloody shirt. It even tried to raise the specter of another Southern rebellion.

The Democratic resurgence felt in Pennsylvania was one common to the nation. Cameron was half right in his prediction. The Republicans and Democrats divided the Western states, 6 to 5. The Commonwealth's neighbors, Ohio, New York, and New Jersey, went Democratic. The Democratic margin of 4,600 votes in Pennsylvania gave the Democracy a majority of Representatives in Congress and a combined majority of 11 in the state legislature. The Democrats would elect a United States Senator in January, 1875.[44]

The elections of 1874, charged the Democracy, defeated the hope of Simon Cameron to install his son as

[43] Evans, *op. cit.*, 192.
[44] *Ibid.*, 185-87, 197-98; Edward McPherson, *A Handbook of Politics For 1876* (Washington, 1876), 255.

his colleague in the Senate in 1875. It is doubtful whether even a subservient legislature would have submitted to the spectacle of a father-son team in the Senate; and it is even more unlikely that Cameron desired it. His hope was to give Don national stature by introducing him into the Grant cabinet and to keep him there into another administration until he should choose to retire. Then Don would succeed him at his leisure.

When Grant returned to the White House in 1873, Cameron journals expressed the hope of seeing Donald Cameron represent Pennsylvania in a newly reconstructed cabinet. Since the days of Lincoln, Pennsylvania's Republicans always insisted the state should be represented in the Presidential cabinet because of its importance in national affairs. Cameron's announcement in the summer of 1873, rather prematurely it would seem, of his wish to see Grant elected for a third term, was interpreted as a move to get Don into the cabinet. In the spring of 1874, Grant suggested either Don Cameron or Joseph Patterson, another Pennsylvanian, for the treasury post. The mention of Patterson, formerly a professed Democrat, spurred William Kemble, Republican National Committeeman, into action. If Pennsylvania was to be represented in the cabinet, wrote Kemble, it must be by a Republican. The appointment went to Kentucky.[45]

A repeat performance on the cabinet question took place after Postmaster General Creswell was ousted from Grant's cabinet in July. The proposal of Fish to place Wayne MacVeagh in the cabinet, contrary to prejudicial Democratic accounts, could not have been pleasing to

[45] New York *Herald*, July 29, 1873; Nevins, *Fish*, 711; Kemble to Cameron, April 20, 1874, Cameron MSS, LC. J. P. Barr editor of the Pittsburgh *Post* wrote an article on the subject.

Cameron. He wanted his son, not his son-in-law, in the cabinet. Moreover, MacVeagh had wandered from the tent of his patriarch to that of an alien tribe, the reformers. Two cabinet posts had gone by the board and still there was no place for Donald. Although the Republican National Convention still lay two years in the future, the exasperated machine leaders rejected a resolution, introduced at the state convention, to endorse Grant for a third term. Instead it pledged its votes to a favorite son, Governor Hartranft.[46]

Although the Republican state organization had never been more firmly held within the hand of Simon Cameron, his fortress had been breached. Conceivably, the break with Grant could lead to serious patronage problems, but the politico was saved by a sudden quirk of fate; the President dared not allow the state's patronage to be channeled through the new Democratic Senator from the Commonwealth. The real crisis lay within the state. It was imperative, if the machine was to maintain its existence, to wipe out, within a period of two years, the Democratic majority in the General Assembly.

[46] Nevins, *Fish*, 719; Evans, *op. cit.*, 386.

11
The Passing
of the Scepter

FASHIONING OF THE STAGE FOR THE PASSING OF THE SCEPTER of state bossism from Simon Cameron's hands to those of his son was the goal of Cameronian planning during the concluding years of the Grant era. The machine succeeded easily in retaining complete control of the party's organization. It checked the recent Democratic gains and elected its candidate for governor. Before leaving Washington, Grant invested J. Donald Cameron with the office of Secretary of War, a key post during the Hayes-Tilden post-election crisis in the South. President Hayes, it was assumed by the Cameron coterie, would in some manner recognize Pennsylvania and its party leaders for their contribution to his victory. When the new President failed to do so, Simon Cameron resigned from the Senate, thereby terminating his political career.

With the Democrats in control of the legislature in 1875 and there being no chance of the election of a Republican United States Senator, courtesy decreed that the minority party should endorse the outgoing incumbent in recognition for his services. Scott had taken care of the bill (one on which Cameron did not vote) for suppression of the Ku Klux Klan and party reformers had mentioned his name for the Vice-Presidency in 1872. The party's failure to concede John Scott the empty honor aroused speculation and some indignation among his followers.

In March, 1874, the Harrisburg reporter of the Huntingdon *Globe* wrote: "the very keenest and best men here smile sardonically at the mention of Scott's name for re-election." The reporter's observation followed the contest in the Congress over the currency bill, a measure Scott had opposed.

The misrepresentation of Scott's position by leading Republican organs, especially the *Press* of Forney, now at peace with the Camerons, led the Senator to retort with indignation on the subject of Forney's plan to "systematically defame him." He likewise had some strong words for Cameron: ". . . on the subject of specie payment my colleague equally misapprehends my position. I am not in favor of *immediate* resumption . . . [nor] do I think it possible . . . to resume specie payment . . . in the near future." He agreed with Cameron on the subject of resumption, insisted Scott, but not on expansion.[1]

The Senator's rejection by the machine, "an outrage upon every sense of propriety and duty," claimed Scott's mouthpiece, was because he would not become a party to the ring—another way of saying he had his own ideas on patronage. Two factors often overlooked in the case of Scott's rejection are the factional split in Scott's own bailiwick, brought on by a feud with the editor of the Huntingdon *Globe* (recently ousted from his superin-

[1] Huntingdon *Journal*, March 18, 1874.

tendency of the state orphanage at Cassville) and the wish of Matthew Quay of Beaver County to move one of his neighbors into a higher echelon.

In the Republican caucus, Scott's few adherents remained faithful during the two ballots it took to nominate Quay's close friend John Allison, a federal treasury executive.

The victory of William Wallace over former Senator Buckalew had apparently brought to an end a feud in the Democratic ranks; but the enemies of Wallace found a new giant, Samuel J. Randall, to contest his position. The inveterate strife between Wallace and Randall became comparable to that between Cameron and Curtin. There is a good chance that Judge Jeremiah Black, an outstanding Democratic leader since the days of Buchanan, could have been the new Senator had he not chosen to wait until he was "drafted." In January, 1875, the victory of Wallace over Allison gave the Democracy its first Keystone State Senatorial election in twelve years.[2]

In the spring of 1875 Simon Cameron accomplished a goal he had fought for persistently over a period of thirteen years—a rescinding of his censure by the House in April, 1862. The politico's famous feud with William D. Kelley, it will be recalled, had its origin in this drive.

On March 2, 1875, concurrently with a proposed law changing the name of the pleasure yacht from "Dolly Varden" to "Clochette," Pennsylvania's Glenni Scofield urged the passage of a resolution to bestow "justice long

[2] Black to Cass (copy), Nov. 17, 1874, Wallace to Black, Nov. 19, 1874, Black MSS, LC; Philadelphia *Age*, Jan. 1, 15, 19, 1875; Evans, *op cit.*, 226-28.

deferred." A Committee member who had recommended the censure, William S. Holman, recalled that at the time, "passion incident to a state of war" could have made a mistake possible. On his part he was willing to see the "bitter memories of the war fade into oblivion." Henry L. Dawes, the nemesis of the retiring Secretary of War in 1862, rose to admit a "possible injustice" of the past. Breaking the solemnity of the occasion, William E. Niblack of Indiana asked whether the resolution was to be considered a part of the series of amnesty measures. At the conclusion of remarks by three members, the House adopted, by unamimous consent, the following resolution:

Whereas the House of Representatives, on the 30th day of April, 1862, adopted a resolution censuring Simon Cameron for certain irregular proceedings as Secretary of War in the matter of purchasing military supplies at the outbreak of the rebellion; and whereas on the 26th day of the ensuing month the then President of the United States, Abraham Lincoln, in a special message to Congress, assumed for the Executive Department of the Government the full responsibility of the proceedings complained of, declaring in said message that he should be wanting equally in candor and in justice if he should leave the censure to rest exclusively or chiefly on Mr. Cameron, and added that it was due to Mr. Cameron to say that, although he fully approved the proceedings, they were not moved nor suggested by him, and that not only the President but all the other heads of Departments were at least equally responsible with him for whatever error, wrong, or fault was committed in the premises; therefore

Resolved, That this House, as an act of personal justice to Mr. Cameron and as a correction of its own records, hereby directs that said resolution be rescinded, and that "rescission" be entered on the margin of the Journal where said resolution is recorded.[3]

[3] *Cong. Record,* 43 Cong., 2 Sess., 2084-85; McPherson, *Handbook of Politics,* 1876, 204-05.

In the meantime Cameron was planning a new excursion to Mexico. The list of twenty included Zachariah Chandler, Oliver P. Morton, Thomas Scott, Wayne MacVeagh, and their wives. In New Orleans Cameron's group was to be joined by others. The party arrived at the New Orleans rendezvous to hear of a new yellow fever epidemic raging in the Caribbean, and like their predecessors of 1874 discreetly refrained from boarding the steamer for Vera Cruz.

The contemplated week of rest, warmth, and play at the gay city was not without its problems. The Senators found themselves in company with a potential Louisiana Jonah. The honorable Pinckney Benton Stewart Pinchback, a claimant for a seat simultaneously in the House and Senate at Washington, paid assiduous court to the party. The cunning Morton and Cameron made a brief visit to the factional leader's residence thereby eluding a staged dinner meeting with "black and tan" politicians. But a year later, on March 8, 1876, both Morton and Cameron voted to seat Pinchback, who was forced to retreat to his demesne with only the salary for his pseudo term in the Senate.[4] Before leaving New Orleans, Cameron renewed his acquaintance with the widow Oliver and pledged his efforts in her behalf.

While still in the South, Cameron received word of the death of his sister-in-law, Mary Schulze Cameron, the widow of his brother John. Mary was a sister of Governor Andrew Schulze, the official responsible for Cameron's life-long rank of "General"—the title by which he was always addressed.

The chief assignment of General Simon Cameron's task

---

[4] *New York Times*, March 25, 1875; Philadelphia *Times*, March 25, 1875, Oberholtzer, *United States*, III, 232, 245, 265.

forces for the campaign of 1875 was to repel the serious inroads of the Democracy within the state. What with a governor, a state treasurer, and a few all-important legislators to be elected, the machine must go to work early and relentlessly. Although the Liberal Republican Party was dead, there was a plentiful sprinkling of reformers, especially the opponents of dram drinking, to cause trouble. The discredited chairman of the party's state central committee, Russell Errett, called his group together and set the state convention for May 26, an unusually early date, for the purpose, so said his enemies, of forestalling any attempt at control from the grassroots of the party.[5]

There was no question of Hartranft's renomination at the Republican State Convention. The military hero's portrait was paraded through the streets of Lancaster with great enthusiasm and the following day he was nominated by acclamation.

The all-important question was the naming of a success to Cameron's leading strategist, state treasurer Mackey, now constitutionally ineligible to succeed himself. Matthew Quay, the political magician of Western Pennsylvania, reached into his bottomless chapeau to pull out another hopeful from neighboring Lawrence County. The Philadelphia coterie led by Mann and Mackey favored Senator Butler B. Strang of Tioga County; but the Camerons wished to inject a lily-white strain into the slate with their endorsement of Henry Rawle, Mayor of Erie.

At this juncture the mailed fist of the heir apparent

[5] Evans, *op. cit.*, 255-59, 334-35. Election figures for 1875 showed that the prohibitionists held the balance of power in the campaign.

was revealed. Unlike his father, who usually employed veiled threats to discipline recalcitrant party disciples, the new Caesar, J. Donald Cameron, peremptorily ordered Rawle's nomination. Charlemagne Tower's disappointed sponsor of 1873, Lin Bartholomew, made the most of an opportunity to sow dissension within the Cameron machine and nominated Strang. The Cameronian fiat was a move in the right direction—Rawle, the honest businessman, gave respectability to the state ticket. The names of G. Dawson Coleman, Cameron, Hartranft, Rawle, and John Cessna associated with the convention made it look as if the leadership constituted the old Democracy under a pseudonym.[6]

The convention, although calling for "free banking and a safe and uniform national currency," refused to endorse the federal act of January 14 providing for future redemption of greenbacks in coin. The state's Republicans had repeated their straddle of the previous year and sagely failed to recognize any existing currency issue; and again, for the second year, the convention, tactlessly it would seem, needled Grant with its resolution against a third term for "any person."

Grant's broadside against the Cameronian-inspired statement of principles had to be read by the Pennsylvanians after their return home. The nation's hero, who (in his own opinion) had sacrificed himself for the public good by accepting the Presidency, was not a candidate for renomination—that is; unless tendered under circumstances "making it an imperative duty."[7]

[6] Philadelphia *Times*, May 25-27 1875; Philadelphia *Press*, May 26-27, 1875; New York *Herald*, May 26, 1875.

[7] "Letter" of U. S. Grant to General Harry White, May 29, 1875, Philadelphia *Weekly Press*, June 5, 1875.

For its gubernatorial candidate the Democracy nominated Cyrus L. Pershing, judge of the troublesome Mollie Maguires in Schuylkill County. The party adopted a greenback platform, declared itself against contraction of the currency—"a disaster to the country," and rather peculiarly proclaimed war on inflation.[8]

An amusing political interlude of the season was provided by "Pig Iron" William Kelley, at the moment a rabid exponent of "rag money." His Independents, an anti-monopoly group, met in convention at Mt. Union on the blue Juniata River to organize a new party representative of the people. Not even a scant dozen delegates could agree on a platform.[9]

Cameron's leading journalistic enemy, A. K. McClure, got back in business in time for the campaign of 1875. Possessed of little capital of his own, he called on Jeremiah Black and William Wallace, two leading Democrats of the state, for assistance in raising the required $100,000 for a press. At first he proposed to buy out the Philadelphia *Press* of Forney, who was once again in trouble; this time, rumor had it, because of $25,000 subtracted from the assets of a mail company.

McClure's Philadelphia *Times*, successor to the Democratic *Age*, appeared on March 13. Styled an independent paper dedicated to war on public corruption, the organ at once trained its sights on the Cameronian-sponsored rings. The first issue described disgraceful legislative scenes of adjournment and then recall, and of bills passed in the darkness without the benefit of either gas lights or a quorum. His hope of getting MacVeagh, a newly

[8] Harrisburg *Patriot*, Sept. 10, 1875; Harrisburg *Telegraph*, Sept. 10, 1875.
[9] Huntingdon *Journal*, Aug. 4, 1875.

recognized liberal, to write for his paper failed. Mac-Veagh's reason was a good one—he disliked the editor. McClure placed on reserve some choice derogatory items on Cameron which he intended to air at the strategic moment.[10]

McClure's former chief, A. G. Curtin, had remained politically silent after his participation as a Democratic delegate to the Constitutional Convention of 1873. In the spring of 1875 he emerged to campaign for the Democratic ticket in Connecticut. The observation that "poor Andy" was comparable to the indecisive ass that starved between two bales of hay may have stirred him to action.[11]

The Democratic campaign of 1875 was largely repetitious in nature. Through execution of "operation exposure," so they believed, the stigma of corruption was about to be pinned upon Mackey's Treasury Ring. But Mackey had anticipated the move and the Democrats were trapped. The outgoing treasurer proved he had paid off a portion of the state debt and submitted a certified report on the Sinking Fund. Neither could the Democracy stamp a derogatory label upon Rawle, a man without a record.

The Republican new state chairman, Henry Hoyt, conducted an energetic campaign. He arranged to have Senator Morton speak at Pittsburgh and moved to action that dependable adjunct of the party since 1863, the Union League. A leading representative of the reform wing of the party, Rutherford B. Hayes, toured the Common-

[10] McClure to Black, Dec. 11, 18, 1874, Feb. 18, 1875; Mac-Veagh to Black, Nov. 17, 1875, Black MSS, LC; Philadelphia *Times*, March 13, 1875.

[11] Evans, *op. cit.*, 301.

wealth in company with Governor Hartranft. Two exciting days were spent in Philadelphia and Columbia, where
Hayes addressed 5,000 people. However, the political
evangelists could not match the record of the gospel twins,
Moody and Sankey. One hundred thousand enemies of
Mammon gathered at Armageddon (Philadelphia) to
chorus "Hold the Fort" in doing battle for the Lord.[12]

The "No Popery" slogan of the Ohio group, emphasizing
the attitude of the Catholic Church toward public schools,
was transferred to Pennsylvania. Cameron organs joined
in the attack upon the Catholics and Democrats, "American allies of Vaticanism."[13] In 1855, it will be recalled,
Cameron made a confession of his beliefs in the tenets of
the Americans and for years was close to Isaac Hazlehurst, the Know-Nothing chieftain of Philadelphia.

On Sunday, October 24, Hartranft was host to Hayes
and in the afternoon, in company with Simon Cameron,
paid his respects to the J. Donald Camerons. Although
Conkling men, the Camerons were too astute politically
not to consort with a likely dark horse.[14]

The election of Hartranft and Rawle was narrow but
complete. To have carried Philadelphia by a large majority without the help of the Registry Act must have
been a source of great relief to the Republicans. The
Democratic floodtide of 1874 had been checked and the
machine breathed easier. Now the Republican state of
Pennsylvania was in position to exert a commanding voice
at the coming Presidential convention.

Probably Hamilton Fish acted as an intermediary in
bringing about a rapprochement between Grant and

[12] Hoyt to McPherson, Sept. 9, 1875, McPherson MSS, LC;
Harrisburg *Telegraph*, Oct. 23, 1875.

[13] Evans, *op. cit.*, 303-07.   [14] Williams, *Hayes*, III, 296.

Cameron. The influential secretary of state was likely to have a voice in the selection of any candidate for a foreign appointment or for any cabinet changes. The placement of Quay's defeated candidate, John Allison, in the Philadelphia collectorship and of John Cessna, a Democratic renegade, in the administrative family of the attorney general indicated once more the President's amenability to Cameron's wishes, but the zenith of his many designs—a cabinet post for Donald—remained uneffected.

In September, 1875, Secretary Fish, in response to Grant's wishes for a worthy successor to Secretary Delano, suggested five names, three of them from Pennsylvania. One was Wayne MacVeagh, Cameron's son-in-law. In spite of the correspondence and public comment on the subject it is impossible to believe that at this particular time Cameron desired MacVeagh's entrance into the Grant cabinet, because it would mean the debarment of Don. Neither was MacVeagh a member of the Cameronian machine.

In April, 1876, fortuitous circumstances provided another vacancy in Grant's ephemeral cabinet. The poker-playing discredited minister to England, General Robert C. Schenck, resigned his post and Grant offered the vacancy to Richard Henry Dana, Junior, of Massachusetts. Dana's enemy, Benjamin F. Butler, had no difficulty in persuading his cronies, Cameron and Conkling, to assist in defeating Dana's confirmation. Possibly with the idea of removing MacVeagh from the scene, Cameron suggested him for the English mission; but the President's attorney general, weary over the Whiskey Ring prosecutions, asked and secured the English mission. Again MacVeagh was mentioned for the cabinet vacancy. Following

a tête-a-tête between Grant and Cameron, Alphonso Taft
was transferred voluntarily to the legal department from
his war post and now the spot for which Don Cameron
could qualify had been created.[15] On May 22, 1876, J.
Donald Cameron became the new Secretary of War.

Cameron's contention, two years later, that he was
ignorant of Donald's appointment is very likely true, but
certainly he had the best of reasons to expect it. The
night before his name was sent to the Senate, related
Cameron, "I had dined with President Grant, but he told
me not one word of what he intended to do." The following day Grant's son laughingly asked Cameron if he approved of the new appointment and questioning revealed
the President's recommendation. "At the time," concluded
the politico very truthfully, "I suppose most people
thought that I had asked for the appointment." Actually,
Donald's candidacy for the War Department was first
initiated in 1869. Blaine turned down an excursion to
Niagara Falls with Simon Cameron because he did not
wish to endanger Don's chances for the post.[16]

From the Presidential viewpoint, one could interpret
Donald's appointment as a protest by Grant against the
move to name James G. Blaine his successor. The public
knew it—the Camerons were backers of Roscoe Conkling
for the Presidency. The delegation pledged to Governor
Hartranft was actually intended for bargaining purposes
at the coming convention. Grant's wishes in the matter,
party leaders well recognized, would have little influence
on the proceedings in Cincinnati. Simon Cameron properly

---

[15] Nevins, *Fish*, 776-77, 831.

[16] Cameron to H. C. [*sic*], special correspondent, *New York
Times*, June 3, 1878; Blaine to Cameron, Sept. 22, 1869, Cameron
MSS, LC.

appraised the situation: "The President's forces, if he ever had any—are in a scattering condition." [17]

Simon Cameron's well educated, reticent son had attained national leadership in the Republican Party not on his record of public service, because he had none, but solely on the basis of his position in a political hierarchy that controlled one of the most powerful states in the Union and because of the power his father exercised in national administrative circles. A later generation of Americans, presented with the spectacle of Supreme Court appointees who had never tried a case in their lives, would not have been shocked by J. Donald Cameron's appointment.

In the Presidential year of 1876, both political parties of the Commonwealth met in state convention early for the purpose of selecting Presidential electors and of instructing state delegations for the national conventions, the latter burden hardly necessary in the case of the Republicans, who had instructed their delegates in 1874.

Simon Cameron chose not to attend the Republican National Convention. It was Secretary of War J. Donald Cameron who was generalissimo of the state's delegation. Here was forged another link in the chain of circumstances leading to a dynastic political succession. Few times in the party's history had a manager been presented with so formidable a problem. Here was a Conkling man presenting Hartranft for the Presidency, backed by a Blaine delegation. If Hartranft were to stand any chance for the Presidency he must show consistent gains through several ballots, the effect of which, it was hoped, would create a boom in his favor. The gains were managed by

[17] Cameron to MacVeagh, April 8, 1876, MacVeagh MSS, HSP.

Southern votes. Mr. P. B. T. Pinchback, grateful to Cameron and Morton for their support when he sought a Senatorial seat, promised with Morton's consent some of the latter's delegation, and the carpetbagger Senator J. Patterson gave assistance.

Hartranft's name was the last of seven placed in nomination at the national convention. Pennsylvania's favorite son started with the state's 58 votes and after four ballots rose only to 71. On the second ballot four of Pennsylvania's members protested their right to be counted independently of the unit rule and the chair sustained them.[18] The bolters had torpedoed the machine's plan and Morton, now in desperation, had to recall his borrowed delegates. Fourteen Blaine men were already out of hand and the manager had to decide where to concentrate his shattered forces.

The Cameron hostility to Blaine may have had a personal note. The Plumed Knight had extended patronage to critics of Cameron's regime in the War Department. Blaine recognized the antagonism of the Camerons and tried his best to get on better terms with them. His proposed tour with Cameron to Niagara Falls and his invitation in 1873 to have the politico vacation with Grant is evidence of his efforts.[19]

The extent of the Cameron-Blaine breach was not sufficient to preclude bargaining. The terms were much like a repetition of 1860, but this time the bargainer was thinking of himself when J. Donald Cameron at the end of the fifth ballot proposed to Blaine's manager to ex-

[18] McPherson, *Handbook of Politics*, 1876, 212. McPherson was the chairman.

[19] Evans, *op. cit.*, 394; Blaine to Cameron, July 28, 1873, Cameron MSS, LC.

change the vote of the Pennsylvania delegation (thirty of it was going to him anyway) for a pledge to have the state represented in Blaine's cabinet. But the overconfident Eugene Hale thought he could win without the additional 28 votes it would bring Blaine and rejected the offer.[20] Ironically, Blaine was exactly 28 votes short of winning on the last ballot, which nominated Hayes. The Stalwarts, led by Conkling and Morton with some assistance from Don Cameron, had concentrated on Hayes.

After the election, Matthew Quay was not hesitant in letting the victor know how it happened: ". . . for I am immediately responsible for the action of the Pennsylvania delegation at Cincinnati which resulted in your nomination. Mr. Blaine will tell you this if ever the subject is discussed between you." [21]

The choice of Hayes was a good one. The Old Guard could not harbor the crusader Bristow nor could the reform element have taken Conkling, Morton, or Blaine. The latter's bitter tea was a logical finale to his "Mulligan Stew," a concoction of his own preparation.[22]

For the third consecutive year Simon Cameron made another trip South, but this time it did not include a pleasure trip to New Orleans. A Republican counterthrust for campaign purposes was needed and his mission was to secure it.

[20] Theron C. Crawford quoted in Charles E. Russell, *Blaine of Maine* (New York, 1931), 316.

[21] Quay to Hayes (copy), Dec. 16, 1877, Letters of Matthew Quay, Library of Congress. Not until a decade later did Donald and Blaine celebrate a "Love Feast" in Harrisburg.

[22] On Republican Convention see Evans, *op. cit.*, 404-07; McPherson, *Handbook* 1876, 211-12; Foulke, *Morton*, II, 400-01; Russell, *Blaine*, 315-17. J. D. Cameron's contention that enforcement of the unit rule would have brought victory to Hartranft is incorrect; it would have instead resulted in Blane's nomination.

In the Mississippi town of Vicksburg, under the governorship of General Adelbert Ames, son-in-law of the notorious Benjamin F. Butler, a municipal carpetbag ring had raised the debt of the town from $13,000 to $1,400,-000, elected a full council of illiterates, and installed a villainous sheriff to supervise its operations. The taxpayers rose up against the "People's government" and Ames called out Negro militiamen to restore the "supremacy of the law." The following year, under the able leadership of L. Quintus Cincinnatus Lamar, the Democrats regained control of the state government without bloodshed. Ames, in company with his state superintendent of education (a fugitive from a larceny indictment in New York), packed his carpetbag.

A House "Report," tinged with Democratic bias stated their opponents, had disclosed the abuses of carpetbag government in Mississippi and the Republican dominated Senate saw need for a true appraisal of election irregularities and discrimination. The investigating committee under Boutwell and Cameron took testimony from 162 witnesses and issued its report just prior to the Presidential campaign. The "Report" proved that Negroes by various methods were restrained from voting the Republican ticket. The minority report of the committee pointed out that thousands of spurious directives from President Grant were distributed among the Negroes ordering them to vote Republican. The partisan majority "Report" had discovered one of the "darkest chapters in American history" and recommended remedial measures to Congress —the remanding of Mississippi to territorial status if necessary.[23]

[23] Oberholtzer, 211-19; Foulke, *Morton*, II, 365-76.

Instead of enjoying a well-earned vacation, Cameron spent a large part of July in the smothering Washington heat listening to lengthy testimony and argument relative to the impeachment and trial of former Secretary of War Belknap. Allegedly, the secretary was guilty of accepting bribes from an Indian Trader, but actually he seemed to have been scalped by two sisters of expensive tastes. Belknap had married both of them (singly), thereby doubling his pleasure, at least temporarily. Belknap resigned immediately upon exposure, but the House, feeling that justice had been cheated, relied upon good old English precedent and impeached him anyway. Cameron, becoming impatient with wrangling, three times made motions to adjourn.

Finally on August 1, the vote was taken. Each Senator was allowed in one sentence to state the reason for his vote. Many Senators voted "not guilty" because in their opinion the court could not exercise jurisdiction over a private citizen. Cameron showed no special interest in the case and gave no reason for his vote of "guilty." The total was not sufficient to convict Belknap. The preceding October Belknap had thanked the politico for his kind expressions and concluded: "Devotion to your friends is a trait in your character so plainly marked," and signed the letter, "Your friend very truly." Did Cameron suffer conscience pangs over his vote, or was it true that Belknap had not really crossed into Cameronian communion? [24]

[24] *Cong. Record*, 44 Cong., 1 Sess., Vol. IV, Part 7, 342-55; W. Belknap to Cameron, Oct. 17, 1875, Cameron MSS, LC. The prejudiced Claude Bowers wrote (*Tragic Era*, 472): "Humerously enough, it was Simon Cameron who fumed and cursed the loudest."

The campaign of 1876 was the last one which Simon Cameron managed for his party. Although most of the work was delegated to his able lieutenants, he would, nevertheless, receive the credit for a victory or censure for a defeat.

Prospects for success within the state were encouraging from the beginning. In Allegheny County the successor to Errett's mantle, Christopher L. Magee, carried the spring municipal elections for the Cameron machine. In Philadelphia, the quartet of Kemble, Mackey, Mann, and James McManes, the chief luminary of the Gas Trust, performed equally well.

Federal legislation outlawing campaign levies on office holders did not deter enforcement of the time-honored custom. The Pennsylvania politico worked with Zachariah Chandler of the Executive Committee on the national level, and with chairman Hoyt of the state organization, making assessments. "Our rooms are fitted and machine running," boasted Hoyt at the beginning of the campaign season. Quay, besides acting as liaison between the Hayes managers and his own organization, supervised a statewide drive to register every qualified Republican voter.[25] The experienced old-line politicians were carrying the ball; the reformers sat on the sideline.

The Democrats were led by Samuel J. Tilden, erstwhile Barnburner, Free Soiler, Copperhead, and old-line Democrat. Tilden was a man who could fashion himself into elegibility for high office at a given time and had adeptness in "appropriating to himself," said Blaine, "the credit . . . of reform already planned by his political opponents."[26] The Democratic opposition could find little

[25] Quoted in Evans, *op. cit.*, 436-37.
[26] Blaine, *Twenty Years*, II, 575.

fault with Hayes. His rather obscure record to date defied scandalous revelations. But it was Conkling, Chandler, Cameron, and Morton who had made Hayes' nomination possible and his political enemies predicted another regime of Grantism under a new name. But the reformers took heart at Hayes' public advocacy of civil service reform and home rule in the South.

The old issues emerging from the Civil War again dominated the campaign strategy of the Republicans. Even Grant, who possessed no talents for campaigning, performed yeoman's service, calling the nation's attention to the "cruel blood-thirsty, wanton, unprovoked and uncalled for" massacres in the South.[27] Not only alarmists, but many serious thinking men actually believed Tilden's election would undo the gains of the conflict and Confederates would rule the nation. The militant Republicanism of Thaddeus Stevens was still on the march.

Because Pennsylvania was no longer an "October State," national attention was concentrated upon the early elections in Ohio and Indiana, which the parties split between them. Intense suspense prevailed throughout the nation.

Early telegraphic returns on the night of November 7 indicated a Democratic victory. The next day, the Chandlers, Zachariah and William, realizing that Tilden needed only one vote from the cloudy returns from three Southern states to insure him the Presidency, claimed a victory for Hayes, thereby getting credit for a challenge quite likely to come anyway. That same night Simon Cameron joined Grant at the residence of publisher

[27] Quoted in Hesseltine, *Grant*, 409.

George W. Childs. In spite of the politico's arguments, the President remained unconvinced of a victory for Hayes.[28]

Both sides sent observers, advisors, and supervisors south to insure "honest returns"; and both parties employed unscrupulous and dishonest methods, but in such a contest the Republicans had the advantage. The crucial struggle took place in Louisiana and Florida. The Cameron machine dispatched Quay to Louisiana and Mackey to Florida to assist W. E. Chandler. In Louisiana, Senator John Sherman bribed two members of the election board. The board altered the returns by 12,000 votes and gave Hayes a 3,000 majority. Z. Chandler wrote to the governor of Florida that the three Southern states must be secured "by fair means or foul." [29]

The man in control of Federal troops, J. Donald Cameron, was in the nation's key spot to insure the purity (from his party's viewpoint) of Southern election returns. His effort to place Pennsylvania on a war footing through a legislative appropriation of one million dollars, said his enemies, was actually a scheme to aid unscrupulous contractors. It was Donald Cameron's purpose, charged A. K. McClure, to force, with the aid of troops, favorable returns and thus insure victory to his party. Could Hayes be ungrateful to the cabinet member making him President? With Grant's permission, Secretary Cameron ordered four additional companies of troops to the Florida state capital, and informed General Sherman to retain troops at Columbus, South Carolina. ". . . But for the partisan

[28] Harry Barnard, *Rutherford B. Hayes and his America,* (Indianapolis, 1954), 321-22; George W. Childs, *Recollections. . . .* (Philadelphia, 1885), 10.

[29] Hesseltine, *Grant,* 415; Norbert C. Soldon, "James Donald Cameron, Pennsylvania Politician," (M. A. thesis, Pennsylvania State University, 1959), 31.

aggressiveness of Secretary of War Don Cameron, there would have been no electoral deadlock following the Presidential election of 1876." "Hayes' presidency," observed John Bigelow, "is truly the creation of the War Department." [30]

Technically, it was the task of the electoral college to elect the President, but a case had been presented where it was not possible to identify all its members. There was talk of war and of two contesting governments in Washington. Many Southerners, however, were willing to see Hayes President if only they could rid themselves of bayonet-supported carpetbag government. Saner heads, especially that representative of business, prevailed and a compromise solution was suggested—to select a commission empowered to determine the true electoral vote of a controversial state. Only Congress could authorize such a procedure.

Throughout the controversy Simon Cameron opposed any type of compromise. "If any such bargain was made," he wrote two years later, "it must have been negotiated by that new school of politicians who indulge in modish sentimentalism and cowardice calling them statesmanship, and go about sneering at obsolete courage and political conviction, calling them 'radicalism.' " [31]

The bill authorizing an electoral commission was reported out of a special committee on January 18, 1877. The following day the lower house of the Pennsylvania General Assembly endorsed it "fully and unequivocally." At the same time the legislative members opposed to it sent a petition to Cameron. He read it to the Senate with-

[30] *Ibid.*, Philadelphia *Times*, Jan. 18, Feb. 24, 1877; Evans, *op. cit.*, 445, 480, 482.

[31] Quoted in *ibid.*, 489.

out comment. Grant worked aggressively for the bill and engaged Donald Cameron in debate regarding its merits. The President had always exhibited a penchant for misunderstanding conversations and in this case he ran true to form. Donald's father, he believed, would abandon his hostility to the bill.[32]

One of the most persistent misrepresentations of Cameron by historians arose out of his stand on the electoral bill. He is usually represented as speaking "at length" and of having put in a plea for "purity of elections" that moved the Senate to laughter. One can read his speech in less than three minutes and his theme was *not* purity of elections. A New York paper was probably the first to relate the tale and Claude Bowers was one of the first to accept and embellish it.

On January 22, just as the Senate was ready to go into executive session, Cameron received permission to say a "word." The proposed bill was wrong for two reasons: it was extra-constitutional and it was designed to elect Tilden President. He was prejudiced, perhaps because of his age, against all compromises. Every concession, American history had shown, made by a majority to a minority had been destructive of the interests of the majority. This Clay, Webster, and Douglas had learned to their sorrow. The speaker, perhaps unconsciously, was applying the same philosophy of containment to public issues as he always used in individual cases—never extend, gratuitously, an advantage to your opponent.

Next Cameron examined the merits of having Supreme Court justices sit on such a proposed commission. Without question, the commission was being organized on a

[32] Harrisburg *Patriot*, Jan. 20, 1877; *Cong. Record*, 44 Cong., 2 Sess., 736; Nevins, *Fish*, 855.

partisan basis and it gave one the impression of being a political court. If four of the Supreme Court justices were expected to act on a partisan basis would not the fifth be expected to do the same? Consequently, every justice on the commission becomes a common politican. "They are but men and will act as men when you take from them the dignity which the constitution and high office gives them. I want them to be pure for all time to come." Obviously, Simon Cameron was not arguing for the sanctity of elections but for maintenance of the high standards traditionally upheld by members of the nation's highest court.

Regardless of the motives ascribed to the speaker, hindsight revealed the truth of his argument that the bench was to be prostituted to partisan purposes. This is the argument that allegedly created much merriment in the Senate.

After an all-night session, the Senate passed the bill on the morning of January 24. Fifteen other Republican Senators voted nay with Cameron; ten found it convenient to be absent. The five Supreme Court justices, three Republicans and two Democrats, along with the other five Republicans and five Democrats from the Congress, on three occasions voted a straight party ticket. In a sense, Hayes' election was determined by the vote of one man, Justice Joseph P. Bradley, whose son later married the daughter of J. Donald Cameron.[33]

President Grant left office in a blaze of glory. On March 2, the day before Hayes' election was announced, he prepared a telegram ordering the commandant in Louisiana to withdraw military protection from the carpetbag regime. But J. Donald Cameron went to the telegraph

[33] *Cong. Record*, 44 Cong., 2 Sess., 808, 913.

office and countermanded the orders of the commander-in-chief of the army and navy. All orders from the War Department, he asserted, must go through him.[34] His purpose was to preserve the dilemma for the Hayes administration. In this he was successful.

For purposes of orientation, Hayes met with the retiring Grant cabinet on March 6. Four members joined with J. Donald Cameron in insisting upon recognition of the Republican regime in Louisiana, which meant retention of Federal troops. At this time Cameron knew that he was not slated to remain in the cabinet.

From the Cameronian point of view no President holding office through the efforts of the Secretary of War could possibly prove himself such an ingrate as Hayes did. From the time of the election until his induction into office, Hayes was not allowed to forget the preeminence of Pennsylvania. In December he was reminded of the block of electoral votes, the largest he received, from the Keystone state. Later state delegations visited the President-Elect in Ohio to remind him of his political debts to the Cameron organization.

When it became apparent that Hayes was likely to emerge victorious over Tilden, the machine staged a concerted drive for J. Donald Cameron rivaling the one faced by Abraham Lincoln in 1861. Only one Republican in the state senate dared not to sign a petition to place Don in the cabinet. Immediately on Hayes' arrival in Washington the state's entire Republican Congressional delegation called on him in a body. Matthew Quay accompanied by Governor Hartranft personally urged Donald's appointment and reminded the President-Elect that he "must rely upon the state administration" of Pennsylvania "as his

[34] Bernard, *Hayes*, 420.

friends." According to Hayes, Donald Cameron and General John A. Logan were urged upon him all day. Hayes would not dare pass Pennsylvania for a cabinet post, believed the *New York Times*. Very accurately, the Philadelphia *Times* pointed out: "Republicanism in Pennsylvania is Cameronism, and the stream cannot rise above its fountain." [35]

Had such an appointment been acceptable for the state, the President-Elect would have taken Galusha Grow or even Governor Hartranft, but J. Donald Cameron, he bluntly told in person, he could not appoint. He had announced his intention to start with a fresh cabinet and to accept Donald would allow other claims to remain. One force within the state Republicans had been working to keep Donald out of the cabinet. Louis Hall, hoping Hayes would not fall into the trap of Pennsylvania politicians "who seek but to promote their selfish ends," was urging former national convention chairman, Edward McPherson of Gettysburg, to have Blaine speak to Hayes on the subject. Hayes had criticized Grant for allowing himself to be branded with the Cameronian stamp and could not afford to lay himself open to the same charge. It should be noted however that Hayes was not above rewarding the "visiting statesmen" who steered the canvassing boards which brought him victory.[36]

On March 6, when it was publicly known that Donald would not enter the Hayes cabinet, the Hartranft Club, in company with Benjamin Brewster and Senator Patter-

[35] Evans, *op. cit.*, 481-82; Quay to Hayes (copy), Dec. 16, 1877, Quay Letters, LC; *New York Times*, March 3, 1877; Philadelphia *Times*, March 2, 1877; Williams, III, *Hayes*, 426.

[36] *Ibid.*, 136, 426; L. Hall to McPherson, Feb. 17, March 5, 1877; McPherson MSS, LC.

son, serenaded Simon Cameron at his Washington residence. His few remarks on the occasion revealed his bitterness and disappointment. Pennsylvania had demonstrated its power to make Presidents, he said, but Presidents were not always ready to recognize the state's claims.[37]

Certainly Cameron was no happier when his hometown paper soberly bestowed credit upon the "8 by 7" President for sparing Pennsylvania the disgrace of being represented in a fraudulent cabinet. "Was this not a pretty dish to set before the king"—a Confederate who tried to destroy the Union, a Liberal Republican who had bolted the party, and a lawyer who had defended the detested Andrew Johnson.[38]

Cameron did not want to see Evarts, an enemy of his friend Conkling, or Schurz, the bolter, enter the cabinet, but the appointment especially irritating to him was John Sherman's nomination to the Treasury post. He could rely upon the bullying tactics of Blaine to aid him but the deplumed knight made the mistake of trying to block en masse the cabinet nominations.

In executive session Simon Cameron spoke at length against the nominations. He held that a Republican President should appoint only Republicans to office, and that there was no warrant or excuse for the Southern policy adopted by the President. He was successful in not having Sherman's name reported out of the Finance Committee. When asked if it was not unusual to refer cabinet nominations to committees, he retorted: "Yes, but this is a very unusual administration." When Cameron saw he could not command the votes to block the nomination (he

[37] Philadelphia *Times*, March 6, 1877.
[38] Harrisburg *Patriot*, March 7, 1877.

could not plead Senatorial prerogatives because none were from his state), he voted to confirm them.[39]

Cameron's determined opposition to his nomination shocked Sherman because their personal relations in the Senate had been friendly. Sherman was Hayes' first choice for his cabinet and it was believed Sherman's influence, largely instrumental in fashioning the cabinet, had been directed against Donald Cameron. But there also remained a wound dating back to 1862. When Lincoln nominated his fallen Secretary of War for the Russian mission, Sherman, although not voting against Cameron's confirmation, had urged postponement of a vote in executive session until charges could be aired.

Two days after attaining his 78th birthday, Simon Cameron penned his resignation to Governor Hartranft:

I have the honor to herewith tender to you my resignation as a Senator of the United States, from the State of Pennsylvania, to take effect the twelfth day of March, 1877. In thus withdrawing from active political life, I deem it fitting that I shall cherish in my retirement, and I venture the hope that I have represented their interests and their aspirations with some measure of success. I am conscious that I have constantly aimed to do this.[40]

When the news was made public, the press agreed unanimously on three items: Cameron had resigned in protest against the Hayes regime and non-recognition of Pennsylvania's cabinet claims; the politico wished to demonstrate his political strength; and this demonstra-

[39] *New York Times*, March 8, 1877; Philadelphia *Times*, March 8, 1877; Albert V. House, "President Hayes' Selection of David M. Key for Postmaster General," *Journal of Southern History*, IV (Feb. 1938), 87-93.

[40] Archives Division, Manuscript Section, Collection "C," Pennsylvania State Library.

tion would consummate his desire to see his son succeed him in the Senate. None questioned his power to name his successor. Simon Cameron, it seemed to the Philadelphia *Press*, had made public the first provisions of his will with the understanding that his son, Donald, would do the same for his son. The New York *Tribune* contributed a prophesy: "The voice in the convention may be the voice of Don, but the hands in the back room will be the hands of Simon. He will live a pleasant life on his farm smelling the clover and the cows, and watching from a distance the vexations of the reformers."

Publicly, the retiring Senator gave no intimation of his disgust with the incoming administration; in fact he denied that dissatisfaction had anything to do with his resignation. A proud, self-respecting politician of the old school, he could not confess himself a sorehead, or admit his consumption of a disagreeable menu of boiled crow, sour grapes, and humble pie. He was tired of public life and needed a rest. Relaxed on the same farm on which his grandfather had toiled and died, he, like the retired Caesars of old, would be happy alone with his cabbages. No longer would he have to turn good people away or be annoyed by unscrupulous petitioners seeking only to make use of him. Never in his 32 years of public service, he was proud to state, did he ever use his position to make a dollar for himself. A few days later, after Donald was nominated for the Senatorship, he admitted gracefully that his son's election in his place would be "very gratifying to him." It seemed to him, as it did to his friends and enemies alike, that he could not have selected a more propitious moment to retire.[41]

[41] Philadelphia *Press*, March 13, 1877; New York *Tribune*, March 13, 14, 1877; *New York Times*, March 13, 1877.

Events of the next few days confirmed what the public assumed. No one, not even the most naïve, believed that Simon Cameron would arrange to have his resignation accepted and announced without first establishing guarantees of his son's succession. In spite of last-minute machinations to pressure Hayes into taking Donald, his father was proceeding on the assumption of his rejection. Machinery must have gone into operation early, because the wife of one of his best friends, Mrs. E. B. Moore of West Chester, "left the cat out of the bag" when she wrote on February 20 of her sorrow in hearing of his resignation from the Senate. Evidently Mrs. Moore had received enough information to confuse her. It was her husband's paper, it will be recalled, that properly predicted the successful Senatorial nominee in 1869. Mr. Moore wrote a lengthy essay on the "Life and Public Services of General Simon Cameron" after his ideal's death.

The Republicans had a majority of 50 on joint ballot in the General Assembly, so there was no question of a Republican victory in a special election for United States Senator. The genial publisher of the protectionist Philadelphia *North American,* Morton McMichael, in jest it would seem, announced his candidacy before the Republican caucus and marshalled his forces, "even less numerous and more ridiculous and contemptible" than Falstaff's array.[42]

The same night that Cameron's resignation was delivered by special messenger to Governor Hartranft, the Cameron mansion on Front Street in Harrisburg was the scene of continuous visitations from darkness until dawn.

[42] *Ibid.,* March 13, 1877.

The faces of Stockley, Hill, Mackey, Kemble, Quay, William Leeds, David H. Lane, J. A. Hiestand, Colonel E. W. Davis, Christopher Magee, and James Rutan, Quay's lieutenant, made the city look like the scene of Cameron Old Home Week. Pages were delegated to contact Republican legislators as they emerged from trains or at their hotels. They were requested that same night, at the hour stated, to honor former Secretary of War Cameron with their presence at his residence. Who could dare to refuse?

J. Donald Cameron entertained with an imposing array of refreshments, but on this occasion the *pièce de resistance* proved to be the "guest register." Personally, to small groups, J. Donald Cameron explained the coming announcement of his father's resignation and his wish to see his son succeed to the Senatorship. Before leaving, each guest was requested to sign a register pledging his vote to J. Donald Cameron. Before morning, more than a majority of the Republicans in the state legislature had signed.[43]

The following afternoon, March 13, at 1:00 P.M., the Republican faithful assembled in Senatorial caucus at the state library. One hundred thirty-two were present. Only two men, J. Donald Cameron and Morton McMichael, were nominated. The vote tallied: Cameron 131; McMichael 1. The nomination was made unanimous without opposition. One member emerged saying he dared not run the risk of life-long persecution by the "clan." The body, needlessly it seemed, had rubbed salt into Haye's wounds; it passed a resolution endorsing his policies. The Republicans also spread rumors of the Presi-

[43] Sam Hudson, *Pennsylvania and Its Public Men* (Philadelphia, 1909), 203.

dent's intention of sending the retiring Senator Cameron on a mission to England.[44]

Editor J. W. Forney saluted the feudalistic ceremony of Lord Cameron transmitting his Duchy of Pennsylvania to his son and legal heir, J. Donald. Old-fashioned folks, predicted the Philadelphia *Public Ledger*, would be puzzled to find that proprietary government in Pennsylvania had not come to an end in 1776. The New York *Tribune* related a brief biography of the new Senatorial nominee. Possessing administrative ability of a high order, this widower of "large fortune" was considered the "shrewdest and most influential politician in Pennsylvania." [45]

There was no manifestation of excitement, pleasure, or displeasure when, on March 20, 1877, every Republican in the House voted for J. Donald Cameron for Senator. During the roll call Simon Cameron came into the chamber. One Democratic assemblyman voted for Andrew G. Curtin—a tribute to a fallen warrior. The same routine followed in the Senate. The announced election of J. Donald Cameron over his Democratic opponent, 146 votes to 93, to fill the unexpired term of Simon Cameron contributed not even a mild anti-climax.[46] Perhaps in this one case the historian can be excused for saying the scepter of power had passed from father to son without creating a ripple.

The appearance of the most propitious moment for the succession was, of certainty, the leading factor in bringing about Simon Cameron's resignation in March, 1877; but

[44] *New York Times*, March 14, 1877.
[45] New York *Tribune*, March 14, 1877.
[46] Philadelphia *Press*, March 21, 1877; Philadelphia *Times*, March 21, 1877.

there were other factors which had made his office less desirable. His chairmanship of the Foreign Relations Committee would bring him into daily contact with Secretary Evarts, whom he disliked; he was not in sympathy with the declared policies of the Hayes administration; he was the oldest member of the Senate, with almost all his old associates gone; and he was having embarrassing domestic litigation on his hands. Physically, he showed the vigor of a man ten years his junior.

For decades the General Assembly of Pennsylvania suffered ridicule throughout the land for its servility to the Clan Cameron; but at the moment there was more involved than liege homage to a political dynasty. The just claims of the Commonwealth, so it appeared to Pennsylvanians, had been consistently ignored and its leading political figure snubbed by the incoming Hayes administration. Here was provided the opportunity to express an aroused provincial patriotism, and the majority of Republican legislators were pleased to register their dissent. Even in a so-called free caucus nomination, one cannot envision, with the possible exception of Galusha A. Grow, any candidate who had attained the national stature of J. Donald Cameron. Seven months following his election, Senator William Wallace presented the credentials of Pennsylvania's junior Senator.

Simon Cameron's last days in the Senate were marked by a short special session of the Forty-fifth Congress. On March 5, following a brief session, the Senate proceeded to the platform on the central portico of the capitol and heard the delivery of Hayes' inaugural address. Unsympathetically, the Stalwart Senator received the new Presidential dictum: "He serves his party best who serves his country best."

On March 7, Cameron delivered his last phrases on the floor of the Senate. When he argued to seat William Pitt Kellogg, a former carpetbag governor supported by Grant, he was forced to sit down because of a demand for a roll call. But he added, with the persistence for which he was famed, "I have something to say about that [communication sent to South Carolina] and I *will* say it." But the veteran politico's words were never forthcoming—his active participation on the floor of the Senate was ended forever.[47]

During the last few years, Cameron's record in the Senate was largely negative in character. He had refused to allow himself to be disgorged of the back salary gratuity. On the questions of specie resumption, inflation, the electoral commission, continued Federal protection of the Republican regimes in the South, and the civil service, he had been defeated or checkmated. He had witnessed James Blaine leading the Republicans to a reduction of his sacred protective tariff and the restorations which followed were totally unsatisfactory to him. Surely, as he confessed in private, he must have resigned in disgust.[48] His chairmanship of the Foreign Relations Committee for a period of six years was the one bright spot in an otherwise mediocre performance.

The epilogue of the father-son political drama was enacted in October, 1877. This time the action demonstrated the son's gratitude to his father.

Hayes had been under continuous fire because Pennsylvania did not possess either a cabinet post or a first-class foreign mission. The President decided to fill the gap

[47] *Cong. Record*, 45 Cong., I Sess. (special), 1-3, 23.
[48] Stewart Pearce to Cameron, Aug. 1, 1878, Cameron MSS, LC.

with a diplomatic post and found among the names suggested that of Wayne MacVeagh, a hardy perennial. The administration, not being able to arrive at a decision, was seeking an easy solution and hoped to find it by throwing the burden of choice upon Pennsylvania. "Evarts in his gushing way said in the presence of Don Cameron, that Pennsylvania was entitled to one of the great missions, and as that to England was vacant, if the Republicans there could agree among themselves, it could be had." The Camerons, masters of political chicanery, could not have laid a better trap for the Secretary of State than he did for himself.

J. Donald Cameron called a meeting of Pennsylvania's Congressional delegation at his residence in Washington. An informal poll favored Wayne MacVeagh and Morton McMichael. Representative Thompson, probably by prior arrangement, delivered a prepared speech eulogizing Simon Cameron's services and his voluntary retirement. His appointment, claimed the speaker, would have the effect of uniting the party and healing old wounds. No one spoke against the motion to make Simon Cameron the choice of the group and the politico, by default, became the unanimous choice of the group. Each member of the delegation was required to sign the petition requesting Simon Cameron's nomination.

J. Donald Cameron presented the paper directly to the President and said "this is what Pennsylvania wants." William D. Kelley (for purposes of humiliation, claimed the Democratic press) was delegated to carry the suggestion to Evarts. According to one source, Evarts gave assurances that the wishes of the Pennsylvania delegation would be carried out. The following day a majority of the state's delegation called at the White House, claimed they were coerced into signing, and agreed that the appointment was not really proper.[49]

The enemies of the Hayes administration welcomed the new Presidential dilemma. Under the circumstances, if the mission were not tendered to Cameron, the state of Pennsylvania could consider itself insulted. The Cameronian John A. Hiestand quiped: ". . . the administration has been asking for harmony—now they have it." Hiestand was enjoying the dicomfiture of Hayes, Evarts, and Schurz.

Hayes made a quick decision. Better incur the wrath of one state than become the laughing stock of the nation. A face-saving device was discovered. The Congressional petition, Secretary Evarts reminded the delegation and press, was only advisory—no one was bound by its provisions. On October 30, Hayes announced the nomination of John Welsh of Philadelphia to the English mission. J. Donald Cameron was "shocked," but "Pig Iron" Kelley was "satisfied." According to Washington patter, Senator Roscoe Conkling intended to lead the fight against the confirmation of Welsh, but dropped it after taking stock of his strength.[50]

In the meantime, the subject of the controversy had spoken at a dinner in Virginia. Pennsylvania was willing to forget its animosity toward the South and the new Hayes administration; nevertheless, his state had not been "rightly treated by him whom she has put in power." The question of his acceptance to the English mission is conjectural, but he was blessed with good health; he especially wished to visit England and Scotland, the land

[49] Williams, *Hayes*, III, 515; Philadelphia *Times*, Oct. 24, 1877; Harrisburg *Patriot*, Oct. 25, 1877.
[50] Philadelphia *Times*, Oct. 27, Nov. 1, 1877.

of his reputed illustrious ancestor, the Gentle Lochiel; and a ministership to the world's leading nation was an honor not lightly to be cast aside.[51]

But the fact remained that Pennsylvania's most powerful political figure had disappeared from the scene and his heir must now accept full responsibility for maintenance of the most consummate political machine the Keystone State had ever witnessed.

[51] Harrisburg *Patriot*, Oct. 20, 1877.

12
The Good Neighbor

IT WOULD HAVE BEEN EXTREMELY DIFFICULT FOR ANY MAN still endowed with an active intellect, good health, and continued prestige, whose very life *was* politics, and whose son now occupied a commanding position in his old political hierarchy, to have withdrawn completely from political life.

People continued to speak in awe of the omnipotent Cameron machine. During the remaining years of his life, Simon Cameron saw his machine still dominating his party and, usually, the Commonwealth. The rise of the Greenbackers and the Independent Republicans brought temporary setbacks and even the election of a Democratic governor, the first since ante-bellum days, but both times his son sought re-election to the Senate, in 1879 and 1885, the Republican majority in the legislature supported him. In 1887, Matthew Quay, who in 1866 had rather thoughtlessly named his second son Andrew Gregg Curtin, joined J. Donald in the Senate.

The year following Simon Cameron's retirement was a particularly crucial one for the organization—its prestige under new management was at stake. The new Democratic gains must be reversed and a favorable legislature returned which would pass on J. Donald's determination to try for election in his own right; and the Commonwealth would elect a governor to succeed the strong Cameron man, Hartranft. The Cameronian candidate for governor, General Henry Hoyt, had little opposition at the convention and won an easy victory over his Democratic opponent in the fall. Quay was rewarded with an exceedingly lucrative position in Philadelphia—an office especially created by the Republican legislators for his benefit.

Cameron must have derived special satisfaction from the election results in the Twentieth Congressional District. There, former Governor A. G. Curtin, running on the Democratic ticket, was defeated by an unknown Greenbacker, Seth Yocum. The outcome represented distrust and resentment against a man who as late as 1866 had severely castigated the Democratic Party.

The beginning of the new year was marked by the death of the Cameron machine's ablest manager, Mackey, "one of the safest of advisers in finance as well as politics," and the equal of Quay "in boldness of conception and execution." During the last ten years of his life, admitted the opposition Harrisburg *Patriot*, "no man exercised so much influence in management" of the dominant Republican Party. It will be long before one is found, predicted the organ, "who possesses the capacity, the courage and organizing skill of Robert W. Mackey." [1]

Mackey's last political assignment was to make certain that no strong combination of bolters would be organized to unite with the Democrats for the purpose of defeating

[1] McClure, *Notes* II, 505; Harrisburg *Patriot*, Jan. 2, 1879.

J. Donald's re-election to the Senate. The end results of his efforts were successful, although three weeks after his death five Republican legislators refused to vote for Donald Cameron.[2]

State Chairman Quay, disappointed at finding the lucrative Philadelphia recordership did not bring him political dominance of the city, resigned, became Secretary of the Commonwealth, and hindered by no new Mackey, took active charge of the Republican organization.

When Cameron attended a Philadelphia dinner in the fall of 1879, the Philadelphia *Record* published a fictitious interview allegedly having taken place at Girard House. Asked if he contemplated buying out Tom Scott's stock in McClure's *Times* he answered, "Well that's rich." McClure suspected the "interview" was spurious and called Cameron's attention to it. At any rate, the old politician's "prediction" of the machine's drive to install Grant for a third term had a ring of truth in it.[3]

J. Donald Cameron's position as chairman of the Republican National Committee gave him a powerful voice in the drive to renominate Grant. The old Cameron allies, Conkling of New York and Logan of Illinois, joined in directing the last stand of the stalwarts of the party. Much interested in witnessing his son's prominence at the nominating convention, the old politician made arrangements to attend as the guest of Robert Todd Lincoln.[4]

But J. Donald's arbitrary tactics in refusing to accept motions or to allow appeals from his decision were fruitless, and Garfield emerged the victor over Grant after 36 ballots. A trusted leader of the Philadelphia ring, James

[2] Soldon, "Quay," 47.   [3] Philadelphia *Record*, Oct. 13, 1879.
[4] R. Lincoln to Cameron (telegraph), May 27, 1880.

McManes, dared break the unity of the state's delegation by supporting Blaine.[5]

Rather strangely the unwanted Presidential candidate James Garfield gave indications he might prove amenable to Cameronian persuasions. General Thomas L. Kane, having made his peace with Simon Cameron following the Liberal fiasco of 1872, was again acting as a self-appointed liaison for his close friend. Following a visit to the Republican Presidential candidate he wrote: "[Garfield has] an earnest desire if elected to profit by your counsel." After his election over Pennsylvania's favorite son, General Winfield S. Hancock, Garfield requested a visit from Simon Cameron.[6]

The entrance of Cameron's son-in-law Wayne Mac-Veagh into Garfield's cabinet was actually a victory for the insurgents of the party. Simon did not extend any congratulations to him, but the editor of the Lancaster *New Era* welcomed him "on behalf of the Independent Republicans of the 'Old Guard'" as a man who had "never recognized a political boss." At first, the Cameron machine had urged General Harry White for Garfield's cabinet, then, following a compromise parley, had expected Galusha Grow to get the Pennsylvania appointment.[7]

In 1885, J. Donald Cameron was again returned to the Senate in spite of the careful plans of the Independents under John Stewart to unseat him, and the next year,

[5] Gillett, *Hoar*, 101-03; John J. Serff, "The Life of James Beaver" (Ph. D. thesis, Pennsylvania State University, 1955), 67.

[6] Kane to Cameron, Oct. 29, 1880, J. D. Cameron to S. Cameron, Nov. 23, 1880, Cameron MSS, LC.

[7] MacVeagh MSS, LC; Quay to Garfield, Jan. 31, Feb. 25, 1881, Quay Letters, LC. Cameron extended congratulations to Benjamin H. Brewster when he succeeded MacVeagh in Arthur's cabinet.

General James Beaver, who had affiliated himself with
the machine in 1880 and had suffered defeat in one
gubernatorial contest at the hands of the Democrats, was
easily elected governor. When Simon Cameron requested
Beaver to make Thomas V. Cooper Secretary of the Commonwealth, the incoming governor replied that he'd be
pleased to do so if there were no constitutional objections.[8]

It is apparent, therefore, that official retirement did
not bring an end to Simon Cameron's political activities,
that, working behind the scenes, he continued to exercise
powerful influence upon the functions of the machine
which bore his name, and that patronage hunters often
preferred to seek rewards through the time-tested efforts
of Simon Cameron rather than through the titular leaders,
J. Donald Cameron and Matthew Quay.

All activities, political and social, of Senator J. Donald
Cameron now became front page news. In February,
1878, the wealthy widower, who reputedly had experienced an "affair" with Judge Black's daughter, formally
announced his engagement to Elizabeth B. Sherman at a
dinner party given at the residence of her uncle, Secretary John Sherman. J. Donald's fiancé, the daughter of
Judge Charles Sherman of Cleveland, was 22 years of
age, tall, graceful, already recognized as one of Washington's most accomplished young ladies. Hundreds of
invited guests attended the marriage ceremony performed
by the bishop of the diocese in Cleveland's St. Paul's
Episcopal Church. The couple received gifts worth more
than $100,000. The report that Simon Cameron did not
attend his son's nuptials because he feared a railroad acci-

---

[8] Serff, "Beaver," 69, 81; Beaver to Cameron, Dec. 6, 1886,
Cameron MSS, LC. Soldon, *op. cit.*, 67, attributed the machine's
defeat in 1882 to a combination of reformers and oil men.

dent is strange indeed; a much better reason could have been given—the attendance of Secretary John Sherman, whose entrance into the cabinet Cameron had bitterly opposed.[9]

Two years later Simon Cameron was able to attend the marriage of his granddaughter, Eliza, Don's eldest daughter, to William Hornblower Bradley of Newark. The bridegroom was the son of Supreme Court Justice Joseph Bradley, who, it will be recalled, received credit for "electing" President Hayes in 1877. Beside the venerable Simon Cameron, seated in the front pew, notable guests were George W. Childs, Anthony J. Drexel, and Governor Henry Hoyt. The marriage was performed by the president of Lafayette College and three of the ushers were sons of Senators. It was the stunning figure of Mrs. J. Donald Cameron, however, attired in a white corded silk gown with diamonds, which stole the show. Simon's gift to the newlyweds was a silver coffee urn. General U. S. Grant expressed regrets at his absence—he had intended to come but forgot.[10]

The several spacious residences and estates of Cameron made it easy for him to play the good neighbor and host. Before the Civil War he had purchased three farms near Harrisburg called, collectively, Lochiel. On the estate he built a large red brick two-and-one-half story mansion with a wide Southern-style porch. After his return from Russia in 1862 he purchased the old John Harris mansion (now the headquarters of the Dauphin County Historical

[9] Philadelphia *Record*, March 5, 1878; Philadelphia *Times*, Feb. 25, May 9, 1878; Harrisburg *Patriot*, May 10, 1878.

[10] Philadelphia *Times*, Nov. 18, 1880; Grant to Cameron, Nov. 21, 1880, Cameron MSS, LC. Eliza Bradley died at Donegal in 1955 at the age of 98. Her sister and companion at Donegal, Mary Cameron, died in 1959.

Society) on Front Street in Harrisburg. The former served as his summer residence, the latter as his winter residence.

As Simon Cameron became older he showed more pride in his Scotch ancestry and exhibited a sentimental attachment for the area around Donegal Spring and Maytown, the site of his birth. In 1872 he purchased the Dr. Nathaniel Watson farm adjoining the spring and the Donegal Presbyterian Church and cemetery. He set to work purchasing the old glebe farms of the church, on which his grandfather and great grandfather had worked, until he had nine farms totaling 1,200 acres. The old Watson farmhouse, enlarged and renovated, became "The Mansion," regarded with admiration and wonder by the people of the countryside. Its elaborately constructed bar, stocked with the finest imported wines and liqueurs, served an almost continuous stream of guests. The many rows of maple trees seen on the farms today were planted under the personal direction of the proud owner. Cameron lost interest in Lochiel and J. Donald took charge of it.[11]

The accumulation of broad, fertile acres in Lancaster County allowed Simon Cameron to take on some of the trappings of the aristocratic English gentleman-farmer. There was much interest in new crops among the progressive land-owners of region and under the able direction of his farm superintendent, Captain Henry Haines, more and more acres were planted in tobacco. By 1880, the Donegal Farms were producing 35,000 pounds of tobacco annually, in spite of the obnoxious tobacco worms and other agricultural hazards. Catering to the demands of the expensive cuisines of metropolitan areas, Cameron shipped watercress directly from Donegal to New York

[11] Beck, "Camerons," 91-95; Ziegler, "History of the Donegal Presbyterian Church," 38-51.

hotels. He imported chickens from Cuba and the finest breeds of cattle from Europe for experimental and gift purposes.

Cameron likely lost money as an agriculturist because of the mismanagement of tenant farms operated under the direction of his grandson, Simon Brua Cameron. At one time, $14,000 was needed to balance the books.[12]

Cameron belonged to the Farmers Club, a select group of gentlemen well known to fortune and gracious of mien. Its members, which included industrialists W. G. Moorehead and Thomas Scott and publisher Charles A. Dana, usually met at Donegal or at Colonel Duffy's home in Marietta. The extraordinary extrovert, Duffy, had engaged in engineering, water transportation, and railroad construction. During the war, Colonel Duffy had supervised the transportation of westward-bound government supplies. In 1868 he returned to agricultural pursuits and became the largest tobacco grower in the state. No one, it seemed, envied the good fortune of this huge man, renowned for his liberality, graciousness, and hospitality. He was Cameron's chief companion during the politico's last years. Three of his sons were named James, Donald, and Cameron. On one occasion, at a party held in Duffy's park, a most distinguished guest, General U. S. Grant, imbibed too freely of the liquid refreshments and suffered himself to be carried prone on a door to a spring wagon for transportation to the Marietta railroad station.[13]

Charles A. Dana wrote of a little party "in lilac time"

[12] Beck, *op. cit.*, 97; Cameron to Haines, Aug. 19, Nov. 15, 1880, Nov. 5, 1885, Cameron Letters of Captain Henry Haines, Maytown; Cameron to MacVeagh, May 2, 10, 1885, MacVeagh MSS, HSP.

[13] Henry Haines to writer, Maytown, July 14, 1964.

given by Cameron at Donegal and attended by more than 30 gentlemen, including two leading Democrats of the Commonwealth, Samuel Randall and Governor Pattison. The "descendant of Irish kings," Colonel James Duffy, occupied the post of honor at the end of the table.[14]

All citizens of the Maytown area were invited to Donegal to celebrate the Centennial of Independence from Britain. More than 600 guests were served from tables on the lawn of the mansion. Donegal's Presbyterian minister read the Declaration of Independence and the host recited the story of his life and of the difficulties encountered in buying all the farms on which his grandfather had worked. Donald had sent word that he might not be able to attend and the host delighted the people with his answer: "you'd better wait till you get an invitation—you ain't a Donegaler." At Thanksgiving time, the people of Maytown went in carriages to nearby Elizabethtown for a banquet served by their good neighbor.

The next year, Maytown's grateful citizens decided to reciprocate their benefactor's hospitality. Committees were formed to take care of all details, such as ice cream, small beer, etc. It is doubtful whether the honored guest ever revealed his payment of $158 for the unpaid picnic bills.[15]

Public entertainment constituted but a small portion of the old politico's benevolence. Many aged folk would have lacked the necessities of life had it not been for the generous heart of Simon Cameron. An old newspaper clipping related: "the people near Maytown will tell you here of a mortgage lifted, and there of a kind deed done,

[14] Lancaster *Examiner*, May (?), 1879.
[15] *Maytown Bicentennial*, 55-56; W. M. Larzelere to Cameron, Sept. 3, 1877, Cameron MSS, LC.

that made life lighter and its burdens easier." Several
indigent widows in Maytown had their coal bills sent
each year to the good neighbor at Donegal. The distressed
widow of his Democratic friend Lebo, who had aided his
election in 1857, was still having her coal bills paid.
Cameron was one of the leaders in the move to buy a
house for Mary Lincoln and gave $1,000 to the cause.[16]
He gave another $1,000 for the relief of the earthquake
sufferers in Charleston and one of the last financial transactions of his life was a generous contribution to the
victims of the Johnstown flood. It would have taxed the
ingenuity of a Philadelphia lawyer to have separated,
from the numerous requests for aid, the worthy from the
fraudulent.

Cameron's habit of offering aid and succor to the needy
almost led to his victimization by scheming and unscrupulous women. The politico liked to think of himself
as possessing a propensity for gallantry toward the fair
sex—a trait attributed to his illustrious ancestor, the
Gentle Lochiel. In ante-bellum days he negotiated a
transaction with the Wetzel family which, on paper, looks
suspiciously like blackmail. On April 1, 1854, he signed a
note to pay Elizabeth Wetzel $6,000; but if in one year he
paid $3,000, the whole debt would be discharged. Three
years later, however, Cameron was still paying to Martin
Wetzel. In 1869 he paid a coal bill amounting to $65 for
Miss Tabitha Wetzel (or Weitzel), once his ideal beauty.
His nostalgic reflections recorded on the back of the bill
read: "coal for poor woman once rich . . . the 'admired of
all admirers' . . . one so generous when she was courted
and admired."

In February, 1877, scandal-mongers were pleased to

[16] Lancaster *Examiner*, May (?), 1879; Lancaster *Sunday News*,
April 30, 1961

hear of a $50,000 damage suit instituted against Simon
Cameron by Mary S. Oliver, an employee in the treasury
department at Washington.

The plaintiff, styling herself the "Widow Oliver," had
a most intriguing background. In 1850, while modeling
clothes for a New York house, the beautiful young manne-
quin met Thomas M. Oliver of Cincinnati. The following
year Oliver sought her out, learned that she had been
seduced by an admirer, and saw the fruit of her sin, a
baby. Oliver transported her to Louisville, Kentucky,
lived with her for seven years—although he "never introduced her as his wife"—and discarded her to marry
another woman. Years later the "widowed" Mary Oliver
enjoyed a free European tour in company with a wealthy
elderly gentleman and his daughter. If Cameron had met
Mary in 1853, conjectured Mr. Oliver, she would have
ruined him; in fact she was "one of the *very worst women*
on this continent" and it was to be doubted whether she
had "an equal on the habitable globe."

The "Widow Oliver," under oath, submitted a sorry
story. She had made the acquaintance of Mr. Cameron
at the Congressional Hotel in New Orleans in 1874,
shortly before the death of Mrs. Cameron. The acquaintance was renewed the following spring in New Orleans.
He spent a night with her at the St. Charles Hotel, enjoyed "improper privileges," and gave her a "dose intended to destroy her." Before leaving New Orleans he
made an offer of marriage, claimed the injured party, and
gave her a letter with which she procured a position in the
treasury department. The following September from
Harrisburg he wrote: "I will carry you to a better home
than Washington . . . you will be my wife." Later she
received $300 from him. She had decided to bring suit
when, after one year's delay, he failed to marry her. It

had been her intention to have a baby delivered to him on the floor of the Senate.

Poor Cameron became the subject of much ridicule from his contemporaries. The disreputable Orville E. Babcock, soon to be relegated to the superintendency of lighthouses, wrote: "As you know I am the friend of all good young men who get into trouble." Senator John Percival Jones jested: "Bless you my boy, it isn't every man who has $50,000 worth of affection at 78." Jeered the New York *Tribune*: "If Simon Cameron had promised to marry anyone, he is going to do it or die in the attempt." Another journal mocked: ". . . old Simon, you gay old dog, you!" But the pastor of his Harrisburg church, taking a dimmer view of his predicament, invoked the divine comforts of the "good Father in heaven."

A veritable battery of first-rate attorneys offered their legal services to the defendant. One counsellor, William Cook, who procured $300 from Simon in November, 1877, to be used at his "discretion"—the end would justify the means—pressed to bring the case to early trial and began ferreting out the past "doings" of Mrs. Oliver.

The case was not decided until April 1, 1879. After several hours deliberation the jury pronounced Simon Cameron an honorable man, guilty of no wrong to the "widow." The emotional judge received the verdict with tears in his eyes. Mrs. Oliver had failed to produce a bona fide letter from her suitor. Cameron was thankful to be relieved from the "vile and groundless persecutions of a dishonest combination" and hoped to punish the "dirty conspirators," but he did not institute any counter suits. Attorneys' fees alone had cost him over $2,000.[17]

[17] Washington *Post*, March 18, 22, April 2, 1879; Babcock to Cameron, Feb. 9, 1877, Cook to Cameron, Nov. 2, 1877, C. A.

Retirement allowed the wealthy Simon Cameron to indulge in one of his greatest interests—travel. Enjoying the pleasures of companionship, he often planned excursions calling for an entourage of considerable size. The politico planned his trips late in the year and would start south after the Christmas holidays. Business interests in the areas added incentive for such trips. The summer vacations were spent at the country's best known spas—Hot Springs, Saratoga Springs, Bedford Springs, and White Sulphur Springs. At the latter resort, in 1881, he noted the presence of over 1,000 guests, enjoying daily horseback rides, bakes every night, and absence from the cares of "hail storms and tobacco worms."

During his Senatorial years, proposed trips to the Caribbean and Mexico had been postponed, but now he determined not to be denied. In January, 1881, his crony, General Benjamin F. Butler, now an "old-fashioned Democrat" invited him for a Caribbean cruise on his private yacht, "America," but he preferred to plan his own itinerary. In middle February he left Fernandina Beach, Florida, for the West Indies. From Latin Cuba came words of warm greetings and the hope of entertaining the distinguished General Cameron together with the other *amigos* from Pennsylvania. The next year again found him in Florida for a winter vacation, enjoying fresh strawberries, early radishes, and beets, before moving on to his favorite rendezvous, New Orleans. General Grant was hoping he would arrive back in time to spend some time at Long Branch.

Holmes to Cameron, Feb. 10, 1877, Thomas Oliver to Judge Marshall, Sept. 27, 1878, Cameron MSS, LC; Cameron to A. G. Riddle, May 5, 1880, Simon Gratz Autograph Collection, HSP; Evans, *op. cit.*, 489-90.

The long deferred trip to the Southwest and Mexico was carefully planned for March, 1883. Charles Dana expected to see the "author and patron" of the expedition at El Paso, but Cameron suffered a fall at his home and wrote his regrets. But early the next year, fortified with letters of introduction from U. S. Grant and President Arthur to President Manuel Gonzales, he made his way to the Mexican border in a private railroad car. He was back home before the middle of February.

His greatest dream, a voyage to Europe, became a reality in 1887. Not many men in their late eighties would have dared such a trip. His party, composed of Colonel Frank A. Burr, J. M. Forster, Leonard Jerome, and Colonel James Duffy, his genial neighbor, sailed from New York on Her Royal Majesty's Ship "Brittanic." "I am going for pleasure," reported the excursionist, and "have no plans mapped out."

The same day the party arrived on foreign soil, Simon had a great-grandson born to him in London. Thomas Burnside, son of Simon's daughter, Rachel Burnside, was living in England at the time. Other relatives to greet him were Virginia and Wayne MacVeagh.

En route from Liverpool, the successful businessman enjoyed seeing the butcher shop kept by the bard's father at Stratford-on-Avon. He spent a night at Kenilworth Castle, the medieval estate once owned by Simon de Montfort and Elizabeth's favorite, Leicester. In London he established his headquarters at Morley's Hotel in Trafalgar Square.

His most brilliant social fête of the season was a banquet in honor of General Joseph R. Hawley of Connecticut. In attendance were such notables as Francis Bret Harte, Murat Halstead, and the Lord Mayor of London.

When the incomparable Chauncey Depew called on General Cameron he responded with a toast to Her Majesty the Queen. "I am going about all the time to dinner parties and I never enjoyed myself more in my life," wrote the tourist. Verily, such a round of daily dinners must have tested the gastronomic limit of the octogenarian to its utmost.

Two top-ranking noblemen, the Duke of Marlborough and the Duke of Beaufort, were Cameron's hosts. The New Yorker Leonard Jerome, grandfather of Winston Churchill, paved the way for a vacation at Blenheim. At Badminton, the summer residence of Beaufort, Cameron was awed by the sight of the duke's "Little Park" of 20,-000 acres—the habitat of 2,000 deer, 20 hounds, 80 horses, and an undetermined number of foxes.

The old politico cancelled his trip to Paris and chose to spend the extra time in Scotland, the land of his paternal ancestors. He enjoyed the many sights of Edinburgh and its environs, but the visit giving him the greatest satisfaction must have been the one to Inverness, ancient stronghold of the Clan Cameron, a region rich in Highlander and Jacobean lore. Here the regicide Macbeth committed the foul deed so graphically recorded by Shakespeare. Most of his time was spent at the estate of Andrew Carnegie. Purposely or not, James C. Blaine left the steel magnate's residence before the next guest arrived.

On September 5, the returning party stepped off the boat at New York. Jokingly, Cameron warned the customs officer that Jerome's huge Waterbury watch was jammed with diamonds. The new York *Graphic* saluted the return of the "Eagle of the Susquehanna," the patriot who was surer than ever that "America was the greatest land on earth." The aged excursionist had returned "greatly improved." To him the European trip "was in all things very pleasant." [18]

Soon after his return to America, Cameron made plans to play the good host to Marlborough, who had been so very "civil" to him at Blenheim. He planned a dinner party for the Duke at his Donegal mansion in late November. The few invited guests included the MacVeaghs, who had met the Churchills in England.

The aged traveller made his last Southern trip in 1888 with a Senatorial party. He enjoyed the oranges of Indian River but missed his usual fare of strawberries and pineapples. Charles A. Dana had been unable to accompany him and the fat Colonel Duffy was "too old and trifling" to make the effort.

The leading role which Simon Cameron had played in the Lincoln administration during the crucial war years led, after an interlude of two decades, to his being looked upon as a authoritative historical contributor to, and interpreter of, the events of the era. Historians, engaged in the task of recording the story of the period, called upon him for aid. His criticism in 1878 of Meade's tactics following the third day at Gettysburg aroused considerable comment. General Frémont, wishing to clarify in his favor the circumstances surrounding his dismissal by Lincoln, received a tart reply from the former secretary of war. It was true that he carried a dismissal order dated October 17, 1861, but his position gave him discretionary

[18] On Cameron's travels see letters in the Cameron Collections, 1880-1887; Captain Henry Haines Letters of Simon Cameron, Maytown; Harrisburg *Telegraph*, July 13, 14, 22, 26, Aug. 13, Sept. 6, 1887. None of the three leading London journals took cognizance of Cameron's visit.

powers and on that particular occasion he was not acting as General Scott's messenger boy.[19]

One of Cameron's bitterest political foes of the past, A. K. McClure, now editor of the Philadelphia *Times*, requested: "I want from you the inside history of the desperate struggle of which the world knows but little. . . . You are entitled to much honor because of that achievement and no person now living can write the story truthfully but yourself." On the reverse side of McClure's letter, Cameron noted: "this is not *the time* for me to be heard." But Lincoln's first Secretary of War never did find the time propitious for the report of his stewardship to the nation. There is no reason to believe that he was reluctant to give such an account.[20]

On several occasions Simon Cameron remarked that had he chosen to remain out of politics he would have been a much richer man, and this statement must not be taken lightly. During the decade following his retirement at the age of 78, he increased his wealth over 50 per cent. At the end of 1877 his personal inventory totaled $1,100,000; in 1887 it was approximately $1,700,000.

His investments were varied in nature: coal lands, railroad stocks, oil fields, United States bonds, banks, canals, real estate, and a quarter of a million dollars in mortgages and notes. The list of holdings names such interesting items as the Magnetic Telegraph Company, the Peach Bottom Slate Company, and an Arizona cattle ranch. Cameron listed Lochiel, Donegal, and his two Harrisburg residences at $235,000—an amount considerably above actual sale value.

[19] Fremont to Cameron, Aug. 24, 1885, Cameron to Fremont (copy), Aug. 27, 1885, Cameron MSS, LC.
[20] McClure to Cameron, Nov. 20, 1880, Cameron MSS, LC.

Very late in life the politico made large investments which he knew could benefit only his heirs. At 83 years of age he paid $25,000 for an island in the Susquehanna River and three years later made a private loan of $125,-000. He usually consulted his son-in-law MacVeagh before making heavy investments.

One of Cameron's chief disappointments in later life was the lack of business acumen and the irresponsibility shown by his many cousins, grandsons, and nephews who were ever besieging him for financial aid. These "poor relatives" cost him at least $50,000. From far away Shanghai he was presented a bill for $291, the cost of one night's frolic for his grandson, Cameron Burnside.

Another family frustration was the mental retardation of his son Simon, born in 1844. Before the Civil War the boy was given treatment at a special school in Germantown. Even at 30 years of age, "Uncle Simon," as he became dubbed, looked forward to his annual birthday party and his father would take pains to be home on that date. To keep him occupied, Simon, Junior, was allowed to assist in the "management" of the great Donegal estate. The Duffy family at Marietta showed much kindness and interest in the younger Simon, and Cameron was so gratified that he willed Mrs. Duffy $5,000. Under the careful supervision of Donald's son, James McCormick Cameron, the younger Simon remained at Donegal until his death in 1908.

Although Simon Cameron was an elderly man during most of his Senatorial service, his unusually long span of life allowed him to witness the passing of many of his associates. Among the first to go were Charles Sumner and Oliver P. Morton. Senator J. Donald Cameron represented the family at the funeral of the latter. In November, 1879, Cameron thanked a member of the Democratic Party for "pairing" with him at the election so he could attend the funeral of Zachariah Chandler. "In all the long years of our public life," recalled the old politico, "we were intimate friends." He was "stunned" by the news of Grant's death in July, 1885. For this man of "simple honesty—not cunning like . . . Lincoln" he had found a "warm attachment." [21]

He renewed his former close relationship with Benjamin H. Brewster and wrote of his desire to again tour the countryside in a buggy with his old friend, and to strike new friendships with the younger generation. When Brewster died, not long after leaving Arthur's cabinet, his aged friend served as his pall bearer.

Cameron's will, drawn in 1886, left most of his estate to his children J. Donald, Virginia, and Margaretta. For five of his grandchildren he placed in trust large sums totaling almost $400,000. The grandson in whom he placed his greatest confidence, James McCormick Cameron, was entrusted with $100,000 to be used for the care of Simon, Junior. His small endowment of $5000 for the pastor's salary of Maytown's Reformed Church was still being appreciated three-quarters of a century later. [22]

One of his last gifts, to be used as a parsonage, was the house located alongside the spot of his birth.

The people of Maytown over a period of fifteen years had seen much of their good neighbor from Donegal. Occasionally he would walk the distance of 5 miles for

[21] Cameron to A. B. Hamilton, Nov. 3, 1879, Correspondence of A. Boyd Hamilton, HSP; Cameron to MacVeagh, July 23, Aug. 7, 1885, MacVeagh MSS, HSP.

[22] Copy of the will of Simon Cameron, courtesy of Mrs. Henry Haines, Maytown.

exercise and pleasure. On one of his last visits he was spotted leaning on his cane and laboriously pushing a rose-bush into the soil of Maytown's public circle.[23]

The finale of the drama of the aged politico's life began in 1889, much like preceding years; his mind was clear, he could still write a legible hand, and he walked with the aid of a cane. He recognized, however, that he was "getting older pretty rapidly." The old general must put his house in final order and be ready for the command to march. In order to insure a home for Rachel's grand-children in Bellefonte, he arranged to have the property there placed in the name of Cameron Burnside's wife.

Weatherbound in his Front Street mansion along the icy Susquehanna, burdened with the cares of ninety years, and disgusted with the financial ineptitude of his many relatives, the old man was impatiently waiting for the "ides of March to bring pleasant weather" and permit his return to his beloved Donegal.

Cameron would soon celebrate his ninetieth birthday, and his many friends determined to make it the most memorable in his career. On March 7, the General Assembly of Pennsylvania passed a resolution congratu-lating him upon attaining his ninetieth year. The pro-tectionist Philadelphia *North American* hailed him the "grand old man of Republican politics."

March 8, 1889, was a bleak, dreary day with squalls of flying snow in Harrisburg, but there was much sunshine and joy in the old Harris House. Simon Cameron spent most of his morning hours reading the dozens of con-gratulatory telegrams from across the nation, including one from the famous Buffalo Bill. The most sentimental

[23] Henry Haines, IV, to writer, Maytown, July 14, 1964.

one came from the survivors of the Cameron and Lincoln Club of Chicago—in 1860 an organization of 700 members. When the time came to pose for his photo he remarked: "I remember the first picture I ever saw of myself in a newspaper. It was when I was elected U. S. Senator the first time. A New Jersey printer had no picture of me, so he just took an old wood cut of a murderer who had been hanged, cut the whiskers away, and printed it as my picture."

Before noon the legislature, led by the lieutenant governor and the two speakers, arrived in a body. He stood in his parlor to receive the Senators, but fatigue compelled him to remain seated while the House members slowly filed by. His remarks on the occasion were few: "Gentlemen, I am very glad to see you all and I am very much obliged for the honor done me. I don't know what more I can say, except that I'll behave myself as long as I'm here." Then the group assembled on the front lawn for a photograph.

The program of honor continued during the afternoon. Governor James A. Beaver and his official family paid their respects. Only the presence of Matthew Quay, it seemed, was necessary to make the visitations complete, but that worthy was in Washington giving advice to the incoming Republican president, Benjamin Harrison.

The gifts and symbols of sentiment included baskets of tropical fruits and many floral tributes, especially gifts of roses, his favorite flowers. The legislative shield of white roses, bordered in pine, red, cream, and pink roses was inscribed "SC—1799-1889." The Cameron Club of Philadelphia (William D. Kelley was a member!) did not forget him. And over the *Telegraph* building waved a flag honoring the president of the state's press club. At the conclusion of such unusual honor the recipient could only say: "It is one of the happiest days of my life." [24]

In a few weeks, while the countryside was in its "most attractive dress," Simon Cameron moved to his Donegal Farms, where he could sit on the wide porch and view the spring, the little Presbyterian Church, and the cemetery where his great-grandfather's pastor rested. Had it been given to him to envision the future three-quarters of a century hence, he would have been pleased to see his great mansion a home for children like his own son Simon, who lacked the intellectual capacity to make his own way in the world.

Shortly after his arrival the "Sage of Donegal" suffered hemorrhages and a partial collapse. His daughter Maggie took care of his mail. Not until June 10 was he able to come downstairs and then he was "glad to get back to bed." Still concerned with the welfare of his neighbors, he was trying to secure appointments for two of his Maytown friends, one of them the young son of his farm superintendent, Captain Henry Haines. The hard-headed businessman to the last, he wondered how Donald (at the time making a carriage tour in Europe) could leave the Middleton Bank in such a mess.

It was on June 20, exactly 16 years after the death of Margaretta Brua Cameron, when Simon's man John noticed his master rubbing the right side of his face. About noon he asked John to get his mail. Simon Cameron had spoken his last words. When John returned he found his master paralyzed—unable to speak although conscious. Unable to take nourishment, the politico became weaker and sank into a coma. His last act was to hold up a red rose placed in his left hand. On the evening

[24] Lewisburg *Saturday News*, March 16, 1889; Harrisburg *Telegraph*, March 8, 9, 1889.

of June 26, surrounded by his two daughters, three grand-children, and other members of the family, Cameron expired.

Because J. Donald was still in England, the deceased's grandson, Simon Brua Cameron, took charge of arrangements. The following morning the body was taken from Donegal Farms by carriage to Marietta and from there to Harrisburg by special train. The oak casket was placed in the large parlor opposite the library of his Front Street residence. The deceased wore a black suit, an old-fashioned high collar, and a scarf of black silk tied under his chin. One floral design read "Statesman" and another honored the late president of the press club. All visitors had to pass under the scrutiny of John, the one man who could recognize all his master's friends.

The last rites, in accordance with Cameron's expressed wish, were simple. The Reverend Dr. Chambers of the local Pine Street Church conducted the services at the mansion. A Presbyterian church quartet sang the deceased's favorite hymns, "Jesus Lover of my Soul" and "Abide With Me."

Leading the funeral cortege across the tiny valley in full view of the state capital flying its flag at half-mast was the carriage of Governor Beaver of Bellefonte. Many dignitaries and friends were included in the long procession. At that very moment the courthouse bell in Sunbury was tolling in memory of the town's good neighbor.

The family plot in which the Commonwealth's most astute political figure was placed at rest came to include the bodies of his wife, two of his daughters, Rachel Burnside and Margaretta Haldeman, and his son Simon.[25]

Simon Cameron was one of the most controversial

[25] Philadelpia *Press*, June 29, 1889; Harrisburg *Telegraph*, June 28, 29, 1889; Lewisburg *Saturday News*, June 29, 1889.

figures of his age; loudly acclaimed by his supporters and as ardently vilified by his enemies. Because with the passing of time, passions soften and perspectives broaden, abused personages are generally content to be judged by posterity, and so it was with Cameron.

But the passing of a century found almost no one willing to do honor to a name repeatedly used for the purpose of symbolizing the worst in political machinations. The modern historians, following a stereotyped pattern established by the writers of the muckraking era, have consistently presented the politico in the most unflattering terms. Herbert Agar and George F. Milton found him unscrupulous; Allan Nevins termed him unprincipled, and the soul-searching Carl Sandburg considered him a cheap trickster and a master of the "weasel word"; T. Harry Williams labelled him "an inefficient and corrupt administrator." Other less harsh terms—wirepuller, Senatorial satrap, old intriguer, astute manipulator, and slippery opportunist, have been used by critics of his career.[26]

The bitterest invectives directed against Cameron usually came from members of his own party whom he had outgeneraled. Forgetting the politico's efforts on behalf of Van Buren in 1832, Andrew Jackson spoke of him as a "renegade politician" not to be trusted by anyone in any way. After Cameron procured his own election to the Senate in 1845 in the place of the candidate designated by the Democratic regulars, and successfully defended his Senatorial prerogatives against President Polk, James Buchanan denounced him as a scamp, an

[26] Agar, *Price of Union*, 408; Milton, *Eve of Conflict*, 455; Nevins, *Emergence of Lincoln*, II, 237; Sandburg, *Lincoln: War Years*, I, 149; T. Harry Williams *Lincoln and His Generals*, 57.

unprincipled radical, and a disorganizer. Polk readily concurred in these opinions, picturing him as "managing tricky man in whom no reliance can be placed." [27]

In early 1861, Thaddeus Stevens was almost at a loss to find words from his voluminous vocabulary to describe Cameron when the politico changed his mind and decided not to support the Commoner for a spot in Lincoln's cabinet. Again in 1867, when Stevens found himself easily outgeneraled by J. Donald Cameron in his fight for the Senatorship, he attributed Simon Cameron's success to his conquerer's gold. The charges directed against him by erratic John Wien Forney, who periodically waxed hot and cold, can hardly be taken seriously. Secretary Gideon Welles, whose passion ran high against his cabinet colleague, judged him equal to the average in the Senate, and conceded that his instincts were "usually right." [28]

If any public figure had a right to pass an opinion, based upon forty years of personal observation and contact, that man was Alexander K. McKlure. During the years when he was a publisher of the *Franklin Repository*, the venom directed against Cameron literally poured from his pen; yet three decades later he commented: "It was often complained by his foes that Cameron fought and won unfairly in his political contests, but the defeated generals of Europe made the same complaint against Napoleon." [29] Here was a tacit admission—a concluding verdict—of the fairness of Cameron's victories over his political opponents.

An observation written by one of Cameron's friends is

[27] Quoted in Hendrick, *Lincoln's War Cabinet*, 51.
[28] Stevens to Washburne, Jan. 19, 1861, Lincoln MSS, LC; Welles, *Diary*, III, 20-21.
[29] McClure, *Lincoln and Men of War Times*, 138.

so amusing, and at the same time so revealing of the politico's character, that it is deserving of special notice: "The worst I ever heard of you was that as an electioneering tactician you were so shrewd and cunning that the very Devil himself could not circumvent you." [30]

Apparently there is no basis for the definition of an honest politician commonly attributed to him—"An honest politician is one, who when he is bought, stays bought." This slanderous reflection upon the character of Simon Cameron has appeared in the pages of reputable encyclopedias and monographs.

The subject of this biography did not lack for defenders among his contemporaries. Ben: Perley Poore, General George McClellan, L. E. Chittenden, and three members of Lincoln's cabinet, John P. Usher, William H. Seward, and Salmon P. Chase, defended him. Chase wrote: "You are unjust to Cameron and I am bound as a man of honor to say so. I have seen him closely as most men here, and I am sure he has acted honorably, and faithfully and patriotically . . . he more than any other man here, has always acted toward me the part of a frank, manly, and generous friend." The Puritan Charles Sumner, a specialist in the art of ferreting out public evil-doers, remarked that Cameron had never enriched himself in public services.[31]

Simon Cameron achieved great success in the two worlds in which he lived and worked—politics and busi-

[30] Dr. John Cameron to Cameron, Aug. 15, 1865, Cameron MSS, LC; *Encyclopedia Americana* (1957) V, 264; Clarence E. Macartney, *Lincoln and His Cabinet*, 51.

[31] Chase to Murat Halstead, Dec. 25, 1861, quoted in J. W. Schuckers, *Life and Public Services of Salmon Portland Chase* (New York, 1874), 281; Joseph M. Medill to Cameron, June 15, 1878, Cameron, MSS, LC.

ness—and few possessed his skill in combining the two. He practiced the philosophy of the rough-and-tumble Jacksonian era—one democratic in the sense that all men were considered equally fit to qualify for public service if they had supported the victors.

If the politico succeeded in earning a special niche for himself, it must have been in the field generally designated state bossism. More than one competent observer spoke of him as the ablest political manager of his day. Although his methods usually deviated from those of his contemporaries, his great success testifies to their effectiveness. The personal factor was the key to a "management" which lacked management. In each locale he preferred to deal directly with his "man" rather than using the circuitous approach through committees on the various levels. Possessed of almost unerring judgment in the selection of able lieutenants, he allowed them the freedom of making important decisions.

Many factors contributed to his success: the practical aspects of his bossism; ability to adapt quickly to new conditions; public confidence in his power to reward faithful followers and the certainty of punishment for the unfaithful; patience and persistence; dogged determination never to accept defeat; and good health, a blessing denied his greatest opponent, Andrew G. Curtin. Although he never submitted his name to the electorate, he had most of the earmarks of a stumping politician. In his expressions of friendship there was a ring of genuineness, and he kissed little girls because he was really fond of them. Cameron was a man who first of all wanted to be liked.

One of the chief reasons for his success—his ruthlessness and persistent "hounding"—was invariably employed against members of his own party who defied or contested his leadership. He always maintained nostalgic memories of his affiliation with the old Democratic Party, and some of his closest associates in business and society were members of that party. In fact, among his "secret weapons" were his close ties to members of the Democracy. It was this factor which gave him a Senatorial victory in 1857, a process which would have been repeated in 1863 had not the "friends" feared for their lives.

Simon Cameron played a part in the economic development of his state and nation and was closely associated in the post-bellum age with the so-called "robber barons." He expressed faith in canal and railroad construction when other faint hearts feared to make investments. No member of the Senate exceeded him in his zeal or efforts to secure a tariff affording protection to America's industry—a boon he considered as beneficial to the working man as to the owners. He boasted that through his long political career he had never been false to his constituents.

No phase of Cameron's career suffered greater criticism than his conduct of the War Department in 1861. Here was a man poorly equipped for a super-human task. His appointment, in view of the existing national crisis, was a mistake. If any man had an opportunity to fill his pockets from the nation's war chest it was this "corruptionist," yet even his bitterest enemies could charge him only with poor management and judgment, the censure for which Lincoln accepted a share. It is one of the ironies of American history that other leading public figures who found their appointed friends betraying public trust were excused on the basis of ignorance, good intention, or weakness of character, but not so in the case of Simon Cameron.

The thesis that Cameron's successful career was based upon corruption is unacceptable. Only one possessed of great abilities could have matched his accomplishments. The rewards enjoyed by his clientele were varied in nature but not often were they of a strictly pecuniary character. Witnesses were not lacking, however, to testify to his purchase of votes, a practice common, in one form or another, in this entire period of American history.

Simon Cameron was not one to shield himself behind a façade of self-righteousness. He once philosophized: "There is no rest for the wicked and who is not wicked?" [32] An evaluation of his great political victories he summed up in the words of the preacher: "All is vanity."

In his ninetieth year, the aged politico expressed to Rufus Wilson what he hoped would constitute posterity's verdict:

From my youth up it has been a rule with me to be kind to everyone. Still I have made enemies because I had opinions and the courage to assert and defend them. I am an old old man now, who has lived through the most wonderful days in our history, and when I am gone all I ask is that people may say that I did the best I could and was never untrue to a friend.[33]

[32] Cameron to MacVeagh, May 8, 1870, MacVeagh MSS, HSP.
[33] Cameron to Rufus Wilson in Philadelphia *Press*, Jan. 20, 1889.

Bibliography

MANUSCRIPTS

Dauphin County Historical Society, Harrisburg
  Correspondence and Papers of Simon Cameron
Dickinson College Library, Carlisle
  Slifer-Dill Manuscripts
Historical Society of Pennsylvania, Philadelphia
  William Bigler Papers
  Henry C. Carey Papers
  Salmon P. Chase Papers
  Simon Gratz Autograph Collection
  Correspondence of A. Boyd Hamilton
  Historical Society of Pennsylvania, Autograph Collection
  Papers of Wayne MacVeagh
Historical Society of Western Pennsylvania, Pittsburgh
  Papers of John Covode
Library of Congress
  Jeremiah Black Papers
  Simon Cameron Papers
  Simon Cameron Letters to Mrs. S. C. Burnside
  Papers of William E. Chandler
  Papers of John Covode
  Hamilton Fish Papers

Letter Copy Books of Hamilton Fish
John W. Forney Papers
Andrew Johnson Papers
Robert Todd Lincoln Collection
Edward McPherson Papers
Papers of John G. Nicolay
Letters of Matthew Quay
Papers of Thaddeus Stevens
Papers of Benjamin F. Wade
Elihu Washburne Papers
Lincoln Memorial University, Harrogate
Cassius M. Clay Manuscripts
Pennsylvania Historical and Museum Commission, Harrisburg
John White Geary Letters
Sylvester K. Stevens Checklist of Pennsylvania Newspapers
Pennsylvania State Library, Harrisburg
Pennsylvania Scrapbook, Volume IV
Wyoming Historical and Geological Society, Wilkes-Barre
Hendrick B. Wright Papers

PRIVATE COLLECTIONS

Captain Henry Haines Letters of Simon Cameron, courtesy of Henry L. Haines, IV, Maytown.
Notes of the late Lee F. Crippen, taken from the James M. Cameron Papers, in possession of the author through the courtesy of Cathell C. Crippen.

NEWSPAPERS

The newspapers, including microfilm reproductions,

with the exceptions listed in parenthesis after the place of publication, are located in the Library of Congress, Historical Society of Pennsylvania, Pennsylvania Historical and Museum Commission, Pennsylvania State Library, and the Pennsylvania State University Library.

Altoona, Pennsylvania
  Tribune (Blair County Historical Society)
Beaver, Pennsylvania
  Argus
  Radical
Bedford, Pennsylvania
  Gazette
Bellefonte, Pennsylvania
  Central Press
  Democratic Watchman
  Republican
Bradford, Pennsylvania
  Reporter
Chambersburg, Pennsylvania
  Franklin Repository
Clearfield, Pennsylvania
  Raftsman's Journal
Erie, Pennsylvania
  Observer
Greenville, Pennsylvania
  Argus
Harrisburg, Pennsylvania
  Democratic Union
  Patroit
  Patroit-News
  Patroit and Union
  Pennsylvania Intelligencer
  Telegraph

Huntingdon, Pennsylvania
  Globe (Juniata College Library)
  Journal (Juniata College Library)
Lancaster, Pennsylvania
  Intelligencer (Lancaster Newspapers, Inc.)
  New Era
  Sunday News
Lewisburg, Pennsylvania
  Saturday News
Lewistown, Pennsylvania
  Gazette
New York, New York
  Herald
  Times
  Tribune
Philadelphia, Pennsylvania
  Age
  Bulletin
  Inquirer
  North American
  Press
  Public Ledger
  Record
  Times
  Weekly Press
Pittsburgh, Pennsylvania
  Gazette
Pottsville, Pennsylvania
  Miners' Journal
Reading, Pennsylvania
  Eagle
Washington, District of Columbia
  Post

West Chester, Pennsylvania
  American Republican
Williamsport, Pennsylvania
  Gazette and Bulletin

OFFICIAL DOCUMENTS

Pennsylvania
  Journal of the House of Representatives
  Journal of the Senate
  Laws of the General Assembly of the Commonwealth of Pennsylvania
  Legislative Record
  Pennsylvania Archives, Fourth Series, Papers of the Governors, VIII (1858-1871), Harrisburg, 1902
  Smull, John A., *Pennsylvania Legislative Handbook*, 1873
United States Government
  Congressional Globe
  Congressional Record
  Executive Journal: United States Senate
  McPherson, Edward, *Handbook of Politics*, 1876
  Papers Relating to Foreign Affairs, Executive Documents, 37 Cong., 3 Sess.
  "Records" of Militia Appeal Docket for Lancaster County, Archives Division, Pennsylvania State Library
  Richardson, James E., ed., *A Compilation of the Messages and Papers of the Presidents, 1789-1897*
  War of the Rebellion: . . . *Official Records of the Union and Confederate Armies*, 130 vols., Washington, 1880-1901

BOOKS

Albert, George D., *History of the County of Westmore-land*, Philadelphia, 1882.

Armor, William C., *Lives of the Governors of Pennsylvania*, Norwich, 1874.

Bancroft, Fredrick, *The Life of W. H. Seward*, 2 vols., New York, 1900.

Barnard, Harry, *Rutherford B. Hayes and His America*, Indianapolis, 1954.

Barnes, Thurlow W., *Life of Thurlow Weed, II, Memoir*, Boston, 1884.

Bartlett, Marquerite G., *The Chief Phases of Pennsylvania Politics in the Jacksonian Period*, Allentown, 1919

Basler, Roy P., *et al.*, eds., *Collected Works of Abraham Lincoln*, 9 vols., 1959.

Bates, Ernest S., *The Story of Congress: 1789-1935*, New York, 1936.

Battles and Leaders of the Civil War, introduction by Roy F. Nichols, 4 vols., New York, 1956.

Beale, Howard K., ed., *Diary of Gideon Welles*, 3 vols., New York, 1960.

Benton, Thomas, *Thirty Years in United States Senate*, 2 vols., New York, 1856.

Beveridge, Albert J., *Abraham Lincoln*, 4 vols., New York, 1928.

Bigelow, John, *Retrospections of An Active Life*, 5 vols., New York, 1909-13.

Bining, Arthur C., *Rise of American Economic Life*, New York, 1949.

Bradley, Erwin S., *The Triumph of Militant Republicanism*, Philadelphia, 1964.

Bucknell University Alumni Catalogue, 1851-1926, Lewisburg, 1926.

Butler, Benjamin F., *Butler's Book*, Boston, 1892.

Callahan, James M., *Russo-American Relations During the Civil War*, Morgantown, 1908.

Carman, Harry and Luthin, Reinhard, *Lincoln and the Patronage*, New York, 1943.

Chittenden, L [ucius] E., *Recollections of President Lincoln and His Administration*, New York, 1891.

Clay, Cassius M., *Life, Memoirs, Writings and Speeches*, Cincinnati, 1886.

Cox, Samuel, S., *Eight Years in Congress from 1857-1865*, New York, 1887.

Crawford, Samuel W., *Genesis of the Civil War*, New York, 1887.

Crippen, Lee F., *Simon Cameron: Ante-Bellum Years*, Oxford, 1942.

Cushing, Thomas, *et al.*, *History of Allegheny County*, Chicago, 1889.

Davis, Stanton L., *Pennsylvania Politics, 1860-63*, Cleveland, 1935.

Dennett, Tyler, ed., *Lincoln and the Civil War in the Diaries and Letters of John Hay*, New York, 1939.

DeWitt, David M., *Impeachment and Trial of Andrew Johnson*, New York, 1903.

Donald, David, ed., *Inside Lincoln's Cabinet: The Civil War Diaries of Salmon P. Chase*, New York, 1954.

Dunaway, Wayland F., *History of Pennsylvania*, New York, 1948.

Eaton, Margaret, *Autobiography of Peggy Eaton*, New York, 1923.

Egle, William H., ed., *Andrew Gregg Curtin: His Life and Services*, Philadelphia, 1895.

Eagle, William H., *History of the Counties of Dauphin and Lebanon* . . . . , Philadelphia, 1883.

Elliott, Charles W., *Winfield Scott*, New York, 1937.

Ellis, Franklin and Adams, Samuel, *History of Lancaster County*, Philadelphia, 1883.

Flower, Frank A., *Edwin McMasters Stanton*, New York, 1905.

Ford, Worthington C., *A Cycle of Adams Letters*, 2 vols., Boston, 1920.

Forney, John W., *Anecdotes of Public Men*, New York, 1873.

Foulke, William D., *Life of Oliver P. Morton*, 2 vols., Indianapolis, 1899.

Garrison, George P., *Western Extension, 1841-1850*, New York, 1906.

Gillett, Fredrick, H., *George Frisbie Hoar*, Boston, 1934.

Gilmore, James R., *Personal Recollections of Abraham Lincoln and the Civil War*, Boston, 1898.

Going, Charles B., *David Wilmot: Free Soiler*, New York, 1924.

Hansen-Taylor, Marie and Scudder, Horace, eds., *Life and Letters of Bayard Taylor*, 2 vols., Boston, 1884.

Harris, Wilmer C., *Public Life of Zachariah Chandler*, Lansing, 1917.

Hart, B. H. Liddell, *Sherman-Soldier-Realist-American*, New York, 1929.

Hendrick, Burton J., *Lincoln's War Cabinet*, 1946.

Hesseltine, William B., *Ulysses S. Grant: Politician*, New York, republished 1957.

Hollister, Ovando J., *Life of Schuyler Colfax*, New York, 1886.

Hudson, Sam, *Pennsylvania and Its Public Men*, Philadelphia, 1909.

Josephson, Matthew, *The Politicos, 1865-1896*, New York, 1938.

Julian, George W., *Political Recollections*, Chicago, 1884.

King, Willard L., *Lincoln's Manager—David Davis*, Cambridge, 1960.

Kleeburg, Gordon S. P., *The Formation of the Republican Party as a National Political Organization*, New York, 1911.

Klein, Philip S., *Pennsylvania Politics, 1817-1832: A Game Without Rules*, Philadelphia, 1940.

Korngold, Ralph, *Thaddeus Stevens*, New York, 1955.

Macartney, Clarence E., *Lincoln and His Cabinet*, New York, 1931.

McCabe, James, *Behind the Scenes in Washington*, n.p., 1873.

McClellan, George B., *McClellan's Own Story*, New York, 1887.

McClure, Alexander K., *Abraham Lincoln and Men of War Times*, Philadelphia, 1892.

———, *Old Time Notes of Pennsylvania*, 2 vols., Philadelphia, 1905.

McCormack, Thomas J., ed., *Memoirs of Gustave Koerner*, 2 vols., Cedar Rapids, 1909.

McLaurin, John J., *Sketches in Crude Oil*, Harrisburg, 1896.

McNaire, Hiram S., *et al.*, *Biographical Encyclopaedia of Pennsylvania of the Nineteenth Century*, Philadelphia, 1874.

McNair, James B., *Simon Cameron's Adventure in Iron*, Los Angeles, 1949.

Marshall, (Mrs.) Jessie A., ed., *Private and Official Correspondence of General Benjamin F. Butler*, 5 vols., Norwood, 1917.

Meneely, A. Howard, *The War Department, 1861*, New York, 1928.

Miers, Earl S., editor-in-chief, *Lincoln Day by Day*, 3 vols., Washington, 1960.

Moore, Frank, ed., *The Rebellion Record*, 11 vols., New York, 1861-63.

Moore, John B., ed., *The Works of James Buchanan*, 12 vols., Philadelphia, 1910.

Morse, John T., *John Quincy Adams*, Boston and New York, 1899.

Mueller, Henry R., *The Whig Party in Pennsylvania*, New York, 1922.

Nevins, Allen, *Fremont, the West's Greatest Adventurer*, 2 vols., 1928.

——, *Hamilton Fish*, New York, 1937.

——, *Abram S. Hewitt*, New York, 1935.

——, *Ordeal of the Union*, 2 vols., New York, 1947.

——, ed., *Polk, The Diary of a President*, New York, 1952.

Nichols, Roy F., *The Democratic Machine, 1850-54*, New York, 1923.

——, *The Disruption of American Democracy*, New York, 1948.

Nicolay, John and Hay, John, *Abraham Lincoln*, 10 vols., New York, 1904.

Nicolay, Helen, *Lincoln's Secretary: A Biography of John G. Nicolay*, New York, 1949.

Oberholtzer, Ellis P., *Jay Cooke, Financier of the Civil War*, 2 vols., Philadelphia, 1907.

Oberholtzer, Ellis P., *History of the United States Since the Civil War*, 5 vols., New York, 1922.

Page, Elwin L., *Cameron for Lincoln's Cabinet*, Boston, 1954.

Pike, James S., *First Blows of the Civil War*, New York, 1879.

Poore, Ben: Perley, *Sixty Years Reminiscences*, 2 vols., Philadelphia, 1886.

Randall, James G. and Donald, David, *The Civil War and Reconstruction*, Boston, 1961.

Randall, James G. and Current, Richard, *Lincoln the President: Last Full Measure*, New York, 1955.

Rhodes, James F., *History of United States from the Compromise of 1850*, 7 vols, 1893-1906.

Richardson, Robert D., ed., *Abraham Lincoln's Autobiography*, Boston, 1948.

Riddle, Albert G. *Recollections of War Times*, New York, 1895.

Russell, William H., *My Diary North and South*, New York, 1954.

Sandburg, Carl, *Abraham Lincoln: The War Years*, 4 vols., New York, 1939.

Savidge, Eugene C., *Life of Benjamin Harrison Brewster*, Philadelphia, 1891.

Schurz, Carl, *Reminiscenses, 1829-1869*, 3 vols., London, 1909.

Seward, Frederick W., *Recollections of War Times*, New York, 1895.

———, *Seward at Washington, as Senator and Secretary of State*, 2 vols., 1891.

Shannon, Fred A., *Organization and Administration of the Union Army, 1861-65* 2 vols., Cleveland, 1928.

Shea, John G., *The Fallen Brave*, New York, 1861.

Sherman, John *Recollections of Forty Years*, 2 vols., Chicago, 1895.

Sherman, William T., *Memoirs, Written by Himself*, 2 vols., New York, 1890.

Smith, William E., *The Francis Preston Blair Family in Politics*, 2 vols., New York, 1933.

Smith, Donald V., *Chase and Civil War Politics*, Columbus, 1931.

Snyder, Charles M., *The Jacksonian Heritage*, Harrisburg, 1958.

Stanwood, Edward, *A History of the Presidency from 1788 to 1897*, Boston and New York, 1898.

Storey, Moorfield and Emerson, Edward, *Ebenezer Rockwood Hoar*, Boston and New York, 1911.

Swanberg, W. A., *First Blood*, New York, 1957.

Taussig, Frank W., *Tariff History of United States*, Fifth ed., New York, 1909.

Tribune Almanac, 1866.

Usher, John P., *President Lincoln's Cabinet*, Omaha, 1925.

Van Deusen, Glyndon G., *Thurlow Weed*, Boston, 1947.

Watterson Henry, *"Marse Henry"*, 2 vols., New York, 1919.

Weber, Thomas, *The Northern Railroads in the Civil War, 1861-65*, New York, 1952.

White, Horace T., *The Life of Lyman Trumbull*, Boston, 1913.

Williams, Charles R., ed., *Diary and Letters of Rutherford Birchard Hayes*, Columbus, 1922-26.

HISTORICAL ARTICLES, INTERVIEWS, PAMPHLETS, UNPUBLISHED ACADEMIC THESES

Barrett, Eugene A., "John Frederic Hartranft," Ed.D. thesis, Temple University, 1950.

Beale, Howard K., ed., "Diary of Edward Bates, 1859-1866," *Annual Report* of American Historical Association, 1930, Washington, 1933.

Beck, Herbert H., "The Camerons of Donegal," Lancaster County Historical Society *Papers*, LVI (1952) 85-109.

Beers, Paul, "It was an Outstanding Family," Harrisburg *Patriot-News*, Jan. 26, 1964.

Bradley, Erwin S., "Post-Bellum Politics in Pennsylvania, 1866-1872," Ph.D. thesis, Pennsylvania State University, 1952.

Brown, Ira V., "William D. Kelley and Radical Reconstruction," *Pennsylvania Magazine of History and Biography*, LXXXV (July 1961), 316-29.

Burr, Frank, "An Old-Time Statesman," Philadelphia *Weekly Press*, April 13, 1882.

Clark, Marth B., "Donegal Church, Colin McFarquhar," Lancaster County Historical Society *Papers*, XVII (1913), 254-59.

Cottell, W. C., "Remarks made at the funeral of Mary, daughter of James and Eliza McCormick and wife of J. D. Cameron," HSP.

Dudley, Thomas H., "Inside Facts of Lincoln's Nomination," *Century Magazine*, XL (July, 1890), 477-78.

Evans, Frank B., "Pennsylvania Politics, 1872-1877: A Study in Leadership Without Responsibility," Ph.D. Thesis, Pennsylvania State University, 1962.

Everett, Edward G., "Pennsylvania Raises an Army, 1861," *The Western Pennsylvania Historical Magazine*, XXXIX (Spring, 1956), 83-108.

[Frauds]: "Report of the Committee on Frauds," 1863, PSL.

Glonek, James F., "Lincoln, Johnson, and the Baltimore Ticket," *Abraham Lincoln Quarterly*, VI (March, 1951), 255-71.

H. C., special correspondent, "Simon Cameron at Home," *New York Times*, June 3, 1878.

Hellerich, Mahlon H., "The Pennsylvania Constitution of 1873," Ph.D. thesis, University of Pennsylvania, 1956.

Kelley, Brooks M., "Simon Cameron and The Senatorial Nomination of 1867," *Pennsylvania Magazine of History and Biography*, LXXXVII (Oct., 1963), 375-92.

Luthin, Reinhard H., "Pennsylvania and Lincoln," *Pennsylvania Magazine of History and Biography*, LXVIII (Jan., 1943), 61-82.

"Maytown Bicentennial: 1760-1960," Maytown, Pennsylvania.

Pease, Theodore and Randall, J. G., eds., "The Diary of Orville Browning," Illinois Historical *Collections*, XX, XXII (1925, 1933).

Phillips, Ulrich B. "The Central Theme of Southern History," *American Historical Review*, XXXIV (Oct., 1928), 30-43.

Pratt, Harry E., "Simon Cameron's Fight for a Place in Lincoln's Cabinet," Abraham Lincoln Association *Bulletin*, 49 (1937), 3-11.

Russell, William A., "A Biography of Alexander K. McClure," Ph.D. thesis, University of Wisconsin, 1953.

Serff, John J., "The Life of James A. Beaver," Ph.D. thesis, Pennsylvania State University, 1955.

Snyder, Charles M., "Pennsylvania Politics, 1833-1847," Ph.D. thesis, University of Pennsylvania, 1949.

Soldon, Norbert C., "James Donald Cameron: Pennsylvania Politician," M.A. thesis, Pennsylvania State University, 1959.

Wilson, Rufus, special correspondent, "Interview With Simon Cameron," Philadelphia *Press*, Jan. 20, 1889.

Ziegler, J. L., "History of the Donegal Presbyterian Church to 1902," in C. B. Segelken, Compiler, *The Donegal Presbyterian Church* (1935), 38-70.

Index